Henry Dunant

Henry Dunant
The Man of the Red Cross

Corinne Chaponnière

Translated by Michelle Bailat-Jones

BLOOMSBURY ACADEMIC
LONDON • NEW YORK • OXFORD • NEW DELHI • SYDNEY

BLOOMSBURY ACADEMIC
Bloomsbury Publishing Plc
50 Bedford Square, London, WC1B 3DP, UK
1385 Broadway, New York, NY 10018, USA
29 Earlsfort Terrace, Dublin 2, Ireland

BLOOMSBURY, BLOOMSBURY ACADEMIC and the Diana logo are
trademarks of Bloomsbury Publishing Plc

First published in 2010 as *Henry Dunant: La croix d'un homme*
by Éditions Perrin, Paris
Copyright © Éditions Perrin, 2010
Published in 2018 as *Henry Dunant: La croix d'un homme*
by Éditions Labor et Fides, Geneva
Copyright © Éditions Labor et Fides, 2018
First published in Great Britain 2022

Cover design: Graham Robert Ward
Cover image © Henry Dunant, 1862. Photopress Archiv/Keystone/Bridgeman Images

A catalogue record for this book is available from the British Library.

Library of Congress Cataloging-in-Publication Data

Names: Chaponnie`re, Corinne, author. | Bailat-Jones, Michelle, translator.
Title: Henry Dunant : the man of the Red Cross / [by Corinne Chaponnie`re] ;
[translated by Michelle Bailat-Jones].
Other titles: Henry Dunant, la croix d'un homme. English
Description: New York : Bloomsbury Academic, 2022. |
Includes bibliographical references and index.
Identifiers: LCCN 2021028847 | ISBN 9781350253438 (hardback) |
ISBN 9781350253452 (pdf) | ISBN 9781350253445 (ebook)
Subjects: LCSH: Dunant, Henry, 1828-1910. | Red Cross and Red Crescent–Biography. |
Red Cross and Red Crescent–History.
Classification: LCC HV569.D8 C4313 2022 | DDC 361.7/634092 [B—dc23
LC record available at https://lccn.loc.gov/2021028847Edit

ISBN: HB: 978-1-3502-5343-8
        ePDF: 978-1-3502-5345-2
        eBook: 978-1-35025-344-5

Typeset by RefineCatch Limited, Bungay, Suffolk
Printed and bound in Great Britain

To find out more about our authors and books visit www.bloomsbury.com
and sign up for our newsletters.

'. . .the line separating good and evil passes not through states, nor between classes, nor between political parties either – but right through every human heart . . .'

ALEKSANDR SOLZHENITSYN
THE GULAG ARCHIPELAGO

CONTENTS

PLATES

ACKNOWLEDGEMENTS

I would like to express my deepest gratitude to the Bogette Foundation. This book would not have been possible without their generous support.

This project also received strong support from a few friends and followers of Henry Dunant's work. I am especially indebted to Pierre Keller, former Vice President of the ICRC, who enabled this book to be published, along with Thierry Lombard, honorary member of the ICRC, who was the first champion of an English translation and generously contributed to funding it. François Bugnion, also honorary member of the ICRC, encouraged the project from the very beginning through his constant attention, useful contacts and friendly advice. I am extremely grateful for the extraordinary support I received from these three former members of the International Committee of the Red Cross, and which I consider a great honour.

I would also like to extend my gratitude to Michael Meyer, of the British Red Cross, who has been very supportive and helpful from my first steps towards an English publication; to Helen Durham, member of the ICRC, and to David Forsythe, emeritus researcher in Human Rights Studies, whose careful reading and useful advice were a great help.

I am immensely grateful to my translator Michelle Bailat-Jones, whose outstanding professional skills, matchless patience and ongoing availability over many months made this translation a great journey as well as an enthralling intellectual experience.

I am also grateful to Maddie Holder, from Bloomsbury, whose close reading and ingenious editing will certainly help this book reach a wider public.

I cannot end these acknowledgements without paying tribute to Roger Durand, who helped me begin this research and whose work in Geneva as a historian and president of the Henry Dunant Society has enormously enriched the scholarship surrounding Henry Dunant and the origins of the Red Cross.

ACKNOWLEDGEMENT TO THE RED CROSS

The Red Cross designation and design are used on the cover with kind permission from the United Kingdom Ministry of Defence and the British Red Cross.

NOTE TO THE READER

All quoted citations from written sources are included in this text verbatim, unless explicitly mentioned otherwise. At times, inner thoughts or oral dialogues between the protagonists have been reconstructed according to meeting minutes, reports, correspondence, memoirs, etc. and done so with express consideration for historical accuracy.

Introduction

Henry Dunant is one of Switzerland's best-known citizens. A hundred years after his death, his work has withstood the test of time. So has his mystery.

Even while alive, the founder of the Red Cross was a controversial figure. And his death neither softened his detractors nor lessened the fervour of his supporters. How could he not be divisive? Yet, despite questionable moments in his life, his legacy is immense. By introducing the very idea of brotherhood into war, Henry Dunant became one of the few people in history to move humanity one step forward. In June 1859, he happened to be in the right place at the right time for an event which inspired his specific genius. The experience occurred in a small town in the north of Italy, near Solferino. The moment? The aftermath of a bloody battle. The man? A Genevan citizen travelling around for business.

Dozens, hundreds, thousands of men have been up-close witnesses to the cruelties of war. Why was he the one who learned a lesson from this experience, and then turned that lesson into action? Red Cross historians have been looking for an answer to this question for a hundred and fifty years.

All biographies include an invariable series of events: childhood, formative years, active life, maturity, old age. Dunant's life adds a few syncopated beats to this ordinary tempo. There is definitely a before Solferino and an after Solferino. There is also a before bankruptcy and an after bankruptcy. There is a Geneva of happiness and then a Geneva of humiliation. There is a Red Cross as a source of pride, and a Red Cross as a source of bitterness. There is a devoted Christian and an angry Christian. And finally, after oblivion and misery, a time for resurrection and honour.

In all truth, the history of the Red Cross and the history of its founder only briefly coincide: the lives of heroes rarely conform to the myths they engender. It only took five short years, between the shock of Castiglione and the signing of the Geneva Convention, for Dunant to imagine, and then christen, the Red Cross that would make him so famous. And then for the next forty years, this same man was condemned to bear another cross – red like his bank statements, red like the iron with which he was branded, red like the shame, anger and hatred that filled him so relentlessly. And yet this other cross is barely visible behind the first, as if it didn't matter when compared to the real cross of the "great" and peerless Dunant.

I have opted for a strictly chronological structure in this biography, as impartial as possible in its themes and in the weight of its different parts. This means there are other themes running alongside the adventure of the Red Cross: three should be mentioned here.

His birth in 1828 into a bourgeois Genevan family immediately saddled him with some unmistakable baggage: Dunant grew up immersed in the Protestantism of his family, his milieu and his city, giving him not only a religious interpretation of the world, like most other nineteenth-century children, but one that was specific to his brand of religion. The division of the Christian world between Protestants and Catholics was especially deep in Geneva, and Dunant would never escape this distinction, not in his way of seeing the world and not in the complex game of his alliances and his mistrust, even when at the end of his life his preferences would be reversed. From his attitude with the wounded soldiers of Solferino in 1859 to the refusal of a pastor at the hour of his death, Henry Dunant would be intimately marked by the religious nature of his era, his milieu and his place of birth – this is one of the most consistent features of his entire life.

Like each of us, Henry Dunant is a combination of historical being, social animal and unique individual. Yet his social persona played a highly determining role in his destiny. Without his extraordinary skill in creating, maintaining and employing relationships, he would be missing from the history of the Young Men's Christian Association (YMCA), and perhaps the Geneva Convention might not yet exist, a truth both his contemporaries and historians have all recognized. But when misfortune came to shadow the second half of his life, it was the social animal who would experience such profound despair. The man who had laid his success at the altars of so many different 'networks' would experience his disgrace in the same way: Dunant could only understand his enemies in the form of a shadowy, Machiavellian network striving to persecute him in any way it could. In this way the two halves of his life, as opposed as they may seem, do in fact reveal two sides – dark and light, worldly and misanthropic – of a single trait without which Henry Dunant cannot be wholly understood.

Finally, the singular individual. The one who managed to transform chance into fate; the one who translated the emotions of a single day into an unprecedented historical agreement. Dunant isn't exceptional only because of his humanitarian vision and his instinctive understanding of when a utopia could become a reality. His own genius also relied on a method that he applied in every single one of his various projects from the YMCA to the Nobel Prize. That method can be described in three words: desire, convince, disseminate. As much as he was a man of vision and of faith, of tenacity and enthusiasm, he was also a matchless propagandist – a quality without which all the others would have failed.

When considered as a whole, Henry Dunant's life thus reveals driving forces other than those he is most often credited with. While the spectacular chain of events between Solferino and the Geneva Convention crowned him with laurels, the rest of his existence, with its zigzagging path, mostly bears witness to his vulnerability as well as his constant resilience. Henry Dunant was a pioneering visionary and a spiteful wheeler-dealer, a great man who was not always great, an exemplary figure and an ordinary man – all of these things at the same time. The goal of this biography isn't to knock an idolized figure off its pedestal; in portraying him as he was and telling the story of his life as it happened, it's my hope his example will serve readers as a reminder that single, ordinary individuals – and not only geniuses or saints – can indeed take humanity one step forward.

1

The Happy Eldest (1828–47)

The hillside

In 1828, the small city of Geneva had only been part of Switzerland for thirteen years. Like most feudal cities, its hierarchy was visible in its topography. Instead of a fortress, however, the cathedral stood at the city's highest point. Clustered closely around it were a series of upper-class family homes – dynasties of bankers, lawyers, doctors, pastors and professors. Two centuries on, the 'Rome of the Reformation' still prized the Church that had endowed it with the talent and knowledge of waves of Protestants escaping persecution elsewhere. Owing their Church a fair measure of their prosperity, Genevans of the period would never have been so ungrateful as to temper the fervour of their faith.

The small hilltop *haute ville* (upper city) housed an aristocracy of only a few dozen families, descendants of the city's burghers who had ruled uncontested up until the eighteenth century. The steep flanks of the hill accommodated a series of tiered neighbourhoods that mirrored the descending steps of the social ladder all the way down to the *basse ville* (lower city) with its minor bourgeoisie, merchants, artisans and day labourers.

It was on one of these hillsides, exactly halfway between the upper and the lower city, that Jean-Henri Dunant[1] was born on

---

[1] Henry Dunant's birth name was Jean-Henri Dunant. He would later shorten and change its spelling. Accordingly, this biography will opt for Henry at the moment that Dunant himself chooses his first name with its English spelling.

8th May 1828. His parents were thrilled: less than a year of marriage and already the gift of a son. Exactly what was needed to bring them closer, something that their hurried engagement had not been able to do.

Like most marriages of the time, theirs was arranged. Poor academic results had sent Jean-Jacques Dunant out of Geneva as soon as the first bristles of a beard had sprouted on his chin, and he'd been travelling the world ever since. Initially hired by an uncle in Marseilles with a merchant company for colonial goods, he'd visited many countries, crossed many seas, suffered through hurricanes and storms before setting up his own business in Marseilles where he'd remained for the next ten years.[2]

Until, one day, it struck him that he might end up living out his final years alone. His business was stagnating, his income less certain, his future growing dim on its Mediterranean horizon. The associate with whom he'd founded his company had returned home. 'I'm a bachelor,' he finally admitted to one of his uncles, 'maybe I was wrong not to think earlier about marriage; I would have more confidence and ambition, yet now it seems unlikely.'[3]

This admission made its way to his two sisters in Geneva who'd been waiting just for this. Behind the closed doors of the Dunant family home, they had begun to worry about the future of their family name. Their older brother had married a Catholic, a heresy in Geneva at that time, so nothing could be left to chance now that the younger brother was finally thinking about settling down.

The younger sister, Anne-Jeanne Dunant, struck first: 'You must absolutely come home and choose a wife,' she wrote to him in 1823, 'but she must have property so that you can set yourself up here [. . .] What could be more natural than to live and die in one's own country?'[4] From letter to letter, the sisters' intentions became increasingly clear – not only did they want their brother to marry, they wanted him home, something which entailed finding him a

---

[2] The most informative book about Dunant's childhood, family and religious development is Gabriel Mützenberg, *Henry Dunant le prédestiné* (Geneva: Société Henry Dunant, 1984).

[3] J.-J. Dunant to J.-F. Dunant, 20 April 1823, *Bibliothèque de Genève, Département des manuscrits* (Library of Geneva, Manuscript Department, from now on: BGE), Family correspondence Dunant-Colladon, BGE, Ms. fr. 3257, f. 257.

[4] Anne-Jeanne Dunant to her brother Jean-Jacques, 27 February 1823, BGE, Ms. fr. 3257, f. 114.

Genevan woman with enough of a fortune so that he could close up shop in Marseilles. Six months later the same sister sent a list of names, with supporting files. Among three possible candidates was a young lady from the Colladon family: 24-year-old Anne-Antoinette, although not a beauty, had several solid qualities in her favour. She could run a household with just one servant, play the piano, even speak a little English. She was small but had quite abundant hair, good teeth, good health, black eyes. What else could he want?

But Jean-Jacques kept dithering. It was not an easy decision to abandon the city he'd chosen to make his fortune and where he'd hung all his hopes. Older sister Sophie thus took up her pen to urge him to select a young woman from Marseilles if he could not choose a Genevan. But as nothing seemed to turn up in that direction either, Sophie returned to the question in 1825: 'If you want to marry a Genevan,' she scolded, 'you must not let all the pretty ones get away, there are a lot of marriages right now!'[5]

The death of their mother in early 1826 finally nudged Jean-Jacques to give in to his sisters' entreaties. 'The modest Nancy,'[6] as he'd already dubbed Miss Colladon with no obvious enthusiasm, was still free. Things moved quickly from that moment on until the last spring day of 1827 when the Dunant and Colladon families celebrated the marriage of Jean-Jacques to Anne-Antoinette.

Both families seemed delighted. Admittedly, in Geneva's social geography of the time, the Colladons would have placed themselves higher up the hillside than the Dunants. The father of the bride was a regent at the high-school, had a seat on both the city and the cantonal council, and was also mayor of Avully, a village in the Genevan countryside. Anne-Antoinette's younger brother, Daniel Colladon, was one of the most promising members of Geneva's scientific community. It was logical that the Colladon family would have expected a smart match for each child.

[5] Sophie Dunant to her brother Jean-Jacques, 27 January 1825, BGE, Ms. fr. 3257, f. 152v.

[6] 'The modest Nancy, as you call her': Anne-Jeanne Dunant to her brother Jean-Jacques, 28 October 1823, BGE, Ms. fr. 3257, f. 117v. 'Nancy' was a customary nickname for Anne-Antoinette, in line with Geneva's Anglophilia at the time.

But good alliances don't always make happy marriages. 'You can be sure our first feeling was surprise,' the fiancée's own brother admitted to one of his uncles, yet 'surprise' was quickly followed by relief: 'I was extremely worried that Nancy would end up alone,' he continued. 'Her loving and sensitive heart requires the affections of family and the tenderness of a spouse. Depriving her of these joys would have altered her nature over time.'[7] The truth is that at that time, when a woman reached or surpassed the age of 25, both the woman and her family were generally more flexible in their choice. Having previously dreamt of an ideal husband, the ageing young woman became more ready to settle for the dream of any husband. The Colladon family was no exception.

Young Nancy's dowry granted the couple a house on one of the steep streets of what is still called the Old Town in Geneva. The newly-wed bride was radiant. She'd had her sights set on Jean-Jacques from the very first time her future sisters-in-law had suggested him, and had waited patiently for two long years until he decided in her favour. And now, after barely a year of marriage, the birth of their first son fulfilled all her hopes. They named him Jean-Henri.

Happy times

Henri was not yet walking when the young couple moved from the Old Town to a beautiful country home called La Monnaie, coming this time from the Dunants. The large property included a variety of fruit trees and enjoyed a broad view of the lake and the Alps. The Jura mountain side of the estate boasted several mossy and sheltered spaces, perfect for taking refuge from the goings on of the house. Jean-Jacques had returned from his travels with a love of beautiful trees and several rare species had been planted on the grounds, giving the garden a touch of the exotic.

If you stood at one end of the gardens you could see the Lausanne coach, and from the other, the Paris mail-coach. When the weather was fine, Nancy would sit out on the terrace with her baby to wait

---

[7] Daniel Colladon to his uncle Jean-Pierre Colladon, 21 May 1827, BGE, Papiers Daniel Colladon, Ms. fr. 3742, f. 70.

with childish delight for her brother Daniel, the family genius making his career in Paris. Her letters to him gushed with all the fresh pride of a newly married mother of a sweet chubby boy. 'I must tell you about your fat little nephew: he is delicious. I lose myself entirely when he sets his big black eyes on me.'[8] In page after page, Nancy recorded Henri's slightest utterings for her very learned brother, but also for her schoolmasterish father, and especially for her great traveller of a husband whom she would have liked home with her more often. Yes, Mr Dunant had surrendered to his sisters and put roots down in Geneva, but he hadn't given up his Mediterranean business. He was often in France, leaving his young wife to her melancholy. Not too often, though – the family grew at a steady pace, unseating Henri from his infant-king status as five brothers and sisters arrived in rapid succession over the next six years.

While La Monnaie had ample room for the family to grow, Jean-Jacques's income wasn't growing in the same proportion. Butcher's bills competed with doctor's bills; Nancy was physically and psychologically frail and sent away for her devoted Dr Senn at the drop of a hat. Balancing the budget was delicate: it relied on rental income from various apartments in Geneva as well as on the highly random success of Jean-Jacques's commercial affairs in Marseilles.

But what are monetary concerns to a boy? A happy childhood is more truly remembered through the flavours and fragrances of a man's nostalgia. Henri's memories of La Monnaie were of 'delicious, juicy and sweet, greengage plums'.[9] As well as the scented violets covering the moss, the sound of the mail-coach 'muted in the distance', and of the pristine Mont Blanc, which could easily be seen on clear days from their lawn.

On his mother's side, the harvest at his grandparents' home in Avully was even more voluptuous: lush tarts, holiday cakes and other treats, massive strawberry patches, bushes of red- and

---

[8] Nancy Dunant to her brother Daniel Colladon, 4 November 1828, BGE, Ms. fr. 3742, f. 116v.

[9] Dunant, *Mémoires* (Lausanne: L'Âge d'Homme, 1971), 20. These memoirs correspond to the biographical notebooks prepared by Henry Dunant for Rudolf Müller for his *Entstehungsgeschichte des Roten Kreuz und der Genfer Konvention*, published in Stuttgart in 1897 (according to the decisive discovery of J.-D. Candaux, 1978). These notebooks were then edited by Bernard Gagnebin and published in French under the title *Mémoires, Henri Dunant*. This is the edition we use here. We translate.

blackcurrants, raspberries and blackberries all within reach of his greedy little hands. And more than anything, the attentive love of his grandparents for their daughter Nancy, an affection which stretched naturally to her multiplying brood.

Henri's grandfather, Henri Colladon, had acquired the vast estate in Avully sometime around 1815; it included a manor house and small farm. Henri's mother had lived there as a teenager and young woman, well cared for by her parents and a brother she adored. Despite a nearly hour-long trip between La Monnaie and Avully, she returned as often as she could. As a young mother who was frequently home alone with her children, she sought the comfort of her childhood family cocoon.

In Henri's youthful universe, Avully was a distillation of the noblest elements of his maternal line. This wasn't about wealth, this was a thousand times better – this was productive land, the harmony of a large family, the elevation of a thoughtful elite, the philanthropy of a social caste who believed themselves obligated to give back what they had received. In the purest Protestant tradition, it was most likely at Avully that Henri experienced how charity might be combined with interest – with the young orphans his grandfather took as pensioners in exchange for a daily per capita from the city's Charity Office, but whom he also took care of with great attention to their education and well-being. There is no doubt that Henri Colladon, Nancy's father, had a real social consciousness; it is equally true he had some financial worries that worsened after a few tricky investments made around 1830, only two years after Henri's birth. All of this is to say that Henri had plenty of time before the age of 10 to consider three things with respect to his grandfather's small protégés at Avully: *he* was born on a good rung of the social ladder; many others didn't have the same chance; the aid provided to those less fortunate, whether benevolent or compensated, made a difference.

A time of exaltation

Henri gently closed Mr Bonifas's office door. He stood watching his friends romping about the courtyard on this last day before the holidays. He did not go to join them, preferring the back stairs and the road running alongside the prison to reach the Old Town without being noticed.

He needed to think quickly. He had about three quarters of an hour before his mother would get worried. Three quarters of an hour to figure out how to avoid the worst – tears, smelling salts, an emergency call to Dr Senn. The inevitable drama was a short hour away.

To make matters worse, the weather was splendid. A weather for crowning victories, not for bad news. To continue his dawdling, Henri went left along the La Treille Promenade, where the leaves of the chestnut trees were a vivid, luscious green but not quite the emerald branches of July. Oh, he should have dropped hints to warn his parents what was coming! He'd known he was on thin ice. Why hadn't he said anything? Probably because he hadn't believed it himself. He'd already had to retake the year, and no one had thought, himself included, that he'd fail again. And yet he had. His schooling was finished.

He'd just turned 14. A desperately blank and unknown space now awaited him. He slouched onto the long bench of La Treille. In the distance was the Bastions Promenade where he'd walked so often and so carefree, convinced then that he was facing a path of notoriety, like his grandfather Colladon and his famous uncle Daniel.

But today was different and Henri remembered only his other grandfather's prison sentence, his uncle David's shameful bankruptcy and the recurrent uncertainties of his father's business. And now it was his turn for failure. How upsetting; he'd always seen himself as a man of letters, a scholar, even a pastor!

The sun was setting when he arrived at La Monnaie. His mother called out to him from upstairs, she had been watching for him since the school bell rang at its usual time. There she was coming down the stairs, slowly, as if to control herself. The sight of her so fragile and upset sent Henri, sobbing, into her arms. Gone were the careful explanations he'd prepared on his way home. This wasn't the plan – mute, hiccupping, childish. Yet this was exactly the right way to go about it. No drama, no anger, no scolding. His mother, who'd understood right away, held him in her arms and cried with him.

The narrow door

A half-chance in the autumn of 1843 brought Henri Dunant back into the house where he was born. Now that a higher education was off limits, it was time to find another way forward. By chance, a young couple – a novice pastor married to a young teacher – were renting Henri's parents' first home at the time and supplemented their income with pensioners and private lessons. Exactly what Henri needed, since neither he, nor anyone in the family, could imagine him looking for work at the age of 15.

A few lessons with the Nicoles confirmed the school's judgement: Henri had no head for science! However, his early passion for religion had continued to develop, granting him three prizes when he was still at school. His struggles with academia may have closed the doors of a higher education to him, but his faith would open others.

On a gentle evening in September 1843, Henri went directly to The Oratory. This recently constructed chapel had been hosting the faithful flock of the *Société évangélique* (Evangelical Society) since 1834. Throughout his school years, Henri had eaten lunch each day with his father's sister to avoid the hour-and-a-half round-trip walk from La Monnaie. Aunt Sophie lived in the heart of the Old Town, only five minutes from his school. She was also a member of this newly founded Evangelical Society. It was through his Aunt Sophie that Henri had learned of this community. A practical arrangement soon became a moment of respite and happiness on days when the weather was fine, and Henri's aunt rushed their lunch so they could go outside for dessert and sit on a bench along the Bastions Promenade. At that point the conversation would become more confidential and more serious, a perfect moment for Sophie to tell her attentive nephew about her commitment to the Evangelical Society. Already innately attuned to these religious questions, Henri was captivated by the stories and vocabulary of her community. Its *Réveil* and *réveillés*,[10] its 'brothers and sisters in Jesus', its 'efficient grace'. Predestination, original sin, the divine nature of Christ. With all the passion of the freshly converted, Aunt Sophie wasn't even aware of the extravagance of her jargon nor the theological heights to which she enticed her young disciple. This meant that in only four years, Henri had been gradually drawn into this movement of 'Mômiers'[11] – a dissent from the established Swiss National Church in the name of a more literal and fiery Christianity.

---

[10] TN: the *Réveil*, the Awakening, and the *réveillés*, the awakened, were terms used in Switzerland's evangelical movement. *Le Réveil* is commonly translated as the Swiss Revival.

[11] TN: *Mômiers*, whose closest translation would be 'Puritans', was a pejorative name used in Switzerland for the followers of this brand of Protestantism.

Approaching The Oratory that September evening, Henri remembered his aunt's words from their lunchtime conversations: 'Of course, we're all Protestant,' Aunt Sophie had explained as she rose from the bench and brushed the crumbs off her skirt towards the birds. 'But not in the same way. Some of us live our religion with our heads, and some with our hearts and our faith, do you see? Some understand God with their mind, using knowledgeable texts written by theologians, while others would like to be closer to God through their own means: by reading the Bible, through prayer, by loving one's neighbour, by working in service to Christ at all times.'

When he was 13 or 14, he'd asked Aunt Sophie to bring him to hear the famous Pastor Gaussen, founder of the Evangelical Society. Depending on who you asked, Gaussen was either an Antichrist or a saviour, a wise man or a firebrand, a prophet or a cult leader. His 1830 exclusion from the Fellowship of Pastors had given him the prestigious aura of a martyr which had sharpened Henri's desire to see him in real life. He would never forget the details of that first encounter.[12]

Pastor Gaussen had a memorable face: the nose and chin jutting towards one another, a large forehead and wild unruly hair. The way he spoke set imaginations on fire: incandescent, sometimes soft, sometimes authoritarian, and always terrible. He was skilled at transporting the Holy Scriptures to a 'here and now', and electrified his listeners by bringing Moses, Esau, Amos or Paul back to life. The Pastor also boldly predicted spectacular, apocalyptic events using the prophecies from the Book of Daniel or the Book of Revelation; announcing the impending collapse of the Turkish Empire, the fall of the Latin world and the return of the Jews to the Promised Land.

Henri never recovered from that first meeting. It is what guided his steps that twilight towards The Oratory courtyard, where Pastor Gaussen's familiar voice was carrying to him from the great hall. By drawing him into the evangelical community, his aunt Sophie had offered him a new emotional and intellectual family, other perspectives and a possible future.

---

[12] Seventy years later, Henry's 'diagrams' show evident reminiscences of Gaussen's sermons. See below, chapter XII, 'An apocalyptic hobby'.

A little aristocrat

Although the evangelical circles met Henri's adolescent need for belonging, Geneva's high-society balls were equally useful for making connections. A different September evening, this time in 1845, saw Henri sporting black trousers with a brand-new white jacket and a beautiful satin cravat from his grandmother, fastened with a golden pin. A pair of new dancing shoes completed his outfit, and who cared if his feet were already hurting by the second dance? The evening was magnificent, about three hundred guests comfortably spread throughout the reception rooms. Only a piano accompanied the first dance, just enough for the young dancers to warm up. Then, suddenly, more music began to wind its way from the corridor into the grand salon. The men dropped their hands from the waists of their dancing partners, and all heads turned to see where this new melody was coming from. Off with the pianist! No less than ten musicians entered the room to accompany the dancers who, without skipping a beat, began twirling about the waxed parquet floor. Henri made the best of his dancing lessons that night, accomplishing a number of complicated turns. He didn't miss a step, not during the polkas nor during the mazurka which he was quite proud to have led so flawlessly.[13]

Sometime later another invitation brought him to an exquisite country home nestled among the lakeside vineyards about 20 kilometres outside Geneva. At the end of a late evening, when the city gates would have been already closed, the hosts invited several guests to stay the night. One was Henri Dunant, another a young man named Gustave Moynier. Dunant was slightly in awe; he believed this young man's father was a member of the Genevan government. Although older than Henri, Moynier was extremely friendly. They were sent to a room above the greenhouse where they quickly fell asleep. Little could Henri suspect that this friendly young man would become his closest colleague and then his most bitter enemy.

---

[13] Henri Dunant to his grandmother Colladon, 25 September 1845, 'Letters to various correspondents'', Dunant file, ICRC archives (from now on: ACICR), box 44 (Letters of Henry Dunant).

Of this time in his life, Henri would remember: 'When I was 10, I was a little aristocrat in all that is most respectful of the aristocracy.'[14] He never doubted his belonging to the highest society of his birth city. His family could not claim the wealth of several other dynasties of the period and this difference would haunt Henri for his entire life, but he certainly shared the morality, principles and virtues that distinguished Geneva's republican aristocracy.

For example: dancing the mazurka at a banker's ball didn't preclude – it even implied – the assiduous practice of Christian charity. In this nineteenth-century milieu, a Society of Alms was committed to the flow of responsible generosity from the upper city to the lower city in hope of alleviating its increasing misery. Like others of her station, Henri's mother believed that charity was a given, even from within a periodically restricted budget. She had regularly taken a very young Henri with her into the neighbourhoods on the other side of the Rhône river where labourers and the poor, the disabled and street children often went hungry. When he was older, Henri would continue to make a point to go with her when he had the time. Years later he remembered:

And so I slowly learned to know misfortune and misery in small, dark streets, in homes which looked like stables, seeing men who had nothing of their own, as if attached to a chain of countless sufferings.[15]

Already as a child, something in him shook when confronted with misery and injustice. This was no dream of rebelling against the order of a world he would never question. No, this was more a skin-deep sensitivity, an impatient compassion which wanted an immediate remedy for any unfortunate souls who might cross his path.

Henri Dunant was not even 20 years old when he became a member of the Society of Alms. However, in those years since the 'little aristocrat' had accompanied his mother on her visits to the poor, the face of Geneva had changed. In 1846, the so-called aristocrats were chased out of power, and from one day to the next

---

[14] Dunant, *Mémoires*, p. 22.

[15] Maurice Dunant (ed.), *Les débuts de la Croix-Rouge en France, Extraits des mémoires de Jean-Henri Dunant* (Zürich-Paris: Orell Füssli-Fischbacher, 1918), 5.

the milieu to which Dunant identified so fiercely lost both its prestige and its future. The youth of the traditional ruling families – viscerally opposed to the new regime – were overwhelmed; they no longer knew their place, what model to follow, what career to aspire to. They did have religion, though, and it became one of the last havens for their values and their community, a trend even further reinforced by the city's recent upsurge in piety. Individual charity, the duty of all good Christians, was now filled with a new meaning – it became a kind of opposition to the state-sponsored and secular social action envisioned by the new authorities. A vestige of a world in transformation, the Society of Alms made it possible to pretend that nothing had changed. Dunant was able to continue to practice charity in the way his mother had taught him and which he remembered later, in his memoirs:

> Each active member had his own poor and sick people to visit and to whom he brought a small monthly sum [. . .] Because I felt strongly about it, slowly I found myself taking care of a large number of disabled people and crippled old women with no family [. . .][16]

During this same period, Henri frequently spent his Sunday afternoons reading the Bible to condemned prisoners in Geneva; for this good work, the chapel doors were willingly opened for him. Which is to say that although he was not a pastor, his charitable engagements very much resembled a ministry.

At the age of 20, in a Geneva in which faith had once granted citizenship, Henri placed himself entirely and passionately in the service of Jesus Christ. And although his finances prevented it from being his only activity and his schooling level prevented it from being his profession, this would be his path for the next five years.

---

[16] Dunant, *Mémoires*, 24.

2

The Birth of an Association (1847–54)

The Thursday meetings

Geneva's political context, the pious Swiss Revival, his family background and his own personality – all this had already set the stage for Henri's intense experience of faith. But an event in the summer of 1847, which occurred in the Alps while hiking for a few days with two friends, led him towards new heights of religious practice.

This was not overly extraordinary, really, in the context of Europe's Romantic discovery of the hidden beauty of the alpine landscape. But Henri and his two companions instinctively interpreted the 'sublime' of the Alps through the lens of their faith, recognizing in it the greatness of God and the perfection of his works. One evening, within the rocky summer silence of those high mountain peaks, the three young men performed a small ceremony of thanks to the Lord's power and love. An unforgettable moment of happiness, it seems, because upon their return to Geneva the three adventurers decided to continue their meetings every Thursday evening. To do what? For a Genevan of 1847, the answer was obvious – to read the Bible and to pray.[1]

---

[1] On the beginnings of the YMCA, see Clarence Prouty Shedd, *History of the World Alliance of YMCA* (London: SPCK, 1955); on the Geneva YMCA, Théodore Geisendorf, *Soixante ans de souvenirs, Notice historique relative à L'Union Chrétienne de Jeunes Gens de Genève* (Geneva [no publisher] 1913), and UCJG (eds), *150 ans déjà. . . 1852–2002* (Geneva: UCJG/SHD, 2003).

For even in this pious era, the Protestantism of the Revival was particularly dedicated and diligent, having developed as a response to what was seen as the tepid religion of the 'official' National Church. A group of young Christians gathering each week without a pastor to read the Bible, pray and recite the Psalms was now common in Geneva. Yet the group formed by Dunant and his two friends developed so quickly they rapidly outgrew the private home they were using. The building offered to them as a new meeting place left no doubt as to which spiritual family these young men belonged; the registry of the Evangelical Society noted in 1849 the presence of 'younger brothers who meet on Thursday night at The Oratory'.[2] There were no longer three men, nor five, nor ten, but twenty-six.

What these three alpine backpackers had experienced strongly resembled what they would call a 'conversion'. To the modern reader, this word may seem too strong to describe a group of practising Christians who were not renouncing Christianity nor Protestantism, nor even Calvinism, but reclaiming the same with greater devotion and fervour. The term might seem even more inappropriate in a city terrorized by another kind of 'conversion': from 1816 on, the Genevan population was increasingly threatened by an encroaching Catholicism coming from previously French and Sardinian territories. Despite this, in the spirit of the evangelical movement of 1850, it was indeed a conversion when people from the National Church adhered to the theology of the Revival, as Dunant himself would summarize many years later: 'The Gospel must take possession of the entire man – body, soul, and mind.'[3] A quietly tended and discreet little faith was not enough for the adepts of the Revival. Their mission was to proselytize, to gain ground everywhere, in all levels of society and in all countries, relying upon an army of 'peddlers of faith' who went off toting their Bibles on their backs through wind and rain, sleet or snow, no matter the risk of prison or persecution in imperial France or papal Italy.

It was to this movement that Henri Dunant converted, with all the passion of his youth. 'He jumps from the wall into the water and

---

[2] BGE, Archives of the *Société évangélique de Genève*, Ms. Soc. Ev. 49, f. 44.
[3] Henry Dunant, '*Procès de la Chrétienté*', 2nd part (no date, but surely after 1890), BGE, Ms. fr. 4550, f. 4.

swims,'[4] his mother noted when he was still a teenager, proud of her eldest son who swam in the lake no matter the season. It's hard to imagine a more accurate depiction of her son's personality, from the start to the finish of his life. As soon as he returned from the Alps, Henri was already jumping into the movement of the Revival, with courage, with faith and certainly with delight.

On Thursday evenings when preparing the small room on loan at the end of the Oratory hallway, he often had to fetch extra chairs for the newcomers. He recruited the greatest numbers, he brought new bodies and got them to stay, he reconvinced deserters, he was the one who kept these weekly meetings running. Him, a man less educated and less cultured than many of his friends, a man who wasn't studying theology or law, who was resigned to his modest clerk's job in a local bank, a man without any special talent for speaking. Why him?

His first weapon was the deep conviction that sent the right words to his mouth, convincing words that inspired people to come to the meetings and keep coming. He was not afraid of approaching people directly, he would immediately knock on the doors of complete strangers if he thought they might be interested. In 1851, when Maximilien Perrot, future chairman of the *Union chrétienne de Jeunes Gens* (Young Men's Christian Association, or YMCA) of Geneva, returned to the city after an absence of more than two years, one of his first visitors was a man he'd never met but who invited him to a meeting the following Thursday. And so he went, like many before him and like many would do after him.

What was even more efficient was Dunant's passion – the bright, communicative joy on his face when with his 'brothers'. It would be an understatement to say that Henri loved being in social groups. He was enthusiastic about the very idea of community, and even more so when he was part of a group's foundation and so integral to its growth. This focus occupied him during the five years that followed those first Thursday meetings. While the small city of Geneva was demolishing its ramparts to widen its boundaries, Dunant was working to push back the borders of what the disciples of the Evangelical Society called 'God's dominion', paving the way for what would eventually become the YMCA.

---

[4] Nancy to J.-J. Dunant, 30 August 1843, 'Daniel Colladon Papers', BGE, Ms. fr. 3257, f. 268v.

By 1851, two years after the launch of the Thursday meetings, the small room on the first floor of The Oratory was definitely too small. Dunant obtained permission to use the large hall. The pastors of the Evangelical Society were indeed delighted to see how the young were flocking to their new church, even more so because they were from all levels of society: patricians, watchmakers, teachers, bakers, established Genevans and new residents. Calling each other 'brother in faith' and 'brother in Christ' or 'Jesus's beloved', they were creating a spiritual community that no other social connection would achieve.

But Henri Dunant's eyes were looking further into the distance, and what he could see was his future. His ambitions – which were still perfectly compatible with the ambitions of the movement – lay somewhere off in that foreseeable distance. His humble position in a local bank didn't provide him with many options, which is why he placed all his energy and hopes in his role as 'corresponding secretary' of this group of young activist Christian men that he intended to take beyond a small weekly meeting of friends.

In that same year, 1851, Dunant had heard a pastor from Nîmes, France, preach in a chapel in the lower city. He introduced himself to ask if the man's parish had a group of devoted Christian youth. 'There are three,' the pastor responded, 'who meet to read the Bible and pray.'[5] This was all the information Henri needed. Several days later as the pastor was getting ready to leave Geneva, Dunant handed him a letter addressed to the three young men in Nîmes, whose names he didn't even know.

This was the first connection, the first link in the chain of a network. The men from Nîmes answered Dunant and mentioned a few other small groups dispersed throughout France. Dunant wrote to them as well. His method was simple; each time he got word of a group of young active Christians anywhere, he would send them a warm greeting to open the door for a shared future. Like a forger gifted at crafting 'antiques', Henri was skilled at presenting a potential friendship as something that already existed. It's likely the 'brotherhood in Christ' helped foster an intimacy that otherwise would have seemed inappropriate with young people he'd never met. Although common in evangelical circles, this assumed familiarity

---

[5] Geisendorf, *Soixante ans de souvenirs*, 14.

also had a performative function. Once treated as brothers or friends for life, Henri's correspondents became so. One by one they answered him in kind and Henri's network grew and grew.

In addition to his detailed replies, our tireless letter writer was soon adding a 'newsletter' to his to-do list, thus transforming bilateral connections into a single community, and always with the same rhetoric of taking the future by storm. The result was worth the effort: the burgeoning YMCA would believe in its own international existence before it was formally founded, and much of this was thanks to Henri Dunant's newsletters.

In Geneva, the meetings multiplied, now taking place on Wednesdays and Sundays as well as Thursdays. Dunant was everywhere, involved in all these local activities while simultaneously extending his connections at an international level. All this he did with no other title than 'corresponding secretary', as his movement held to its fraternal roots rather than an organized structure. But not for much longer.

The Young Men's Christian Association

Back in September 1850, two faithful members of the Thursday night meetings, Louis Mercier and Joseph Gibert, had left to study medicine in Paris. Uninterested in the usual distractions for young men of their age, they'd continued to meet once a week to pray and read the Bible. Their first meeting had attracted five participants, and over time had become a group of twenty or so. Quickly outgrowing Louis Mercier's garret, they soon rented a room and filled it with an initial collection of edifying books donated by one of the group's more well-heeled members. By March 1852, at the urging of Jean-Paul Cook, the son of an English Methodist pastor, they were in the midst of founding a Paris chapter of the YMCA closely patterned upon the British model that had been active in London since 1844.

Joseph Gibert mentioned these developments to his Geneva friends. From that moment on, Henri Dunant began chomping at the bit. The 'Thursday meetings' had made Geneva a pioneer, why would it fall behind Paris and London? Couldn't they have a proper association, too, with a permanent space offering heat, light, devotional books and religious journals to young men in need of

spiritual nourishment? But Geneva was neither Paris nor London.
Any long-term financial investment would require some tough
negotiating. It would also involve overcoming the reluctance of
those – and there were many – who felt that any form of organization
was a perversion. Yet, the course was already set: Gibert sent a copy
of the Paris YMCA's draft statutes to Geneva. They were simple and
concise, and would serve as a basis for their own branch:

> Art. 2. The exclusive goal of the Association is the religious
> development of the youth who compose its membership, and
> youth in general. Each member must faithfully pursue this goal
> in all relationships with other youth.
>
> Art. 3. Members shall periodically meet to pray, read the Holy
> Scripture, and gain in knowledge together.
>
> Art. 8. Youth who wish to become members must apply in
> writing to the committee and provide satisfying proof of their
> conversion.[6]

In Geneva, however, those who had been attending the regular prayer
meetings were not keen on something so structured. It wouldn't do
to rush things, and Dunant knew this: he had an innate sense of
timing. But a chain of events would provide the impetus he'd been
waiting for. Over the summer of 1852, he went hiking again in the
Alps with two of his 'Thursday' brothers, his close friends Ernest de
Traz and Louis Rosselet, a hike that was as much for pleasure as it
was for propaganda. The three missionaries intended to distribute
the good word of the Revival along their route.

While crossing over the Furka Pass, they happened to meet two
young men animated by the same religious fervour, full of youthful
energy and their own stack of religious tracts in their satchels.
The men were two brothers from France, Édouard and Frédéric
Monnier.

Édouard was a year younger than Henri, 23, and studying
theology in Strasbourg. His parents were French converts to

---

[6] From J. Gibert to E. de Traz, 'Shortly after March 18th 1852', World Alliance of
YMCA Archives, Geneva. All letters between the members of the YMCA as well as
the documents related to it come, unless otherwise specified, from these archives
(World YMCA Archives from now on). We translate.

evangelical Protestantism, and he had inherited from them a vocation for recruiting new adepts that had him wandering the countryside with his younger brother Frédéric, ready to broadcast God's message to everyone he met.

The five men hiked the mountain and discussed, their conversations gaining momentum like the small stones they sent rolling down the slopes as they passed. Édouard spoke of his professors in Strasbourg whom he considered to be overly dogmatic and rationalist compared to his own faith 'of the heart'. Henri, who since June had been the Geneva secretary for the Evangelical Alliance,[7] told him about the tensions between the theological school at The Oratory and the theologians of the National Church. Keeping pace behind them, Ernest de Traz and Louis Rosselet did their best to describe to Frédéric, the younger brother, the spirit of their Thursday meetings, which, however strange it might seem to someone at this time, were organized by young men, for other young men, without supervision from a pastor, church elders or any other authority.

Dunant considered their meeting a sign from heaven. A few weeks later, he would write to Édouard that 'the Lord, who offers all good things to His children, granted us this meeting on the Furka. [. . .] It was so congenial and pleasant to travel with you, to speak with you in particular, my dear Édouard, (please allow me to call you this) of our good Lord and Father's love.' These effusive comments were certainly part of the religious ideal inspired by the strong fraternity of the movement. However, this wasn't the only message his letter wanted to convey:

> Beyond the love for all that comes from Christ, the Lord himself legitimized more specific affections, provided they are in Him; it is said that John was the disciple Jesus loved best; and so if I ask for your friendship – and assure you of my own esteem for you – which is more real than all the connections of this world and subject to the Holy Spirit – it is because of the pleasure I have had in meeting you, the good that you have done for me, the charm of our conversation, your spirit which is most attractive

---

[7] In 1847, the French-speaking Swiss branch of the World Evangelical Alliance (London, 1846) was created.

to me, and your Christian activity, etc., etc. – I am sure you will
not refuse this to me.[8]

Although particularly striking here, Dunant's correspondence
includes many examples of such declarations. An over-demonstrative
friendship with a person he'd sometimes never even met was part of
his personal style but also of his method to develop the movement.
At the same time, Dunant was already relying on, as he would for his
entire life, the unifying power of exceptional individuals, especially
those with some form of social prestige. In the autumn of 1852,
Dunant found unexpected support in the person of Adolf Monod,
one of the greatest preachers from the French Revival who was
fortunately passing through Geneva. It was under Monod's patronage
that the Paris YMCA had been created. Who better to convince the
young people of Geneva to finally get with the programme? Dunant
arranged a meeting with his friends, during which Adolf Monod
paved the way for him beyond his wildest hopes. The preacher didn't
just encourage his audience, he rallied them so well that the young
Christians were more motivated than ever to get to work; they
decided to organize an end-of-October assembly at one of the city's
concert and meeting halls, the Saint Pierre Casino.

Geneva's winter fog had already begun to settle in for the season
on that autumn afternoon. Members began arriving from every
neighbourhood and from all walks of life. Shaking hands all around,
Henri knew every single person. The meeting opened without any
formal agenda, but a goal slowly emerged. Several individuals wanted
to link the various groups into a common structure, for more visibility.
Henri Dunant and Maximilien Perrot supported this suggestion,
countering the usual arguments against any formal structure. The
discussions were advancing when Henri saw his friend Max stand up,
his face barely containing his emotion and illuminated with fresh
conviction: 'If all of you accept this new organization,' he said as
solemnly as possible, 'I am ready to dedicate myself entirely to it.'[9]

Once the idea was adopted, a project took shape. A provisory
committee was finally placed in charge of establishing the statutes

---

[8] Dunant to Édouard Monnier, 7 September 1852, World YMCA Archives. This
letter has been partly quoted by Shedd, *History of the YMCA*, 51. We use his
translation.
[9] Geisendorf, *Soixante ans de souvenirs*, 19–20.

of the future Geneva YMCA. Now, Henri began to see the achievement of the dream he'd been chasing for months: a true 'religious circle', only for the youth, with a permanent location, and ultimately, an organization that could be extended to other regions or, with enough luck and hard work, even internationally.

The assembly elected their first committee. Two young men received the most votes: Henri Dunant and Louis Rosselet. Despite such encouragement, Dunant wasn't interested in the chairmanship. Yes, he was a talented and enthusiastic networker, but he wasn't a manager. When the functions were divvied up the following week, Henri chose 'corresponding secretary', much more in line with his taste for relationships and the epistolary skills that had already made him a natural ambassador.

The position of Chairman landed upon Maximilien Perrot, the young man Henri had brought into the group the year before. Perrot had given up his studies because of a strange 'brain weakness', after which his father had sent him to 'toughen up' on a farm in Germany. Upon his return to Switzerland, his career prospects were nil. For an emotional man with fragile health, Dunant's invitation was a saving grace. His conversion had been lightning quick: it had only taken a few months for him to become one of the most devoted members of the Thursday meetings alongside Dunant, and when it was time to create something more structured, he was the first to present himself as a candidate for the chairmanship. But unlike Dunant who never looked back once he'd thrown himself into something, Maximilien was struggling with his humility when it was time to take centre stage. Once elected for a task he'd coveted, his anxious modesty forced him to deny he'd even wanted it in the first place. 'You know I was nominated chairman against my own wishes,' he wrote to his brother several days later. 'I don't feel myself advanced enough in my Christian Life to warrant the trust that has been placed in me. I would have liked to refuse, but of all the members I am the one with the most time.' He continued by saying that he only accepted because his friends declared it a 'call from God': 'The chairmanship is a formality and I will efface myself as much as possible and work in absolute humility.'[10]

---

[10] Max Perrot to Adolphe Perrot, 19 November 1852. Alain Perrot, 'Regards de Maximilien Perrot sur le début de l'UCGE de Genève', 150 ans déja, 37. All letters from Maximilien Perrot to his brother Adolphe Perrot are taken from this article.

The association was given a space at the Rue des Chanoines, in the very same house that had seen the birth of the Evangelical Society twenty years earlier. Nevertheless, the young members of the YMCA declared their independence from all authority. Members were defined by this single phrase of Article 7 of their statutes:

> ... young people who recognize the Holy Scriptures as divinely inspired and the only rule of faith; Jesus Christ, the Lord our Saviour, as their only hope; and who would like to work, with the help of the Holy Spirit, to advance God's reign.[11]

Between 1852 and 1853, Henri Dunant sponsored no less than twenty new members. No one else on the committee did as much: it was Dunant who recruited, convinced, assembled – so much so that even Maximilien Perrot would be forced to give credit to Dunant twenty-five years later when telling the story of the group's origins, even if by then he could not bring himself to mention his once dear friend Henri Dunant by name:

> The perseverance of one of the founders of the Association, who was a bank clerk, was extremely helpful. He knew how to rebind ties which were breaking, rally deserters, re-energize the weak, reinspire tepid hearts. We owed God and we owed him for fanning the fire of our Thursday meetings [. . .] It was he who first thought to put us in connection with the Christian youth from other cantons and other countries.[12]

Dunant paid with his time, but also with his pocket. Although he did not earn much at Lullin & Sautter, he donated the remarkable sum of 250 francs to the association, a quarter of the organization's total funds. He was by no means the wealthiest member of the circle – far from it. But the YMCA was his work, his pride and seemingly his hope for a larger future than what might be available to a simple clerk with no connections to any of the banking dynasties. There was one thing he knew for sure: for the first year of the Geneva

---

[11] Geisendorf, *Soixante ans de souvenirs*, 22.
[12] Maximilien Perrot, *Notice historique sur l'Union chrétienne de Jeunes Gens de Genève* (Geneva: Privat, 1878), 8.

YMCA's existence, Dunant could think of no better way to spend his savings.

The twenty-six founding members of the YMCA of Geneva included five merchants, four artisans of the 'Fabrique' (the watchmaking industry in Geneva), two clerks, two pastry chefs, two teachers, one painter, one photographer, one bookbinder, four students and four 'annuitants'.[13] The registry indicates Henri Dunant among this last category. Why did he list himself this way? Why didn't he use his banking clerk title like the two others? His irrepressible snobbism would later see him hunting down his most aristocratic origins; he would even be tempted to separate his name into two words. Here, he was already dreaming of reaching a higher rung on the social ladder where work was not to provide income but to broaden his horizons. Since his position at Lullin & Sautter offered him no such opportunities for the moment, what was the use of writing it down? His true ambitions at this point were wholly with the YMCA and its international development; to this, he dedicated his body and soul. What he did with the rest of his time wasn't worth mentioning.

The Paris controversy

Having added the position of 'corresponding secretary' to his list of achievements, Dunant now focused his attention on the initiatives for an umbrella organization or international assembly. Unsurprisingly, the Paris YMCA was the first to raise the question. Frédéric Monnier had moved to the French capital a few months earlier and now took up the YMCA as 'his' cause. At the end of 1852, he met with Jean-Paul Cook, who was just as ambitious, to discuss assembling the different groups from the various French-speaking countries into one General French Association. All that remained was to convince the Genevans, famously opposed to centralization, and then Henri Dunant, whom everyone agreed was the first to have established an international network.

---

[13] With no salaried employment, given that they live on some family inheritance or income from a fortune.

In truth, there was no need to convince Dunant to work on creating permanent connections between Europe's flourishing groups of Christian youth; this was the international brotherhood he'd been dreaming about since that evening of October 1851 when he handed his letter to a pastor from Nîmes for three young men he didn't know. But where the Genevans and the Parisians disagreed was on the nature of the structure, an issue which perfectly reflected the countries' historical differences. Paris could only imagine a centralized francophone association while the Genevans, with Dunant at their head, were more inclined to an international federation of autonomous YMCAs with a strictly executive centre in Geneva, Paris or any other city. This controversy waged on throughout the first half of 1853, and Dunant found himself in direct conflict with his dearest foreign friends, including his very first correspondent from Nîmes, Eugène Laget, who had since become one of his closest 'brothers', as well as the Monnier brothers, whose respect Dunant was very keen to preserve. On 20th January, even though Henri had really only dipped his toe into the quarrel, Frédéric Monnier was already complaining to his brother Édouard that 'these dear friends' [of Geneva], and 'Dunant in particular',[14] had a regrettable tendency to consider Geneva the centre and origin of everything. Henri attempted to defend himself, but to no avail. The harm was done. Édouard backed his brother Frédéric's project, and the relationship between the two men would never be the same again.

The Paris proposal also caused problems within the Geneva YMCA. Because his foreign correspondents continued to write to Dunant instead of Chairman Perrot, it was Dunant who replied according to his own convictions. 'I do not like your project,' he wrote to the French in February 1853, 'in that you seem to be leaving our dearest and precious friends in England and Scotland to the side, as well as those in Holland, the United States, and elsewhere.' In a vertical postscript alongside his last page, he added 'Our friends Perrot and Lullin agree with me.'[15]

This addendum would cost him dearly. Humiliated about being relegated to the background, Perrot rushed to alert Paris that Henri Dunant's 'personal and unofficial' letters expressed only the author's opinion.

---

[14] Shedd, *History of the YMCA*, 51.
[15] From H. Dunant to E. Laget, 5 February 1853, World YMCA Archives.

Even 'brothers in Christ' could not avoid some rivalries. And this was just the beginning.

The apostolic voyage

Notwithstanding their bouts of temper, Perrot and Dunant were agreed on numerous points, and notably that they must meet other YMCA members in the flesh if they wanted to create a living, breathing international community. Seeing one another, speaking together and praying together were the very foundations of their movement. They turned their words into actions and left together at the end of May 1853 on what Maximilien Perrot called an 'apostolic voyage'. From Saint-Etienne to Marseilles and from Marseilles to Montpellier, with numerous stops along the way, they spent more than a month enthusiastically visiting the existing associations, helping establish new ones and revelling in their awe at a fraternity whose limits seemed to be continually expanding.

How did the two friends get along on their trip? This is a mystery: neither man has left a trace of his thoughts. If 'the Lord himself legitimized more specific affections, provided they are in Him',[16] as Henri had written to Édouard Monnier several months earlier, certainly that same Lord made no guarantees that all friendships in Christ involved affection. It is tempting to imagine Henri on that journey with his arms wide open to his new 'brothers in Christ', men he could treat as old friends because of the connections already made through his letters, while the reserved Maximilien at his side struggled to assert his role as chairman of the YMCA of Geneva.

His rivalry with Dunant was so great that it brought Perrot to condemn Dunant's innovation of a newsletter, while simultaneously recognizing how practical they were in helping unify the various widespread groups. As he wrote to his brother that same year:

> I am surely always opposed to ostentation, but there are particular cases where it is very difficult not to step forward. I would like for us to sustain our relationships without the newsletters, but this is hardly possible since we must correspond

---

[16] See note 8, above.

with seventy-five or more meetings, how could we do it without a general letter?[17]

Although their paths would not yet diverge, their personalities continued to clash in both small and large situations, from the day-to-day office management at the Rue des Chanoines to their strategic vision for the overall movement. Perrot and Dunant would not take a second apostolic voyage together.

The summer of 1853 brought more meetings with other YMCAs. One such gathering was planned for the beginning of August in the Canton of Vaud, in the hills above the lake between Lausanne and Vevey. Travelling in those days required a feat of organization, timing and various methods of transport. Henri Dunant, always in charge of his foreign brothers, organized their arrival with a worrying precision, as if the event's entire success relied upon the presence of the outsiders: 'I will hold our two places, yours and mine,' he wrote to Eugène Laget, 'in the coach that leaves at 10:00 p.m. for Lausanne.' And the passports? Henri hadn't thought of it! So another page was quickly written: 'I'll wait for you at Saint-Genis.' But then he would change his mind, indicating that someone at Saint-Genis would wait for Laget and drive him in his own cart to the Geneva gates.

> Now, dear friend, don't forget anything about your Saturday arrival: what will you do if you only arrive on Sunday? You won't see anyone – but me, of course who will have waited for you – and we'll be kept from the party which I'm so looking forward to, and which you will greatly enjoy.[18]

When this Saturday arrived, as Dunant had feared, everything went wrong. The Saint-Genis coach came too late to meet the omnibus and so they did have to take the last coach for Lausanne, all while collecting a few other latecomers along the way. But the happy crowd managed to assemble on the Sunday morning upon a steep hillside where the newcomers were gifted with a jaw-dropping view of Lake Geneva bordered on one side by terraced vineyards, and on

---

[17] From M. Perrot to A. Perrot, no date, A. Perrot, 'Regards de M. Perrot', 48–9.
[18] H. Dunant to E. Laget, 4 August 1853, World YMCA Archives.

the other by the dark and massive silhouette of the Alps. This was where, following many prayers and thanks to the Creator of such a beautiful place, that the French emissary Eugène Laget launched into a vehement speech in favour of an international 'general association'. The Universal Exhibition, set for Paris in two years' time, was already in everyone's thoughts; the perfect occasion for a first Congress of Christian Youth – organized by and for these youth, an unbelievable novelty for the time.

Dunant had been right to insist Laget not miss the 'party' that day. On his own, he could not have brought his Genevan friends to think beyond their comfortable prayer evenings. An organization? Structures? An international congress? These words alone were enough to frighten off half the group. Only someone from the outside, with a communicative warmth like Laget's, could first soften them up and eventually convince them. Dunant really had little to do with this first success ... except that he'd intuitively understood how to proceed, just as he'd understood the year before how to exploit Adolphe Monod's visit, and just as he would know a few years later how to use the Queen of Prussia and the King of Saxony. Here already, Dunant was fine-tuning his method.

But the summer was nearly over, and there were more practical issues to bring him back down to earth. The following Tuesday, Dunant began his first two weeks of the military service required of all Swiss citizens. The time had passed for dreaming of international brotherhoods.

A faraway mission

Since being hired as a clerk in 1849 by the Lullin & Sautter bank, Dunant had done well. His employers didn't mind that he'd spent most of his energy transforming a small prayer group into an up-and-coming international alliance. This might have even cast him as a trustworthy young man in the eyes of his superiors. The evangelical movement was well-established within Geneva's upper-class circles and included both Lullins and Sautters. Dunant may even have found his position through a connection in the religious community.

In August 1853, 'Sir' Sautter, as Geneva's private bankers liked to be called, invited Dunant to his office for a special meeting.

Henri found his boss alone. What was it exactly in Mr Sautter de Beauregard that impressed Henri so much? The man's noble title, or his great success at such a young age? Likely both. The Count, who was only 27 years old, was among Henri Dunant's numerous role models.

Sir Sautter launched into his reason for calling this meeting.

'You are not unaware, Mr Dunant, of our projects in Algeria. My father taught me to cherish this region when he presided over the Algiers Consistory. Which is why I took an interest in this magnificent country.'

Sir Sautter continued describing the mission of the recently created *Compagnie Genevoise des colonies suisses de Sétif* (The Geneva Company of Swiss Colonies in Sétif), which was to contribute as much as it could to the prosperity of the country and its Christianization.

'Since April, thanks to a concession from the Emperor, we now possess 20,000 hectares of land that we must populate with several hundred settlers. There is a lot to do there before they can arrive, and our agent has been frustratingly delayed. Which is why we'd like you to replace him.'

What kind of delay could get in the way of an order from the 'Sirs' Lullin & Sautter? The death of a parent? A move? But there was no time to think it over. Dunant replied immediately:

'Your trust is an honour, Sir.'

'So, it's done. You will leave for Marseilles on September 1st.'

The few days left before his departure gave him very little time to dedicate to the YMCA. He dropped by the Rue des Chanoines on his last Sunday evening in Geneva; only one or two young men were still reading the newspaper near the windows, alongside the brotherly supervision of Maximilien Perrot.

'I'll be away for a few weeks,' Dunant whispered. 'Count Sautter de Beauregard is sending me on an important mission to Algeria.'

Since their trip south together the previous spring, their relationship had worsened, not with angry words, but irremediably. Possessive of his chairmanship, Maximilien couldn't stand Dunant's public dominance within the movement; certain people in town still continued to ask him if Dunant was 'still the chairman'! And Dunant, unaware of the frustrations he caused, added insult to injury with a frightening naivety.

'I have to leave this Thursday. So I'm sorry but, I won't be here to do the next newsletter . . .'

'Don't worry at all about the next newsletter. They're one of my tasks now. Be reassured that all is in hand here.'

For Perrot, the newsletters were a sensitive subject as another example of Dunant's instinctive flair for unification and connection. It would be unfair to deny the decisive role the secretary's modest paper pamphlets had had in the unifying of what had been a number of small fragile groups into a powerful movement. But why was Dunant always so vain? Why couldn't he just pass on his baton?

On Sunday evenings, Maximilien wrote to his younger brother studying in Paris. 'I am constantly having to temper Dunant,' he would tell him that evening. 'Why can't he be less naive!' He may have felt a little ungrateful because he went on in a milder tone: 'Without this he would be a gem for the Association, he has an astonishing zeal and energy. He is the one who during my absence made and sent the second newsletter which, as you say, is weak. But which was written with good intentions.'[19]

The Algerian dream

Henri closed his luggage very early the next morning to take the coach to Lyons. He stopped only long enough in Marseilles to jump on the boat for Algiers. At the end of their meeting, Count Sautter had offered a few words about the French city where his father, 'just like yours, as far as I know', had spent a portion of his life. As he was walking towards the port, Henri considered the Count's comment. He would have liked to speak of Marseilles with such nonchalance! But no: just hearing the city's name brought a painful constriction to his heart. How many times had his mother cursed the place that had kept his father so often away from home? Indeed, Henri suspected a few other reasons for his father's absences, which in his adolescent imagination took the form of blonde hair, theatres and crinolines. Hadn't Marseilles already, thirty years earlier, trapped his great uncle Jean-François in its snare? Henri's father

---

[19] From M. Perrot to A. Perrot, no date, Perrot, '*Regards de M. Perrot*', 41.

had only followed the family tradition.[20] Which was why Henri was relieved not to spend any more time there, as if he were also afraid of Marseilles's siren song.

The boat lifted anchor that Thursday. A breeze made the heat more bearable, even agreeable when at the front of the boat. Standing at the prow gave Henri, no matter where he was headed, an immediate joy, like a tonic, bracing and exhilarating.

Two days later, the Algerian coastline stretched out along a stunning cobalt blue background. The boat was unloaded at Stora, close to Philippeville,[21] in an incredible commotion of luggage, porters, carts, passengers, soldiers and curious onlookers, both Arab and European. From here, his travels were only just beginning: it took nearly two days to reach Constantine by carriage, and then another two days to travel over a series of steep gorges and through forests filled with the cries of strange animals. In Djemila, he visited some Roman ruins, including a great arch he sketched out in his notebook. The inland journey had taken him nearly 1,000 metres above sea level, which meant the August heat was now much less stifling. All that remained was the last leg of his journey from Djemila to Sétif. After setting out early the next morning, he could soon see the Babor Mountains in the distance. In the evening, having arrived in Sétif, he followed his host's advice to wait for daylight to complete the last stage of his journey to the 'Souissi village', the Sétif name for the Swiss colony of Aïn-Arnat.[22]

Sétif in 1853 had a population of several thousand inhabitants, including nearly 2,000 Europeans. Its exceptional climate was not only a lure for foreign colonials but also the reason for the region's high agricultural yields, something the Romans had already exploited. The city Dunant discovered was rapidly expanding. Over the last fifteen years a fort had been built with a garrison of more than 2,000 men, along with aqueducts, fountains, a bazaar, a church and a mosque. In the detailed travel notebook he kept to report

---

[20] See Mützenberg, *Henry Dunant le prédestiné*, 58–67.
[21] Today Skikda.
[22] The major study on Dunant's activities in Algeria is Jacques Pous, *Henry Dunant l'Algérien* (Geneva: Grounauer, 1979). It is based (among many other sources) on the systematic study of the *Compagnie genevoise* archives stored at the State of Geneva Archives, referencing Dunant's Algerian period. See also Claude Lützelschwab, *La Compagnie genevoise des Colonies suisses de Sétif* (Berne: Peter Lang, 2006).

back to his employers, Dunant noted that Europeans and Arabs seemed to be living in harmony.

The very next day, Dunant left the Sétif citadel through the Napoleon Gate. Then, just beyond the double vault of the Algiers Gate, a 'road' that might more accurately be described as a 'track' stretched off into the distance. The small path wound among sparse vegetation of dry, low-lying shrubs. Dunant's horse took him down an abruptly descending hill to a *wadi* and then rising again, just as abruptly, towards a jumble of buildings. This was El Bez, the Geneva Company's farm, a magnificent domain of more than 600 hectares. Stopping first to speak with the few employees present, Dunant then set off in the direction of Aïn-Arnat.

The road rose towards a small hill which looked out across a vast plain, bordered in the distance by several mountain ranges. From that point, as one of the employees had told him, he would cross the plain to reach the settler village.

When Dunant arrived at his destination in the late afternoon, he walked into a silent construction site that was much less advanced than he'd expected it to be. The imperial decree of 26th April, through which the Geneva Company had been granted a concession of 200 square kilometres, had also included several conditions. The area had to be divided into roughly ten different zones, each of which should contain about fifty colonial homes. The decree also stipulated that the villages be constructed in stone, at the company's cost, with vaulted roofs and tiles. Each house needed to have at least three rooms in order to provide for a European farmer and his family.

But the reality Henri discovered was far from what had been agreed upon. The few finished houses were not stone but earthen, and they were extremely damp despite the season. The French government's requirements were even less in order: none of the fountains had yet been built, neither had the village paths. The deadline for the first fifty houses was so tight that the workers had set up their tents near the construction site to save time.

Back in Sétif, Dunant went to sleep that night hoping for an early start. His employers had given him a month and a half to get the site ready for the first settlers expected at the end of October. Dunant was responsible for the company's payments to the local builder in charge of the few houses already constructed. But wood also needed to be ordered for the winter stocks, a particularly harsh season at Aïn-Arnat's altitude. So that the farmers could feed themselves as quickly as possible from their own products, Dunant proceeded to have a number of gardens and fields prepared behind the settlers' homes. When his employers would learn of this later, they would ask him to temper his enthusiasm. Dunant needed to remember he was now working for a finance company, not a charity.

Time was passing quickly, however, and more difficulties arose due to the remote location and difficult access routes. Aïn-Arnat was only 9 kilometres from Sétif but the road was so bad that it took half a day just to get there. Nevertheless, Dunant didn't limit his travels to the Sétif region. Alongside his professional duties, he was curious to discover Algeria, the Arab world, the Muslim religion and the nomadic peoples. For a man who'd only ever known Switzerland and France, everything was a marvel, revealed in what he wrote to Édouard Monnier, with as much enthusiasm as pride:

> I was received hospitably by both the Arabs and the Kabyles; at the home of a governor, I attended a curious local 'fantasia' – Elsewhere I spoke about the Koran with the marabouts; I have formed strong friendships here, and I even became close with a relative of the former bey of Constantine.[23]

Reading these words, did his friend perceive the true magnitude of the transformation Henri was experiencing during that autumn of 1853? Most likely. First, Henri was writing to his dear friend on the formal letterhead of the Geneva Company of Swiss Colonies in Sétif, as he would do for any valuable business relationship. Also, Henri took his time responding, something which was out of character and may have surprised Édouard Monnier after the previously ardent nature of their friendship. In guise of an excuse, Henri slightly falsified the date of his return to Geneva, which we can place on 28th October at the very latest, and which was certainly when he received Monnier's letter. And yet he only responded to Monnier on 10th December:

> And now you must, rightfully so, have been waiting a long time for my reply! But when your precious letter of 25th October reached me – in Geneva – I was amid the kadis, marabouts,

---

[23] H. Dunant to É. Monnier, 10 December 1853, World YMCA Archives.

sheikhs, agas, kaids, sheriffs and imams of Algeria. I was there representing a powerful Genevan business which has undertaken a settlement in the province of Constantine! I've only just returned, which is why your letter remained without response for so long.

Further on, Dunant explained he had been sent to Sétif, 'to fill in for Mr le Baron Gingins de La Sarraz, General Director of the Swiss Colonies of Sétif'. Finally, after a variety of travel anecdotes, including tales of two car crashes, 'which could have been very serious', he claimed with a complacency that Édouard would not have been able to overlook:

I am extremely interested in this colonization and I hope to return as soon as I can to this country I like very much; if you'd like a position as pastor, I will get it for you.[24]

In trying to make himself look important as a 'replacement' for the Baron de Gingins, when he was actually covering for an employee who'd been detained, Dunant neglected to mention the personal projects he was putting together at that moment.

Alongside his obligations to the Geneva Company, Dunant had explored the province, guided by a resourceful young man from Württemberg he'd met in Sétif named Henri Nick, who knew the region like the back of his hand and had offered him all kinds of not-to-miss business ideas. During one of these prospecting trips, Dunant had set his sights on a piece of land between Sétif and Bougie, opportunistically endowed with a waterfall, meaning that a mill could be built there. Such was his excitement that before the end of his first trip he was already envisioning himself as a bigshot Swiss investor in Algeria. This was the start of his dreams for greatness, which would consume him for the next fifteen years.

The campaign in Switzerland

On 28th October 1853, Mr Sautter was waiting for Mr Dunant in Geneva to hear his trip report. His employee had proven himself

---

[24] Ibid.

adept at completing his different tasks, both at the work site and in
the reports he had sent back. They were so pleased with his work
that the company planned to reward Dunant with a bonus of 200
francs.

200 francs! Dunant thanked him of course, but this didn't exactly
match the height of his dreams at that point. Taking advantage of
the trust his employer had just shown him, he jumped in headfirst
and, speaking as equal to equal, mentioned his plans for land
acquisition and factory projects. The only problem was that no one
knew him there! The Count's support of his request for a concession
from the French authorities would smooth his way forward.

There was no need to beg. Three days later, on 1st November
1853, the chief executive of the Geneva Company wrote the following
letter to Marshal de Saint-Arnaud, who was then the French Secretary
of State for War:

> Mr Jean-Henri Dunant has worked four years in my employ and
> has just spent two months in Sétif working for the Geneva
> Company. He would like to obtain in Aïn-Roua, between Sétif and
> Bougie, a concession of 500,000 m^2 of good land and a powerful
> waterfall, upon which he will construct a European mill.

To add conviction to his message, Mr Sautter ended his letter by
lauding the merits of his protégé:

> By all accounts, Mr Dunant is capable of fulfilling his obligations,
> his proposition is serious and his construction project will
> contribute to the enrichment of the colony, and could one day
> become the base of an agricultural centre.[25]

Did Sautter already know that Dunant's request had no chance of
coming to fruition, despite the support of Marshal de Saint-Arnaud?
If not, he would come to realize this several days later, when the Baron
de Gingins, his friend and current Geneva Company representative in
Sétif, wrote to him about it. He explained to Sautter in no uncertain
terms that young Dunant was reaching too high, much too high, and

---

[25] Count Sautter to Marshal Saint-Arnaud, 1 November 1853, cited by Pous, *Dunant
l'Algérien*, 85.

there was no chance of his request being accepted, because of the 'strongly reasoned objections he will be faced with'. And he concluded, soothingly: 'Mr Dunant should not overly regret this failure, since it would be much less profitable than he believed.'[26] He also suggested that the interested young man spend several more weeks in Algeria to study other new businesses, which would undoubtedly be more appropriate – meaning more modest.

From now on Dunant worked on both his personal projects and for the Geneva Company in Sétif. In November and December 1853, his employer asked him to begin recruiting as many settlers as he could from Switzerland for the new villages of the colony, which, according to the terms of the concession, must be populated as quickly as possible. Dunant first used the media to attract candidates. Contradicting the accusations from a few Swiss newspapers against the Geneva Company, he published a letter in the *Journal de Genève* on 3rd November 1853 asserting that the country 'was already covered with villages, farms and gardens, garnished with excellent high-quality products' to which he added that 'the use of natives guarantees economical labour for growing grain'. Another article was published at the end of January 1854 to highlight 'how much the settlers already on site rejoice in their decision' and to boast of their good reputation in Sétif, with their 'fresh faces, proving their good health'.[27]

But volunteers for this exile were not rushing to the gate. Clearly, a newspaper campaign wasn't enough; a more active propaganda strategy was required, grassroots action involving direct recruitment. Henri took this on himself between the end of March and mid-April 1854 by embarking on a two-week campaign tour in the Canton of Vaud.[28] More than just locating 'agents' for voluntary settlers, he needed to teach them how to actively recruit, which wasn't a simple task. It also involved reconciling the communal and cantonal authorities[29] because the first were interested in getting rid of the

---

[26] Count Sautter to Marshal Saint-Arnaud, 1 November 1853, cited by Pous, *Dunant l'Algérien*, 86.
[27] *Journal de Genève*, 22 January 1854, 4.
[28] The 'cantons' are the member States of the Swiss Confederation. There were twenty-two cantons in 1850. The Canton de Vaud, next to Geneva, is one of the French-speaking cantons of Switzerland.
[29] The 'communes' are the third level of government in Switzerland: cities, towns and villages.

poorest citizens from their communes, while the second were afraid that a mass exodus from the canton might make a bad impression. Furthermore, propaganda for Algeria was becoming more and more difficult as news from the colony arrived back in Switzerland.

Because the reality was less rosy, much less rosy then the Sétif-based Geneva Company wanted people to know. After an exhausting journey, the first Aïn-Arnat settlers had discovered an unfinished village, with muddy pathways and dark, damp houses still lacking essential furnishings. For the shared infrastructures, water and heat, the Company and the State continued to pass the buck back and forth. Unfortunately, the village was quite high up and no one was spared the harsh realities of winter that first Christmas in the south. All this was already known in the green countryside of the Swiss Plateau, where many settlers had left families behind. This meant that recruiters needed to embellish somewhat upon the situation during their campaigns in French-speaking Switzerland, or at least hope to find villages who had not yet heard the rumours returning from the Algerian 'El Dorado'.

Dunant used this professional trip to visit several Christian youth groups in the surrounding areas.[30] But once his tour was finished and he was back in Geneva, he had only one thing in mind: to return to Algeria and get his future started. If the Geneva Company still needed him, so much the better: he declared himself ready to do their bidding. However, he was no longer disposed to give them all his time nor was he content to remain a mere employee. By chance, the new Geneva Company chief executive was a certain Fazy-Alléon whom Henri had known for a long time through the Evangelical Society. He was able to obtain a tailor-made contract allowing him to keep his company calling card along with the freedom to develop his own business. He agreed to fulfill his accounting clerk functions 'with all the zeal and interest they required', but he also stipulated – in black and white and with a self-confident poise earned during a year of experience – his requirements for autonomy:

I would like the flexibility that at any time, of which I will be the sole judge, and in the event of major circumstances, I would be

---

[30] According to a letter to Chauncy Langdon, 15 December 1854, World YMCA Archives.

able to return to Geneva before the end of the six months mentioned in your letter, thus no fixed engagement.

It is understood that I will work as clerk alongside Mr de Gingins, for accounting and all related necessary correspondence [. . .] but with the reservation of the time I need for my own affairs.[31]

Obviously, Dunant felt sure enough of his future success to be so cavalier towards his former employers. Did their evangelical brotherhood make Mr Fazy-Alléon overly indulgent towards him? It's telling that the new chief executive was careful to justify such a curious contract when discussing it with his investors:

You'll understand that anyway we have agreed because he is doing us a favour and we are persuaded that with his good heart and his interest in our company, he will deliver more than he has promised. He will be very useful, by the full trust we can place in him as our proxy, or by his ease with paper negotiations that you remember he did so well with last year. (. . .)[32]

With the conditions for his trip finally settled, Dunant could set off again for Algeria with a keen hope to leave his mark on the world.

---

[31] The letter dated from 22 April 1854 is reproduced *in extenso* in Annex III of Pous, *Dunant l'Algérien*, 212–13.
[32] 26 April 1854, Pous, *Dunant l'Algérien*, 63.

3

Windmills on the Sand (1854–9)

Making his mark

Nineteenth-century travel narratives are all agreed that no one returns unscathed from the desert. Dunant was no exception. What experiences awed or stunned him as he travelled for the first time in a region so weighted with the ardent Orientalism of the period? No record has been left of his own specific fantasies, but there's no doubt Dunant believed in an El Dorado. He definitely returned from his first trip to Algeria with the conviction that the country would give him what Geneva could not: membership in an aristocratic circle of European colonials, recognition, wealth, entrance to the big leagues.

In early May 1854, he set off again, and although his African dreams were foremost in his thoughts, he took the time to stop in several places in France he'd visited years earlier with Max Perrot, delighted now to find that YMCA membership was continuing to swell. He regaled these groups with stories of new associations and growth, but however warmly he was welcomed, he was only passing through: his new horizon lay further south, beyond the blue line of the Mediterranean.

After catching a boat from Marseilles on 7th or 8th May, and a quick stop in Algiers with the Algerian YMCA, he arrived in Sétif towards the end of the month. This second stay would last more than three months. Just like his first trip, Dunant acquitted himself carefully of his various Company missions. But his goals were no longer exclusively about serving his Genevan employers, he now wanted to work for himself, towards establishing his future company, whether in a mill, in forests or in minerals – whatever, as long as it gave him a place in the golden sun of Algeria.

As the Baron de Gingins had warned him, the concession he'd requested was refused.[1] Never mind! Again with his new friend Henri Nick, who was becoming his exclusive adviser and whom he'd soon make his associate, Dunant rapidly discovered a new plot of land that suited his ambitions. In June of 1854, he cast his die for a 17-acre *azel*[2] located 17 kilometres from Djemila, near the Mons ruins, which included a waterfall just perfect for a flour mill. He'd received, at least he believed he'd received, enough assurances that he would obtain concessions for the plot and the water that he went ahead and bought the machinery for an English mill, had the plans drawn up for his future factory and even ordered work to begin. This was certainly a little hasty when considering how slow the administration was in the region, but with his unshakeable optimism Dunant could not imagine he might be refused for what he felt was only the start of his Algerian projects.

The definitive authorization for the waterfall and the land plot were not granted to him until two years later, in June 1856, at which point Dunant had had plenty of time to rethink his request and deem it radically inadequate. Seventeen acres! He needed a hundred times more to cover the investments required for the construction of his splendid flour mill: four storeys high with four mills and a sophisticated French-made mechanism for sifting and cleaning.

For our novice businessman, the main problem arose where he hadn't been expecting it. A mill needed to be located outside a town, meaning the transport of the wheat would require animals. Luckily these animals could be fed on the wheat bran produced in the mill – but! – animals also required grazing land, much more grazing land than could be found on the 17 acres already partly in use by the factory buildings.

To make it all work, he just needed to win a small part of the 3,700-acre *azel* that stretched just behind his factory, opportunely endowed with the waterway for which it was named: Deheb Wadi.

---

[1] We follow Pous, *Dunant l'Algérien*, for the numerous proceedings of Dunant's requests.
[2] Land belonging to the State, usually rented out for farming and other uses.

In that summer of 1854, his hope turned to obsession: he needed more land, considerably more land. He eventually settled upon 1,200 additional acres to be sectioned from the Deheb Wadi *azel*. To Henri, this was non-negotiable and urgent. On 4th September 1854, three months after his initial request of 17 acres (which he'd still heard nothing about), Henri Dunant submitted his name – plans in hand – for a new 1,200-acre concession, with permission to use one of its waterfalls. This time he did all he could to secure the rights. And so he left Africa at the end of September with high hopes of returning as an enterprising colonial landowner.

A difficult report

Count Sautter de Beauregard was expecting Dunant once he'd arrived back in Geneva, eager to receive his report and news of the small Swiss colony. While making his way to the bank, Henri considered his task. How could he honestly describe the situation in Aïn-Arnat without overly dramatizing things? Luckily, Mr Sautter had not invited the other administrators for this first meeting. He received Dunant alone in his office and listened to him for forty-five minutes without interruption, with increasing consternation as Henri's report unfolded.[3]

'The settlers are completely demoralized. It began with a few bouts of illness, caught carelessly by sleeping out in the damp grass after sweating in the fields. Then several cases of typhus appeared. This meant the sick had to be taken all the way to the hospital in Sétif. And there is cholera in town, which the sick brought back to the village.'

Henri went quiet for a moment, looking for an expression on Mr Sautter's face. But the Count remained impassive, giving only a glance to encourage Dunant to continue.

'As you've already learned, the epidemic killed several settlers and sowed real terror throughout the community. Luckily Reverend Curie knows a very efficient remedy, a mixture of cognac and camphor, to which one adds borage, sage and chamomile. I administered this

---

[3] The following oral exchange is based on a written report: A.C.G. PV. 1. fol. A4, 25 September 1854, quoted by Pous, *Dunant l'Algérien*, 66.

myself to several of the sick, and they recovered quickly. Nevertheless, the toll is heavy, especially with settlers who were also housing workers: along with some cases of excessive drinking, the overcrowding and lack of hygiene resulted in many fatalities among the adults, and some children as well.'

Dunant did not mention the increasing anger of the settlers, and how many of them regretted their 'adventure'. He did not mention the delays in land distribution that had so discouraged some of the men that, once they'd finally received their allotment, they actually passed it on to tenant-farmer *fellahs* from Sétif. Nor did he describe the desperation of the Burnens and Sergy families, who'd had to gather together each week for a new burial. The Count knew all of this, of course – why worry him further?

Indeed, August Sautter had heard enough. He accompanied Dunant to the large staircase, thanking him for the faithfulness of the report.

Once outside in the heavy Genevan drizzle, sharp images of Aïn-Arnat came to him through the fog, as if rebuking him for having shut them away during the entire meeting with Sautter. First the faces which, before leaving for Algeria, Dunant had naively imagined as the newspapers had described: 'fresh faces, proof of good health'.[4] Instead, he was met with filthy, gaunt and swollen faces, frightening dark circles around the eyes of children with cholera. Images of disgusting piles of food stocks, utensils, dirty laundry and trash, vagrant children, desperate women, exhausted workers in scandalously overcrowded houses which emanated a fetid stench that the occupants didn't even seem to notice. And, more haunting than the images, the echo of the raspy voice and the barely perceptible weight in his left hand of little Beauvert's head, as he helped him drink some of Pastor Curie's miracle potion.

Dunant took a deep breath. As he walked up the street that climbed to the Old Town, some of the dampness coming from the lake began to dissipate; Dunant tried to forget for a moment the shapes, smells and sounds of Aïn-Arnat – his first Algerian disenchantment. And yet it was a good idea to spread the Good Word of the Lord through an increasing Christian presence in the country! Except that the Europeans ready to live there were not

[4] *Journal de Genève*, 22 January 1854, 4.

the ones Dunant would have chosen to help extend the 'Kingdom of God'. What connection was there between these miserable Swiss settlers, whose places of origin had rushed to be rid of them, and his own Christian friends, men of energetic piety and irreproachable conduct?

It was towards these men he was now walking. Once he reached the Rue des Chanoines, Dunant happily pushed against the door of the place he'd so often thought about in Algeria. Aware of his return, his best friends were waiting for him: Ernest de Traz, Louis Rosselet, Théodore Necker, all of them gathered around, assailing him with questions about his travels, about his chances of Christianizing North Africa, about the reality of the Swiss Colony so disparaged by the newspapers. Shaking hands around the room, Henri revelled in his rediscovery of friendship's warm embrace. This was enough to put him right back in the saddle. He intended to spend the winter in Europe, he said, and he would happily represent Geneva at the General Assembly of the YMCAs in the Netherlands. He would travel himself to encourage the many small groups forming throughout the north, from Leiden to Brussels.

A small ripple of silence delayed the assembly's acceptance of such kindly offered support. Perhaps a touch of relief mixed in with their applause? Quite possibly. Because since his experiences in the North African sands, his 'brothers in Christ' had been a little worried about him. His enterprising spirit looked a bit like social climbing to those born at the top of the ladder. But no: here he was with them again, true to himself, with the same intense, vigorous and communicative faith as those first Thursday meetings! All doubts about him vanished on sight. Dunant was there, Henri had returned to them, all was well.

Northern travels

Henri's journey to the north would be intense. On 31st October, Dunant was in Amsterdam for an assembly of 300 people celebrating the third anniversary of their YMCA. Continuing along, he met with his many 'brothers': merchants in Haarlem and Rotterdam, farmers in the Frise, students in Leiden, salesmen in Antwerp. Along his return route, he stopped in Brussels where the YMCA had been created eighteen months earlier. They welcomed him as the indirect founder of their association, as he discreetly reminded his Genevan friends in a letter: 'I was surrounded and given a warm welcome. Their association was formed after the first newsletters from ours that I'd sent completely by chance to Pastor Durand.'[5]

From Brussels, Dunant went to Paris where the YMCA members invited him to attend their meeting. This was 21st November 1854, the date the decision was made to hold the first General Assembly of all YMCAs for the following summer in Paris.

For Dunant, this decision represented the outcome of five tireless years working to get a worldwide movement of Christian youth off the ground. While he may have been publicly reticent about a centralized organization, the kind that Paris had been lobbying for, he had long claimed to be in favour of a synod or an annual meeting which would make it possible to strengthen the international ties of friendship. He would never express any regret that this first meeting was to be held in Paris instead of Geneva; after vagabonding all over the continent for the last two years, the location mattered very little to him now. Furthermore, Paris had certain indisputable advantages. The entire world was watching the French capital in preparation for the next Universal Exhibition. The Evangelical Alliance had even decided to hold its annual meeting there in the summer of 1855; why wouldn't the Christian youth jump on the occasion to organize their own conference?

His timely presence for that 21st November meeting in Paris meant Dunant had the satisfaction of giving Geneva the good news himself: the next day he sent notice to Chairman Perrot, as if it were a done deal, that all the YMCAs were planning to assemble in Paris the following July. 'Delegates will be sent from the United States, England, Scotland, Holland, Belgium, and Germany. What about Geneva?'[6] he added in the curious form of a question, as if there were any question of Geneva not joining the party.

Did Max Perrot begrudge Dunant's front-row seat? Or his ability to find himself in the right place at the right time? On 26th November, five days after the Paris meeting and while Dunant was spreading the word all the way to the United States, Perrot was reduced to begging for details from his brother living in Paris about what had been

---

[5] H. Dunant to the YMCA of Geneva, 22 November 1854, World YMCA Archives.
[6] Ibid.

'decided in regards to a General Assembly of the U.X.[7] from all countries'.[8] He also mentioned that a pastor from Lyons had suggested he prepare a report for the assembly of the Evangelical Alliance on the origins of the YMCA movement. With his customary reticent humility, Perrot denied having accepted the task, but then went on to describe exactly what shape such a report might take, point by point! A month later, the same equivocation. In mid-December, he wrote to his brother: 'I'll admit that if the Evangelical Alliance decided to give up the report, I would be greatly relieved.'[9] But when he learned that Dunant was about to be mixed up in the business, he made a sudden U-turn and wouldn't dream of letting anyone else do it. 'Dunant seems to have arranged things definitely with Cook and said that he and I must take care of the general report,' he wrote to his brother Adolphe only a day after claiming to be happy to be rid of the task. 'But since I do not much trust Dunant,' he continued, 'I beg you to ask Cook if this report must be done, yes or no – and if he would give me as chairman the final answer so I can show Dunant if he gets upset.'[10] On 20th January 1855, Perrot would finally be relieved: Dunant was not involved, the report would be conferred to him. He would spend the next four months writing it and two more memorizing it.

Perrot's nervousness about this report betrays not only his hunger for recognition but also how exasperated he was with respect to his 'dear friend' Henri, according to what he wrote to his brother in the same period:

'How much I wish my dear friend would have more sense, more tact, and better judgement. He is always the same and, in his usefulness, he often tires me and mostly worries me. Let's pray for him, because he will have trouble in this life.'[11]

Alas, how right he was! And his prayers would change nothing. Dunant would have trouble, much trouble indeed. And Max Perrot's hostility would never turn to pity, it would only get worse.

---

[7] U.X. was a common abbreviation for *Union chrétienne*, the short-form name in French of the YMCA.
[8] M. Perrot to A. Perrot, 26 November 1854, in Perrot, '*Regards de M. Perrot*', 50.
[9] M. Perrot to A. Perrot, 19 December 1854, '*Regards de M. Perrot*', 52.
[10] M. Perrot to A. Perrot, 20 December 1854, '*Regards de M. Perrot*', 51.
[11] Ibid.

At this point in early 1855, however, contrary to Perrot's apparent fears, Dunant was no longer seeking a prominent position in the development of the YMCA. As he wrote to the general secretary of the American YMCA, William Chauncy Langdon, whom he'd never met but to whom he confided most sincerely, he was satisfied with what he'd accomplished:

> For the last six years I've dreamed of the YMCA and this brotherly correspondence, these reports, these relationships being established everywhere; four years ago, I alone began this ecumenical correspondence and early on I alone bore the weight of it. Since then things have changed and I'm happy to relegate myself to the background, seeing that the sacred fire has spread through my friends in Geneva and that all over the continent where evangelical Christians and young people exist, this work has begun.[12]

In closing he recommended 'Mr Max Perrot' to his correspondent, saying he was 'a very dear friend and excellent chairman. He is entirely devoted to the work and has truly understood it.' He evidently had no idea what his 'dear friend' was thinking about him. He would learn eventually . . . but it would be too late.

Troubles in the sand

Henri's letter to Langdon doesn't mention that all his energy was now focused on another future. On 1st March 1855, he left again for Algeria. Although no longer working for the Geneva Company of Swiss Colonies in Sétif, he still had plenty of reasons to pay attention to what was happening in Aïn-Arnat. It was becoming increasingly difficult for the Geneva Company to find new immigrants able to pay the 3,000 francs required by the French administration. Most of the candidates, having left home in total poverty, had no such resources. Consequently, the entrepreneurs of the firm had developed a work-around. The 50-acre lots conceded to the Geneva Company were no longer being bought by the future

---

[12] Dunant to Ch. Langdon, 22 January 1855, World YMCA Archives (in French. We translate).

settlers, but by wealthy Genevan investors, shareholders, friends or close relations of the Geneva Company, who then rented the lots to settler farmers. Inasmuch as the morality of the transaction didn't seem to bother them, neither were they planning to go to Algeria themselves to verify the quality of their investment. But they were delighted that a man they trusted could visit in their stead. Since Dunant was heading to Algeria anyway to advance his own affairs, his Genevan friends charged him to inspect the happiness, health and prosperity of their tenant farmers in Aïn-Arnat.

Describing the moral state of the settlers in an April 1855 letter to the Count Sautter de Beauregard in Geneva, Dunant did not mince his words: 'It couldn't be worse.'[13] A community decimated by illness, settlers detested by the native people, a population racked by depression, skeletal children living in filthy homes – this was the El Dorado he was now introducing to his younger brother Daniel, whom he'd brought with him this time, hoping Daniel might learn the business and join his projects. The shock was even more severe since Dunant's friends were mostly at fault. As well as skirting around the imperial decree of 1852 by buying up the lots meant for colony farmers, the investors were renting those lots at such high prices that the farmers could not keep up; in the end they had to forfeit. The French military authorities were soon alerted and intervened, forcing the Swiss owners to reduce their rental prices by a third, to even forgive some settlers an entire year's rent depending on how far the abuse had gone.

As representative for the Genevan property owners, Dunant's position was a delicate one. Did he perceive the full scope of his friends' responsibility in the catastrophe? Did he sympathize with the resentment of the Aïn-Arnat farmers against the rents which condemned them to fail before they'd even begun? His reports leave us no clues. Certain critical passages from his letter of 2nd April 1855 were read by Sautter de Beauregard before the Geneva Company board of directors. But these gentlemen could not hear the truth; once the letter was read, the managing director hurried to conclude 'that there was some haste in the judgement of Mr J.-Henri Dunant'.[14] And

---

[13] Pous, *Dunant l'Algérien*, 72.
[14] Pierre Boissier, *From Solferino to Tsushima* (Geneva: Henry Dunant Institute, [1963] 1985), 13. When available, we use existing translations.

so Henri understood just as quickly that no one liked the bearer of bad news. Rather than calling a system into question, there were other, simpler explanations for such misfortune. Starting with human nature: intemperance, laziness, lust, negligence – there were plenty of defects to choose from for explaining the woes of the Aïn-Arnat population, from a drunken regent to threats of famine, from abandoned crops to prostitution. And bad luck as well, another guilt-free explanation – the bad luck of the climate, too hot or too cold, the bad luck of epidemics, the bad luck of the hostility of the native people, the bad luck of poor harvests, the bad luck, finally, of misery, which cannot be argued with.

In this moment of his life, Dunant could not have embraced a different view to that of his investor friends or of the world to which he so wanted to belong. His education had taught him empathy when faced with human misery as well as the charity that should relieve it. But it had also instilled in him the rules of a society that believed in its own unshakeable order. Although Dunant was certainly aware of the settlers' hardships, he wore the same blinkers as his employers and endorsed on their behalf the same stubborn optimism that often sidles close to cynicism. Thus, only a month after the shock of his arrival, at the end of April 1855, everything seemed to miraculously improve:

> The current sanitary state of the villages is excellent. [...] In Arnat, the gardens around four or five settlers' homes are beginning to look rather nice. In general, in this locality, the population that have left or died are not to be missed.[15]

What a nice interpretation of natural selection. Death kills off the good-for-nothings, misery chases away the lazy. And for the rest, a hope that human nature might improve and bad luck remain at bay.

> Bouhira is generally well populated, people are active, energetic and working together, exactly what was missing in Arnat. Let's hope that this village, which is located in a lowland, will not

---

[15] Dunant to M. Faesch, 30 April 1855, quoted by Pous, *Dunant l'Algérien*, 214–15, for this quote and the following.

suffer from fevers this summer. [...] The success of the project depends on sober people and much energy.

Following his first stay in Algeria, Dunant still entertained the notion of a missionary project. He had even confided to his friend Chauncy Langdon that he wished to form a small missionary society in Geneva 'for evangelizing the believers of Muhammad'.[16] But this project would slowly dissipate, as if his third trip to Algeria established a definitive break between Henri Dunant's divergent aspirations. Was it the vision of a failing Swiss colony, the discovery of the cruelty of the business world, a simple maturing of his character? The fact is that during this trip of 1855, he seemed to convince himself to separate, both morally and geographically, his Christian evangelism from his professional goals. Africa's fantastic commercial and financial opportunities didn't mean the 'Kingdom of Heaven' would be created there in six days, no matter how many Protestants were settling and no matter how many natives were enticed to convert.

It is also true that his own business concerns were more than enough to keep him busy. There was still no response to his request for the additional 1,200 acres adjacent to his mill. As the weeks passed, his impatience was turning into a deep anxiety. What could he do? Harass the authorities, plead with underlings, pace hallways and antechambers ... only to learn that, yes, the Secretary of State for War had transferred his request to the General Governor; yes, he'd included a favourable opinion; no, still no response from the Governor, and there was no more hope for one. In May 1855, Dunant received a provisional acceptance for his request from the previous year concerning the original 17 acres and waterfall meant for the construction of his mill. But this no longer suited his much larger aspirations. In June 1855, Dunant left Algeria with only one certainty, a piece of land ten times too small for his dreams and his plans.

The Paris Conference

The Conference of Young Men's Christian Associations, originally conceived of at the November 1854 Paris meeting, was finally set

---

[16] Dunant to C. Langdon, 25 November 1854 ('Confidential'), World YMCA Archives.

for the end of August 1955 along with the Assembly of the
Evangelical Alliance. What should have been a shared project for
the two founders of the Geneva YMCA, Dunant and Perrot, would
instead definitively show their diverging paths and temperaments.
Just before his departure for Algeria in May, Dunant had prepared
the sixth 'newsletter' announcing the conference date for August – a
way to leave his stamp on the event before disappearing for three
months. In contrast, Perrot would worry over every detail, nagging
the Parisian organizers to get moving, fussing over delegate housing
as much as debate content. He even went so far as to scold Jean-
Paul Cook, chairman of the Paris YMCA and conference head, for
wanting to get married in April, a most extravagant project in the
eyes of bachelor Perrot just four months before a crucial conference!

The two men did not meet in June when Dunant returned to
Geneva. 'Dunant has returned from Algeria and will spend the
summer here,' Max Perrot wrote to his brother on 22nd June. 'He's
taken a small apartment in town, he receives his friends there; it is
said he has a lackey in livery.'[17] For a young man raised in the
strictest Calvinist austerity, it must have been laughable indeed to
see his 'brother in Christ' trying so hard to play the noble. There
may have been a touch of envy in his criticism: suffering from what
his family called a 'fatigued head',[18] Max Perrot knew he could
never earn his own living – a problem solved first by wealthy
parents, later by a wealthy wife.

Despite Perrot's worries, everything was ready in time: on 19th
August 1855, ninety-nine delegates from nine countries arrived in
Paris for the first worldwide conference of what is now still known
as the Young Men's Christian Association. Following an inaugural
evening at the Paris chapter's headquarters on the Rue Jacob, the
official sessions began on Monday 20th August at the Methodist
chapel on the Rue Royale. Jean-Paul Cook was elected conference
president, assisted by four vice presidents, including Max Perrot.
Dunant had no official function, but like the other founders of the
movement, he received a standing ovation at the end of the
conference by a grateful assembly.

---

[17] M. Perrot to A. Perrot, 22 June 1855, Perrot, *Regards de M. Perrot*, 53.
[18] Francis Chaponnière, *'Maximilien Perrot'*, in *Notices biographiques, Unions
chrétiennes de Jeunes Gens* (Geneva: UCJG, 1902), 10.

The greatest moment of the conference occurred on Wednesday afternoon when the impetus arose to create an international structure out of all these small and large YMCAs formed over the last ten years. Frédéric Monnier read a charter proposal: 'There is no question now of organizing our Association, it already exists,' he said solemnly to the assembly. 'The question is to make it visible.'[19] Listening to him present his project, Dunant tried to remember the juvenile inflections of the young man he'd met three years earlier on the rocky paths of the Furka. Would he be at that pulpit now if they hadn't met in the Alps? A series of events flashed through his mind. But yes, everything had happened in only a few months: as soon as he'd returned from the Alps, Frédéric left for Paris, and quickly became close with Gibert and Mercier, both men Dunant had spoken to him about; the Paris YMCA was founded after this connection, once they'd met Jean-Paul Cook. And here he was helping to lay the foundations for a World Alliance, Dunant thought, moved by the emotion he would later often feel at any thought of universality. But the orator was just finishing his report – following some debate, the ninety-nine delegates applauded Frédéric Monnier, making him the main author of the 'Paris Basis' which is recognized today as the foundational text of the World Alliance of YMCAs.

The very next day, Max Perrot presented his famous report to the delegates of the Evangelical Alliance. The goal of the exercise was to reassure the church elders being confronted with the incredible novelty – for the era – of a Christian youth organization that functioned independently of their churches and pastors. This is what Perrot needed them to understand, and his natural modesty meant he phrased things in just the right way to calm their worries: 'The YMCA unites the classes without confusing them (. . .) We respect the ministry, (. . .) we are not a Church, we are only a youth group (. . .) The only thing we want is to use the youth to motivate the youth.'[20] How better to summarize the movement, in both its novelty and its conformism?

The next day the seventh and final session of the Conference was held, which adopted the definitive text of the 'Paris Basis'. And so

---

[19] Cited in *Déjà cent ans! Aperçu historique de 100 années de l'Alliance universelle des UCJG, 1855–1955* (Geneva: UCJG, 1855), 71.

[20] [M. Perrot], *L'Union chrétienne de jeunes gens, Rapport lu à l'assemblée de l'Alliance évangélique de Paris* (1855), cited in Perrot, 'Regards de M. Perrot', 55.

was born a 'self-directing' – before the term even existed – youth movement, which had no prior equivalent and which would never have a comparable peer in terms of membership and geographical spread. The conference was ending, and emotions were at their peak. Dunant bid the young people farewell. Only five years earlier, from within a small local prayer group, he'd initiated the international correspondence that would weave the first threads of a World Alliance. At that very moment he could not have imagined that a century and a half later it would count tens of millions of members; but this conference was nevertheless a great reward for his inspired vision and dogged determination.

Just as he wrote to his friend Langdon at the beginning of the year, he could now take a step back with the feeling that a page had been successfully turned. So much the better. Because at that end of August 1855, the skies over his future were much more uncertain.

A fickle fiancée

That brilliant summer of 1855 would be followed by a merciless autumn. Like a choosy fiancée, Algeria continued to spurn Henri Dunant's advances. One after another his requests were refused by the administration, obliging him to scale down his ambitions or reattack from another angle.

Did he have a choice, with his investments already reaching 100,000 francs? In September, he reduced his concession request from 1,200 acres to 500, but when a month passed without any reply, he tried something new. In October 1855, he offered to pay cash for 500 acres. This time the response was swift: no.

There wasn't a coherent line between Paris and Sétif in these repeated refusals. Paris wanted to promote French projects, while the local authorities wanted to protect the interests of the natives who had, for generations, worked the land now claimed by the colonizers. Despairing of any French support, Dunant decided to directly address the local authorities, this time to request a second waterfall. This path proved no more successful. The local consulting committee favoured settlement projects and wanted to see villages built, not a foreign businessman taking control of water and land for his own benefit. This meant they continued to prefer another colonial, Joseph-Julien Niocel, a large landowner, and future mayor of Sétif, who had promised to build a village of twenty-five homes on the same plot of land. Dunant had no means to outbid this kind of promise.

The months and years were passing, and nothing was happening. Only the 17 acres he'd requested in 1854, granted conditionally in May 1855, were finally confirmed in 1856. Nothing could be done for the rest. He did not obtain a single additional inch of ground for three years. But Dunant refused to think he'd been beaten. These things take time, damn it! What he needed to do was assert himself, win their trust and overcome both Paris's and Algiers's hesitations. The watermill was turning, wasn't that already something? And the French military administration had just ordered flour from him to shore up a deficit brought on by drought. Didn't this prove, at least a little, the usefulness of his business?

After several months in Algeria, Dunant returned to spend the fall of 1856 in Geneva, as had become his habit. Officially, he was still secretary of the Evangelical Alliance, but his ties with the movement were gradually loosening, as is evident in a letter Max Perrot wrote from Edinburgh to his brother in Paris, in January 1856: 'Is it true Dunant has separated his name in two (Du Nant) or that he sends formal invitations to his friends?' Despite the distance between the men, his jealousy was still burning bright:

'Poor Dunant! One must pray for him because his piety is superficial, and the exaggerated reputation made for him in London does him no good. [. . .] I can assure you it is difficult for me to have such a colleague. He's lost all his credit in the French U.X. by his miserable letters and in Paris because of his silliness.'[21]

Whether or not he'd added a space to his last name, Henri wasn't thinking about the Dunant side of his family in the autumn of 1856. His maternal grandfather, embodiment of the civilized and salt-of-the-earth culture that had given Henri his childhood's most solid values, died in early October. Henri spent as much time as he could with his mother in Geneva, but when winter rolled around, he couldn't stay put any longer. Without the YMCA he no longer had a reason to traipse about Europe, and the dreadful inertia of the

---

[21] M. Perrot to A. Perrot, 24 January 1856, A. Perrot, 'Regards de M. Perrot', 57.

Algerian administration meant it was not quite time to visit Paris, Algiers, Constantine or Sétif. Luckily, a political situation gave him a good reason to leave the country. At the end of 1856, Henri headed south again, this time his course was set for Tunis, via Nice, Naples, Sicily and Malta.

Scientific ambitions

In Nice, Dunant spent several days at the house of his friend Ernest de Traz, who was staying in the south with his mother and sister. Of all of Henri's friends, Ernest was the closest and the most indisputably loyal. They had been in the same classroom when they were 12, together with Louis Rosselet they had founded the Thursday evening meetings, and he'd remained closely associated with Dunant as they set up the YMCA. When Henri began doing business in Algeria, Ernest had been an early enthusiast. Dunant was so good at convincing his entourage that in Nice it took only a single conversation with Ernest's sister Amélie to have her counting all her chickens before they were even hatched: 'His business is working so well he gets 200 francs profit a day,' she wrote to a friend, 'and he will give me 8 per cent return on any money I give him, I think that's not so bad.'[22]

Several days later, Dunant was in Naples. From there he wrote to his friend Chauncy Langdon on 20th January 1857 with an account of the different stages of his trip. The tone of his letters had changed a great deal since 1854 when he was confiding in a 'very dear and affectionate brother' who was still technically a stranger! That was now all water under the bridge. Opening with a simple 'my dear friend', the letter from Naples contains no more traces of the fervent friendship Dunant had used while writing as corresponding secretary for the Geneva YMCA. Here, however, for the first time – perhaps because his recipient was an Anglophone – he ended his first name with a 'y' and not an 'i'. Hoping their paths would cross in Italy, the freshly minted 'Henry' announced to Langdon that his trip would take him to Malta, Tunis and Tripoli, before returning to Italy.[23]

---

[22] Gabriel Mützenberg, *Valérie de Gasparin* (Le Mont-sur-Lausanne: Editions Ouverture, 1994), 173.

[23] Dunant to C. Langdon, 20 January 1857, World YMCA Archives.

Did he actually go so far? Was he travelling as a tourist, an evangelist, a businessman or . . . a deserter? The previous September an anti-Republican insurrection had blazed in the Swiss city of Neuchâtel, a former Prussian principality, led by a small group of nostalgic royalists. The *coup d'état* had failed, and the insurgents were taken prisoner. But Prussia was threatening to take military measures against the Helvetic Confederation and the Swiss army was preparing to defend its borders. December saw 30,000 men posted along the Rhine river under the command of General Dufour, former commander-in-chief of the Swiss Army and a highly respected military officer.

Forty years later when Dunant needed to prove his pacifist sympathies were indeed deeply rooted, he would claim his anti-military convictions were what motivated a trip to Italy that coincided with a mobilization of Swiss citizens. It's an explanation that comes a bit late to be entirely credible. More likely, Dunant preferred sampling the oranges of Palermo to freezing his feet in an uncomfortable mid-December stake-out, eyes peeled for the hypothetical arrival of the spiked helmets.

And so Dunant was in Naples in January 1857, and from there gave his friend Langdon the odd advice not to look him up with the Swiss consulates. Instead, he would leave word of his various addresses with the United States legations. Sometime later, he found himself bedridden in Palermo. He had caught a cold following a foolish trip in an open carriage all the way to La Bagaria, a leisure ground for Palermo's princes. The doctor called to his bedside advised him to head to Malta to get well, a pleasant prescription he followed straightaway. From there, he went on to Tunis for another stay, this time for several months.

These prolonged vacations are quite intriguing when considering his professional embroilments – except the plausible hypothesis of a forced absence in order to escape his civic duties. However, Dunant did spend his time well. He crossed all of Tunisia, gathering anecdotes, witness accounts, documents and observations of the political system, religions, fauna and flora, the various characters, Arabic proverbs, antique ruins, even the colour of the sky: enough to comprise a worthy documentary on a region of the world still quite unknown to most of Europe.

Settling down upon his return to write his narrative, our burgeoning geographer finished off his simple observations with a studied elegy

of the patriarchal society, Muslim hospitality, the humanity of Islam
towards slaves, and above all the sovereign of Tunis, a *bey*[24] who, in
Henry's eyes, embodied the perfect model of an enlightened monarch
and to whom he would dedicate his book. He certainly wanted to
be well regarded in Tunisia, it is also not unlikely he was looking
for a backup solution, an emergency exit in case things went badly
in Algeria. But alongside the businessman's compliments, the
geographer's notations and the anthropologist's observations, there is
also a very clear infusion of the humanitarian's concerns.

Three years earlier, when he'd begun corresponding with the
American chapter of the YMCA, Dunant had tiptoed around the
question of slavery, knowing that the United States was very divided
on the issue. 'I am certain, oh yes, I am certain, that you disapprove
of it! I want to believe it! Will the American Christian youth do
nothing?'[25] In 1857 he returns to the same question with such
vehemence that it's hard not to think this was his main reason for
writing the text.

In the opening pages Dunant praises the previous two *beys* who
had abolished the slavery of Christians and coloured people, as well
as freed the Jews. But then, in a 27-page chapter soberly entitled
'Slavery', he covers Tunisia in six pages and dedicates the rest of the
chapter to the horrors of the American states who, 'far from
preparing the path to abolishing slavery,' were 'walking further into
the shadows of odious, inhumane and anti-Christian laws'.

In the autumn of 1857, Dunant wrote the final word of his
Notice sur la Régence de Tunis:[26] asylum, a prophetic word for a
man who would later spend twenty years in search of this very
ideal. In these early optimistic days, however, he was far from
guessing his own dark future. He contemplated the pages stacked
on the corner of his table, such a thick pile that his heart began to
hammer. The pile of pages was an actual book, and he was the
author of this book. The author!

---

[24] Under the Ottoman Empire, a *bey* was the governor of a province.
[25] Dunant to C. Langdon, 25 November 1854 ('Confidential'), World YMCA
Archives.
[26] There is no existing English translation of the full book, but an extract translated
by Patricia Reynolds, 'Tunis the glorious: Report on the Regency of Tunis', appeared
in Hafedh Boujmil, *In the Warm Shade of Tunisia*, 2017. Most other English mentions
of the report cite it as *An account of the Regency in Tunis*, which we follow.

A few weeks later found him exulting yet again at the sight of the proofs waiting for him at the printers; for the rest of his life the smell of fresh ink would remind him of one of his most intense joys. An unknown in the world of letters, Dunant self-published the work. But he gave his manuscript to the city's best printer, specialist of luxury editions, Jules-Guillaume Fick, to whom he would remain faithful as long as he lived in Geneva.

The book was printed on large paper, with special lettering at the beginning of each section. On the title page was a sticker bearing the arms of the *bey* of Tunis, surmounted by the Islamic cross, along with the following mention in italics: *This work is not for sale.* Indeed, the point of the publication was not to earn royalties but to open new circles, new societies, new worlds.

Turning the pages, Henry was overawed to read his first name in capital letters on the first page: J. HENRY DUNANT. Yes, this final 'y' was decidedly more chic and from this point on Henry would always use it. He had left for Algeria as a lowly bank employee with evangelical ambitions and had returned hoping to soon rank among the great European entrepreneurs and colonizers. A similar pattern marked his experience with Tunisia: he had gone there as a simple tourist and now he expected his *Account* would grant him admittance to the various circles of the scholarly elite. His failure at school had closed the doors of academia to him, but hadn't he gone further anyway? Weren't his travels worth as much as book learning, didn't his membership in so many societies provide him something akin to learned colleagues? He had been a member of a literary society since 1856, as well as the Society of Arts; on 18th March 1858 he would also participate in the founding of Geneva's Geographical Society. The minutes of the meeting leave no doubt as to Dunant's hope of giving credibility to his work through membership: 'Messrs Dunant, Chappuis, de Candolle & Duby,' noted the minute-taker, 'believe that direct communications from our travellers and their correspondence can be used in the meetings of the Society.'[27] What a perfect advertisement for his *Account*! The first print run had emphasized quality over quantity, and so Dunant immediately printed a second edition.

---

[27] Archives of the *Société de géographie de Genève*, 18 March 1858, BGE, Ms. fr. 7998/6.

For the time he remained in Geneva, Dunant was devoted to this society: he only missed one meeting between 1858 and 1859. It's clear the society granted him access to the region's greatest scientific minds, not only geographers but also doctors, judges and engineers – the very same people whom Dunant would soon lead into the adventure of the Red Cross. On 14th December 1858, a young doctor named Louis Appia became a member of the Society of Geography, followed by the lawyer Gustave Moynier at the end of 1859. Finally, proof of the accumulated prestige of this brand-new society, 13th March 1860 marked the membership date of a famous engineer and cartographer, the venerated General Guillaume-Henri Dufour.

The mills of Mons-Djemila

Just as his first book was leaving Fick printers in the winter of 1857, Dunant was already setting up new projects. On the one hand, he had now understood that only solid financiers or large companies were credible in the eyes of the French Administration in Algeria, and on the other, he was aware of the prejudice brought by his Swiss nationality and his connections with the criticized Geneva Company. And so the young businessman Henry Dunant from Geneva decided to change his stature by changing his status. He would become French, and both board director and chief executive of his own company.

Two family circumstances enabled him to put these plans into action. French nationality was accessible through some ancestors who had fled religious persecutions in France. His father's family still owned a house in the Ain, in Culoz, a place where Henry had gone several times as a child. He presented himself to the city hall of Culoz in April 1859 to request 'French papers' and settle his residence at 'la Chèvrerie', as the family estate was called.[28] This naturalization brought the additional advantage of enabling him to dispense with his military service obligations in Switzerland. As for his promotion to the dual function of chief executive and director,

---

[28] See Gabriel Mützenberg, 'C'est là qu'Henry Dunant devint citoyen français', Bulletin de la Société Henry Dunant, 11 (Geneva: SHD, 1988), 11–16.

another development in his family's circumstances allowed him to take these titles. His dear aunt Sophie had died three years earlier and left property in Geneva to her three nephews, Henry, Daniel and Pierre. While the two younger brothers were content with a shared loan of 25,000 francs against the building, the eldest of the nephews borrowed on his own and 'in his personal interest', according to the notary record, the sum of 50,000 francs which, there is no doubt, was to be used as capital for his new company. Because Dunant's entire Algerian project was focused on the flour mill constructed near the Mons ruins, themselves located not far from the city of Djemila, the new company would be called the *Société des Moulins de Mons-Djemila* (The Mons-Djemila Mills Company). The shares were beautifully decorated with palm leaves, exotic animals and romantic-looking ruins. They also included the date the Geneva State Council authorized the company's founding: 8th January 1858.

The new company was endowed with a capital of 500,000 francs and a Franco-Genevan board of directors, a cultural hyphenation Dunant must have relished. Its listed names include a formal colonel of the Swiss army, Charles Trembley; a 'French and Genevan landowner' businessman, Thomas Mac Culloch; the pure Genevan Théodore Necker who was, Dunant underlined, 'grandnephew of the eponymous Minister of Finance';[29] and finally, Daniel Dunant, 'landowner in the department of Ain and Geneva', whom we know already as Henry's younger brother and faithful second in his Algerian activities. The statutes give the company goals as: 'acquisition' of existing installations (the wheat-milling factory), as well as the adjacent land parcels and the waterfall conceded an 1856, all of which now belonged to 'Henry Dunant & Company'. The new company was 'meant to dedicate its capital, which could be later increased, to a vast exploitation in the Deheb Wadi valley', once the French government would finally grant them the land concessions and a new waterfall which Dunant obstinately continued to claim. Once this was achieved, the company could get working on the extensive programme outlined in Point 2 of its goals: 'the commerce of grain milling, as well as raising sheep and

---

[29] Dunant's close friend Théodore Necker was in fact the great grandnephew (and not grandnephew) of Jacques Necker, Minister of Finance for Louis XVI.

other animals, the farming of land, the construction of new factories and any other industrial operations in line with the goals of the company'.[30]

Now in the name of his company, rather than in his own, Dunant relaunched his offensive for the concessions by requesting new recommendations from everyone he could ask, both Swiss and French. Putting in the request as a newly minted chief executive instead of a private individual may have increased his chances, but his ambitions had increased in the same proportion. The company was now requesting 2,400 acres of the Deheb Wadi *azel*, for which it claimed to be ready to pay 20 francs an acre. The letter which Dunant sent in March 1858 to the Governor General of Algeria, Marshal Count Randon, repeated for the hundredth time the same arguments he had been using in vain for the past four years: that 'Mr. Dunant had brought considerable capital into Algeria, that he had used much money to create a large factory',[31] and also that he was the only European settler in the region, which meant he needed to construct a road, at his own cost, etc. But the Marshal didn't even have time to give his response. In the summer of 1858, Dunant received some good news: instead of Marshal Randon, who was rather hostile to Genevans, Prince Jerome Napoleon had just been appointed Minister of Algeria and its Colonies. A long-standing relationship between the imperial family and the Swiss Confederation meant that the tide might be changing for Swiss colonial entrepreneurs.

There was no time to lose. Dunant rapidly requested the support of two shareholders who were a part of the emperor's circle, the Count de Budé de Ferney, grandfather of his friend Ernest de Traz and a family friend of the Dunants, and Henri de La Harpe, brother-in-law of Senator Eugène Haussmann. Armed with these new signatures, Dunant resent two requests in the autumn of 1858 to Prince Napoleon and began to hope again.

During that summer of 1858, Geneva was host to the second conference of the World Alliance of the YMCA. As chairman of the hosting association, Max Perrot gave the opening speech. Who might he have been thinking of while speaking?

---

[30] Pous, *Dunant l'Algérien*, 96–100.
[31] Dunant to J.-L. Randon, 12 March 1858, letter quoted *in extenso* by Pous, *Dunant l'Algérien*, 216–17.

The young who profess to be Christian too often give way to popular trends, seeking too fervently to acquire fortune. They become worried and anxious [. . .] Some of these young men had been working at modest professions but which granted them an honourable life; in doing this they would serve the Lord actively and faithfully. They are then offered a brilliant but dangerous vantage; they will be exposed to great temptations, all their time will be consumed with mercantile tasks, but they will become rich – maybe![32]

Perrot was wasting his breath. Dunant was certainly not in the room to hear his scolding. He was waiting on the results of his new company, the miracles of his new recommendations, the goodwill of the new minister of the colonies. He was as anxious as an ill man waiting for a doctor's diagnosis. Finally, at the end of September, a partial opinion arrived for the chief executive of the Mons-Djemila Mills. The administration consented to the creation of two factories on the Deheb Wadi with the concession of the corresponding land plots, but it maintained that the rest of the *azel* be used for building a village of forty homes, in direct line with the settlement policy consistently held by the Algerian authorities and to which Dunant already owed many of his previous refusals.

For Dunant, the larger problem remained: working the land required the waterfalls, and he still didn't have them. He returned to his offensive with a new letter, this time setting his sights on a new target. One of his shareholders, the Count de Budé, was kind enough to have a nephew by the name of Beaufort d'Hautpoul, who himself was on good terms with the commander-in-chief in Algeria, the Count Mac-Mahon. Upon Dunant's request, de Budé had his nephew send word of Dunant's indisputable merits to Mac-Mahon, 'a talented young man, highly commendable in all respects' and 'already well-known in Algeria'. In other words, General de Beaufort d'Hautpoul presented Dunant as directly representing the interests of his uncle the Count de Budé, using again this family tie to support the Mons-Djemila Mills.

---

[32] M. Perrot, '*Calvin, ses élèves et les jeunes chrétiens d'aujourd'hui*' (opening speech), *Souvenir de la Seconde Conférence universelle des UCJG* (Geneva: Cherbuliez & Beroud, 1859), 45.

As a precaution, Dunant wanted to deliver the letter to General Mac-Mahon himself. He left for Algeria at the end of 1858, but this trip was no more fruitful than his earlier ones. What was worse, he had begun to give himself airs which were not pleasing. Wanting to distance himself from the Geneva Company and his role there of lowly employee, he didn't even bother visiting its representative in Sétif, something he had never failed to do before. The director was offended, while pretending to take 'little account of Mr Dunant's pettiness and little appreciation for his insignificant person'.[33]

'Insignificant person' and 'talented young man': both opinions were definitely valid for Dunant who, depending on the winds of fate, could be either magnanimous or petty, stubborn or charming, blind or visionary.

Several weeks later, on 19th February 1859, when Dunant left Sétif on the back of a mule to catch the boat to Philippeville, he felt the hopelessness of his efforts more than ever. The first regular general meeting of the Mons-Djemila Mills Company would be held in Geneva in less than a month. He had been hoping to arrive a conqueror; instead he was going to have to explain to shareholders why everything was more complicated than expected.

The fateful day arrived, and all initial shareholders were there. Henry Dunant may or may not have explained his difficulties, but he did convince the board that they were surmountable. He ultimately had them vote to double the capital, which would now be a million francs, a considerable sum for the time. His daring relied entirely upon an oral response from Prince Napoleon, which he'd taken as encouraging. But the prince, less than seven months after beginning his duties, had just been replaced by a new minister of colonies, the Count de Chasseloup-Laubat. The shareholders also learned that, although the first waterfall requested seemed to have been acquired, it could not irrigate the fields, which made farming them impossible. More rumours circulated about the imminent loss of the second waterfall to a competitor. Worried about this news, the board decided to enlist, in addition to Messrs de Budé and de la Harpe, the prestigious General Dufour from whom they hoped for a miracle. On 16th April the company sent a new request to Minister Chasseloup-Laubat. The competition was

---

[33] E. Gambini to P.-E. Lullin, 18 February 1859, cited by Pous, *Dunant l'Algérien*, 75.

so fierce surrounding these waterfalls that persistence, even harassment, seems to have been part and parcel of the desperate race towards fortune.

A bow to the emperor

The confrontation with his shareholders created a feeling of urgency that Dunant had never before experienced as a solo entrepreneur. Since his trip to Algeria in March, he had been thinking of all possible ways to achieve what he'd been fighting for these last five years. And no matter when and how he thought about it – by day or night, calmly or in a panic, rational or fantastic, he always came back to the same name, the same man: Napoleon III.

The French emperor. Who else? He was the only fixed star amid a rotating constellation of ministers. All roads led to him. Everything depended on him.

The emperor: he had to see him. He had to tell him. He had to convince him. But how to reach him?

The previous spring Dunant had made sure to send the emperor a copy of his *Account of the Regency in Tunis*. The emperor's attaché had despatched a few words of thanks on a small note, which the author would devoutly safeguard. Is this when a new project took seed in his mind? His tract on the *bey* of Tunis had not yet earned him his first decoration, the 'star of Nichan Iftikhar', which would be awarded to him the following year in gratitude for his obliging study and his flattering comments.[34] Nevertheless, in the spring of 1859, while his Algerian projects were in a state of desperate stagnation, Dunant set off on the same road he had taken with the *bey* of Tunis: he would offer His Majesty Napoleon a book dedicated entirely to his glory, written for him and inscribed to him. All this for his watermills.

Selecting such a moment for this kind of publication was either pure insanity, or a stroke of genius – perhaps both. As of 3rd May 1859, France was at war. In this first chapter of Italian independence, both the Genevan press and population were supporting the French

---

[34] Roger Durand (ed.), *La Tunisie d'Henry Dunant* (Geneva: Société Henry Dunant, 2007), 207–13.

and Piedmont allies against the Austrian invader. Although not
obvious at first glance, religious solidarity seems to have been a
factor since the 'liberal' Piedmont was tolerant of the Reform (the
mother of its Prime Minister Cavour, born Adélaïde de Sellon, was
Protestant) and the surrounding threat was Catholic. The Genevan
newspapers had been publishing a daily notice asking for donations
to be collected in favour of the war wounded. On 13th May 1859,
Dunant read in the miscellaneous items of the *Journal de Genève* a
call for cloth and bandages to be sent to Turin, where a Centralized
Soldiers' Aid Society had been set up. It was Dr Louis Appia,
member of the Geographical Society alongside Dunant and also
involved in evangelical circles, who was collecting the gifts and
taking them into Italy in a process that directly foreshadowed the
vocation of the Red Cross.

Did Dunant take this as a personal call? The fact is that in May
of 1859, what is often referred to as the 'spirit of Geneva'[35] seemed
to rise up at the end of the lake. Donation requests came in for the
wounded of both sides. The city's rival newspapers, the *Journal de
Genève* and the *Revue de Genève*, concurred for once in their
shared admiration of the French emperor's concern for the war
victims of any nationality, and the humanity with which His Majesty
required the Austrian war wounded be treated. In this, Napoleon III
respected the lessons of his former instructor, General Dufour,
who'd recommended in 1847 that his troops avoid harassing or
confining the enemy. All this also bolstered Dunant's veneration of
Napoleon III . . . as well as his irrational project.

That same May of 1859 a new volume by Henry Dunant was
published by Fick printers, even more sumptuous than his *Account*,
and bearing a rather unique title: *L'Empire de Charlemagne rétabli
ou le Saint-Empire romain reconstitué par Sa Majesté l'empereur
Napoléon III* (The Restoration of the Empire of Charlemagne or
The Holy Roman Empire Reconstructed by His Majesty Emperor
Napoleon III). The title page was decorated with the imperial arms,
followed by the dedication: 'To His Majesty Napoleon III': and then
came very visibly the name of the author with the list of his titles: at

---

[35] '*L'esprit de Genève*' (The Spirit of Geneva) is the title of a book by Robert de Traz
tracing the international and peace defender tradition of Geneva through Calvin,
Rousseau and Dunant (Paris: Grasset, 1929).

the top was 'Director and Chief Executive of the Mons-Djemila Mills' – which had nothing to do with the book's subject – and then 'member of the Asian Society of Paris' – his admission dated only a few days prior – along with member 'of the Oriental Society of France,' along with the Geographical Societies of Paris and Geneva, and the Historical Society of Algiers, etc.

This strange booklet is a 46-page 'prophecy' littered with biblical references in which Dunant attempts to trace a line starting with the empires of Romulus and of Augustus straight through to Charlemagne and the Holy Roman Empire, which he then extends to the contemporary era: 'Emperor Napoleon III, as the legitimate heir of Napoleon I and Napoleon II, is the only true successor of the Roman emperors, as well as Charlemagne. [. . .] Napoleon III must save Europe from anarchy, return the "great nation" to its rank in the world and its importance amid the peoples of the universe.'

Having signed the book as 'Director and Chief Executive of the Mons-Djemila Mills' in a rather transparent revelation of his true goals, was Dunant really so oblivious as to think of placing the book in the emperor's hands at this exact moment in time? While he'd been signing his copies, the chief of the imperial army and his cousin Prince Napoleon, recent Minister of the Colonies, as well as Dunant's 'ally' with the imperial government, General de Beaufort d'Hautpoul, and the most recent commander-in-chief in Algeria, the Marshal de Mac-Mahon – all these influential people were, and had been for several weeks at that point, at war in Italy helping the kingdom of Piedmont chase out the Austrians. Did Dunant, a reasonable man on all accounts, really intend to show up in the middle of hostilities to personally deliver his gift to its lofty recipient?

Later on, he would vehemently deny such a crazy goal, not to appear wiser than he actually was but more to avoid tainting his humanitarian role with any personal interests. Despite this, and his later claims, his travels into Italy at this time do seem to have been focused on getting closer to the imperial star, starting with the fact that he took a copy of his book in his luggage. To this main goal, one must also account for two elements of his personality without which his excursion would have been utterly foolish: a traveller's intrepid curiosity, on the one hand, and an authentic Christian compassion, on the other, both impelling him to seek out the unknown and where suffering might be found. In a region at war, with or without the emperor, he was sure to find both.

A fateful meeting in Italy

Governed by the treaties of Paris and Vienna of 1814 and 1815, respectively, by 1859 Italy was divided into numerous political entities. In the north was the independent Piedmont. It belonged, along with the Savoy, to Victor Emmanuel II's kingdom of Sardinia, whose Prime Minister Camillo Benso, Count of Cavour, lead an active policy of country unification. Their neighbours, Lombardy and Venetia, were attached to Austria; Cavour's dream of unifying the peninsula meant his first goal was to throw out the occupying power.[36]

Emperor Napoleon III was favourable to Italian unity. A year earlier, during an interview at Plombières with the Piedmont minister, he'd promised to help liberate the north of the country from its occupier, but this alliance could not take effect unless Austria appeared to be an aggressor.

Cavour increased provocations until he achieved what he wanted: the Austrians invaded the Piedmont on 29th April 1859 and, true to his word, Napoleon III declared war on Austria and sent 120,000 men to Italy.

The first battles were fought in the area between Turin and Milan, where the Franco-Piedmontese troops took the advantage twice. The Austrians retreated towards the Lombardian capital, which they then lost following the Battle of Magenta on 4th June. Knocked back again to Melegnano, the Austrian army was then forced to retreat to the west; it even crossed over the Mincio river, which then remained a symbolic border between the two sides throughout the fighting.

It was amid this extremely tense context that Dunant adventured into Italy in June 1859, going straight for Parma around the 20th – not at all by chance – where Prince Napoleon and General de Beaufort d'Hautpoul were readying to appear with the 5th Army Corps, who had been waiting until then in Tuscany on the emperor's order. The very men Dunant was chasing, as he admits in his *Mémoires*: 'To find this mysterious 5th Army Corps, I was obliged to make numerous zigzags.'[37] Indeed, the emperor, who had finally

---

[36] For the political context of Dunant's travel in Italy, see Mike Wellis, *Unification and Consolidation of Germany and Italy 1815–1890* (Cambridge: Cambridge University Press, 2013).

[37] Dunant, *Mémoires*, 33. The following quotations are from the same source, 32–4.

decided to bring his cousin Prince Napoleon into the war, ordered
him back to Parma, from Florence. Not, however, by the most direct
route but via a much longer and more difficult one, passing along the
edge of the sea and then across the Apennine mountains. Dunant
was perhaps not informed of the emperor's bizarre instructions to
his cousin; he arrived in Parma several days before the corps who
were still struggling through the mountains, and rather than twiddle
his thumbs waiting for them, he decided to make his way towards
them. Which is why he set off bravely in a coach, in a region
inundated by storms and blocked by army traffic, to cross the
Apennines towards the south. He must have known where he was
going: on 22nd June, arriving in Pontremoli, he had 'a stroke of a
luck', because when he got down from his coach, still stiff from the
journey, he 'chanced upon' Prince Napoleon's General Staff and the
famous General de Beaufort d'Hautpoul, the very people he'd been
seeking for at least three days.

Prince Napoleon was in a terrible mood. He quite rightly
considered it a humiliation to have been forced through the
mountains by his imperial cousin. He also guessed he was going to
miss the decisive battle – he was not wrong on either account.
Dunant 'saw' him, he specified in his memoirs, but he certainly
didn't speak to him, because he does not record any exchange. On
the contrary, General de Beaufort d'Hautpoul, exchanging a few
cordial words with him, expressed 'his profound astonishment' to
find him in such a place and at such a time.

Did Dunant truly mention the fate of the war's wounded, as he
affirmed later in his memoirs, only to receive the curious response
from Beaufort d'Hautpoul that 'one does not make an omelette
without breaking eggs'? And did this same general really advise him
not to miss the 'very big battle' that would occur sometime soon on
the other side of the Apennines? No matter how he later edited his
memoirs, it is clear that during this brief encounter Dunant kept in
mind the very reason for his complicated journey. He extracted
from Beaufort a new missive to deliver to Marshal Mac-Mahon.
Whether the general's note was a private message or a letter of
introduction, Dunant never says. But it granted him safe passage as
well as a reason to approach Mac-Mahon – recently named Duke
of Magenta. Exactly what he wanted.

What may have appeared to be a remarkable coincidence to
Beaufort d'Hautpoul and Prince Napoleon could not have been less

so. By virtue of the same step-by-step method he'd applied until
now and would soon apply again with extraordinary success,
Dunant moved steadily forward. He was excellent at working
casual relationships within select circles to achieve new connections
that were a step higher, enabling him to reach what he'd had his
sights on from the beginning. Everything was unsettled in Algeria;
Prince Napoleon had just been replaced by Chasseloup-Laubat
from whom he could hope for nothing; all he needed was to
reach the emperor by climbing up through all intermediate ranks.
This carefully premeditated 'fortuitous' meeting with Beaufort
d'Hautpoul would lead him to Mac-Mahon, who could then lead
him to the emperor. This and only this can explain his extravagant
travels through Italy 'to locate this mysterious 5th Army Corps' as
well as his outlandish whim to immediately retrace his footsteps
from Pontremoli, 'without even taking the time for a meal', to make
the very journey he had just undertaken in reverse.

It was now night-time, but this would not stop him for a second.
The coach recrossed the Apennines towards the north in complete
darkness, still with a single traveller on board, and no one else
around, not even any scouts from the weary 5th Army Corps
Dunant had left behind. But soon enough the roads were too chancy
for the carriage; Dunant exchanged it for a seat in a chaise that took
him painstakingly through the night to Parma, then Piacenza and
then Cremona, until he arrived in Brescia. Getting out of the coach,
he noticed he was soaking wet: what with the heavy rain and the
loss of certain bridges in the fighting, vehicles were forced to drive
(and splash) through very high water.

When he wrote his *Mémoires* in 1895, he remained quite evasive
about the exact dates of his travels in 1859; this was presumably to
avoid contradicting *A Memory of Solferino* (1862), which makes
the plausible claim that he had seen the battle. Yet, if he was at
Pontremoli on the evening of the 22nd, which is now sure,[38] he had
over 1,000 leagues to travel, more than 250 kilometres, to reach
Brescia via Parma and Piacenza. The weather was horrible, the
rivers were overflowing and the roads becoming impassible;
furthermore, his memoirs mention two nights spent on the road, in

---

[38] Dunant most likely purposely omits the date of the meeting in Pontremoli. But the
narratives of a few contemporaries like Bazancourt (1860), Du Casse (1898) and
Deguignet (1904–5) make it possible to reconstruct his itinerary quite exactly.

a coach and then in the chaise. And so he would have arrived in Brescia at the very earliest on 24th June.

But why Brescia? Because the emperor had established his headquarters there several days before, on the 19th and 20th; because the Duke of Magenta was also there; and finally, because it would have been easier to find a driver willing to take him further. And this is exactly what happened. An Italian who'd fled Mantua to avoid forced recruitment by the Austrians agreed to drive the little cab Dunant had rented; the man knew the area very well and he took his client safely from Brescia to where he wanted to go.

But where exactly did Dunant want to go on the night before the 'great battle'? It isn't very likely, even impossible, that General de Beaufort d'Hautpoul had indicated the emperor's exact plans to a Swiss tourist in a white suit, and even less likely that the emperor had set them in stone at that point. The truth is that what would become the decisive battle in the Italian wars took everyone by surprise. At the very most, based on the evidence of the letter handed over when they met, Beaufort d'Hautpoul may have advised Dunant to head back north to find Mac-Mahon.

In Brescia, Dunant must have sought information. He would have learned that Napoleon III had been headquartered for two days in Montichiari, where he'd held a war council with all his army corps commanders on the evening of the 19th. Dunant might also have heard that the emperor had just joined Mac-Mahon in Castiglione, where the Marshal had been waiting for him for two days. On the morning of Friday 24th June they were surveying the region from the bell tower of the Chiesa Maggiore, a church perched atop the city.

When Dunant left Brescia and then Montichiari later that same day, no one could have told him there would soon be a terrible battle, nor how many wounded it would produce. The emperor himself had only been informed in the night that Solferino was heavily occupied and seems to have understood just as he was approaching the town that everything would play out just there. Until that moment, nothing signalled such a strong concentration of Austrians in the region, not even the hot-air balloon Mac-Mahon had had brought to Castiglione to scan the area. All this supported the French hypothesis that the enemy was camped out on the other side of the Mincio river and that the Franco-Sardinian troops would need to cross it to meet the Austrians.

Thus, Dunant arrived 'accidentally' in Castiglione on the afternoon or the evening of 24th June. He was looking for a marshal whose protection he coveted, or an emperor to whom he wanted to give a book, or most likely both. Fate would deal him a very different hand. Just a few kilometres away, one of the bloodiest battles of the century was coming to an end.

4

A Battle for Glory (1859–62)

The Battle of Solferino

All throughout the first battles, from Montebello on 20th May to Palestro at the end of the month, the Franco-Piedmontese army maintained its advantage. The Battle of Magenta on 4th June forced the Austrians to retreat towards the east and take refuge at the Venetia border. Austrian emperor Franz Joseph, who had taken command of his 120,000 men, resigned himself to call upon Prussia for help. The answer came on 20th June: yes, on condition that the Austrian Army step up their offensive.[1]

On 22nd June, the Austrians decided to counter-attack. The next day, their troops turned around, headed back west, recrossed the Mincio river to make a line from Pozzolengo to Medole, passing through the small town of Solferino. Neither camp had any idea of their enemy's movement until the following evening. A few scuffles between reconnaissance patrols led the commander of the 1st French Army Corps, Baraguey d'Illiers, to think he was dealing with a rearguard until he was notified that the Austrians were in Solferino. Unaware of the general assault planned by Franz Joseph, he believed he would easily push them out the next morning.

This meant that in the early hours of 24th June 1859, the soldiers were readying for battle yet neither commander had prepared

---

[1] Henry Dunant, *A Memory of Solferino* (Geneva: ICRC, [1939] 1969), 13–16. See also Th. Falk (ed.), *Précis de la campagne de 1859 en Italie* (Brussels: Librairie militaire C. Muquardt, 1887) and R. Durand, '*La bataille de Solférino*', in R. Durand (ed.), *Le creuset de la Croix-Rouge* (Geneva: SHD/MICR, 1997), 21–3.

manoeuvres for a decisive encounter. The Austrian soldiers were exhausted by the dozens of kilometres they had walked in the days prior, in one direction and then back in the other; and that morning, at the beginning of what would be an endless day, they'd hardly eaten at all. The commissariat had been ordered to replace solid food with a double ration of brandy meant to make them more aggressive. Similarly on the French side, the soldiers fighting under Marshals Baraguey d'Illiers and Mac-Mahon had been given nothing but their morning coffee ration before heading out.

It was barely dawn when the fighting began; the forces gathered were equally matched. On the Franco-Sardinian side were approximately 170,000 men, 16,400 horses and 600 cannons. The Austrians numbered 160,000 men, 10,500 horses and 670 cannons.[2] The two emperors personally commanded their troops. Their armies were lined up in two parallel lines stretching for about twenty kilometres from north to south, between the Chiese and Mincio rivers; San Martino sat to the north and Medole to the south. In the centre was Solferino, nestled between a rise of hills ascending towards Lake Garda and a plain that stretched south all the way to Mantua. These three places triangulated the decisive battles of that day.

At 4:00 a.m., the 1st Army Corps of Marshal Baraguey d'Illiers attacked the 5th Army Corps of Field Marshal Stadion, not far from Castiglione. Napoleon III arrived at 7:00 a.m. and from the bell tower of the city's church measured the scope of the fighting. Judging that the 'decisive point of the battle [would be to] remove the Solferino position',[3] he proceeded to that very location with all his staff.

Solferino's 'Spia d'Italia' tower became objective number one, not only because it offered the best observation point across the region, but also because of its central position on the front lines. When Bazaine's division secured the area and the *Voltigeurs* of the imperial guard took the tower in the early afternoon, the battle seemed to be turning in the Allies' favour.

From this moment on, Napoleon III had no doubt he would win. At 2:30 p.m., he gave the order to his equerry to move the imperial

---

[2] Th. Falk (ed.), *Précis de la campagne de 1859 en Italie*, 203–4.
[3] Report from Marshal Saint Jean d'Angely, commander-in-chief of the Imperial Guard, Cavriana, 25 June 1859, *Le Moniteur universel*, 4 July 1859, 1.

quarters from Castiglione to Cavriana, a position he was now sure to take back from the Austrians.

Around 4:00 p.m. a fierce wind began to kick up. An hour later the soldiers were being pounded by a terrifying storm and cold, horizontal rain. The French Army was suddenly hindered at the very moment the Austrians were attempting a final counter-attack. But soon enough their troops, too, surrendered to the strength of the elements: lightning, thunder and smoke were now obscuring the battlefield.

From his observation post – a chapel perched on a neighbouring hill – Austrian emperor Franz Joseph decided upon a general retreat. Emperor Napoleon went on to set himself up in Cavriana as he'd intended, in the very palace where the Austrian sovereign had breakfasted that morning. From there, he addressed a sober despatch to the empress, summarizing his day: 'Large battle and large victory.'[4]

Both the victorious and the vanquished emperor were exhausted that evening. Their troops had suffered considerable losses. In one way or another, the tally was comparable: between 18,000 and 19,000 men from each side had fallen in a single day of combat.

In his *Mémoires*, looking to justify his presence near the battlefield that day, Dunant describes himself as 'very concerned for the wounded (. . .) Yes, I was a tourist; but a tourist entirely preoccupied with questions of humanity.'[5] If this really had been his primary goal for travelling to the region, his shock upon arriving in Castiglione delle Stiviere would have been less brutal, his trauma less profound, but maybe from a historical perspective, less fertile. Instead, when Dunant appeared in the small town of Castiglione at the end of that Friday, 24th June, he was not prepared for the spectacle awaiting him. He was haggard, overwhelmed, stunned. The town was only a few kilometres from the fighting, and thousands of wounded soldiers had made their way to it on the backs of mules, in carts or on foot when they could. From Castiglione, they should have been taken to neighbouring hospitals: in Brescia, Cremona, Bergamo or even Milan. But the Austrians had requisitioned all the carts during their occupation of Castiglione in the days preceding the battle. This meant the town had now

---

[4] '*Nouvelles de l'armée, L'empereur à l'impératrice*', *Journal de la Guerre*, 11, 29 June 1859.
[5] Dunant, *Mémoires*, 33.

unwillingly become a vast improvised hospital, for both the French and the Austrians.

As nothing of the sort had been planned, the panic was extreme: with nowhere to house or even offer a space to stretch out for the hundreds, the thousands, of bloodied, wounded bodies spilling off the battlefield in an endless parade, the town hastily opened its barracks, churches, convents and cloisters. Anything! Citizens and soldiers raced about searching for blankets, sheets, mats and makeshift mattresses. Eventually they began throwing straw in the streets and plazas and courtyards for bedding, and fashioning shelters out of planks or fabric. The wealthy opened their homes to wounded officers, while others were already working out how to dispose of the corpses. A deafening concert of death rattles, sobs, howls of pain, orders and counter-orders in all languages, shouts of revolt, panic and anger – this is the hell Henry Dunant stepped into upon his arrival at the Castiglione Plaza on Friday, 24th June, dressed in an elegant but now rumpled white suit.[6]

Had Dunant been planning to stop here, intending to spend a single night, or was his plan to continue on immediately to find Marshal Mac-Mahon or the emperor? He has kept this information to himself. But we can be in no doubt that he hadn't dressed in his white suit intending to work as a nurse.

His suit didn't stay white very long. Henry spent all of Saturday 25th June tending the wounded. A frustrating disorganization became immediately critical and then fatal: there were water and supplies, yet the wounded were dying of hunger and thirst; there were dressings at hand but not enough hands to apply them. Dunant noted all of this and saw the urgent, immediate need for a volunteer service. But how to put this in place amid such chaos? His empathy took over, and his compassion and faith guided him. He was surrounded by atrocious suffering – the shrieks of pain from emergency limb amputations, the convulsions of men overcome by tetanus, the spectacle of bones shattered by cylindrical bullets, the haggard eyes of dying men. Such distress on all these faces, young men on the ground begging for water, for medical care, for death.

---

[6] This white suit inspired Dickens to metonymize Dunant as 'the Man in White' in his article 'A Souvenir of Solferino', *All the Year Round*, 16 May 1863, 283–7.

Henry would run from one to the other, giving fresh water to parched lips, writing down a goodbye, comforting a last breath, relieving those he could, without plan or method, following the hands and voices calling out to him. He worked like the passing tourist he was, and like the disciple of Christ he tried to be – like a solitary aid worker, in fact, in the right place at the right time. It was already a lot. But it wasn't enough.

He didn't sleep much that night, lying in the room he'd miraculously found at the Pastorio Palace.[7] It wasn't just the terrifying images of the devastated bodies and the beseeching looks that passed before his closed eyes. It wasn't just the unacceptable waste of so many lives lost or ruined on a single Saturday in June; the lives of young men who were nearly his own age, who could have been his brothers or his cousins. No, what truly haunted him that night was the confusion, the disorganization, the frantic *improvisation* of a city that had known a battle was looming, had even hoped for Allied liberation, and yet was totally unprepared when it arrived. How many extra lives had this cost? Was it inevitable that war continued to kill even days after a battle had ended? Dunant would have closed his eyes that night on these unanswerable questions while the two emperors, each on his side, were taking their own lessons from such a grisly encounter – from the sounds of the painful screams still echoing in their ears.

Tutti Fratelli

In the early dawn hours of Sunday, 26th June, Henry Dunant got to work organizing the most urgent aid, with no concern for which 'side' the wounded were on. French, German, Arab or Slav, they all lay suffering on the cold stone floors of the churches and pavements, their blood pooling together in red rivulets that coursed along the rain-soaked streets of Castiglione. Gathering several women he'd seen already helping, Dunant began distributing first aid as

---

[7] Castiglione's local tradition says that Dunant was lodged at the palace adjacent to the Chiesa Maggiore, the Pastorio Palace. But in a letter to Rudolf Müller, forty years later, he mentions trying to remember the name of the inn where he stayed, so there remains some uncertainty as to where he actually was that evening. Dunant to Müller, uncertain date in 1902, BGE, Ms. fr. 5204, f. 229–39.

methodically as he could: give food and water, dress wounds, wash bloodied bodies. Unable to help the entire city, he focused his work where it seemed most necessary. Coincidently, he established his general quarters in the very church with the bell tower that Napoleon III had climbed just forty-eight hours earlier.

The wide terrace fronting the Chiesa Maggiore overflowed with the dead and dying, hundreds of soldiers stretched out side by side. Inside the sanctuary, there was a striking contrast between the light ceiling with its lime-washed arches and the dark floor with its roiling, indistinct mass of human flesh, skin, leather, straw and blood, reeking of death and echoing with moans and sobs. The French soldiers were placed against the walls in two parallel lines; the Austrians, Germans and Croats were mostly relegated to the back of the church, quite distrustful of any pity they might be offered.[8] Throughout that entire Sunday, Henry walked up and down the nave and the two side wings of the church between the rows of wounded: 'They followed me with their eyes, going to the right if I went to the right, going to the left if I went to the left,' he writes in *A Memory of Solferino*.[9] Taking care that no one was forgotten, he responded as best he could to those with the most pressing needs, to the outstretched hands and cries for help. Young boys ferried water from the fountains to the church, courageously climbing the steep path with buckets larger than themselves. Their mothers and sisters would then rush to bring the water to the men, quenching their thirst and cleaning their wounds.

The town's resources were exhausted by the end of that Sunday. Not a square of cloth could be found, not a single package of tobacco. The next morning Henry sent his coachman to Brescia to hunt out what could be purchased in terms of food and first-aid materials: chamomile and mauve for washing wounds; oranges, lemons and sugar to make lemonade; shirts, sponges, cloth strips, pins for changing bandages and providing clean linens; cigars and tobacco to comfort and soothe. While waiting for his coachman to return – Brescia was a good 20 kilometres away and it would take

---

[8] According to Dr Chenu, chief medical officer of the French Army, there were 630 hospital beds in this single church and attached chapel. Dr Chenu, *Statistique médico-chirurgicale de la campagne d'Italie en 1859 et 1860* (Paris: Dumaine, 1869), 92.
[9] Dunant, *A Memory of Solferino*, 72.

him several hours to get there, gather all he could and return – Henry continued his work in Castiglione. An old naval officer was passing through, along with two English tourists, an Italian abbot, four foreign rubberneckers and a journalist from Paris. Dunant got them working immediately and kept them as long as they could bear it . . . until they would leave, defeated by so much suffering. Only the women and young girls were neither put off nor discouraged, and Dunant would never forget their dedication:

> But the women of Castiglione, seeing that I made no distinction between nationalities, followed my example, showing the same kindness to all these men whose origins were so different, and all of whom were foreigners to them. 'Tutti fratelli,' they repeated feelingly.[10]

Tutti fratelli – all are brothers. That the Lombardian women could use this simple phrase after decades of Austrian occupation, demonstrating an extraordinary impartiality between their old enemy and their celebrated liberator, was nothing short of the victory of compassion over resentment.

A walk in the night

On Monday, 27th June, the streets of Castiglione were quieter again; some of the wounded had been displaced to other surrounding towns and order had slowly returned. The French quartermaster, who had just set up lodgings in Castiglione, authorized prisoners to work in the hospitals: three Austrian doctors and a German surgeon joined the overwhelmed medical teams.

Henry took advantage of the lull to take up his pen. More than ever, he felt the need to write, both to request aid and to express himself. The right name came immediately to mind: the Countess de Gasparin.

Valérie de Gasparin-Boissier belonged to an honourable Genevan family but she was also a writer, a public intellectual and, along with her husband Agénor de Gasparin, an important member of the

---

[10] Dunant, *A Memory of Solferino*, 72.

evangelical church. She had become known for a famous appeal for
the soldiers of the Crimean War. In December 1854, *L'Illustration
Française* had published her open letter, suggesting 'a very simple,
eminently practical idea' of 'sending comfort to the soldiers of both
armies of the east, to the French and to the English, in the form of
cigars, pipes and tobacco'.[11] The appeal hit its mark: donations
came in from all over France, thousands of francs were gathered in
a few weeks.

Five years later, Valérie de Gasparin's gesture was still
remembered, and Dunant referred to it explicitly when writing to
her from Castiglione in June of 1859:

> For three days I have been attending the wounded of Solferino
> and I have looked after more than a thousand victims [. . .]
> Nothing can express the seriousness of the aftereffects of combat
> [. . .] The war in Crimea was small in comparison [. . .] I address
> my entreaties to you, Madam, that you should revive the action
> that you undertook during the Crimean War with respect to
> tobacco and cigars to be sent to our soldiers.[12]

Once his letter was written, Dunant hitched his carriage in the late
afternoon to 'breathe the fresh evening air in the open', if we are to
believe his words in *A Memory of Solferino*, 'and to get a little rest
by staying away for a time from the gloomy scenes which surrounded
one on every side at Castiglione'.[13] This description becomes all the
more curious when we consider that he was accompanied by a
French corporal on this 'relaxing' drive, and that their destination
was the Solferino battlefield which he found to be 'a melancholy
site', without 'any sign whatever of passion or enthusiasm'.[14] This
was certainly the first time he was witnessing the war theatre with
his own eyes despite the detailed reconstruction he gave in *A
Memory*. But this wasn't his only goal that evening. Continuing
along, he arrived at 9:00 p.m. at Cavriana, where he confessed to be
looking for 'Marshal the Duke of Magenta' whom he claimed to

[11] Mützenberg, *Valérie de Gasparin*, 126.
[12] *Journal de Genève*, 9 July 1859. This letter is translated in Boissier, *From Solferino to Tsushima*, 30–1.
[13] H. Dunant, *A Memory of Solferino*, 78.
[14] Ibid.

know personally. This was, of course, none other than Patrice de Mac-Mahon, the addressee of the letter Beaufort d'Hautpoul had given him several days earlier.

Why was he still so obstinately looking for Marshal Mac-Mahon? What authorization, what new favour did he want from the former commander-in-chief in Africa, recently named Duke and Marshal, and soon to be Governor General of Algeria? He never says. However, when mentioning his trip to General de Beaufort d'Hautpoul several days later, he reports that he forgot 'both book and letter'[15] in the wake of the disastrous fallout from the Battle of Solferino. So there was a *book* as well as a letter behind his assiduous quest of Count Mac-Mahon. And what book might that have been?

In Cavriana, he had his carriage stop in front of the palace that had welcomed two emperors in the same day, first Franz Joseph and now Napoleon III. How could Dunant resist stopping near the sovereign he venerated more than anyone else? There was nothing terribly imperial about the place; a long building with a gallery and arcades on the ground floor and fronted with a row of pediment windows. A few officers were seated on stools and chairs outside, calmly smoking their cigars when Dunant got out to question them.

Mac-Mahon wasn't there. Wary and surprised, the officers told the unexpected traveller that Mac-Mahon was in Borghetto. To their continued astonishment, Dunant then headed off again, still accompanied by his corporal and a coachman increasingly terrorized by this nocturnal stroll amid two warring armies. They took the wrong road at first, just missing a French army corps camping in the vicinity, dodging a wayward Austrian blast and rushing full-speed into a sentry who forced them to a halt and was ready to fire when the corporal yelled 'France!' in desperation, granting them a 'Pass'. Finally, a little before midnight, they reached Borghetto. But Dunant didn't achieve his goal until the next day, when the General Mac-Mahon allowed him several minutes of his time at 6 o'clock in the morning.

For a man on a constant quest for titled and high-level connections, even a small meeting with a duke carrying a marshal's baton could only swell Henry Dunant's pride. But this wasn't all he was after. On this very Tuesday, 28th June, Dunant finally managed to do what

---

[15] H. Dunant to H.M. Beaufort d'Hautpoul, 3 July 1859, BGE, Ms. fr. 2108, f. 10.

he'd wanted from the outset, even if he would forever deny it: get his pamphlet to Napoleon. A particular trait of Dunant, and typical for the era, he believed in recommendations as the only way to open doors. And who better than a man recently titled by the emperor to recommend Henry's pamphlet to him? Although Dunant has never admitted this, his determined search for Mac-Mahon had to have been to entrust him with *The Restoration of the Empire of Charlemagne* and, at the same time, the future of his mills.

But yet again, Dunant's destiny didn't exactly follow its expected route. Between his original intentions and his actual outlook, there was a battlefield, a hell, an apocalypse which momentarily placed his Algerian mills in the background. What did these two men talk about? Only briefly mentioning this meeting in his *Memory of Solferino*, Dunant was much more forthcoming in his memoirs, thirty years later:

> I did my best to explain to the illustrious Marshal what I had just witnessed for three days in Castiglione, the lack of sufficient first aid with respect to a considerable number of victims [...] I mentioned, among other things, the horrible state in which I had seen wounded Austrians and the necessity of requisitioning, as quickly as possible, the help of the doctors from Austria who happened to be prisoners.[16]

According to his memoirs, it was Mac-Mahon himself who advised him to retrace his footsteps towards the emperor in Cavriana, something that Dunant did right away with the rekindled hope of placing his gift directly into the emperor's hands.

Because of the vague account of this hypothetical meeting with the emperor, we can suppose Dunant did not see him in person, but rather his personal secretary, Charles Robert, who, it appears, faithfully performed two missions on Dunant's behalf. Three days later, still according to Dunant's memoirs,

> The Emperor of France has taken the following decision: the doctors and surgeons of the Austrian Army taken prisoner while tending the wounded will be unconditionally liberated as they

---

[16] *Mémoires*, 36.

have requested. Those who gave aid to the wounded after the Battle of Solferino in the mobile hospital units of Castiglione are authorized to return first to Austria.[17]

The secretary's second mission – placing Dunant's unsolicited pamphlet into imperial hands – was also performed with the desired precision, as the author would soon discover.

Once he'd completed his strange 'relaxing' evening drive, Dunant returned to his post alongside the wounded of Castiglione. Napoleon's response reached him there one or two days later. It was dated 29th June, the day after his visit to Secretary Robert. With his heart beating wildly, Henry began to read this much-expected response, the proof of imperial recognition he'd so desired:

> Sir,
>
> The Emperor has been made aware of the work which you are planning to publish under the title: *The Roman Empire* – His Majesty has charged me to inform you that while he thanks you for this missive, He cannot accept the dedication and that for current political reasons, He requests you to suspend its publication, which would pose certain inconveniences.[18]

Folding the letter back up, Dunant must have felt Algeria's dust devils rising up to burn his eyes. And the sound of his mill's double axle slowing and then squeaking to a halt. Empty flour sacks, a dried-out waterway, the scowling faces of angry investors. Without the emperor's support, he was utterly lost. And yet this letter signalled the loss of all hope of that very support.

Speechless, he left the Pastorio Palace for fresh air and a walk. He crossed several groups of gentle 'helpers' of the Chiesa Maggiore on their way home from the church, their colourful handkerchiefs tied over their hair. They greeted him with smiles. An immense disappointment overwhelmed him; he would leave Castiglione the very next day.

---

[17] *Mémoires*, 37.
[18] Ch. Robert to H. Dunant, 29 June 1859, BGE, Ms. fr. 2108, f. 8.

Delegates on a mission

Meanwhile in Geneva, everyone was obsessively following the daily updates of the fighting in Italy. The evangelicals were no exception, ready to put their philanthropy into action.

Several days before Madame de Gasparin received Dunant's letter, Reverend Merle d'Aubigné, professor at the Oratory's theological school, used the General Meeting of the Evangelical Society on 29th June 1859 to raise awareness of the suffering on the other side of the Alps. Couldn't they hear 'the staggering cries of the wounded' crossing over 'the Alps and their glaciers'? A high-flown speech followed by an authoritative, urgent and straightforward plea: 'We need prayers, we need men, we need money.'[19] His listeners, comprised not only of evangelicals but also some of Geneva's wealthiest families, left the meeting ready to offer up their connections, money and time. Two thousand francs were gathered in several minutes and a Committee for War Wounded was created on the spot to be presided over by the host of the occasion, Adrien Naville, to 'send spiritual and material help' towards the army hospitals in Italy. Three students of the Oratory's theological school volunteered to leave immediately for Italy and were instructed in bandaging by the aptly named Charpiot,[20] a surgeon and pastor from France who would go with them.

At the very moment his friends from the Evangelical Society were organizing this despatch of volunteers, Dunant had set himself up in Brescia for a week. Momentarily freed from any other concern but charity, he continued going back and forth between the hospitals and improvised dispensaries, handing out tobacco to the wounded of both sides, who all confirmed what he had written to Madame de Gasparin: 'There are soldiers who would prefer not having anything to eat or drink as long as they have something to smoke.'[21]

He travelled from Brescia to Milan in the second week of July. Also in northern Italy at that time was a Dr Louis Appia, one of the first to stand in favour of providing aid to the wounded. Apparently, they did

---

[19] Alexis François, *Le berceau de la Croix-Rouge* (Geneva: Jullien, 1918), 43.

[20] T.N. At the time, bandages were made of a material called *charpie* (lint).

[21] *Journal de Genève*, 9 July 1859. Translation from P. Boissier, *From Solferino to Tsushima*, 31.

not meet up, despite the fact that they knew each other, were both preoccupied by the same questions and were energized by the same faith. Appia was moving in the opposite direction to Dunant. The latter was heading back towards Geneva, and the surgeon heading towards Brescia to conduct a demonstration for his French colleagues of one of his inventions, a device for transporting the wounded on the back of a mule. It is likely they just missed each other.

Things were moving quickly in Switzerland. At the beginning of July, having relocated to her family estate near the Jura mountains, Madame de Gasparin would have been curious to receive a letter from Italy. Both members of Geneva's Evangelical Society, the countess knew Henry as one of the architects of the religious revival occurring among the young people of the city. However, she had no idea he was in Italy at that moment, and she was far from expecting what she was about to read. Her astonishment gave way to rising emotion and then to shock as she discovered the extent of the human disaster following the Battle of Solferino. Profoundly moved by what she read, she immediately took it upon herself to send his letter – minus the passages that would be too painful for readers – to *L'Illustration* in France and the *Journal de Genève* in Switzerland. She informed Dunant of this decision that same evening. She then advised him to form a committee in Italy very quickly so all donations could be sent there directly. She also informed him that she'd left his name out of the newspapers.

By chance, the president of the small and recently formed Committee for War Wounded, Adrien Naville, also went to the *Journal de Genève* in the days that followed to ask if they would advertise the Evangelical Society's initiative. The director was preparing to publish the letter sent to him by Madame De Gasparin and mentioned it would be awkward to publish two appeals for the same cause! Any rivalry was dispensed with immediately – not only members of the same church, Adrien Naville and Valérie de Gasparin were also cousins. Mr Naville suggested they 'combine the two actions' into a single call with a single goal.[22] Madame de Gasparin readily accepted, and on 9th July Dunant's letter appeared in the newspaper's 'Miscellaneous' section:

---

[22] A. Naville to V. de Gasparin, 6 July 1859, BGE, *Papiers de la famille Boissier*, Ms. fr. 7504/13, f. 1v.

M. . ., Permit me to turn to you in the exceptional circumstances
in which I find myself.

For three days I have been attending the wounded of Solferino
in Castiglione and I've looked after more than a thousand
victims. There are 40,000 wounded, both Allies and Austrians in
this terrible situation. There are not enough doctors, and I've had
to replace them, for better or worse, with some women from the
region as well as by a few healthy prisoners.

From Brescia, I went immediately to the battlefield at the time
of the engagement; nothing can express the seriousness of the
fallout from this combat [. . .] I cannot go at length upon all that
I saw, but encouraged by the blessings of hundreds of dying or
wounded men, to which I had the fortune to whisper a few last
words of peace, I am writing you to beg you to organize a funding
drive or to at least gather a few donations in Geneva for this
Christian work.[23]

True, this author had been several leagues from the battlefield at the
time of the fighting, but that wasn't the point! What mattered was
to garner support. After listing the numerous needs – tobacco,
shirts, medicine, bandages – the article finished with a tangled
paragraph on the initiative of 'several individuals' to 'provide
material aid and religious consolation' for the 'wounded of various
nations'. For the material aid, generous benefactors were invited to
send their donations to Adrien Naville or to drop them off directly
at Lombard, Odier and Co., bankers in Geneva.

The day after the letter was published in the *Journal de Genève*,
both Adrien Naville and Madame de Gasparin wrote to Dunant to
give him details of the arrangements. Naville was counting on him
to lead the four Evangelical Society missionaries to hospitals or
other strategic locations for giving aid, to help them get all necessary
authorizations and to facilitate all essential contacts.

Did Dunant receive this letter in Milan? Probably not. He had
quietly left the capital of Lombardy a little before 11th July without
telling anyone his reasons for leaving nor his destination. As
mysteriously as he had 'missed' Appia between Torino and Brescia,
he returned to Switzerland at the exact moment that the small team

---

[23] *Journal de Genève*, 9 July 1859; *L'Illustration*, t. XXXIV, 39.

of voluntary helpers, in accordance with his wishes and repeated claims, were crossing over the Alps into Italy.

Why? His only excuse, as he would later claim, was that 'I felt obliged to breathe the high mountain air to re-establish my health so altered by the painful emotions I had experienced during my trip to Castiglione'.[24] He also briefly mentioned that 'the four gentlemen did not arrive in time' to join him in Castiglione, nor in Milan, 'in the midst of the general confusion'.[25] This did not stop the four volunteers from accomplishing remarkable work during the seven weeks they spent in Lombardy, going from town to town and hospital to hospital, to bring the 'material aid and religious consolation' promised by the Evangelical Society to the wounded of both armies, in the spirit of impartiality that was so important to them. Even in his absence, Dunant's vision had already begun to come to life.

Dunant returned to Geneva by 11th July. Upon discovering his letter had been published in the *Journal de Genève*, he immediately complained to Madame de Gasparin as if he'd been betrayed: betrayal of his modesty, of the 'complete forgetting of himself' and the strict 'Christian point of view' in which he'd written it. He was evidently afraid of being suspected of a lack of humility. So he claimed to be 'disagreeably surprised' by the publication, as if he himself had not begged Madame de Gasparin to do just this.[26]

Madame de Gasparin took his reproaches badly. We do not know exactly how she responded, but however she did, she certainly made herself understood. Five days after shouting about his scorned trust, Dunant apologized to her, as humbly as possible. 'I am begging you to excuse me for a nearly unforgivable lapse,' he wrote, ascribing his forgetfulness to the 'cruel experience'[27] he'd just suffered. Magnanimously, Madame de Gasparin forgave him and declared the affair closed.

Unbeknown to him while still travelling in Italy, Dunant had been co-opted into the brand-new Committee for War Wounded.

---

[24] Cited by Maurice Dunant, *Les débuts de la Croix-Rouge en France*, 20. This phrase is not, however, in the Gagnebin edition of the *Mémoires*.

[25] *Mémoires*, 42.

[26] Dunant to V. de Gasparin, 15 July 1859, BGE, *Papiers de la famille Boissier*, Ms. 7504/13, f. 12–13.

[27] Dunant to V. de Gasparin, 20 July 1859, BGE, *Papiers de la famille Boissier*, Ms. 7504/13, f. 14.

He attended the two meetings which immediately followed his return on 16th and 20th July. With more tact than he had used with Madame de Gasparin, he again insisted his name not be put forward too obviously. Upon learning that Dr Appia had just returned, he passed the leading role to him, asking if he would give his first-hand account to the Genevans still hungry for news. Mindful of the need to separate religious and secular work, Dunant took the risk of insisting, among that pious assembly, that the Evangelical Society's help with relief for prisoners should not turn into preaching. Was he heard? Nothing is less sure. On 1st September, Adrien Naville reported that the Evangelical Society had raised 10,632 francs in donations, efficiently distributed onsite aid, received warm thanks from Italy and, last but not least, spread the Word of the Gospel.

Now that the Committee for War Wounded had fulfilled its mission, it could be dissolved, Dr Appia could return to his patients, and Dunant to his windmills.

A letter from the general

Although his experience in Solferino would soon alter Henry Dunant's future, for the moment it hummed in the background compared to his Algerian worries. Spurred on the previous spring by the eminent nomination of Jerome Napoleon as Minister of Colonies, Henry had pushed the board of the Mons-Djemila Mills to double its capital. Shortly thereafter, Prince Napoleon had left and taken his presumed benevolence with him. A new plea would have to be addressed to his successor, the Count de Chasseloup-Laubat. In vain. And so that summer saw the arrival of some catastrophic news: a Frenchman named Ronsset, a direct competitor of Dunant in the Deheb Wadi region, was about to obtain one of the two waterfalls he wanted. If this news were true, Henry's company had no future.

Who could he turn to? Since his request to two successive ministers of Algeria had not been enough, only the emperor could set things right. His charm offensive using *The Restoration of the Empire of Charlemagne* had unfortunately failed, but this could not mean he'd lost forever. If Dunant the courtier had not found favour with the emperor, then perhaps Dunant the businessman, Dunant the Genevan and friend of General Dufour would be able to convince him of his seriousness and good faith.

Usually reticent to exploit his privileged relationship with the emperor – he'd been his instructor in 1830 – for third parties, General Dufour was swayed by Dunant. It is worth noting that his own interests were in play, however, as he was himself a shareholder in the windmill company. It was nonetheless a rare favour he granted, meaning that he judged the Mons-Djemila affair to be worth the trouble. Dunant's request was the following: convinced he was the victim of a lack of understanding more than hostility, Henry had drafted a detailed memo[28] of how he had spent the last five years attempting to obtain territorial concessions in Algeria, along with all the good reasons to approve him. But after the modest reception of his *Account of the Regency in Tunis*, and the complete flop of his *Restoration*, Dunant could not allow himself to address a third text to His Majesty without accompanying it with a cast-iron recommendation. This was the 'service' Dunant now requested from the untouchable Guillaume-Henri Dufour, General in Chief of the Swiss Confederation: a word to the emperor to help ensure his *Mémorandum* would be read.

The situation was so important that Dunant brought his case in person to Dufour, in his lovely country house built a few hundred metres from the old trenches surrounding Geneva. It was the end of the summer, but still quite hot; the general suggested to Dunant they take advantage of the sunshine. As they took their seats on the sunny terrace, Henry's stress was certainly visible as beads of sweat on his brow.

He expressed his worries as simply as possible, trying hard not to list all the hassles that had afflicted him. Then he handed the general a ready-made letter, signed by the six members of the board of directors[29] who 'begged' His Majesty to please read their *Mémorandum*.

The general invited Dunant to follow him into his office. Behind him, Dunant was not walking, he was flying. His windmills were saved.

A few minutes later, Dunant read what the general had added to his letter, a phrase that should change everything:

---

[28] J. Henry Dunant, *Mémorandum au sujet de la Société financière et industrielle des Moulins de Mons-Djémila en Algérie, Exposé des démarches* (Paris: Renou et Maulde, 1859).

[29] Alongside Henry Dunant and his brother Daniel were his friends Necker, Mac-Culloch and both father and son Trembley.

The signatories of this letter are all well-established in Geneva and deserving of consideration: I know them all personally. I shall therefore join my instances to theirs.

[Signed:] General Dufour.[30]

Standing on the front porch, Dunant thanked the general effusively. Although there was no family connection between the two men, they had a long-standing affection for one another. Dufour, who had no son, may have developed paternal feelings towards his enterprising young friend who, conversely, had possibly dreamed of having such a successful father.[31]

Autumn in Paris

At the end of September 1859, Dunant left for Paris with two decisive documents inside his luggage meant to secure land in Algeria: his *Memorandum* on the Mons-Djemila Mills, a single copy lavishly printed on parchment, and the letter signed by Dufour. There is nothing to indicate, however, that these documents ever made their way to the emperor. During that autumn in Paris, Dunant knocked on every door he could, from cabinet chiefs to company presidents, hoping for meetings, promises, letters of recommendation, certificates and references. In November, as a practical measure, he had his *Memorandum* reprinted as a simple business document, into which he inserted the letter with Dufour's additional note, as well as a strongly worded protest against a possible adjudication of the second waterfall to his rival Ronsset.

Refusing to grant one of two waterfalls will not only be disastrous for the discouraged shareholders but will further assault the company with a blow from which it will not be able to recover, creating a deplorable effect through its very disaster in the eyes of the French and foreign public interested in Algeria, and will

---

[30] Letter of 6 September 1859, added to the *Memorandum* (no pagination).
[31] See Roger Durand and Felix Christ in R. Durand (ed.), *Guillaume Henri Dufour dans son temps* (Geneva: Société d'histoire et d'archéologie, 1991), 384–96 and 419.

push the capitalists further than ever out of a country that treats them so badly and yet which needs them so much.

The government should beware: these considerations deserve the trouble of an attentive examination – the various and successive administrations of Algeria in Paris for the last few years have all taken the same approach, and it is not in acting as they have for the last six years that the formal will of the emperor will be fulfilled.[32]

Dufour's first intervention might have been the result of a disinterested benevolence, but a second suggests that the general didn't want to see a business in which he had invested fail. And so, in December, he put a new letter of introduction in Dunant's hands, this time for Mr Mocquard, Napoleon III's Chief of Cabinet. He also recommended Dunant present his case 'as clearly and briefly as possible' and not to forget, if Mr Mocquard sent him an invitation, that he should bring it with him as an 'admission ticket'![33] Following this advice to the letter, Dunant apparently managed to place his *Memorandum* with someone high-up in the administration. And so it was on 21st February 1860 that he finally received a small item of good news: the first waterfall had been granted, as well as the surrounding 206 acres plus three farms totalling 370 acres. However, the second waterfall had been conceded to Mr Ronsset, who had already constructed a factory and several other buildings at the site.

The extension of his land plot meant Dunant could solve at least two of his major problems. He now had enough land to raise animals, so he could not only transport his flour, but also use the wheat bran produced by the mill to feed them. Despite losing the second waterfall, the French decision gave Dunant enough confidence to launch a new advertising campaign lauding an 'excellent manager in Algeria' (who was none other than Henri Nick) and its 10 per cent yields to entice shareholders in the early spring of 1860. The Genevans rushed to sign up.

---

[32] Appendix and Protest added to the *Memorandum* (no pagination).
[33] According to a note from Dufour to Dunant, 4 December 1859, BGE, Ms. fr. 2108, f. 27.

Writing *A Memory*

Henry Dunant began to write *A Memory of Solferino* probably a year and a half after the battle. This need to write, he said later, did not come only as a result of the trauma he'd experienced in Lombardy, but was also encouraged by the interest his humanitarian projects had awakened in Paris's political circles, eventually convincing him to write his memories and ideas down for posterity. He began to do so in 1860 and continued throughout 1861.

The task was more difficult than he'd first imagined. He could not simply jot down his impressions randomly like some ordinary travel notebook. Aiming for the same accuracy and seriousness of his *Account of the Regency in Tunis*, he began documenting all possible sources to embellish his own observations with knowledge provided by renowned men of his time, from military strategists to surgical experts in amputation.

Convinced that illustrations would help his readers – even though the printer Fick warned him this would seriously increase the bill – he went ahead and included two colour lithographs of the battle site and troop movements. This detail would tack on the extravagant sum of 450 francs, nearly a fifth of the total printing cost.

His other obsession was impartiality, as difficult as that might have been for a child of Geneva naturally disposed to take the side of the French and Sardinian Allies. However, he made it a point of honour to immortalize the bravery, and even more the suffering, of both sides. Without muting the horror of the carnage, Henry attempted to describe as objectively as possible the 'horrible and frightening body-to-body combat':

> Austrians and Allies trampling each other underfoot, killing one another on piles of bleeding corpses, felling their enemies with their rifle butts, crushing skulls, ripping bellies open with sabre and bayonet. No quarter is given; it is sheer butchery; a struggle between savage beasts, maddened with blood and fury. Even the wounded fight to the last gasp. When they have no weapon left, they seize their enemies by the throat and tear them with their teeth.[34]

---

[34] Dunant, *A Memory of Solferino*, 19.

A fascinated reader of *Uncle Tom's Cabin*, Henry knew very well that beliefs are born of emotions. It wasn't his rational mind alone that had first made him hate slavery but his heart, his young man's heart discovering the immensity of America, its cotton fields and human ferociousness through Harriet Beecher Stowe's pen. He clearly remembered this in the winter of 1861–2 when he moved his desk closer to the window to catch every last ray of daylight; he remembered it when he continued, page after page, to describe live amputations, jawbones being ripped away, exploding brains splattering uniforms: all the bloody, ordinary cruelty of war.

However unbearable this depiction may have been, he knew that his ideas would gain ground by sprouting first in the heart before blossoming in the brain. The horror, the blood, the violence of battle had to be told – using second-hand accounts when needed – and so did the miserable disarray of the days that followed with their improvised aid, the wounded to tend, the dead to bury, the families to console. But he also had to tell of the devotion of the few who, from Castiglione to Milan, had already made all the difference in turning hell into chaos, and who could have been able to do more if only, if only . . .

If only the message he delivered in the fourteen last pages of *A Memory of Solferino* would be taken as seriously as it should be, and which already constituted, although in rudimentary form, the guiding principles of the future Red Cross:

> Would it not be possible, in time of peace and quiet, to form relief societies for the purpose of having care given to the wounded in wartime by zealous, devoted and thoroughly qualified volunteers? [. . .][35]
>
> On certain special occasions, as, for example, when princes of the military art belonging to different nationalities meet at Cologne or Châlons, would it not be desirable that they should take advantage of this sort of congress to formulate some international principle, sanctioned by a Convention inviolate in character, which, once agreed upon and ratified, might constitute

---

[35] Dunant, *A Memory of Solferino*, 116.

the basis for societies for the relief of the wounded in the different
European countries? [. . .]³⁶

And do not these considerations alone constitute more than
adequate reason for taking precautions against surprise? [. . .]³⁷

Dunant's entire future work is included in these few paragraphs,
whose novelty comes from just one or two words: that relief societies
could be prepared for war, *in times of peace*, in order not to be taken
by *surprise*; the *international principle, sanctioned by an inviolate
Convention* making it possible to send relief forces without fear of
hostile fire from either side. If the neutrality of this aid is not yet
explicitly formulated, it can be deduced from the 'international
principle' upon which the countries would have to agree.

The publication

Wanting to make the work as up to date as possible, Dunant was
still inserting recent events from that summer of 1862. Finally, in
the autumn, he distributed several pages to his friends, beginning
with General Dufour, whose approval he needed and for which he
waited anxiously.

On 19th October 1862, the General wrote to his protégé that he
had read the work 'with much interest' and completely approved of its
content. However, he contested the very points that ensured its novelty,
and expressed profound doubts about the feasibility of his ideas:

> Doubtless an association of the kind you envisaged would be
> most desirable, but its setting up would be problematic. It could
> hardly be [anything] other than both temporary and local [. . .] It
> is difficult to imagine how similar bodies could be permanent
> and follow armies to war in distant places.³⁸

Dunant was not fazed. This was both his weakness and his strength:
when he was sure he was right, he heard and saw only what suited

---

³⁶ Dunant, *A Memory of Solferino*, 126.
³⁷ Ibid., 128.
³⁸ G.-H. Dufour to Dunant, 19 October 1862, BGE, Ms. fr. 2108, f. 33–4.

his plans. Dufour had reservations about three of Dunant's key ideas: the permanent nature of the relief societies; their collaboration with the army; and the international character of the institution. OK. But didn't the first part of Dufour's letter praise the usefulness of testifying to 'what the glory of the battlefield costs in terms of torture and tears'? This was enough to justify including part of Dufour's letter in his book. Without thinking twice, Dunant folded up the general's letter and took it to the printer: there was thankfully still time to add a page to *A Memory of Solferino* with several flattering sentences from one of the most unanimously respected figures in Switzerland.

The book was published by Fick printers in November 1862; the first 400 copies carried the words *Not for Sale* on their title page. A selection of these were distributed to his friends in Geneva, but the rest were meant for the great leaders of the world. Searching through his connections for anyone with a title or some form of renown or power, Dunant targeted the highest level of the pyramid – sovereigns, chancellors, ministers. It did not take long for him to receive his first congratulations: by mid-November, Dunant knew he'd hit his mark.

There was not a minute to waste. He had a second edition printed in December. The *Not for Sale* label had vanished and according to advertisements in Geneva newspapers, the book could now be found 'with all main booksellers' for a price of 5 francs. In February 1863, 3,000 copies of a third edition were printed in a small paperback format, at an affordable price of 1.50 francs and with several substantial modifications: factual amendments, less fawning praise of the French army, more specific proposals.

After three French editions, Dunant went after Europe. Starting in 1863, translations appeared in German, Dutch and Italian; despite all his efforts, Dunant did not manage an English or Russian edition.

The media response was positive. A first article appeared in the *Journal de Genève* on 26th November 1862, then the *Journal des Débats* presented *A Memory of Solferino* to the French on 15th February 1863. On 16th May an article accompanied by large extracts appeared in Charles Dickens's mass-produced periodical *All the Year Round*. Responses were numerous, always positive, and often enthusiastic. Officers, clergymen, historians, philosophers, ladies and gentlemen, everyone approved of Henry's audacity in presenting the war as it was – atrocious. In the months that followed the book's publication thirteen sovereigns expressed their interest in the project mentioned in the book's conclusion.

Amid the clamour, a voice of caution made itself heard. In January 1863, echoing General Dufour's early reservations, an 'expert' on the subject called Dunant a dreamer in barely concealed terms. The legendary 'woman of the lamp', a great heroine of the Crimean War, an uncontested authority on humanitarian ideas and a figure venerated by Dunant for fifteen years – Florence Nightingale. The august lady did not write personally, but via a third party;[39] she made it clear that Dunant's approach was misguided. He wanted to internationalize the problem and its response, while Nightingale wanted to treat it nation by nation, and within each army. Point by point, she claimed that it was the government's task, and only the government's, to address these issues, that England had all the resources necessary during times of peace, and that if a system must be put in place, it would be the one already established in Great Britain, which was so perfect it could be applied anywhere else. Mr Dunant, she kindly made known in the conclusion of her response, had not quite understood England's extraordinary advances since the war in Crimea – thanks to her, naturally.

Dunant did not risk arguing with her, she was too well known to be contradicted. Up until the end of his life, he would go on claiming her great influence on him, and the convergence in their opinions. He omitted the strong critiques contained in her letter and retained only her phrases of polite approbation, converting them into 'precious support' from the Crimean heroine, who would have 'highly' approved 'of the excellence of the goal'[40] suggested in *A Memory*. Nightingale's brother-in-law had written her letter in English; let's grant Dunant some liberty with the translation.

The Akfadou forest

Over the months of writing *A Memory*, Henry hadn't lost sight of his Algerian concerns. The series of failures he'd already lived

---

[39] Sir Harry Verney (Florence Nightingale's brother-in-law) to Miss Gaussen (Louis Gaussen's daughter, close to Dunant), 14 January 1863, BGE, Ms. fr. 2108, f. 183–4.
[40] Dunant, *Mémoires*, 56.

through didn't yet rattle his nerves – quite the contrary! By gradually increasing his financial pressure each time, the setbacks only had him engaging in riskier and riskier bets. A first fiasco in silver-lead mining in 1854, then a second in copper mining in 1856, both the result of advice from the imaginative Henri Nick,[41] prompted Dunant to try his luck elsewhere and with someone else. He turned his attention to the jewel of colonial capitalism – the cork oak forests, Algeria's goose with a golden egg, shared by a few dozen happy shareholders.

This time things were well-run and seemed to promise a more optimistic future. In the spring of 1862, the *Moniteur de l'Algérie* announced that a certain Mr Doulouze, a merchant from Constantine, and a Mr Dunant, 'a rich landowner from the department of Ain, connected to some of Geneva's wealthiest families', had just been granted the management of lot number one in the Akfadou forest. The article that followed leaves little doubt as to who wrote it:

> Mr. Dunant is not only a capitalist; member of a great number of learned societies in Paris and abroad, and a tireless traveller, he has toured through Algeria but also through other parts of northern Africa. His recently published book on Tunisia shows him to be a serious observer as well as scholarly writer.[42]

The style of this sentence reeks of Dunant himself, who continually asserted, alongside his financial activities, his status as a man of letters, if not a man of science.

The new project of our erudite financier was, in theory, neither unreasonable nor eccentric; a few other wise Genevan patricians were also involved at that time in harvesting cork oak in Algeria, lured by the same promises of profits as Dunant. Did they have a more solid financial base with which to shore up the significant

---

[41] This is at least what Dunant said later, when he needed to defend himself. A recent book by a descendent of Henri Nick makes clear that in Nick's family, the worries were the other way round: Nick's father-in-law, namely, was very anxious about Dunant's megalomania in business. See Grégoire Humbert, *Faillite en Algérie* (Paris: Ampelos, 2018), 93–144.

[42] *Moniteur de l'Algérie*, 134, 25 May 1862, quoted by Pous, *Dunant l'Algérien*, 113.

investments required for this particular product? Ditches, logging, pruning, trimming, construction and maintenance of roads – and, above all, to wait out the ten or fifteen years needed before receiving any initial dividends? It's probable. Although Dunant did, two years later, send 4,000 cubic metres of wood to the Imperial Navy, he was still lightyears from recuperating the gigantic investments that forest management required. Only a perpetual concession would make the situation profitable, and yet he'd only obtained an eighteen-year permit in the spring of 1862. By the time he realized that a longer-term lease was needed, and had even taken steps to obtain it, it was already too late. The decree granting him an almost limitless forest concession came on 7th August 1867 – but by this date, alas, there was no longer anyone matching the description of a 'wealthy landowner from the department of Ain' by the name of Mr Dunant.

5

Europe Around One Table (1862–3)

The evening visitor

Obtaining the concession to the Akfadou forest, even if only for a limited period, calmed Dunant down. At least for 1862, the skies seemed to clear over Africa. He could now dedicate himself to promoting *A Memory of Solferino*. In Dunant's view, he'd written a call to action, a manifesto, a foundational text from which a movement would be launched. Which is why he'd so widely distributed the first edition: he was waiting for the sap to rise in one of the philanthropists, pastors, jurists, professors, humanists, princes, countesses, ministers and high officers to whom he'd sent a copy.

Was he hoping for a sign from Geneva, the city of his birth? Over the last two or three years, Henry had increasingly developed his relationship with France; he'd acquired French nationality and remained an unabashed admirer of Napoleon III. And so Geneva wasn't quite at the top of his list when, in November 1862, he set to work transforming the ideas he'd laid out in his writing into actual policies. A tour was planned, and it seems it would be launched in Paris where he was planning an early-December visit to present the key points of his project to one or two scholarly circles and distinguished aristocrats.

Meanwhile, several noteworthy individuals to whom he'd sent his book in French-speaking Switzerland had already seized upon the innovative nature of his proposals. The chairmen of three different charities contacted him almost simultaneously to say they were strongly interested and would like to contribute in some form or another. One of these individuals was the chair of the *Société genevoise d'utilité publique* (Geneva Society for Public Welfare), a lawyer named Gustave Moynier with no taste for the courtroom but a remarkable talent for philanthropy.[1] Dunant knew of him through several societies to which they both belonged. Moynier visited Dunant at the end of November to discuss how they might collaborate.

As Dunant shook Moynier's hand that afternoon in the fading light, an image crossed his mind like a spark from the past. There was something aquiline in Moynier's face; at first it seemed only to be the sharp angle of his nose, but upon closer scrutiny it was his extraordinary eyes which flitted so sharply from one object to another, exactly like a bird whose head moved atop a quiet, motionless body. Then it came to him! He'd seen this gaze fifteen years earlier at a high-society ball outside the city. Moynier had been among the group of several young men who'd stayed the night in the improvised dormitory above the greenhouse. Since then their paths had crossed in various societies but they had not spent much time together. The divide between a degree-holding attorney, who stubbornly resisted his banker in-laws' offers of employment in the world of finance, and a self-taught entrepreneur looking for any way into the very same world had been much too vast for friendship or complicity.

'I've come to congratulate you, Mr Dunant. What a moving story, and I also firmly believe in your idea of a volunteer nursing corps. This seems to merit the most attentive consideration. Which is why I'd like, with your permission, to submit the project to my society.'[2]

'This is the Society for Public Welfare?' Dunant asked him, standing to fix the flickering light of the lamp on the side table and get out from beneath those eagle eyes for a moment.

'The *Geneva* Society for Public Welfare,' Moynier gently corrected. 'By its statutes, the society is devoted to social issues and focused on local interests. But I have high hopes that it will agree to turn its attention to the fate of wounded soldiers. I do not expect

---

[1] André Durand, '*Gustave Moynier: retour à Genève et recherche d'une vocation*', *Cahiers du Centenaire*, 4 (Geneva: Association Dunant-Moynier, 2008), 2–12.
[2] This dialogue follows Gustave Moynier, *La fondation de la Croix-Rouge* (Geneva: Soulier, 1903), 4–5; Jean de Senarclens, *The Founding of the Red Cross, Gustave Moynier its master builder* (Geneva: Slatkine, 2005), 98; and Dunant, *Mémoires*, 51.

any great insights or practical guidelines, of course, but I can at least initiate a debate on the subject. I'd like to put this item on the agenda for our next meeting.'

After an hour of conversation, Dunant walked Moynier to the door. The most contradictory thoughts were swirling through his mind. Was it a good idea to engage with a local society, or should he look for direction in Paris? Moynier had highlighted the different international congresses at which he represented the Society for Public Welfare, convinced that one of these future gatherings might be interested in Dunant's proposals. But was this the best forum in which to defend his ideas? Was Moynier the right ambassador? Was Geneva the right place to launch his project? A concerning association popped into his mind. There was something of the same enthusiasm and good will in this Moynier as in his old friend Perrot, before envy had made a mess of things.

But no. This was absurd. Moynier was nothing like Perrot, Henry thought, bringing his lamp to his work table. He sat down and began to write. Encouraged by Moynier's excitement, he still wanted to check if France might consider his project, thus giving it the support of a great nation. That evening he confirmed all his meetings in Paris.

At that very moment while walking home, Moynier was putting the final touches to his own strategy. It hadn't escaped his notice that Dunant was still focused on Paris. He knew he must move quickly. To ensure the project could be defended as a member's proposal, giving it a greater chance of success, he would immediately present Mr Dunant's candidacy to the Geneva Society for Public Welfare as well as include the proposals listed in *A Memory of Solferino* on the agenda. Clearly, the question of wounded soldiers could not be further from his society's usual field of action; although its statutes were quite broad – issues related to education, poverty and industry – no matter how you looked at it, wounded soldiers were an awkward fit. Well, he would just have to convince his colleagues: establishing the unanimously heralded vision of *A Memory of Solferino* was an opportunity the Geneva Society for Public Welfare should not overlook.

Moynier executed his plan in record time. On 8th December 1862, Dunant was welcomed as a member of the society. A week later, on 15th December, Moynier delivered Dunant's proposal to his executive committee: organize volunteers in peacetime so that, when war did break out, they would be able to help the wounded and thus save numerous lives. Among the ten or so members of his committee, one was listening to the chairman with palpable interest. At the end of the session, all eyes turned towards him – everyone was waiting to hear what General Dufour would say.

'Who would pay for the volunteers?'[3] the general asked immediately. 'How will they work alongside military medical services? Won't their position be difficult?' Other objections were raised, less about the premise and more about whether it was the place of the Geneva Society for Public Welfare to consider such grand proposals. And the verdict inevitably fell: 'This is not for our Society to deal with,' as was noted diligently by the secretary of the session.[4]

The Society for Public Welfare

Wounded soldiers weren't the only thing on Gustave Moynier's agenda at the end of 1862. Alongside his other social commitments, the fight against alcoholism would dominate his programme throughout 1863; he had a report to give in January on 'the abuse of intoxicating beverages in Geneva', a speech to prepare for February on drunkenness, followed by a public reading in March of a treatise on alcoholics. But none of this could distract him from the issue raised by Dunant: he had to find a way to put it back on the table with his hesitant society. Until now he'd focused on what were surely noble causes but restricted to the more grassroots miseries of abandoned children, drunks, illiterates, indigents. The case for wounded soldiers gave him the feeling of a window suddenly opening out onto a newer, bolder, wider world. This was his call to a larger issue. Overriding his committee's first refusal, Moynier decided to place the plight of wounded soldiers back on the agenda for the following session on 28th January 1863.

These were, obviously, the very same people who'd swept his proposal aside a month and a half earlier. But Moynier was planning to get their consent another way. If he couldn't force his local society

---

[3] Geneva Society for Public Welfare Archives (*Commission d'économie domestique*), 15 December 1862, *Archives d'Etat de Genève* (Geneva State Archives, AEG from now on), AP241.2.1, 212.
[4] Ibid.

to take up a challenge as important as the victims of war, well then, he would simply suggest they establish a smaller working group to tackle the question.

This time the committee accepted their chairman's proposal. Moynier quickly convoked the entire membership of his Society – 164 in total – to a debate on 'the attachment of a corps of voluntary nurses to armies in the field', which, being a new field of activity, required the consent of a general meeting. Moynier was twitching with impatience to get to work. 'This is why I have placed this subject on the schedule for the next meeting of the Society for Public Welfare on Monday, 9th February, at six o'clock,' he wrote to Dunant at the beginning of February 1863. 'I hope you will be able to attend to give me a hand and help me obtain the formation of the commission in question.'[5]

How could Moynier worry for a single second that Dunant might skip this meeting? It seems unthinkable from our perspective now that Henry Dunant would not attend a meeting whose objective included a defence of his own ideas. But Moynier's question reveals how much these two men's schedules differed. While the professional philanthropist could dedicate both body and soul to the projects that interested him, the striving entrepreneur could only grant the crumbs of his time to anything but his business in Algeria which required travel, decisions, arbitration, negotiations, accounting, recommendations, endless approaches, not to mention the complicated reports he had to deliver to increasingly nervous shareholders. Dunant may also have had some reservations about linking the future of his international movement to the Geneva Society for Public Welfare, whose tiny white invitation card for its next meeting wedged Henry's grand project for 'wounded soldiers' between a debate on 'a popular edition of the French classics' and 'the setting up of a farming community for juvenile delinquents'. Was Dunant afraid his idea might be taken from him if he let Gustave Moynier run with it? Or did he simply believe he might be condemning it by setting it in Geneva? In any case everything indicates that, on the eve of that general meeting, he was not entirely ready to give up on France: he warned Moynier that having received 'many notes of approval and precious encouragement from all

---

[5] Gustave Moynier to Dunant, 2 February 1863, in Senarclens, *The founding of the Red Cross*, 100.

sides, especially in Paris', he hoped to create a committee there with
'a certain number of influential individuals belonging to both the
city's scholarly societies and its upper class', to whom he'd already
expressed his intentions.[6]

Geneva in the starting blocks

However, a bird in the hand is worth two in the bush. Since nothing
concrete was coming to fruition in Paris, Dunant did attend the
general meeting of the Geneva Society for Public Welfare on 9th
February 1863. It was held at the Saint-Pierre Casino, in the very
same room that had witnessed the creation of the Geneva chapter
of the YMCA, eleven years earlier.

The meeting was held on the ground floor. As was customary, the
older men would have arrived first to sit in the front rows, with
their hands crossed over their canes, talking while waiting for the
meeting to begin.

The first subject of debate, 'a popular edition of French classics',
clearly energized the meeting, eliciting nearly a dozen comments
and discussions. And then came the second object of discussion: 'the
attachment to armies of a corps of voluntary nurses (Conclusion of
the book by Mr Henry Dunant, entitled *A Memory of Solferino*)'.

Attempting to avoid any ruffled feathers, Moynier had settled for
an apparently inoffensive proposal: Dunant's project for granting
aid to wounded soldiers could be presented to an international
welfare congress to be held in Berlin the following September. The
idea would be to lobby the various countries through their delegates
to hold a conference on the subject.

Just as he had done in a smaller circle, during the committee's
December session, General Dufour expressed his reservations. He felt
executing such an idea would be difficult, and it required them to
'think big'.[7] An international congress would indeed be the lowest-
level echelon at which such a proposal could realistically be defended.

[6] Unpublished 'Fragments' of Dunant's memoirs, BGE, Ms. fr. 2096, f. 22.
[7] Geneva Society for Public Welfare Archives ('*Procès-verbaux*'), 9 February 1863,
AEG, AP241.1.6, no pagination. About this meeting, see Roger Durand, '*Le "non-
événement" du 9 février 1863*', *Bulletin de la Société Henry Dunant*, 10 (Geneva:
SHD, 1985–8), 33–47.

In all, Dunant's proposal elicited only six comments, an obviously less passionate debate than the one on French classics. Nonetheless, the idea was accepted. The meeting readily consented to the creation of an ad hoc drafting committee to deal with the question, and even more readily to the consignment of any concrete plans to the faraway Berlin congress. Quite keen to be done with a subject that so exceeded the Society's mandate, the assembly was even happy to forgo any future follow-up reports from the new committee.

This time, however, the time-worn strategy of 'referring to committee' wouldn't bury the issue for good. On the contrary. The five men gathered that night – chairman of the Geneva Society for Public Welfare, Gustave Moynier; General of the Swiss Army, Guillaume-Henri Dufour; the doctors Théodore Maunoir and Louis Appia; and our Henry Dunant – were about to change history, though none of them could imagine it yet. For the moment, their sole task was to write a report for the international congress in Berlin, six months later.

The meeting then moved on from this question to its next matter: 'setting up a farming community for juvenile delinquents in French-speaking Switzerland'. But Henry was only listening with one ear. Now the die were cast. If his vision would come to pass, if it would one day lead to the international agreement he'd felt the urgency for in Solferino, it had just taken form that evening at the foot of the cathedral before a handful of individuals who perhaps did not recognize its novelty nor the stakes involved. Right then, the compliments he'd received in Paris the month before sprang to mind. Had he hit the wrong target? Had he just committed the worst mistake of his life through the same impatience that so often led him astray? The scraping of chairs brought him out of his thoughts. The meeting was adjourning. Dr Appia came to shake his hand, followed by General Dufour and then Mr Maunoir. His doubts vanished. Geneva had won this first round.

The first meeting of the International Committee of the Red Cross

Eight days later, on 17th February 1863, the members of the drafting committee or 'Committee of Five' – today recognized as the ancestor

of the International Committee of the Red Cross (ICRC) – gathered
for their first meeting. Gustave Moynier opened with a reminder of
their mission: to prepare a report for the international welfare
congress in Berlin. The purpose was to present Mr Dunant's book
and its goal of promoting the creation of relief societies to send
volunteer nursing corps for wounded soldiers.

The first thing the report must emphasize, General Dufour calmly
stated, was the need for unanimous consent from the princes and
nations of Europe, followed by the formation of national committees
that would establish close cooperation between the volunteers and
military staffs.

Dunant paused in his note-taking: in just one week, Dufour's
hesitations had certainly vanished! The general even went a step
further, lending his support to the idea of a symbol, a uniform or an
armband, 'distinctive and universally adopted insignia' which
would make the volunteers recognizable and thus accepted by the
armies.

'It would also be good if the committee would *"agitate"*,'[8]
Théodore Maunoir said, 'in order to win everyone over, among high
and low, with the rulers of Europe as well as the masses.'[9]

Appointed secretary of the new committee, it was Henry Dunant's
task to write the report for Berlin. But he was hoping for more than
these initial suggestions. Why not aim higher? Why not see bigger?
Alongside the subjects mentioned, he wanted to advocate for better
military hospitals, to improve transport methods, even for a
museum of rescue equipment! 'And more than anything,' he added
after a pause, 'I would like to insist on a most crucial point. In *A
Memory of Solferino*, I expressed a wish that the civilized powers
would adopt an international and inviolable principle, which would
be guaranteed through a kind of covenant among the governments.
This would serve,' he went on, 'to protect all individuals, official or
not, who treat the victims of war.'

General Dufour and Gustave Moynier kept silent, visibly
sceptical. Who could imagine the great armies of Europe handing

---

[8] Maunoir would have said today: 'create some buzz'.
[9] Meeting minutes from 17 February 1863 (signed by 'the secretary Henry Dunant'),
Jean-François Pitteloud (ed.), *Procès-verbaux des séances du Comité international
de la Croix-Rouge 1863–1914* (Geneva: SHD and CICR, 1999), 18.

over their health services and medical staff to a third party? But there was probably no need to argue as reality would soon bring Mr Dunant back to earth.

Moynier was, however, in complete agreement with Dunant on a point mentioned earlier in the session: the committee should declare itself 'permanent and international'.[10] None of the four other members around the table seemed the least bit shocked by the boldness of the suggestion. By creating a structure with an *international* scope and with *permanent* status, each of them were well aware that they were breaking with all previous customs of humanitarian assistance. Up until then, once hostilities were over, relief societies or charity committees were usually dissolved and every nation, whether at war or not, went back to minding its own business and its own casualties.

Each member recognized how monumental this suggestion was, but nonetheless the motion was unanimously adopted.

What remained now was to adapt the name of this new committee to live up to its new ambitions. They hesitated and brainstormed for some time, leaving their brave and careful secretary with a mess of superimposed headers all over his notes.[11]

This first session of what would become the International Committee of the Red Cross finished by divvying up a number of tasks. Under the presidency of General Dufour, Gustave Moynier became vice president and Henry Dunant was confirmed as secretary.

Ten years before, another meeting had named him corresponding secretary of the Young Men's Christian Association of Geneva, a

---

[10] Based on the meeting minutes from 17 February 1863, *Procès-verbaux du CICR*, 16–19, and François, *Le berceau de la Croix-Rouge*, 109–15.

[11] The manuscript of the 17 February minutes shows this hesitation (ICRC Archives [AICRC from now on] A PV, 'February 1863–March 1864', f. 1, facsimile in the *Revue internationale de la Croix-Rouge*, 360, December 1948, no page number). It would only be in 1876 that the committee would take its current name, more widely known through its acronym, ICRC. Until then the committee would be called *Comité international de secours aux blessés*, variously translated as International Aid Committee for Wounded Soldiers, for (the) Relief to Wounded Soldiers, for Assistance to Wounded Soldiers, and more and more frequently International Committee of the Red Cross. To harmonize for English readers, as well as distinguish it from the eventual Swiss Red Cross, we use 'International Committee', 'Geneva Committee', or ICRC.

very successful appointment indeed. While gathering his papers that evening, he revisited that earlier role with calm certainty. He would do even better this time.

Some agitation

Maunoir's advice to 'agitate' would be followed beyond all expectations by the frenzied secretary of the International Committee. Dunant went immediately to Paris after that meeting on 17th February. Instead of launching his international movement from there, as he'd once planned, he went about setting up a central committee for a French Soldiers' Aid Society as quickly as possible, with some heavyweight personalities.

A Memory of Solferino had garnered him many testimonies of support and interest, as well as a string of articles in the press. But it was the article written by the scholar Saint-Marc Girardin in the *Journal des Débats* which made him an overnight celebrity in the capital city of France exactly at the moment he happened to be there: letters poured in, calling cards were constant. He was no longer waiting around for his moment of glory, it had arrived.

This favourable welcome had Dunant hoping for a visit card embossed with imperial arms. The first on the list of recipients of *A Memory*, Napoleon III had already expressed his thanks via his secretary but without any commentary. Dunant was yearning for something more tangible. He'd even perhaps boasted a little prematurely in Geneva, since we know his friend Appia gave him a message to pass to the emperor while in Paris! But Dunant would not meet His Majesty, not this time, nor on his future visits to Paris, no matter how many reasons were pushing him to seek the emperor's support: wounded soldiers, yes, but Algerian windmills, too, and all his other pressing financial entanglements.

On 17th March, Dunant returned to Geneva for the second meeting of the Committee of Five. Since their first session, the stack of congratulatory letters for his *Memory of Solferino* had grown a good 10 centimetres, so much so that Dunant had to hire two secretaries to deal with the abundant correspondence. With a trace of bitterness that only Dunant would have missed, Moynier mentioned it would be useful to everyone if these expressions of support were recorded into the Committee minutes, perhaps hinting to the author that the glory of *A Memory of Solferino* should, from now on, work to the benefit of the International Committee.

War hero General Guillaume-Henri Dufour also did not seem much impressed by all of Dunant's praise. 'We must lay the markers, and then others will come to pave the road,'[12] he stated with a firm confidence in the future of an idea he'd not thought possible only six months earlier.

Hearing this, Dunant brusquely recognized the very words he'd written in 1855 to his friend Chauncy Langdon, on the eve of the first conference of the YMCA: 'I'm happy now to step into the background, seeing that the sacred fire has won over my friends in Geneva.'[13] His work then had been accomplished; his task completed. But here, but now, everything was still waiting for him, it was just beginning! How could the general even be thinking of stepping back already when nothing was yet settled?

'Mr Dunant remains in charge of writing the report which will be read in Berlin,'[14] Gustave Moynier said, cutting off Henry's internal argument. Yes! Everything was still to be done.

But Dunant had other fish to fry. At the end of April, he was on the road again to Marseilles and Algiers. His affairs could no longer wait: the news from his associate Nick was not all terrible, but it was also not good. He had to return to Algeria to see for himself how his mills were turning, how the land was being managed and where his concession requests stood. All this would take time. May passed, and then June, two long months during which the secretary of the International Committee became a hard-pressed entrepreneur, beset with unbearable financial deadlines, moving forward like a tightrope walker on the tense cord of his ambitions.

An admirer in Holland

While Dunant's stay in Algeria stretched on, a man in Europe was waiting impatiently for him to return. Chief surgeon of the Dutch army, Johan-Christiaan Basting had devoured *A Memory of*

---

[12] Meeting minutes from 17 March 1863, *Procès-verbaux du CICR*, 18.

[13] Dunant to Langdon, 22 January 1855, World YMCA Archives.

[14] Based on meeting minutes from 17 March 1863, *Procès-verbaux du CICR*, 19.

Solferino and been so enthusiastic about it he'd written to the author the moment he'd finished reading it, offering to complete a Dutch translation and bring it to the attention of his sovereigns. From this first contact a thorough correspondence had developed between Geneva and The Hague. Dunant's immediate response was positive, giving Basting permission for the translation on the condition that his name 'be correctly spelled',[15] no doubt worried of seeing his *y* turned back into an *i*. In the same mailing, he sent gilt-edged copies to be passed on to the queen, the king and to the Prince of Orange – just the thing to seal the beginnings of a promising friendship.

Dr Basting fulfilled Dunant's wishes to the letter. He wrote to his new friend with a surprising freedom and affection for a man he'd never met, in a style which echoed the warm familiarity between the children of the Protestant Revival. The two men would soon discover they shared a similar emotional and compassionate nature, the same Christian fervour, but also the same abolitionist convictions. Dunant sent him his most recent publication, a chapter on slavery taken from his *Account on the Regency in Tunis* and published on its own. The American Civil War was raging at the time, making this older pamphlet newly topical, an opportunity that Dunant's editorial flair had not missed. Entitled '*L'esclavage chez les Musulmans et aux États-Unis d'Amérique, par l'auteur de* Un Souvenir de Solferino'[16] (Slavery in the Muslim world and in the United States of America, by the author of *A Memory of Solferino*), Dunant's text bluntly condemned the cruelty of the American slave institution. The tone of the book was quite Crusade-like, but the 'good guys' and the 'bad guys' were reversed: the Muslims of Tunis had given up what the 'civilized' nations of the New World continued to accept. Dr Basting could not have agreed more, his own anti-Americanism making him even more severe: in his Pietist eyes, slavery was just one of the United States's many vices.

Dunant must have mentioned his projects from the International Committee for the Berlin congress to Basting. The military doctor

---

[15] Dunant to Basting, 31 January 1863, private collection Dortmund/Bilthoven, BGE copy.
[16] Geneva: '*Chez les principaux libraires*' ('to be found at mainstream bookshops'; no publisher), 1863.

did not need to be told twice. He would go as well to support his Genevan friend and offer his assistance.

Things were starting to look up. Upon his return from Algeria, with his business concerns somewhat calmed, Dunant took up his mission where he'd left it: he began to write the report to be read at the Berlin congress.

One congress is worth another

For Moynier as much as for Dunant, the shock must have felt like freezing rain on a hot summer day: in the middle of July, both men learned that the Berlin welfare congress had been cancelled.

It was likely Basting who told them. But the Dutch surgeon didn't want to just be the bearer of bad news; he had a Plan B. His government had asked him to represent the Netherlands at an international congress on statistics to be held in Berlin at the same time. Part of this congress would be dedicated to comparative data of health and mortality between military and civilian populations. Could this be the right place to launch Dunant's proposals onto the international scene? Basting was a speaker; he could present the project somehow. And Dunant could use the opportunity to connect with the military doctors who would be there. After several back-and-forths, Basting and Dunant made a decision: down with the welfare congress, long live statistics!

Moynier, however, had other plans. No matter what Dunant said, even if the statistics congress might offer good networking opportunities, they could not count on it to launch the widespread action General Dufour was rightly pushing for. Furthermore, let's be clear, Moynier was also no longer available around those dates because his wife was due to give birth! No, he wanted to advance his pawns in a different direction.

In early August, Gustave Moynier set up a new strategy that he felt was the only viable one. He went to see Dunant at home just a few days before the Five were set to meet at the end of the month. Did he arrive with the idea completely settled, or did the two of them encourage one another to make such a bold move? There is no way to know. The fact is that on 25th August, Gustave Moynier opened a new session of the International Committee by announcing soberly to his colleagues that the welfare congress would not be taking place that year 'because of various circumstances'. Then he continued in the same matter-of-fact tone: 'Mr Dunant and I have been thinking that the only way to get this business to work is if we ourselves convene an international conference in Geneva.'[17]

This proposal was all the more daring in that it came from the chairman of the Geneva Society for Public Welfare himself. The green light from the General Meeting of 9th February could not have been clearer: yes to a new working group but only a temporary one, focused exclusively on the Berlin congress. Since then, although that congress was no longer taking place, the ad hoc committee had been very quick to transform itself into a permanent and international structure, which now intended to call for an international conference well beyond its mandate.

None of the five committee members seems to have dithered for a second over these lowly procedural concerns. A conference in Geneva? What a good idea! Moynier and Dunant's three colleagues were enthusiastic and offered their full support. After only six months and three meetings, they were now so convinced of their project's viability they couldn't imagine dropping it at the first sign of a hurdle. Yes, the welfare congress had been cancelled but so much encouragement had reached them in Geneva, from the King and Queen of the Netherlands, from Prince Alexandre of Hesse, from the Grand Duke of Baden, and this was just the tip of the iceberg! If Berlin was no longer offering them an international arena, well then, they would simply create one themselves.

They may not have hesitated, but the project did give our five commissioners a bit of vertigo. Who were they to invite the great powers to question their manner of conducting warfare? Dufour's status surely gave the committee an unshakable confidence: if the general was ready to preside over the conference, then the conference could take place. They just needed to send invitations and organize the proceedings.

Once the idea of the conference had been accepted, Henry stood up. He placed in front of him a large handwritten paper, resembling an agenda, with numbered paragraphs, and began: 'Since this is about gathering people together to move my ideas from theory into practice, it would be preferable to discuss not just abstract ideas but

---

[17] Based on meeting minutes from 25 August 1863, *Procès-verbaux du CICR*, 23.

concrete proposals. With this in mind, I've prepared a draft concordat which could be used as a basis for discussion at the conference.'

With the poise of a man who clearly knew his subject, he read the paper to the other four commissioners. In it, they recognized several of the conclusions of *A Memory of Solferino*; no one interrupted him. Gustave Moynier blackened an entire page with notes while Dufour scribbled a few words from time to time.

When he'd finished, Dunant sat down. It was clear his text didn't elicit much enthusiasm. First, there was nothing of the lawyer in Dunant. His prose would need to be revisited article by article. Also, the scope of Dunant's project was probably frightening for the other committee members. While the four commissioners were set on creating relief committees for wounded soldiers and that was it, the philanthropist of Castiglione wanted to implement the key conclusions of his 'manifesto' – not only the fate of those wounded in battle, but also of soldiers taken prisoner, the role of civilians, medical supplies and more.

As the discussion dragged on, the commissioners delegated the task of drafting everything, letter and concordat, to 'Messrs Moynier and Dunant'.[18] Next up was to select the date for the conference, somewhere towards the end of October, and send the invitations as widely as possible with the reworked draft agreement.

Dunant and Moynier had not a single quiet moment in that last week of August. After a final revision, they had the letter of invitation and draft concordat printed. The letter, dated 1st September, convoked 'an International Conference in Geneva, in order to examine the means of remedying the insufficiency of sanitary service of armies in the field'.[19] It explicitly referred to both the desire expressed by Mr Henry Dunant in *A Memory of Solferino* and to the initiative of the Geneva Society for Public Welfare. The letter bore the signatures of the five members of the *Comité international de secours aux blessés* along with their titles: 'General Dufour, President; Gustave Moynier, Chairman of the Society for Public Welfare; Doctor Maunoir; Doctor Appia, Henry Dunant, Secretary.'

---

[18] Based on meeting minutes from 25 August 1863, *Procès-verbaux du CICR*, 23–4, and on François, *Le berceau de la Croix-Rouge*, 129–31.

[19] Dunant, *Mémoires*, 74.

As they waited for the proofs, Dunant and Moynier made a list
of who should be invited. It would be sent, of course, to anyone
with 'a heart for philanthropy',[20] but with more urgency, it would
invite the governments to send representatives, as 'their participation
was essential to the success of the Work'.[21]

General Dufour's signature, sitting alongside that of the author
of *A Memory of Solferino,* would hopefully prompt recipients to
consider this invitation from a completely unknown 'Geneva
Committee'. On 1st September, the envelopes were ready, bearing
their prestigious names and addresses – palaces and chancelleries,
ministers and high-level staff – all delicately handwritten by Dunant.
He sent them out himself, at his own cost.

The Berlin Congress

With the letters in the mail, Dunant headed off to Berlin. The project
of an international conference in Geneva hadn't swept aside the
International Statistics Congress, where Dr Basting was waiting for
him. The two men had agreed to work together beforehand so as to
make their case as effectively as possible.

Mr Basting and his wife were settled in a slightly outdated
establishment, the Hotel Toepfer, on the Karlplatz, where Dunant
had also reserved his room for efficiency's sake. The congress began
on 6th September, but Dr Basting was not meant to speak until the
session focusing on civil and military populations, two days later.

On the evening of the 7th, in the blue velour salon on the hotel's
ground floor, the two men, who had only met each other a few days
before, sat together plotting away in low voices like two old
comrades in arms. Their work that night was to finalize what
Dr Basting would say in front of his colleagues from the different
armies of Europe, in the name of the author of *A Memory of
Solferino.* For Dunant, there was much at stake: unlike his co-
committee members in Geneva, his new Dutch friend understood

---

[20] Ibid.

[21] TN: Dunant's humanitarian project is referred to by himself and by others as
'*l'Œuvre d'humanité*' or simply '*l'Œuvre*' with the same implication. We translate
both with and without capitalization as 'the work' or 'the Work'.

that his idea of an 'international, sacred and government-ratified principle' was the central premise of A Memory. It was exactly this point he intended to champion before the 4th Section of the Statistics Congress, a section comprised of civil and military physicians likely to appreciate the extraordinary benefits of such a proposal.

On the morning of 8th September, the hotel concierge hailed them a cab to get them to Herrenhaus, where the congress was being held. They had to cross the Spree river to get there, but as they reached the bridge a gust of wind slammed against the open windows of the cab, carrying away a happy whirlwind of pages containing the speech that the doctor and his companion had recklessly left on the seat! The two passengers jumped from the carriage, rushing to collect the papers before they fell into the river. A beggar watching the scene joined in and, without his help, the actual goal of the journey might have quite literally been washed away.[22]

How was Basting's speech received? The minutes of the fourth section don't mention any discussion related to his proposal, nor any note recording the intervention of a certain Mr Henry Dunant, 'delegate from Switzerland, in Geneva'. Dunant was properly registered for the congress, but he doesn't appear to have been very conspicuous as his name is missing from the lists of any of the six sessions of the 4th Section. It was only on the last day of the congress, Saturday 12th September, that Congress President Engel opened the plenary session by reading various communications including one from J. Henry Dunant, 'the author of A Memory of Solferino', who begged the congress to 'officially express' its interest and sympathy for an international conference that would take place in Geneva in October. When he was finished, the president prudently pushed the entire question to the 4th Section to deal with and went on to something else.

Basting, however, didn't take it this way. Sometime later, when he could speak again, he returned to the question:

Gentleman! [. . .] Alongside my mandate as rapporteur for the 4th Section, I also have a more intimate relationship with the subject of which I would like to communicate the following. I translated

---

[22] Dunant, Mémoires, 77.

Mr Dunant's eloquent book, *A Memory of Solferino*, into Dutch,
and by this recommended to my compatriots the proposals of Mr
Dunant's book: the formation, out of civil society, of international
aid societies for the wounded in times of war.

In Holland, and in nearly all of Europe, we are unanimously
agreed upon the necessity of these aid societies. Princes and
populations, journals and digests, everyone has strongly
applauded, but everywhere the same question is being asked:
how to organize these very societies?

To discuss this 'how', the Geneva Committee will convene an
international conference next October on this subject in their
town. It is in the name of this committee, and on behalf of my
honourable friend Mr Dunant, that I invite the gentlemen
members of this congress to attend and to reward that conference
with their wise counsel.[23]

The assembly honoured the speaker with several bravos, but the
president showed no more enthusiasm for the subject than he had
earlier that morning. In reply to Basting's speech and as if to curtail
any engagement on behalf of the assembly, he said: 'The congress
should, I believe, be happy to take note of Mr Dunant's efforts,
show him its recognition and hope that the planned meeting in
Geneva will contribute to diminish the sacrifices in life and health
suffered as a result of war.'[24]

However modest they were, these few polite wishes were enough
to bolster our two men. They'd been wondering for days how best
to use this congress to promote 'the Work' and an opportunity was
now knocking.

'All the same, President Engel's approval was very cautious,'
Basting pointed out to Dunant as they stepped into one of the cabs
waiting outside the congress.

Dunant withdrew his notes from a case. 'Perhaps, but the
congress did explicitly give me its recognition, upon the president's

---

[23] Sources for the Berlin congress are Dr Ernst Engel, *Rechenschafts-Bericht*, Band II
(Berlin: R. Decker, 1865), 490f., and its French version, *Congrès international de
statistique à Berlin, Cinquième session* (Berlin: R. Decker, 1865) and Carl Lueder, *La
Convention de Genève* (Erlangen: Besold, 1876), 62f.
[24] Engel, *Rechenschafts-Bericht*, 500, and Dunant, *Mémoires*, 76.

invitation, and wished full success to the conference. I think that this is an excellent result, which we should make widely known to the general public!'[25]

As the cab rushed back across the Spree Bridge, making the two passengers worry their pages might be taken for a second dance across the water, they decided to write a communiqué detailing their positive reception at the statistics congress. Back at the hotel, they began to compose the text. It was hard going; they needed to say enough to claim a victory but without too obviously contradicting any future meeting minutes. Here is the result:

> His Excellency, the Count of Eulenburg, Prussian Minister of the Interior, solemnly concluded the Berlin Congress of Statistics on Saturday, 12th September. In this session, the Congress, which had been approached with the subject of the formation of aid societies for wounded soldiers during times of war, took an entirely favourable resolution to this project.[26]

What followed was a reference to the author of this proposal, Henry Dunant, and an explanation of the famous 4th Section, 'composed in part of military physicians', in front of whom Mr Basting had explained Mr Dunant's proposals, before reporting to the General Meeting. With that, the two delegates finished their communiqué with this vigorous but admirably vague affirmation: 'The conclusions of the 4th Section were unanimously adopted with signs of strong approval.'[27] What conclusions? This is exactly what Dunant and Basting agreed not to mention. Because in reality, not a single one of these conclusions concerned wounded soldiers, nor the creation of aid committees, nor the Geneva Conference. But why would that need to be specified?

---

[25] Cf. Dunant, *Mémoires*, 77–8.

[26] Dunant, *Mémoires*, 78–9.

[27] This 'communiqué' was attached to the letter Dunant sent to Moynier on 13 September to announce it had already been sent to the *Journal des Débats* ('Correspondence received by the Committee, 1863–80', AICRC A AF, 20,1-003). Its wording is known by the Berlin Circular, which most likely quoted it word for word.

The Grand Tour

The social programme that came with the congress was, for Dunant, much more exciting than long discussions between medal-bearing army officers. Before leaving for Berlin, Moynier had given him a letter of recommendation for several German friends involved in philanthropic circles. But the author of *A Memory of Solferino* was now aiming higher. Kings and princes had written to him following the publication of his book, and it was these same kings and princes he planned to contact without the slightest hesitation. Over the previous year, he had garnered attention from Europe's elite. He now moved to harvest the fruits of his fame and make it work for his project. If a door was left ajar for him, he'd walk right through, if a hand stretched towards him, he saw more than a greeting, he saw consent, approval and support. This was his mode of action; it would prove to be extraordinarily fertile during the three weeks that followed.

On 13th September, the congress delegates were received at a luncheon in Potsdam. Though the president of the statistics conference had specified that formal attire was not necessary since the royal family had not announced it would attend, the crown prince of Prussia and future emperor of Germany, Frederick III, did show up.[28]

According to Dunant's memoirs, the crown prince indicated that he wished to exchange a few words with the author of *A Memory of Solferino*. The two men were about the same age, the prince had inherited liberal ideas from his mother, and his first words moved their conversation away from the formalities of the official banquet.

'I have the greatest sympathy for your work, both as a soldier and a prince,' said Frederick of Prussia to Henry Dunant. 'As you know,' the Prince continued, 'my mother the queen supports your views with the same enthusiasm as I do. You can be assured that Prussia will send a delegate to Geneva next month.'[29]

On the return journey from Potsdam, seated across from the Bastings in a comfortable carriage, Dunant was still moved by the honour of this meeting. More trusting of women on the subject of appearances, he asked Mrs Basting in a playful tone: 'How did I look when the crown prince addressed me?'

---

[28] Engel, *Rechenschafts-Bericht*, 491.
[29] Cf. Dunant to Moynier, 13 September 1863, AICRC A AF, 20,1-003.

The lady turned a questioning face towards him; the sound of the hooves and cobblestones was so loud that Dunant had to repeat his question. Retying the ribbons of her hat, which seemed to want to return to Potsdam, Mrs Basting smiled and replied, 'For a man who claims only to work for the honour of God, my dear Sir, you seem to put much store in the honours of men . . .'[30]

Mrs Basting said nothing else; she believed Henry Dunant was blushing. But he was already turning to look at the road, while the doctor's wife looked at her husband. Had she vexed him by daring to tease his dear, his venerated, his untouchable friend Dunant?

Once back in Berlin, Dunant sat down to one of his favourite tasks: writing to Gustave Moynier and his other colleagues in Geneva. He had no trouble finding something to say: conclusions from the statistics congress, 'the enthusiasm' of the 4th Section physicians for a project deemed 'practicable', 500 invitations distributed for the Geneva conference, and finally, meeting the royal family of Prussia in Potsdam who offered their support. But he also made sure to include the communiqué prepared the night before with Basting on the congress's conclusions, asking Moynier to have it inserted into the *Journal de Genève*, 'before all the other journals are talking about it'.[31]

This same letter of 13th September also mentioned his next appointment: a supper the following day at the home of the Count of Eulenburg, Prussian Minister of the Interior, with Minister of War General von Roon, specifically 'to discuss the question', Dunant assured Moynier.

And discuss the question they most certainly did during this memorable evening of 14th September. The Minister of the Interior had planned things well: he'd placed Dunant between a Spanish senator and a state councilor from Munich, and opposite a noble adviser to the king of Saxony, the son of the composer Carl-Maria von Weber. Seated nearby were a Russian and two high-ranking Swedish and Norwegian officials.

During the supper, Dunant defended his cause so well that he managed to obtain a promise from all six congress participants to request that their governments send someone to Geneva the

---

[30] Mrs Basting recalled their years-ago conversation in two letters (8 and 14 November 1895), quoted in François, *Le berceau de la Croix-Rouge*, 322.
[31] From Dunant to Moynier, 13 September 1863, AICRC A AF, 20,1-003.

following month. Finding his listeners so well disposed, Dunant went further: he also spoke about the necessity of an agreement between the sovereigns of Europe to establish 'either the neutrality of the wounded, and of those who brought them aid, or the adoption of a unique medical aid flag for all armies'.[32] Dunant felt the guests reacted so favourably to these ideas that he left the supper more sure than ever that he was on the right path – a path still entirely his own.

A royal request

On the morning of 15th September, Minister of War von Roon sent his aide-de-camp to the Toepfer Hotel with a request for the representative from the Geneva Committee. The emissary explained to Dunant that His Majesty Wilhelm I wished for 'a more specific note'[33] on the powers or instructions he would have to give his delegate to the conference in Geneva. Apparently, the official invitation was not precise enough for him and he wanted a few more details.

Not needing any more encouragement, Dunant immediately dashed off several proposals that he felt 'well summarized the *desiderata*'[34] of the Geneva Committee, as he wrote that very evening to Gustave Moynier, but which in reality clearly exceeded them. It wasn't disloyalty that had Dunant moving forward like this without consulting his colleagues in Geneva. It's just that he was a lap ahead on the track. He'd been brilliantly received at the Prussian court and, the night before at the Count of Eulenburg's, he'd been able to test the receptibility of his idea of neutrality for medical volunteers, while his Geneva colleagues were still, inevitably, focused on the initial steps. But more than anything else, Dunant saw in the king's request a unique and unexpected occasion to achieve the goal he'd been chasing for ten days.

For the duration of the congress, both Dunant and Basting, in their separate areas, had worked hard to defend the principle of neutrality for military medical personnel on battlefields, alongside the proposal of voluntary nursing corps. 'Neutrality' in the sense

---

[32] Dunant, *Mémoires*, 81.
[33] From Dunant to Moynier, 15 September 1863, AICRC A AF, 20,1-004.
[34] Ibid. Dunant uses the Latin word for 'wishes', customary in the committee setting.

that the medical teams would be distinguished from the rest of the troops and that their function as doctors, surgeons, nurses and stretcher-bearers would grant them a special status set apart from the warring parties and thus shielded from the fighting. This was the famous neutrality for medical personnel that Dunant and Basting had been tirelessly advocating for all week, and which they hoped the delegates might officially consider.

This was in vain, unfortunately, because the congress had finished without a line on this point in its minutes and the Count of Eulenburg's closing speech did not refer to it at all.[35] Although more qualified than anyone else to understand the major progress this neutrality would represent, the assembly of doctors and senior officers in Berlin had not deemed it the right time to declare themselves in its favour.

Although Dunant and Basting had significantly exaggerated the success of their proposals with the congress, they had not dared to pretend in their press release that the neutral status of the medical personnel had been adopted. But now? Perhaps it was time to take advantage of the king of Prussia Wilhelm I's request to strengthen their original press release with the addition of this essential, primordial and decisive idea.

The Berlin Circular

After scribbling his proposals on paper, Dunant went to find Dr Basting to show him the note he'd just prepared for King Wilhelm I.

The two men sat down again in the salon of their hotel and, doubtless with their hearts beating in unison, Dr Basting read Dunant's text.

First, governments were requested to sponsor the aid societies meant to be instigated in Geneva in October. Secondly, governments would be expected to 'declare that military medical personnel and their assistants, including members of recognized voluntary aid detachments, are neutral and will be regarded as such by nations at war'. Thirdly, governments would commit to enable the operations of these national societies during wartime, by giving facilities for

---

[35] Engel, *Rechenschafts-Bericht*, 549–84, and *Congrès international de statistique à Berlin*, 8.

the transport of medical personnel and donations to be sent to countries at war.

'Perfect, perfect,' Basting said, handing the text back to Dunant, 'the King of Prussia already approves all of this, you are right to make it clear in writing. Send a copy to his ministers von Roon and Eulenburg as well; yesterday they seemed quite favourable. We must take advantage of their good dispositions.'

'Yes, indeed. But I was wondering if . . .' Ordinarily so confident, Dunant seemed nervous to go on.

'I was thinking we could put these proposals together with the conclusions of the statistical congress, and send everything, composed into a single text, to the various European governments. What do you think?'

'How would it be signed?' Basting asked immediately.

'From the Geneva Committee, of course. This letter would be nothing more than a necessary supplement to the conference invitation or, more exactly, an *addendum* to the draft concordat that will be presented in October.'

'And so we would add medical staff neutrality to the agenda of the conference? Magnificent!' Mr Basting yelled, shaking Dunant's hand with a soldier's grip.

It was probably that very afternoon of 15th September that Dunant raced to the royal printer von Decker to have 500 copies of his famous missive printed – known in the history of the Red Cross as the 'Berlin Circular'.[36]

Beneath a heading of 'International Conference of October 26, 1863, International and Permanent Aid Societies for wounded

---

[36] Twenty-seven years later, Dunant would remember in his memoirs the day he brought his famous 'Berlin Circular' to the printer on Saturday 12 September before even the end of the congress *(Mémoires, 77)*. Dunant had likely condensed two successive and distinct events into a single episode. According to his letters to Moynier, on Sunday 13 September, Dunant and Basting had still not had anything printed; they were happy to write a triumphant press release regarding the conclusions of the congress. Then, to answer the request made by the king of Prussia, Dunant rewrote his proposals, including the idea of neutrality for all medical and relief services. The Berlin Circular brought the two texts together, thus adding the principle of neutrality to the programme of the impending Geneva Conference. The Circular was printed on 15 September, and sent to Moynier the same day (from Dunant to Moynier, 13 and 15 September 1863, AICRC A AF, 20,1-003 and 004; cf. Dunant to Müller, March 1894, BGE, Ms. fr. 5201, f. 242–3).

soldiers in times of war', the letter began with the Statistics Congress' flattering opinion of these societies, just as Dunant and Basting had written several days earlier for the press. Then, 'as a result' of this favorable reception, the 'Geneva Committee' was pleased to suggest to all governments, 'in addition to the draft convention', the three points presented to the King of Prussia:

'The Geneva Committee wishes that the governments of Europe will give their conference delegates the necessary instructions on these subjects.' Signed 'the secretary of the Geneva Committee, J.-Henry Dunant.'[37]

Of course, the author of this missive wasn't completely oblivious: he knew that acting alone would greatly offend his colleagues at the Committee. But well, one needed to strike while the iron was hot! When Dunant wrote to Moynier that very evening – putting the entire affair before him as a done deal – he was careful to include the text of the Berlin Circular, justifying its content not with the King of Prussia's personal request but with a generalized, universal request: '*They* found our draft concordat project excellent, but *they* expressed that the governments needed something even more specific with respect to the instructions they would need to give to their delegates.'[38]

At the end of the letter, Dunant added that he hoped it would 'encourage our colleagues by its good news'. He had garnered so much prestigious support in less than a week, surely his colleagues would forgive him for going ahead without consulting them.

Two days later, Dunant wrote to Moynier recounting his latest victory in Prussia: the new proposals had earned him an audience with Count von Roon, Minister of War, along with the head physician of the army, Dr Loeffler. Unbelievably, the minister, who'd only a few days earlier expressed his doubts about Dunant's 'charitable ideas', was now very excited about a neutral status for medical corps during war, and had no quibbles at all, even with the idea of using volunteers to support the military! Further emboldened by such enthusiasm, Dunant then asked von Roon about neutrality

---

[37] '*Supplément à la convocation d'une Conférence internationale à Genève*' (Addendum to the convocation to an International Conference in Geneva), 15 September 1853, in *Actes du Comité international de Secours aux militaires blessés* (Geneva: Soulier & Wirth, 1871), II, 5–6.

[38] Dunant to Moynier, 15 September 1863, AICRC A AF, 20,1-004.

for the wounded themselves, prompting him to add the idea of an international flag to the list of objectives! Dunant sat exalting at his table that night, writing about the details of his victory: 'You were so right in wishing our project could be brought to Berlin!'[39] he wrote to a Moynier who would be surprised to see himself credited with the idea of a trip he hadn't been so keen on. Proud of his success, Dunant even included the freshly printed version of his Berlin Circular, the very document Moynier had yet to see and which contained, Dunant reminded him ingeniously, 'the small appendix that you know, and which is in complete harmony with your views'[40] – in other words, the proposal for aid-worker neutrality, for both military and volunteer personnel. Was he acting in bad faith? Had the success of his two-week tour led him to disregard the fact that this solitary initiative could anger his colleagues in Geneva? It's impossible to know. Dunant – supported by Basting, bolstered by the honours of his royal meetings, carried away by his own certainties – was walking ten paces in front while believing his four other colleagues were right beside him.

Visit to Dresden

Of all the events connected to the Berlin congress, the dinner at the home of the Count of Eulenburg surely reaped the best rewards. One of the guests, Baron von Weber, counsellor to the king of Saxony, had promised Dunant he would arrange an interview for him with His Majesty. When he arrived in Dresden on 1st October, Henry was surprised to see the Baron had kept his word: he came to find him at the Hotel De France with an invitation from the king for an appointment the next day at the royal palace, at 10:30 a.m. precisely.

Thirty years later, Dunant would return to savour the details of this interview that his memory had embalmed like a relic: each smile, each reply, each step echoing through the palace were crystallized in his memories like precious shiny jewels. He reconstructed his extraordinary interview with the king of Saxony, with his kindly persona and his unforgettable last words that

---

[39] Dunant to Moynier, 17 September 1863, AICRC A AF, 20,1-006.
[40] Ibid.

Dunant took away with him and then repeated 'like a talisman'. 'Without any doubt, a nation that does not support this humanitarian work,' the king of Saxony said to him as they parted, 'will incur the censure of European public opinion.'[41] At least this is what Dunant would remember, writing it down in his memoirs as fact. This is also the version historians have echoed, trusting a narrative crafted by the hero of the story himself.

And yet when Dunant sat down at his desk that very evening to send a summary of his last two days to Moynier, he didn't mention this important sentence from the king of Saxony. No. He wrote down another, a single sentence, of a surprising insignificance:

> I'm writing to let you know that our business has much interested Dresden. They have already decided that the delegate will be sent to Geneva[42][. . .] The king of Saxony asked to see me, and His Majesty received me already today. He said: 'This question interests me very much and I have already spoken with my ministers [. . .][43] etc.

This was all he had to report about his audience in Dresden! The rest of the letter re-describes the Prussian court, clearly more interesting in his view.

Why did Dunant say nothing about that key phrase in their conversation, the one which later he would claim he used as a 'talisman'?[44] There is no doubt that the king of Saxony delivered some encouraging remarks. But it is quite likely that Dunant later confused the king's words with his own prose. Two days after the meeting, on 4th October, he wrote to Moynier:

> If you have the occasion to see the general [Dufour], will you please speak to him of the letter that must be written to the emperor [Napoleon III], that he might only speak a little bluntly (!) because now after what the king of Saxony has said to me a

---

[41] Dunant, *Mémoires*, 84.

[42] Again, the memoirs tell another story, which is that the king needed to consult the Chambers to decide whether to send a delegate. And yet on the very day, Dunant told Moynier that the decision had been made.

[43] Dunant to Moynier, from Dresden, [1 or 2] October 1863, AICRC A AF, 20,1-008.

[44] Dunant, *Mémoires*, 88.

nation that does not support this universal humanitarian work
will incur the censure of European public opinion.[45]

Some years later, Dunant dived into his archives to establish his own
version of the history of the Red Cross, archives that included copies
of his own letters. Did he take his own summary about the Dresden
interview (*a nation that does not support . . ., etc.*) for a quote from
the king of Saxony? This is more than likely: if it was a direct quote,
the phrase in French is faulty and incomplete, and Dunant rarely
commits this kind of syntactical approximation. He does, on the
other hand, more easily arrange his memories to suit his needs.

A growing wave

That night, a square of light beamed out into the darkness from the
facade of the Hotel de France into the early hours of dawn. The ideas
Dunant had put forth in *A Memory of Solferino* were taking shape
in the European mind, creating a single growing wave. Dunant,
persuaded that the support of the Prussian and Saxon courts had
given his work a final stamp of approval, trumpeted it to every
European capital in a handful of letters. And especially to Paris:
Dunant remained faithful to his view that France must have a seat at
the conference table in Geneva. According to his memoirs, he directly
repeated the king of Saxony's alleged phrase to Baron Darricau, the
general steward to Emperor Napoleon III, with whom Dunant had
been corresponding for several months. Darricau seems to have
showed his letter to the emperor, who replied: 'You will go to Geneva,
my dear Darricau, and represent France at this conference.'[46]

Again, Dunant's *Mémoires* seem to embellish this scene. The
correspondence reveals that in September, while resting in the
Pyrenees, Baron Darricau had already warned Dunant he would not
return to Paris before mid-October, meaning he would not attend
the conference in Geneva. Neither could he promise to send someone
else, as this could only be decided by General Randon, Minister of
War. But Randon, who'd already been subject to Dunant's entreaties
in Algeria, was just as hostile to his philanthropic views as he was to

---

[45] Dunant to Moynier, from Vienna, 4 October 1863, AICRC A AF, 20,1-009.
[46] Dunant, *Mémoires*, 85–6.

his colonial ambitions, something which Darricau knew perfectly well. Darricau suggested General Dufour, not Dunant, write to the Minister of War in order to persuade him.[47] Dunant followed his advice[48] but could not resist taking up his own pen to 'beg' General Randon, 'in the interest of France and in the interest of humanity', to send an official delegate to Geneva. Working on the Franco-German rivalry, he added that the subject had been extremely well received in the German-speaking world: the 'protection' of the entire Prussian royal family, the 'very special' interest of Archduke Reinier, in Vienna, without forgetting 'the very particular sympathy' and the 'great benevolence'[49] of the king of Saxony. Again, there is no mention of the king's magic sentence, supposedly pronounced six days earlier, even though Dunant would have desperately needed any argument to convince a tough customer like Randon.

From Dresden, Dunant had left for Vienna where the Swiss ambassador had arranged an audience for him with Archduke Reinier, as the emperor was not in the capital. According to Henry, the archduke consented on the spot to send a delegate to Geneva: 'It's such a beautiful idea ... and not at all impractical,' he said, adding another gem to Dunant's collection of royal slogans.

In Munich, he was received on 12th October by a senior member of the Ministry of War[50] who was the first to deliver a diplomatic objection, one which appears obvious to us today: how could a government allow itself to be convened by 'unknown private individuals'? Dunant was happy to remind this misinformed general that 'it was a question of international charity that had already received strong support from several august protectors'.[51] The argument proved its efficacy: the general promised to send a Bavarian delegate to Geneva, as would the kingdom of Württemberg,

---

[47] Darricau to Dunant, 17 September 1863, BGE, Ms. 2109, f. 15–16.
[48] Dufour would write to Napoleon III on 8 October, cf. Micheline Tripet, '*La création de la Croix-Rouge*', in *Guillaume-Henri Dufour dans son temps*, 399–400.
[49] Dunant to Marshal Randon, from Vienna, 8 October 1863, Historical Archives of the French Ministry of War (BGE copy).
[50] In his handwritten '*Mémoires*' (BGE) as in his *Mémoires* translated by Rudolf Müller (*Entstehungsgeschichte* ... 112), Dunant names this general 'Frankh, Minister of War'. It was most probably Siegmund von Pranckh, who in fact would only become Bavarian Minister of War three years later.
[51] Dunant, *Mémoires*, 87.

the grand duchy of Hesse, and the grand duchy of Baden. Trumpeting the support from the royal families of Prussia and Saxony, Dunant managed to unite the German states on an issue, the protection of wounded soldiers, in a way Bismarck could only dream of.

The day before the Geneva Conference, eleven of the twenty-four registered delegates were German-speaking. This might have been an important warning sign for Dunant, one that he did not yet fully understand. Though he'd wanted to see France at the head of this work, it was obviously taking root and flourishing in the German courts. Did a Protestant affinity between Geneva and most of the Germanic states play a significant role? The only French correspondent who'd shown any enthusiasm from the beginning was Baron Darricau, who was – by chance? – Protestant. Was it also just chance that the great powers had so much trouble accepting the idea of *neutral* health services, while the smaller states could see this more easily?

A brutal landing

On 20th October 1863, Dunant had barely dropped off his luggage in Geneva when he could be seen walking jauntily to the fourth meeting of the International Committee. He was anticipating the congratulations his colleagues would surely give him for his extraordinary campaign with the European courts.

But the welcome he received from Moynier and Maunoir instantly shattered his illusions. Neither man had recovered from the shock of reading the Berlin Circular, in which Dunant had so cavalierly added aid-worker neutrality to the agenda. What had got into their secretary? By what right had he acted without first consulting the Committee? How presumptuous was he to entice governments with such unrealistic proposals? Despite their composure, Dunant could feel the disapproval literally seething from his colleagues.

The meeting went ahead as if nothing had happened, because there were still numerous details to settle before the conference would open the following Monday. But at the end of the session, Dunant could no longer stand it. Mostly addressing Moynier, he articulated the question on everyone's lips: 'What did you think of my Berlin initiative on neutrality?'

'We thought you've asked for the impossible!' Gustave Moynier exclaimed, more sharply than he meant to.[52]

'You have forced us, sir, to issue our greatest reservations with respect to your proposal. A proposal you deemed fit to sign in all our names!' Maunoir added.

To cut short a discussion whose tone was rising quickly, General Dufour broke in with calm authority. 'Mr Dunant's specific approach does not compel us to modify the agenda of our conference. We will restrict ourselves to the subjects included in our draft concordat. Gentlemen, the meeting is adjourned.'[53]

Dunant escaped first, eager for fresh air and the open street.

Enraged and fuming, he argued with them in his head. So he had convinced Prussia, Saxony, Austria, Hesse, as well as Spain, Russia and Sweden while the other Genevans had only convinced the Swiss – the Swiss! – to attend a conference they were hosting on its own territory. Two days earlier, while still in Karlsruhe and having obtained the public support of Germany's main royal families, he'd had to politely suggest Moynier write to the consulates of France, Italy and England in Geneva. In vain! If Henry hadn't taken his exhausting seven-week tour, all at his own expense, who would have even answered the Geneva Committee's invitation? A few chairmen of a handful of charities from Lausanne or Neuchâtel? A bunch of philanthropic dilettantes? It was with government representatives, and only with government representatives, that this kind of conference could take place!

But he needed to write up the minutes of the meeting, and to do that he needed to calm down. Back at home, after many crossings-out, he wrote:

After the Statistical Congress, Mr Dunant had thought it wise to print, at his own expense, a new circular dated 15th September, in which neutral status was requested for the wounded,[54]

---

[52] Dunant, *Mémoires*, 91 (footnote).

[53] Cf. François, *Le berceau de la Croix-Rouge*, 146, and Boissier, *From Solferino to Tsushima*, 67–8.

[54] In reality, the circular of 15 September 1863 only requested neutrality for personnel ('*Supplément à la convocation . . .*' in *Actes du Comité international de Secours aux militaires blessés*, 5–6). At what time were 'the wounded' also added to these meeting notes, and by whom? We don't know.

dispensaries,[55] hospitals, medical corps and officially recognized voluntary relief services.

Finally, Mr Dunant wrote directly to nearly all of Europe's sovereigns, and to the Ministers of War of various states, in order to respectfully solicit the despatch of a delegate from each European government.[56]

Here was a true account of the facts. While blotting the last paragraphs, Dunant thought: If one day a neutral status was recognized for wounded soldiers and those who helped them, well then, the world would know who'd had the idea and the initiative.

It was the 20th of October. The conference would begin in less than a week; there was no more time to argue. Fifteen days earlier, Henry had reminded Gustave Moynier to please take care of 'the Latins' because he was taking care of the 'Germans'.[57] But he was now discovering that while he'd been moving heaven and earth in the north, nothing had been done further south and west. So he got to work: over the next five days he contacted the consulates of Great Britain, France and Italy, to ensure their presence at the conference. The first two were a mere formality as their governments had already agreed to be represented. The third, however, posed a greater challenge because Italy was reluctant to send an official delegate; Dunant would also be credited with getting someone from the Italian consulate in Geneva to fill that empty chair.

An unforgettable Sunday

The location selected for the October conference of 1863 could not have been more appropriate. What better place to attempt to heal the wounds of war than a building constructed on the city's old defensive ramparts? With its neoclassical elegance, the Athénée Palace offered the requisite solemnity for this kind of assembly.

---

[55] TN: the French word is *ambulance* and it designates any mobile or temporary medical unit for treating wounded soldiers. We use either 'field hospital', 'dispensary', 'mobile hospital' or 'medical unit', depending on the context.

[56] Meeting minutes from 17 March 1863, *Procès-verbaux du CICR*, 24–5.

[57] Dunant to Moynier, from Dresden, [1 or 2] October 1863, ACICR A AF, 20,1-008.

Owned by a rich widow[58] and friend of Dunant's family, it also spared the Committee the humiliation of having to ask a government they detested – the Radicals, the 'reds' of the time who had ousted their friends or cousins.[59] The rest followed suit: from the first to the last day, the organizers managed to avoid any compromise with the Genevan authorities, a true achievement given the political importance of the event.

On Sunday evening, the night before the conference was due to open, Dunant received the delegates in his home for a first informal gathering. While he may not have known each guest personally, he usually knew their sovereign, which gave him a royal ease with all of them. No matter what might happen, he was already savouring the success of this simple evening – this incredible gathering in Geneva of delegates, military men and philanthropists from all corners of Europe, who had come to discuss *his* idea.

The list of participants was enough to make a man proud: Austria, the grand duchy of Baden, Bavaria, Spain, France, Great Britain, Hanover, the grand duchy of Hesse, the Netherlands, Prussia, Saxony, Sweden, Württemberg and the Swiss Confederation had all sent a delegate. Italy was represented by its consul from Geneva, Russia by Captain Alexandre Kireiew, aide-de-camp of Grand Duke Constantin. Non-governmental institutions rounded out the official group. The very powerful Order of St John of Jerusalem had sent Prince Henri XIII of Reuss, who would be named conference vice president. On the other hand, the Society of Social Sciences of Neuchâtel and the Vaud Society for Public Welfare had sent their delegates as part of the Swiss cohort.

The list of excused delegates can be quickly summarized: a few minor German states, Denmark, Belgium, Portugal and the Papal States, who would not accept an initiative coming from 'Calvin's Rome'.

There was, however, a noticeable absence for anyone who knew something of the Conference's origins. The Geneva Society for Public Welfare, where everything had begun, was not on the list of

---

[58] Mrs Eynard-Lullin, widow of a well-known Genevan philanthropist and philhellene named Gabriel Eynard.

[59] In 1846, a revolution had brought the Radical Party to power in Geneva, ousting the conservative elite from all political, cultural and academic institutions.

participants. From their very first meeting, the five members of the future ICRC had stubbornly claimed their independence, a courageous move by Gustave Moynier, considering he was still chairman of the society. The members of this organization made their reaction clear at the following General Meeting, when they expressed their indignation at having been left out.[60]

The Conference of October 1863

On Monday 26th October at 9:00 a.m. exactly, thirty-one delegates hailing from sixteen countries were sitting in silence as General Dufour opened the 'Geneva International Conference to Study Ways of Overcoming the Inadequacy of Army Medical Services in the Field'. A true soldier, the speaker began by acknowledging that, while the total abolition of war was but a pipe dream, together they could work towards the common goal of reducing war's harm:

> Gentlemen, do we harbour a vain utopia? Is our objective so elevated and so far beyond our means that by uniting our efforts we cannot succeed? If this is the case, we must recognize that it is so; but we will at least have had the merit of having tried.[61]

The general then handed the chairmanship over to Gustave Moynier, who introduced the main themes for debate, namely the organization of the national committees and the feasibility of sending volunteer nursing corps to follow the armies. While his speech highlighted the sacred character of the individuals who brought relief to the wounded as well as the need for them to wear a distinctive symbol, he said nothing on the question of their status, thereby stubbornly dodging the Berlin Circular.

It was time for a word from the secretary of the committee. Between the first sessions of the year and that day, Henry Dunant's role on the committee had considerably changed. He had been in

---

[60] François, *Le berceau de la Croix-Rouge*, 66.
[61] *Compte rendu de la Conférence internationale d'octobre 1863 pour étudier les moyens de pourvoir à l'insuffisance du service sanitaire dans les armées en campagne*, Newsletter 24 of the Geneva Society for Public Welfare (Geneva: Jules-Guillaume Fick, 1863), 5.

charge of writing the report for the original Berlin Congress, hadn't he? But now, Dunant contented himself with reading long extracts taken from the Committee's correspondence. What had happened to his painstakingly crafted report?

The first in a long series of snubs, his colleagues had decided it should not be presented to this noble assembly. Why not? Perhaps because the author had buried the main subject beneath a glut of historical, national and lofty considerations inappropriate for an introductory exposé. Also because he himself was far too prominent within the text – a good portion of his report had been written in the first person. His colleagues felt the need to push Henry gently into the background, relegating him to the role of corresponding secretary that suited him so well. This meant that, apart from reading the Committee's prestigious letters of support, Henry Dunant would not speak again until the end of the conference.

After the letters, the first discussions began, followed by the general recommendations, and then the work itself. Several delegates gave their respects to those who had invited them. Surgeon General Landa from Madrid: 'Mr Dunant contemplated [the battlefield of] Solferino and it brought from him this heart's lament which has found so many echoes.'[62] Even greater praise came from Captain Van de Velde, one of Basting's compatriots, now a passionate advocate for the aid societies: 'What has brought this assembly together is a movement stemming mostly from Mr Dunant who has done immense work as a private individual.'[63]

Others were not so enthusiastic. The United Kingdom's delegate, in particular, had some reservations, which strongly echoed the objections Florence Nightingale had expressed against *A Memory of Solferino*. The medical services of the British Army were perfectly able to handle their wounded soldiers, according to Dr Rutherford, since they had been improved and enhanced after the lessons of the Crimean War. The speaker's silence regarding the soldiers' aid societies was nothing but a polite way to dismiss them as useless, or even inopportune.[64]

---

[62] Ibid., 40.
[63] Ibid., 104.
[64] Ibid., 57-8.

The French were even harsher. Mr Preval argued that 500 mules would be far more helpful than 15,000 volunteers, while Dr Boudier drew a miserable portrait of these volunteer nurses as illiterate, ignorant and unprepared for the tumult of wartime.[65]

After Dr Maunoir, a member of the Committee of Five, cleverly turned the tide of the argument, the assembly arrived at the primary purpose of their debate: the wording of the final concordat. The question of medical-service neutrality, so cherished by Dunant and his accomplice in Berlin, would have been simply passed over if Dr Basting's patience hadn't been running out. On the third day of the conference, he was there to remind the president, as if in passing, how necessary it was to discuss the proposals that had come out of Berlin. To this Mr Moynier responded that he hadn't thought to bring it to discussion as he believed it was included in the draft concordat project.

Condemned to silence, Dunant was powerless. But Basting showed up for them both. 'I fear that our honourable steering committee has not quite understood why the delegates have taken up its invitation.' There was no doubt that the second point of the Berlin proposal (the neutral status of medical services) was of the 'greatest interest' to most of the delegates. Given this, he was 'most surprised to hear' that they did not intend to put the matter up for discussion.[66]

Finally, Dunant and Basting's burning question was raised by the Prussian delegate, Dr Loeffler, who proposed to 'emit the wish for the governments to declare that from now on military medical personnel, and the personnel that depended upon them, including volunteer nurses, would be considered *neutral parties*'.[67] When he finished speaking, he looked for Dunant, who gave him an imperceptible nod of gratitude. Dr Loeffler had been present on 17th September in Berlin alongside Basting when Dunant won over von Roon to the idea of neutrality for the wounded and for doctors and nurses. When Dr Loeffler sat back down, it was as if the three men exchanged an invisible handshake over the heads of the other delegates.

---

[65] Ibid., 53, 62.
[66] Ibid., 113.
[67] Ibid., 118.

After three and a half days of lively debates, the initial 'draft concordat' was transformed into ten resolutions on the creation of relief committees, followed by three 'wishes'. The first 'wish' was for governments to give these committees their highest protection. The second was for dispensaries, military hospitals, medical personnel and local inhabitants to hold neutral status in times of war. Beyond Dunant's greatest hopes and far beyond Moynier's pessimistic view, this second 'wish' referred also to the neutral status of wounded soldiers themselves. Revolutionary for the time, this meant that a soldier would transform from being an enemy combatant to a wounded individual at the very moment he could no longer fight. The third wish encouraged the adoption of a distinctive sign for the persons and places involved in granting aid to the wounded, following up on General Dufour's suggestion from the first meeting of the Committee of Five, in February 1863, for 'a badge, uniform or armband, so that the bearers of such distinctive and universally adopted insignia would be recognized'.[68] Dr Appia eloquently defended this point during the third conference session, on 28th October. He proposed a white band on the left arm, but 'after some discussion' a red cross was added to the white background. The reasons for this choice were not specified in the minutes of the meeting nor in the resolutions or the final wishes. So we do not know today how the debate led to the adoption of one of the most universally recognized symbols; we are reduced to nothing but hypotheses.[69]

---

[68] Meeting minutes from 17 February 1863, *Procès-verbaux du CICR*, 18.

[69] The colour white traditionally signals surrender or parley, or the request for parley and ceasefire, and so it isn't surprising that Appia would have suggested this colour to protect medical services. The addition of a red cross is open for all sorts of speculation. According to Dunant's memoirs, published by his nephew Maurice Dunant in 1918, it was General Dufour who made the suggestion (Maurice Dunant (ed.), *Les débuts de la Croix-Rouge en France*, 16 n. 1). In the *Mémoires* published by Gagnebin (1971), Dunant specified that the 'white flag, with an isolated red cross' was decided 'spontaneously and unanimously' during the conference 'to honour Switzerland' (*Mémoires*, 95). We also know that General Dufour had been instrumental to the adoption of the Swiss flag in 1840. While the symbol was perhaps not directly suggested by Dufour, either clue may be interpreted as meaning that the symbol may indeed have been in homage to the 75-year-old who presided over and supported the conference with all his power and renown. The explicit reference to the inversion of Switzerland's federal colours was only inserted into the Geneva Convention on 6 July 1906 (art. 18). François Bugnion, *Le CICR et la protection des victimes de la guerre* (Geneva: CICR, 1994), 1168.

And so ended the conference of 1863. Everything that Dunant
had hoped for came to pass. An international conference had settled
on a slate of principles that would then be sent to a series of
governments. The conclusions of *A Memory of Solferino* were now
heading towards a future international convention. A distinctive
symbol was even accepted: a red cross on a white flag. This was
enough to compensate Henry for how excluded he'd felt over the
last forty-eight hours. But there was more to come from his most
faithful, even if most recent, friend in the assembly. As soon as the
president's concluding remarks were finished, a strong voice was
raised, marked by a familiar accent:

> In view of the extreme importance that must be attributed to the
> generous initiative taken by Mr Dunant and by the Geneva
> Society for Public Welfare, on the question of relief to those
> wounded on the battlefield, and in appreciation of the immense
> impact these proposed measures will have in all countries,
> especially upon the classes most interested in the question, I
> propose that upon its closure this International Conference
> declare . . .

Johan-Christiaan Basting had prepared his speech, this was clear.
Too emotional to speak without notes, he held his paper tightly and
read the following without raising his head:

> . . . that Mr Henry Dunant, who has instigated through his hard
> work the study of assistance for war wounded, and the Public
> Welfare Society, by supporting Mr Dunant's generous desires,
> have both done mankind a great service and fully deserve
> universal recognition. Gentleman, please join me in standing to
> bear witness of our approval.[70]

The meeting quickly stood as one and applauded the two men,
loudly and warmly.

---

[70] *Compte rendu de la Conférence internationale d'octobre 1863*, 145.

RESOLUTIONS OF THE GENEVA INTERNATIONAL CONFERENCE GENEVA, 26–29 OCTOBER 1863[71]

The International Conference, desirous of coming to the aid of the wounded should the Military Medical Services prove inadequate, adopts the following Resolutions:

Article 1. Each country shall have a Committee whose duty it shall be, in time of war and if the need arises, to assist the Army Medical Services by every means in its power. The Committee shall organize itself in the manner which seems to it most useful and appropriate.

Art. 2. An unlimited number of Sections may be formed to assist the Committee, which shall be the central directing body.

Art. 3. Each Committee shall get in touch with the Government of its country, so that its services may be accepted should the occasion arise.

Art. 4. In peacetime, the Committees and Sections shall take steps to ensure their real usefulness in time of war, especially by preparing material relief of all sorts and by seeking to train and instruct voluntary medical personnel.

Art. 5. In time of war, the Committees of belligerent nations shall supply relief to their respective armies as far as their means permit: in particular, they shall organize voluntary personnel and place them on an active footing and, in agreement with the military authorities, shall have premises made available for the care of the wounded. They may call for assistance upon the Committees of neutral countries.

Art. 6. On the request or with the consent of the military authorities, Committees may send voluntary medical personnel to the battlefield where they shall be placed under military command.

---

[71] English translation by the ICRC.

Art. 7. Voluntary medical personnel attached to armies shall be supplied by the respective Committees with everything necessary for their upkeep.

Art. 8. They shall wear in all countries, as a uniform distinctive sign, a white armlet with a red cross.

Art. 9. The Committees and Sections of different countries may meet in international assemblies to communicate the results of their experience and to agree on measures to be taken in the interests of the work.

Art. 10. The exchange of communications between the Committees of the various countries shall be made for the time being through the intermediary of the Geneva Committee.

Independently of the above Resolutions, the Conference makes the following Recommendations:

(a) that Governments should extend their patronage to Relief Committees which may be formed, and facilitate as far as possible the accomplishment of their task.

(b) that in time of war the belligerent nations should proclaim the neutrality of ambulances and military hospitals, and that neutrality should likewise be recognized, fully and absolutely, in respect of official medical personnel, voluntary medical personnel, inhabitants of the country who go to the relief of the wounded, and the wounded themselves;

(c) that a uniform distinctive sign be recognized for the Medical Corps of all armies, or at least for all persons of the same army belonging to this Service; and, that a uniform flag also be adopted in all countries for ambulances and hospitals.

Conference Secretary J.-Henry Dunant Geneva,
October 1863

6

A Question of Honour
(1863–7)

The fruits of success

The day after the October 1863 conference, Dunant and Moynier's collaboration was running like a well-oiled machine. And there was indeed much work to be done. The Geneva Committee needed to distribute the 'resolutions' and 'wishes' as widely as possible, encourage the establishment of national committees and eventually prepare for a true diplomatic conference. Their goal was no longer a question of simple resolutions but of leading the representative governments into an actual international treaty.

Over the next few weeks, the efficiency of the Moynier–Dunant duo was stupefying. By 4th November Henry had already received the conference proceeding proofs back from Fick printers: a 150-page summary meticulously composed by his lawyer associate Moynier, who had excused the secretary from this delicate and burdensome task. This didn't stop Dunant from offering his twopenn'orth on one of his pet subjects, formatting. He felt the cover didn't look 'quite right' and he suggested a few modifications. Furthermore, he asked Moynier whether it was necessary to include 'The Society of Public Welfare' on the back cover: it was now time for the Red Cross to leave the nest and fly on its own.

The text was published soon after, with no author listed on the cover. Only the resolutions were signed by 'Conference Secretary, J. Henry Dunant'. Despite this, as of the committee meeting of 9th November 1863, it was becoming clear to everyone that Moynier was now in charge. It was he who took care of the orders granted to the committee, sent out the proceedings, ensured a follow-up with the delegates and approached the states who hadn't attended. It was also he who wrote the memo to be sent to all conference participants reminding them of their engagements. The tone had none of Dunant's obsequious deference and all of Moynier's straightforward precision: 'Please let us know if you are interested in working to create a relief committee in your country, and whether we may rely on you to oversee its organization.'[1] The memo was despatched on 15th November, and its effect soon felt.

Gustave Moynier's rise to power didn't overly disturb Dunant. He'd already given enough of his time as corresponding secretary; it suited him to move on to something else for a bit. His new goal was to bring France to the foreground of any future strategies by forcing it to assume its role as a great power and by hurrying along the creation of a prestigious France-based committee. He was off to Paris before mid-November, with plans to spend the winter there. He took up rooms at the Hotel de Bade on the Rue des Italiens, a slightly outdated establishment but well-located in the heart of the city.

Hustle and bustle in Paris

Dunant immediately put his genius for publicity to work, prioritizing a campaign to get the red cross on a white background into everyone's mind – especially the elite – and in all countries – especially in France. An intuitive and early adept of the virtues of *merchandising*, he had white armbands with a red cross made and distributed widely, encouraging the ladies he knew to leave them lying about their salons 'with the premeditated intention of exciting the curiosity of her French friends and inciting questions as to the use of this strange and new ornament'.[2] Among this advertising squadron was Germaine de Staël's daughter-in-law, Adelaïde de Staël, who, despite being in her eighties, roused for her compatriot's cause, convincing her brother-in-law, the Duke of Broglie, to stir up

---

[1] Model letter of 15 November 1863, AICR, A AF 21–2, 1863.
[2] Dunant, *Mémoires*, 133.

the Institut de France[3] on their behalf. A propaganda campaign got underway, eventually reaching the press. On 12th December 1863, in an article about the Geneva Conference, *L'Illustration* published a front-page engraving of these 'Swiss first-aid nurses'(!)[4] wearing their white armbands with the cross.

It took Dunant's media storm only ten days to secure him a meeting with the general steward to the emperor, Charles Darricau, and the Swiss plenipotentiary minister Jacques-Conrad Kern. On 23rd November, the three men settled on a plan to convince the French Empire to 'take up the issue'[5] of an international flag and armband, and then persuade the other great powers to follow suit.

Emboldened by his success, our titleless ambassador was also begging Moynier and Dufour for 'a manner of delegation' from the conference in his favour, what he called 'a sort of title' or 'a form of power', which would enable him to present their request himself to the Minister of Foreign Affairs Drouyn de Lhuys. In the same letter he announced that Darricau had given Empress Eugénie a summary of the conference and that she wished to 'take on the patronage of this work in France'.[6] He was extremely excited, and understandably so. But once again, Geneva took it upon itself to rain on his parade. Moynier tempered Dunant's 'success' by return post, stating that this approach to France was premature and that the committee did not believe they had 'ever expressed the wish you think you remember that a major power should take up the issue of the international flag and armband'.[7]

There are better ways to encourage a man. But it would take more than this to unsettle Dunant, especially since right then his

---

[3] Founded in 1795, the *Institut de France* (Institute of France) is a French learned society, similar to the British Royal Society. It includes the *Académie française*. Germaine de Staël was a Swiss political woman of letters, daughter of Jacques Necker, finance minister to Louis XVI.

[4] Although the illustration caption in *L'Illustration* wrongfully named the 'Swiss first-aid nurses' (Swiss delegates to the ICRC did not yet exist), the body of the article accurately cited the formation of 'companies of first-aid volunteers'. What is likely is that when the page editor saw the armband with the cross, he concluded these were Swiss nurses, a mistake he would not be the last to make.

[5] Dunant to Moynier, 25 November 1863, ACICR A AF, 20,1-016.

[6] Ibid.

[7] Moynier to Dunant, 27 November 1863, ACICR A AF, 20,1-017.

energy was required elsewhere. At that point he'd been canvassing for a year and a half with every upper-class Protestant or blue blood he knew in Paris to create the central steering committee of a French Soldiers' Aid Society. It was high time to launch one more blitz in his tenacious siege of the emperor! On 5th December, he sent a new letter, drawing His Majesty's attention to the conference's 'wishes', a letter that also included a word from Dufour – a 'silver bullet' that reached its target. The hoped-for reply arrived on 21st December: 'His Majesty highly approves of the objectives of the conference and the resolutions passed in order to further these objectives. He wishes to contribute to your efforts by encouraging the creation of the aid committee that you are presently trying to set up in Paris; accordingly he willingly authorizes you to make known the sympathy with which he regards this enterprise.' The emperor would also instruct Marshal Randon to 'authorize a few high-ranking army officers'[8] to become members of the future committee.

As he folded up this missive, Dunant could believe his path forward to a French Soldiers' Aid Society was now paved in imperial flagstones. Still, Marshal Randon's grumpy face flitted across his thoughts. It was such bad luck having to deal with him again! As we saw in 1858, our ambitious Genevan colonial had already been on the receiving end of the Governor General of Algeria's disdain; now, five years later and in completely different circumstances, the secretary of the future ICRC was to be newly confronted with the Minister of War's hostility. The marshal felt the very idea of voluntary medical personnel was a criticism of the army's health services, implying a criticism of the army, and thus of France itself! The emperor may have been charmed by Henry Dunant's youthful face, but not he, the Minister of War. Charm wasn't enough and he wouldn't be pushed around. He needed clear information, precise explanations, convincing guarantees. Several days later Randon asked Dunant through his aide-de-camp: 'What will be the goal of this Committee? Who will be members? Who will preside? Where will it assemble?'[9]

Henry provided the answers he could. Writing to Randon on 26th January 1864, he thoughtfully included a comprehensive list of the

---

[8] Colonel Favé to Dunant, from Paris, 21 December 1863, BGE, Ms. 2109, f. 118.
[9] General Castelnau to Dunant, 29 December 1863, BGE, Ms. 2109, f. 120.

favourable reactions from Russia, Prussia, Württemberg, Oldenburg, Belgium and all the other nations ready to barter their souls for wounded soldiers. This may not have convinced the Minister of War, but it did calm him for a time. Meanwhile, the emperor was still forging ahead: on 19th February he approved a meeting between Dunant and his Minister of Foreign Affairs Drouyn de Lhuys 'so that he can examine your proposal for the neutrality of ambulances, hospitals, the wounded and the medical corps'.[10]

Dunant had won the first battle of his Parisian offensive.

A war committee

February saw Dunant home in Geneva. An ill Gustave Moynier had momentarily stepped back, giving Henry a chance to return with more enthusiasm to his post as secretary of the International Committee. While Dunant had been riling up his prestigious Parisians for the French committee, not much had been happening on the Swiss side of the border except the formation of an honourable group of Genevan ladies bent on preparing wound-dressing supplies and organizing 'bandage soirées'. Yet in these early moments of 1864, the marching of military boots could be heard near Schleswig-Holstein, two duchies connected to the Danish crown but claimed by Prussia because of their majority German-speaking populations. Prussia and Austria had delivered an ultimatum on 16th January 1864. By early February, their troops were entering Denmark – a new war was beginning.

The ladies' group in Geneva hadn't been formed in light of these specific events, but it could definitely demonstrate its usefulness sooner than planned. Indeed, the International Committee encouraged its founder, Madame Eynard, to call for more 'bandage soirées' among her connections, and even urged her to somehow formalize the various groups into a 'Ladies' Auxiliary Committee'.

Despite his boundless respect for their work, Dunant couldn't imagine that a band of willing ladies would constitute the first Swiss – or Genevan – Soldiers' Aid Society. Was it so impossible to do in his own city what he was already accomplishing in France? In

---

[10] Colonel Favé to Dunant, from Paris, 19 February 1864, BGE, Ms. 2109, f. 153–4.

March, under his own initiative but in the name of the International
Committee, he began contacting a short list of well-reputed men to
become a 'Geneva branch'.

The first polite refusal arrived on 2nd March; two more came on
the 7th; a fourth on the 11th; another on the 12th; and, finally, the
last on the 19th. Certainly not concerted, these responses were all
consistently negative. The doors of royal palaces and chancelleries
had opened to him in all of Europe's capitals, but Dunant was
struggling in his own city to find a handful of gentlemen who might
consider his offer an honour.

It was a situation that would discourage anyone – except Henry
Dunant. On 13th March he suggested to the three International
Committee members present – with Moynier still unwell, this meant
Dufour, Maunoir and Appia – to go ahead and create a Geneva
branch with the few men who'd responded favourably.[11] Luckily,
because current events were pressing: the war between Denmark
and Germany had been raging now for six weeks, and the
International Committee had no mandate to act or launch activities
on its own. Only a properly constituted Soldiers' Aid Society,
whether Genevan, Swiss or French, could send volunteers into the
field. Personally, Dunant was tempted to set off towards the war
theatre on his own. But Napoleon III had just informed him that
France was prepared 'to have its Minister of Foreign Affairs
diplomatically address the subject of neutrality with the other
European courts'[12] – a bit of news he proudly announced at that
same meeting of 13th March. This was crucial information from at
least two perspectives. It indicated, on the one hand, that the
emperor now agreed with the controversial Berlin Circular on
medical-staff neutrality and, on the other, it meant the 'resolutions'
and 'wishes' from the 1863 conference would achieve diplomatic
engagement at the highest level.

But these advances in France didn't distract Dunant from his
immediate goal. Four days after the committee's decision to establish
a local branch, the handful of Genevans who had said yes assembled

---

[11] About the foundation of the Genevan Red Cross, see R. Durand, 'Symbolique,
éphémère et éternelle, la Croix-Rouge genevoise a 125 ans', Bulletin de la Société
Henry Dunant, 12 (Geneva: SHD, 1989), 37–59.
[12] Meeting minutes from 13 March 1864, Procès-verbaux du CICR, 26–7.

at his home at teatime. Overriding procedural minutiae, General Dufour quickly declared the 'Geneva branch constituted',[13] thus enabling it to immediately address the situation at hand: the war of the duchies on the Danish border. Not even half an hour old, the brand-new Soldiers' Aid Society of Geneva decided to send two delegates to the Schleswig-Holstein region. What's interesting to note is the concern for impartiality already anchored in this nascent Red Cross: Doctor Louis Appia would go to the Austro-Prussian side and Captain Charles Van de Velde to Denmark. Their mission was to 'enquire into the voluntary field hospitals and act if needed'.[14]

Their priority was clearly action, not renown: the members agreed not to announce the creation of their Genevan Aid Society before the delegates returned from their mission, as this was the only *raison d'être* of this newly founded branch.

Appia left on 22nd March and Van de Velde on the 29th. If we count from 13th March, the day he advocated for establishing a Geneva branch, it took Henry Dunant only twelve days to give the world its first two Red Cross delegates.

France to action

The creation of a Genevan Soldiers' Aid Society, the sending of two delegates to a battlefield: Dunant's successful agenda during his stay in his home town enabled him to leave for Paris with a light heart. Even more so because he now had an audience set for 22nd April with Drouyn de Lhuys, a vital step for the future diplomatic conference. Indeed, although most of the governments had agreed to form domestic aid societies, were united on the principle of neutrality and believed it wise to adopt a uniform symbol, it was proving much more difficult to convince them on the idea of a meeting between states. A favourable signal from one major power would surely bring the others in line.

---

[13] Meeting minutes from 17 March 1864, *Procès-verbaux du CICR*, 28.
[14] Ibid., Charles Van de Velde was the delegate from the Netherlands to the 1863 Conference. His devotion to the project made him a kind of sixth ghost member of the Committee of Five.

Henry Dunant went alone to the Ministry of Foreign Affairs on 22nd April 1864 to discuss the terms of the diplomatic conference intended to pave the way forward for the Geneva Convention. Although the Swiss minister Jacques-Conrad Kern had helped with the preliminary diplomatic dealings, he didn't accompany Dunant to the interview. So we must trust Dunant's memoirs as the sole record of what was said.

The French minister began straightaway with the question of who was in charge; it seemed evident for him that the ball was in the Swiss court:

> If, with the view to transform the idea of neutrality into international law, the Swiss Confederation wants to invite the civilized states to assemble together in a Swiss city, France is ready, as a great military power, to second the initiative and encourage the invited states to accept the Swiss invitation.[15]

Listening to the minister's firm introduction, Dunant would have been pleased to find two problems immediately resolved: first, France wasn't clamouring to organize the diplomatic conference itself; secondly, it was ready to give its support. However, the devil is always in the detail. The minister seemed to think it was a given that the conference would take place in the Swiss capital city of Berne, the seat of the Federal government. But this wasn't what Dunant had in mind:

> The project was conceived in Geneva, Your Excellency. That is where the first conference was held, that is where the International Committee has its headquarters, and finally, as promoter of this work, I would be extremely honoured that the conference take place in my home town . . .

Did the minister bristle at the suggestion? For a Frenchman of old stock, Geneva, 'the Protestant Rome', was still tainted by its religious dissidence. But courtesy won in the end: after a few arguments in favour of the capital, Drouyn de Lhuys ended up conceding, and

---

[15] The whole meeting is reported by Dunant in his *Mémoires*, 105–6.

passed to the next question – just as delicate – of which states to invite. Here again, Dunant's reply, with its unending guest list, upset the minister: 'What? You want to invite all the little German states?'

To which our ambassador from the International Committee pointed out that the states who'd attended the preparatory conference in October 1863 had a full right to join the second round of talks. He won this last point. However, he would not win when it came to the South American republics, which he'd wanted to include as well: the French minister would only consent to invite Brazil and Mexico. Dunant gave in. He was going to have his conference in Geneva, and it was being supported by France – this was already extraordinary!

How did Dunant present the fruits of his harvest to the Committee this time? The letter he posted to Moynier the next day speaks of sending documents, paperwork, instructions to soldiers, but says nothing about his meeting with Drouyn de Lhuys. Not a word. Not even a hint! Did he fear he'd be chastised again, or was there a letter that's since been lost? Either way, what mattered now was preparing for the event.

Between Paris, Berne and Geneva everything suddenly moved very quickly.

The International Committee sent two official letters, one to the emperor and one to Drouyn de Lhuys. By 19th May Moynier was getting worried; he complained he'd received no reply to either of the letters, he knew nothing and no one was telling him anything! By return mail on 21st May, Dunant answered with the following: Kern and Drouyn de Lhuys agreed that the Swiss should convoke the conference. Dr Lehmann, head physician of the Federal Army and Swiss delegate to the October conference, was also in favour. Kern had suggested that the Committee ('General Dufour and you, dear sir', Dunant specified) make an official request to the Swiss Federal Council in Berne to convene a new conference in Geneva, a letter which Dunant dictated to Moynier nearly word for word. He also indicated that Kern was writing that very day to the president of the Swiss Confederation, a way to prepare him to favourably receive the committee's request, and that Drouyn de Lhuys was simultaneously telling his ambassador in Berne to encourage the Federal Council as well. 'Now,' Dunant concluded, 'all that remains is to write a letter to the Federal Council to respectfully and officially request they convoke the Conference.'[16]

Curiously, Moynier – the man this entire intricate edifice was resting on – took his time fulfilling the task. He followed Dunant's suggestions and did write a letter to the Federal Council, but he couldn't make up his mind whether to send it. Why not?

Because he was obviously wary of Dunant's ever-optimistic reassurances. Before sending his letter, he went to Berne on 25th May to do his own reconnaissance. He went first to see the French ambassador, and then via Dr Lehmann's introduction he met with the president of the Confederation and the head of the Military Department. And thus he was finally reassured: everything was presented just as Dunant had said, all the higher-ups had written or responded or encouraged in every which way. The only thing missing was the official request to the Swiss government, that Moynier would have already supplied if he hadn't been so distrustful – sometimes correctly, sometimes wrongly – of 'his dear secretary'. As soon as he returned, he convoked the Committee and finally sent his letter, just as Dunant had asked him to.[17] But the decision had to come from he himself, based on his own information and validated by his own conclusions.

First squabbles

While Moynier had been playing detective in Berne on 25th May 1864, Dunant was already busy with other things. The Swiss question handled, he returned his energy to the French situation. This very same day marked the founding of the *Comité provisoire de France de la Société de secours aux blessés militaires* (Provisory Committee of the French Soldiers' Aid Society).

As we've seen, Dunant had been working like a dog on this for months – making the rounds of upper-society Protestants, the nobility and the literary and scientific circles. He'd successfully recruited some illustrious names: Count de Flavigny, Colonel Huber-

---

[16] Dunant to Moynier, 21 May 1864, ACICR A AF, 20,1-026.
[17] This exchange of letters was published in the *Revue internationale de la Croix-Rouge*, 427, July 1954, 587–600.

Saladin, Augustin Cochin, Théodore Vernes and the always willing Baron Darricau. For the first assembly, Dunant asked François Bartholony, uncle of Gustave Moynier's wife and a long-time acquaintance, to lend him one of the splendid meeting salons of his railway company, the *Chemin de fer d'Orléans*.

At the assembly Dunant gave a short and convincing speech. He summarized the future society's goals and provided a draft of the statutes. The provisory committee was formed around General de Montesquiou, Duke of Fezensac, and under imperial patronage. The secretary of the International Committee was euphoric amid this assembly of title holders, renowned scholars, generals and great financiers. The world was smiling on him, in both Switzerland and France. At least he believed so, as they applauded him warmly beneath the golden panelling of that prestigious room. The rest could wait.

Indeed, the rest was waiting and had been for nearly two years. The whirlwind following the publication of *A Memory of Solferino* had pulled Dunant away from his business affairs. His position as Algerian landowner may have appeared enviable, with his mills valuing around 200,000 francs, his mines and a large, promising forest. But this outlay was constantly begging for new capital, new capital that was harder and harder to find. In fact, he'd just realized that the individual stocks guaranteed by the members of his board of directors would not be enough. A few months before, in January, a new 500,000-franc appeal to facilitate the harvest of his cork oak forests had not found any takers for the sum requested. And his right-hand man in Algeria, the indispensable Henri Nick, was losing a considerable amount of money on wheat speculating, which seemed to be depleting not only his own resources but the Mons-Djemila Mills's accounts as well. Dunant was considering aligning himself with a more solid company or creating something even bigger himself, able to bring in enough capital to match the size of his projects. In this context, the benevolence of the emperor and the French nobility, coupled with all his hobnobbing among the great names in Franco-Swiss finance, could only help his Algerian businesses, over and above the French Soldiers' Aid Society. At least this is what he still believed in May 1864, just when everything could still be saved.

As had now become his habit, Moynier dampened Dunant's optimism yet again. Writing to Dunant on 28th May, he ingeniously reported the details of his trip to Berne. Of course, Dunant was perfectly aware that Moynier's visit had been a supervisory operation, even intended as a corrective of Dunant's initiatives. Moynier went on to cannily reproach the entire Swiss team in Paris – Kern and Dunant – of having said too much; he also adopted Berne's point of view on limiting the guests 'to the European powers', pretending there wasn't enough time to invite Brazil and Mexico, two countries Dunant had wanted to include from the beginning.[18]

This time it was too much. By return post, Dunant responded first that he'd had 'great pleasure' from his 'good letter'. He proceeded with other news, and then this in the final paragraph:

> Now, dear Sir, I believe that I have done everything I can to make our efforts successful and ensure their continuity; I now wish to fade completely out of the picture; please do not count on me for active support; I am returning into the shadows; the work has been set on course and, in this, I was merely an instrument in the hand of God; it is now up to others, better qualified than myself, to push it forward and make it work.[19]

And just as he'd always done, but would not do again, he assured Gustave Moynier of his 'affectionate friendship'.

Upon reception of his secretary's sudden resignation, the president immediately tried to smooth things over. He responded on 1st June:

> Unfortunately, your letter ended with news that caused us great consternation. We still find it difficult to believe that you are seriously thinking to deprive us of your indispensable assistance. We are simply your assistants and cannot be considered your substitutes; to abandon us is the surest way to jeopardize the success of our work at the very moment when it seems to be coming to fruition.

Despite his words, did Moynier really want to keep Dunant? With his right hand, yes; with his left hand, however, he also sent a (well-deserved) slap to his correspondent. Shortly after his meeting with Drouyn de Lhuys in April, Dunant had been unable to resist

---

[18] Moynier to Dunant, 28 May 1864 ACICR A AF, 20,1-032. See also François, *Le berceau de la Croix-Rouge*, 238–341.

[19] Dunant to Moynier, from Paris, 29 May 1864, ACICR A AF, 20,1-034.

informing the Genevan government how he'd so brilliantly defended his birth city as the headquarters of the next diplomatic conference. Along with the vanity that had grown, alas, with his mounting successes, he couldn't help putting himself forward: 'the emperor of France made it clear to *me* that he was well disposed to do what *I* was asking'; '*I* was eager to designate Geneva'; 'His Excellency Mr Drouyn de Lhuys, whom *I* saw again today'; etc.

Unfortunately, General Dufour, who'd known nothing of Dunant's one-man show, had gone several days later to the same government with a formal notification of the next conference. 'I will not hide from you,' Moynier wrote, 'that the General was very put out about this role he'd had to play, not to mention the fact that your letter had more likely irritated the State Council rather than win it over.' And he concluded with the following lecture:

> You should now understand how difficult your position has become, if we must be wary of your overzealousness, and so you will, I hope, forgive me if I reiterate to you the sincere recommendation not to undertake any approach of any importance (except emergency situations, that goes without saying) without informing us or consulting us, if needed; because we are the ones carrying the responsibility, at the very least we should be informed.[20]

Dunant gave in. He would obey. He would remain on the Committee, but he now knew what to expect. In the race for leadership of the Red Cross, the writing on the wall was clear: the International Committee would now be managed by Gustave Moynier.

Final touches

The diplomatic conference was set for 8th August 1864 in Geneva. The invitations left the Swiss Federal Palace on 6th June. Several days later, the French government sent a note to the invited countries in support of the initiative but without thinking to communicate the text to the Geneva Committee, one more cause of frustration for President Moynier.

---

[20] Moynier to Dunant, 1 June 1864, ACICR A AF, 20,1-035.

Of the twenty-five States invited, sixteen responded that they would be sending a representative. Austria, Bavaria and the Papal States (still in defiance of the Protestant Rome?) expressly refused to participate. Some others sent their good wishes but no one to represent them.

The Confederation had sent the invitations, the Genevans would do the receiving. But not just any Genevans! Although they disagreed on several points, Moynier and Dunant were on the same page when it came to keeping the Geneva government at bay as much as possible. Did they imagine a cruise on the lake for the gentleman delegates? 'Perhaps we should ask the Federal Council for this,' Moynier wrote to Dunant during those preparatory weeks, 'but we must not let the State Council be involved, who would only attract their acolytes and lend the party a whiff of "democrashitty".'[21] To which Dunant responded that he 'agreed a thousand times':[22] it would not do to transform this distinguished reception into a common village fair.

As a result, the festivities would be essentially private – private, sumptuous and numerous, even 'a little too much', according to General Dufour, and to Moynier who believed they should not 'overload the participants with entertainment from morning until night'.[23] But with Henry Dunant as head of festivities, the programme would be quite full indeed. To begin, the delegates would be received at Moynier's – or more accurately, at his in-laws' splendid estate – for a 'gentleman's meeting'. The next morning, the delegates would sail the lake all the way to Théodore Vernes's house in Versoix, where they would then reboard the *Helvétie* to take them back to Geneva for supper at the beautiful home of Colonel Favre. On Friday evening, they would watch a naval parade from François Bartholony's mansion. Finally, the Federal Council would offer supper at the Hotel de la Métropole, with a choir and fanfare after the meal.

---

[21] TN: Moynier makes a pun in the original letter on the words *démocratie* (democracy) and *crapule* (thug), *démocrapule*, which we have adapted into our own pun to translate his feelings towards democracy. Moynier to Dunant, 25 June 1864, ACICR A AF, 20,1-039.

[22] Dunant to Moynier, 9 July 1864, ACICR A AF, 20,1-050.

[23] Dufour to Moynier, 5 July 1864, and Moynier to Dunant, 3 July 1864, ACICR A AF, 20,1-048 and -045.

This lovely programme would be modified several times before the conference actually opened. But the menu of events would keep all its courses. Dunant may have forced his hand a little, probably because he'd been given no other role. Since Moynier had refused his resignation but sanctioned him all the same, it seemed Dunant decided to dig his heels in.

In mid-June, Moynier went for a bathing cure in Schinznach, leaving behind all kinds of complicated instructions on how to put the room together for the conference. Dunant docilely acquiesced to everything: 'I will supervise Derabours [their handyman] as you ask, and I'll follow your instructions.' A little later, in July, he maintained the same tone: 'I am at your beck and call,' he wrote to him in Schinznach, 'Send me your good ideas from the waters and I will have them carried out.'[24]

Only once that summer, out of the blue, did he rebel. Moynier was still in Schinznach, and Dunant may have grown a little sick of taking orders like a secretary or a servant. He wrote this prickly reply to Moynier on 9th July:

I am looking forward to your return, because only you can organize all of this. I am no good at these details; I have too much to do. For the important matters, you can count on me, but the details are not my business and I do not have the time [. . .] I offer you my two secretaries, my servant, to help you with the details and other local things, as the big days approach, but do not count on me.[25]

He could throw his hands in the air; he could raise his voice. Alas, Moynier and Dufour did not give him a single 'important matter', not before, during or after the conference. Together, the general and the lawyer constructed a draft convention in a 'legislative style' that was beyond Dunant's reach. Dufour had already been asked back in May to preside over the conference, and Moynier would be the plenipotentiary delegate from the Federal Council, alongside the army's chief surgeon, Dr Lehmann.

---

[24] Dunant to Moynier, 22 June 1864 and no date ('Thursday', in July), ACICR A AF 20,1-028 and A AF, Box 44, 'Letters of Henry Dunant'.
[25] Dunant to Moynier, 9 July 1864, ACICR A AF, 20,1-050.

Dunant could light up the lakeshore from Versoix to Evian if he wanted to, but it wouldn't change the fact that he'd lost the upper hand for his conference.

The Diplomatic Conference of 1864

'We seek only one thing: the neutrality in war of ambulances and medical personnel.'[26] This was how General Dufour summarized the goal of the diplomatic conference to the thirty-five individuals present in the former courtroom of Geneva's city hall on 8th August 1864. At a small desk, a short distance from the large table where the official delegates were placed, sat the man who had conceived and ceaselessly defended the idea of this neutrality. But he wasn't allowed to speak. A mere Committee member, like Louis Appia and Théodore Maunoir, Henry Dunant could only passively watch the proceedings. The Geneva Convention would be created in his presence but nearly without him.

A first series of sessions ran from 8th to 12th August; then a second round from the 16th to the 18th, the date which the 'Diplomatic Committee' – Moynier among them – established the final text. The Geneva Convention was signed on Monday 22nd August 1864, the same day that an electoral incident unleashed a riot which happened to arrive at the door of the city hall. As the Convention was being signed, shouting and sounds of shoving filtered in to interrupt the solemn moment. The rioters entered the courtyard: Dunant, who didn't have much to do during the signing ceremony, went outside the room to lock the doors of the antechamber. Once the delegates were sheltered from the demonstration, he began to speak with the overexcited protestors, trying to convince them to change their route. But to no avail. Some of them made it to the first floor to confront the government. But at least Dunant had prevented

---

[26] Opening of the first session of the Geneva Conference of 1864 by General Dufour, 'Conference internationale pour la neutralisation du service de santé militaire en campagne' in Revue internationale de la Croix-Rouge, 424, May 1954, 422. Dufour did not mention the neutrality of volunteers, probably on purpose, so as not to upset the French: see Véronique Harouel, Genève-Paris 1863–1918, Le droit humanitaire en construction (Geneva: SHD/CICR/CRF, 2003), 95–6.

a clash; he returned to the conference room, where the delegates had barely noticed the agitation surrounding them.[27]

Once the convention was signed and the delegates had left, Dunant took the time to accompany General Dufour – saddened by the tumultuous end to the conference – back to his home. Then he returned to the city hall to check that nothing was left behind. The shuffled chairs, overturned desk blotters and forgotten papers in the silent, empty room gave the impression of a morning after a riotous party. Beyond a sense of completion, was this moment also marked for Henry with a slight feeling of frustration or ill-use? The most important thing was that he and the delegates had shared a historic moment. Before and during the conference, all the different gentlemen had exchanged their portraits, some of them even carrying albums with multiple frames so as to say later, either in a few years or in a few decades: 'This man was there,' 'That man was there,' and above all, 'I was there.'

CONVENTION FOR THE AMELIORATION OF THE CONDITION OF THE WOUNDED IN ARMIES IN THE FIELD. GENEVA, 22 AUGUST 1864[28]

ARTICLE 1. – Ambulances and military hospitals shall be recognized as neutral and, as such, protected and respected by the belligerents as long as they accommodate wounded and sick. Neutrality shall end if the said ambulances or hospitals should be held by a military force.

ART. 2. – Hospital and ambulance personnel, including the quartermaster's staff, the medical, administrative and transport services, and the chaplains, shall have the benefit of the same neutrality when on duty, and while there remain any wounded to be brought in or assisted.

---

[27] Dunant, *Mémoires*, 111–12. On this riot, see also André Durand, '*La journée du 22 août 1864 à Genève*', *Bulletin de la Société Henri Dunant*, 13 (Geneva: SHD, 1989), 6–21.

[28] English translation by the ICRC.

ART. 3. – The persons designated in the preceding Article may, even after enemy occupation, continue to discharge their functions in the hospital or ambulance with which they serve, or may withdraw to rejoin the units to which they belong. When in these circumstances they cease from their functions, such persons shall be delivered to the enemy outposts by the occupying forces.

ART. 4. – The material of military hospitals being subject to the laws of war, the persons attached to such hospitals may take with them, on withdrawing, only the articles which are their own personal property. Ambulances, on the contrary, under similar circumstances, shall retain their equipment.

ART. 5. – Inhabitants of the country who bring help to the wounded shall be respected and shall remain free. Generals of the belligerent Powers shall make it their duty to notify the inhabitants of the appeal made to their humanity, and of the neutrality which humane conduct will confer.

The presence of any wounded combatant receiving shelter and care in a house shall ensure its protection. An inhabitant who has given shelter to the wounded shall be exempted from billeting and from a portion of such war contributions as may be levied.

ART. 6. – Wounded or sick combatants, to whatever nation they may belong, shall be collected and cared for.

Commanders-in-Chief may hand over immediately to the enemy outposts enemy combatants wounded during an engagement, when circumstances allow and subject to the agreement of both parties.

Those who, after their recovery, are recognized as being unfit for further service, shall be repatriated.

The others may likewise be sent back, on condition that they shall not again, for the duration of hostilities, take up arms.

Evacuation parties, and the personnel conducting them, shall be considered as being absolutely neutral.

ART. 7. – A distinctive and uniform flag shall be adopted for hospitals, ambulances and evacuation parties. It should in all circumstances be accompanied by the national flag.

An armlet may also be worn by personnel enjoying neutrality but its issue shall be left to the military authorities.

Both flag and armlet shall bear a red cross on a white ground.

ART. 8. – The implementing of the present Convention shall be arranged by the Commanders-in-Chief of the belligerent armies following the instructions of their respective Governments and in accordance with the general principles set forth in this Convention.

ART. 9. – The High Contracting Parties have agreed to communicate the present Convention with an invitation to accede thereto
to Governments unable to appoint Plenipotentiaries to the International Conference at Geneva. The Protocol has accordingly been left open.

ART. 10. – The present Convention shall be ratified and the ratifications exchanged at Berne, within the next four months, or sooner if possible.

In faith whereof, the respective Plenipotentiaries have signed the Convention and thereto affixed their seals.

Done at Geneva, this twenty-second day of August, in the year one thousand eight hundred and sixty-four.

The family photo

The delegates to the 1864 Conference wouldn't have parted ways without a souvenir: a family photo in which they all stood together, just as is done today at the end of world summits.

Every single one of the delegates is in the photo, along with conference president General Dufour. But Dunant is absent: since he wasn't representing a government, he was excluded from the group pose. He had been there, however, when the photo was taken, surely joining in with the good humour that always accompanies this kind of closing ritual. And it was only afterwards, when he returned to the empty room, that an idea took shape in the wake of his regrets. Since he was in charge of the conference's side programming – festivities, publicity and the rest – he was also responsible for the photographs; this is how he managed to slip into the official picture of the 1864 Conference.

Without a magnifying glass, it is easy to believe – and be astounded – that a portrait of Dunant was there, and that all of the delegates, Moynier included, so solemnly posed beneath it. But if you look at the photo very closely you can see it has been edited, from the arrangement of the individuals around the table all the way to the portrait, which clearly never hung on the wall of the former courtroom above Dufour's head. Of course Dunant didn't show up at the courthouse on the first or last day of the conference carrying a large oval portrait of himself. It was added later, directly onto the photo – photographic retouching was common at that time.

However, when Dunant left the building that evening, he had other worries than how to add his face to that 'family' photo: there was a rumour that his brother Pierre, the doctor, had been hurt while caring for the victims of the demonstrations in the lower city. Violence had been raging all day throughout Geneva, leaving several wounded from gunshots. Dunant collected snatches of details as he hurried towards the lower city. The banks of the river were deserted, and it was only after he'd crossed over to the other side that he heard, 'with inexpressible joy',[29] that the rumour regarding his brother was false. And so he calmly recrossed the river and retraced his steps to exactly where he'd begun, back to his own apartment at the Puits-Saint-Pierre which was a mere 30 metres from the same city hall that had just witnessed such a historic day.

The Convention for the Amelioration of the Condition of the Wounded in Armies in the Field had ratified into international law the proposals laid out two years earlier by Henry Dunant in *A Memory of Solferino*. The treaty stipulated neutrality of field hospitals, dispensaries, hospitals and their personnel; 'respect' of the inhabitants of the countries who would bring aid to the wounded, and the safeguarding of their homes; impartiality in care for the wounded; the adoption of a flag and a distinctive armband, displaying a red cross on a white background, for hospital and medical personnel. While the treaty did not explicitly mention the neutral status of voluntary medical personnel nor those of the wounded, the report that Mr Moynier sent to the Swiss Federal Council sometime later seemed to consider both of these things a given: '[T]he neutral personnel,' he wrote, 'include three categories which are the following: one, those engaged in the care of the wounded; two, the inhabitants

---

[29] Dunant, *Mémoires*, 113.

of the country; three, the wounded.'[30] And so Dunant could be wholly satisfied, even if he was no longer leading the movement.

The month that followed would see Henry Dunant and the other committee members scrambling to have the Convention adopted by the greatest possible number of countries. Among the sixteen states present at the conference (the duchy of Baden, Belgium, Denmark, Spain, the United States, France, Great Britain, the grand duchy of Hesse, Italy, the Netherlands, Portugal, Prussia, Royal Saxony, Sweden and Norway, Switzerland and Württemberg), twelve had accredited delegates to sign the Convention. There remained many more countries to convince, and although it was not its official role, the International Committee made every effort to achieve this goal. They also had to push the diplomats so that the Convention could be ratified as quickly as possible, send out the conference proceedings and get back to working the French side, where the Provisory Committee of the French Soldiers' Aid Society had hardly advanced since its inception back in May. But Dunant was already planning to move back to Paris for the winter. He felt his place was there now, more than in Geneva.

The two lives of one man

During the winter of 1864–5, more than at any other moment of his life, Dunant attempted to unite the founder of the Red Cross and the Algerian investor into a single persona – a man sought after by all of Paris. He was already well-integrated into its upper-class Protestant society, whose connections with Geneva were numerous, but that winter he introduced himself into new settings. He gave a conference on aid work to war victims for the Catholic circle of Paris which, according to Dunant, gathered together the 'best families of France'. He was invited to the general assembly of the Universal Israelite Alliance, where he earned the sympathy of Baron James Rothschild whom he would then persuade to join the Central Committee for the French Aid Society. Noblemen, scientists, clergy and more showed him their interest with a sentence or a note, all of whom Dunant would remember when he sat down years later to detail the great moments of his Parisian glory. Everywhere he went he was astonished

---

[30] *Congrès de Genève*, Report addressed to the Federal Council by Messrs Dufour, Moynier and Lehmann (Geneva: Fick, 1864), 6.

to meet 'civility, urbanity and the greatest kindness towards a simple Genevan, who was still too stilted and awkward himself'.[31] The most heavily locked doors opened to him one after the other that winter until he was eventually awarded France's highest distinction – the Legion of Honour.[32]

Even Marshal Randon, the man so obstinately deaf to Dunant's early work in Algeria, would soften for his 'Work', although not for its apostle. The same man who'd read *A Memory of Solferino* and claimed it was 'a book written against France'[33] ended up accepting the title of honorary chairman of the future French Soldiers' Aid Society . . . although not without a last dig at its founder. In February 1865, a month before the French society was officially founded, the provisory committee formed the previous year brought a delegation to the Ministry of War to thank it for its support. The old marshal, with a cruel malice, pretended to ignore Dunant's presence in the assembly, and launched the following diatribe towards the Duke of Fezensac: 'I believe you have nothing in common with these people in Geneva who meddle in matters which do not concern them.' Then, without paying any attention to the embarrassed glances of his listeners, continued to malign 'that Mr Dunant, a Swiss, who permitted himself to criticize the French Administration'![34] The members of the assembly probably kept their gazes on their shoelaces while Dunant stood in silent mortification.

Bursting the bubble he'd been constructing over the last six months, this incident affected him profoundly. But – a clear sign of his humiliation – there was not a word of it in the account of the episode he sent to Moynier right after. 'His Excellency the Marshal Randon received us well,' he reported cheerfully; 'he accepted our programme, he accepted the honorary presidency.'[35] He even allowed them to choose which generals they wished to become part of the committee of the future Aid Society. What else could they want? A tiny thorn amid the petals of his rose-strewn path wouldn't

---

[31] Dunant, *Mémoires*, 164.
[32] By a imperial decree of 18 January 1865, French National Archives, File LH /849/51, available on: http://www2.culture.gouv.fr/LH/LH056/PG/FRDAFAN83_OL0849051v001.htm.
[33] Maurice Dunant (ed.), *Les débuts de la Croix-Rouge en France*, 30.
[34] Dunant, *Mémoires*, 177.
[35] Dunant to Moynier, 18 February 1865, AICRC, A AF, 20,1-059.

dampen Dunant's optimism. Taking over for the provisory committee of 1864, the French Soldiers' Aid Society was formally established on 11th March 1865, again in one of the rooms of the Orleans railway company benevolently provided by François Bartholony. The new Society's Central Committee included a number of prestigious names, some of which would be found again, over the next few months, mixed up in Dunant's Algerian adventures. While this overlap was certainly not purely coincidental, it was also not the result of cold calculation either. In fact, Dunant's active snobbery provides him with his best excuse. His obsessive quest for approval from renowned figures, and from the nobility in particular, came, first, from his own social ambition and, secondly, from a conviction that only these great names could help him get the red cross emblem into France. That this snobbery led him to use his philanthropic relationships to also serve his financial affairs is beyond any doubt. Dunant was naturally attracted by great people, and he needed them.

March 1865 saw Dunant's philanthropic-financial connections becoming increasingly intertwined. At the same time that the French Soldiers' Aid Society was being created with, among others, the Franco-Genevan banker Théodore Vernes and General de Chabaud-Latour, Dunant was establishing a large holding company with, among other founders, the Franco-Genevan banker Théodore Vernes and General de Chabaud-Latour! Ambitiously named *L'Omnium Algérien* (The Algerian Omnium), the future company was meant to 'promote the development of industry, commerce and agriculture in Algeria'.[36] The shareholders included names often cited in Dunant's business affairs: along with the two Parisian associates were Thomas Mac-Culloch, already on the board of the Mons-Djemila Mills company, and the Count of Angeville, whom we will meet later.

The Algerian Omnium was designed to save, even *had* to save, the Mons-Djemila Mills whose windmills had decidedly lost all their wind. In terms of the aid societies, Dunant could now breathe a little easier; Moynier was in complete control of the International Committee, and the French Soldiers' Aid Society was up and running in Paris. Finally, Dunant could put all his energy into this new project

---

[36] Statute of the *Omnium Algérien*, 3, quoted by Pous, *Dunant l'Algérien*, 122.

and its impending deadlines. Indeed, the French emperor was due to visit Algeria in May to evaluate the tense situation his new governor general had recently reported. This new governor was none other than the Duke of Magenta, the Marshal Mac-Mahon who'd briefly received Dunant in Borghetto, several days after the Battle of Solferino. Contrary to Randon, Marshal Mac-Mahon was naturally more friendly and held a certain respect for the founder of the Red Cross; enough to invite him to the ball he was planning in Algiers in honour of the sovereign's arrival on 9th May. Never before had such an easy opportunity to meet the emperor presented itself to Dunant. A chance to explain everything to him, to convince him in favour of his windmills and, more than anything, to talk up his new project: he needed the emperor's blessing, he needed the emperor's sceptre pointed at his Algerian Omnium. Throwing his best clothing into his trunk, Dunant was off yet again to Algeria.

That 1865 spring crossing from Marseilles to Algiers featured none of the worries that had plagued his previous travels. He was no longer expecting any miracles from his associate Nick, whom he should have been wary of for a long time; he was no longer waiting on the Algerian administration, who had transformed his patience into resignation; and it was too early to hope for any financial windfalls from his forest of cork trees, whose profitability would take years. No. This time his sails were billowing with the intuition of an impending victory, with the certainty that the wind would finally turn because of the emperor's infallibility, the certainty that His Excellency would be able to distinguish – from among all the projects paraded before him – that Dunant's Algerian Omnium would be the one best suited to His Majesty's plans for Algeria. This time Dunant felt it, knew it, was already savouring it. In any case, he was far from suspecting that this would be his last crossing to Algeria.

As soon as Napoleon III arrived in Algiers, the sovereign's words were on everyone's lips. In response to the mayor's welcoming speech, the emperor had announced that an agreement was being prepared with a 'powerful company' to 'accomplish great things or continue advancing great things already undertaken'[37] in Algeria, bolstered directly by a huge loan for the country and another one for its colonization.

---

[37] René de Saint-Félix, *Le voyage de S.M. l'Empereur Napoléon III en Algérie et la régence de S.M. l'Impératrice, mai-juin 1865* (Paris: Eug. Pick, 1865), 207.

Dunant believed he could see his star rising again in these very words. He had just received the Legion of Honour; the governor general of Algeria had invited him to his reception; the General de Chabaud-Latour, senior commander of engineering in Algeria, was one of his Omnium associates, and the emperor's dear General Dufour was a shareholder of the Mons-Djemila Mills. Everything would come into play that very week in Algiers, as long as he could obtain a private audience: he absolutely had to speak to the emperor in person.

The evening of the ball arrived at last. The summer palace of the governors general of Algeria was situated on the Mustapha hillside, with the Bay of Algiers lapping at its feet. There was nothing imposing about the building itself, but its mosaics and delicately sculpted white marble Moorish motifs, its orchards of orange trees, sparkling fountains, terraced verandas and free-roaming gazelles all transported the European guests into an oriental fairy tale. Mingling among the military uniforms, rich Arab costumes and crinoline dresses, Henry felt the magic of the place and the moment. He was back in a country he loved, it was 9th May, the weather was fine and Algiers's purple-blue sky was sparkling with lights from the hillside all the way down to the port where a multitude of vessels decorated in honour of the sovereign added their Bonapartist fervour to his own.

As the famous author of *A Memory of Solferino*, Dunant would have wandered among the other guests responding to greetings and compliments, smiles and nods. He moved from group to group; this was his world: aristocratic and international, European and oriental, political and military, humanitarian and financial – he was feeling quite at home. That evening he found himself thinking back on the path he had travelled, from his small clerk's job at Lullin & Sautter to the man of the Geneva Convention, at the height of his celebrity.

Napoleon III made his entrance around 10:00 p.m. A display of fireworks suddenly erupted from the emperor's fort, the city's rejoicing could be heard all the way at the palace. A mind-blowing supper followed: tortoise soup, porcupine garnished with antelope liver; galantine of gazelle, Bustard cakes, wild boar and ostrich filets; minced deub, a delicate lizard from the south; and finally, Arab desserts with extraordinary names – onidax, macroûdes, scerakborach, oribias.[38]

---

[38] Saint-Félix, *Le voyage de S.M. l'Empereur*, 125–8.

Madame Mac-Mahon was a perfect hostess and spoke with everyone, including Dunant 'at length' (in his estimation) about aid to wounded soldiers. 'I am one of your disciples, Mr Dunant,'[39] she reportedly declared. The discussion with Napoleon III, apparently briefer, seems to have also focused on the success of the institution he had protected. In the paragraph from his *Mémoires* dedicated to this meeting, Dunant says nothing – not a word about boasting the merits of his Algerian Omnium to the emperor, nor requesting one, two or three additional waterfalls.

Did he find an elegant way in that conversation to move from the necessary aid for wounded soldiers ... to the necessary aid for imperilled colonials? It seems he didn't need to. In unpublished notes classified as a 'Financial file', Dunant claims to have been received in 'private audience in Algiers' by the emperor, who guaranteed his 'special protection' to a larger company, if one was about to be set up in Geneva, the emperor going so far as to affirm: 'Your new Company will be protected by my government.'[40] But the emperor's account of this meeting is quite different, as he wrote to his friend General Dufour:

> Mr. Dunant does not seem to have brought clear and precise projects. It isn't enough to build castles in the air and then refurbish them. One must show the practical methods for a company to prosper and succeed. I will grant him any desirable protection, but once again he must know what he wants.[41]

These differing interpretations make it easy to imagine Dunant's shock, ten days later, when he received word that the French government had signed an agreement with Louis Frémy, governor of France's *Crédit Foncier* bank, and Paulin Talabot, chief executive of the private railway company, *Paris-Lyon-Méditerranée* (PLM). The objective of this agreement was the rapid formation of a large new company, the *Société Générale Algérienne*.

Clearly, Dunant's Omnium was not the emperor's preferred company and was now being threatened before it had even really

---

[39] Dunant, *Mémoires*, 181.
[40] BGE, 'Financial File', Ms. fr. 2116 G, f. 39 and 80.
[41] Napoleon III to Dufour, 7 May 1865, BGE, Ms. Dufour 166, env. 7.

got off the ground. With this agreement the *Société Générale* would take over entirely: according to the programme defined by Napoleon III, it would spend 100 million francs to modernize the country's agriculture and industry, and through loans of another 100 million francs enable the state to undertake large infrastructure projects. Faced with this news, Dunant had one hope left: to have his company absorbed into the *Société Générale* and get himself onto the board of directors in any way he could.

It was obvious the emperor was in a hurry to get his new company up and running, and so Dunant needed to find a position as quickly as possible. Before even returning from Algeria, he urged his Omnium associates, Théodore Vernes and Chabaud-Latour, to sing his praises to Mr Talabot.[42] Not wanting to leave anything to chance this time, Dunant also went to his friends from the French Aid Society, Bartholony and Baron Rothschild, to help champion his cause with Frémy and Talabot; and finally, yet again, to General Dufour, as a last resort, when he began to feel the cord tightening around his neck.

A new vein

It wasn't like Dunant, however, to chase a single rabbit at a time. While attempting to move both heaven and earth to introduce himself into Frémy and Talabot's imminent *Société Générale Algérienne*, he believed he was making the deal of a lifetime in acquiring a marble quarry located in east Algeria, which, following the defection of two insolvent buyers, was being offered to him for the modest sum – or what he thought was modest – of 98,000 francs. The sale was undertaken in equal shares with his old accomplice Nick who had no more money than Dunant to invest in the running of a quarry, the extraction of marble being notoriously difficult and costly. But this probably wasn't their intention. It was more likely they were planning from the outset to resell the quarry as soon as they'd purchased it, pocketing a nice profit in the transaction.

This new investment was another of Dunant's many endeavours to meet his engagements and lessen his debts. Following his initial

---

[42] BGE, Ms. fr. 2116 G, f. 134–5.

difficulties with the Mons-Djemila Mills, he'd shifted his hopes first towards an increase of the company's capital (in vain) and then onto a silver lead mine (a disaster), which was followed by two of Nick's brilliant ideas, speculating on the wheat from their own mills and setting up a cattle farm, and, finally, onto the Akfadou forest of cork oak, which had been just as devastating in terms of investments as it had been in bribes, according to its buyer. And between each venture, to catch up with the previous one and enable the next, Dunant borrowed. In Geneva, in Paris, from family, from banks, from friends, from philanthropic connections, for his own business or in the name of his company, against the house in Puits-Saint-Pierre, against the windmills, against the good name of his company shareholders, with the guarantee of this or that person, and more than anything – more than anything – with the certainty that each new deal would put things right. But now he had no more time to watch oak trees grow or wait for the concession of another waterfall. He needed money and he needed it yesterday: though his investors were mostly family and friends, the shareholders of the Mons-Djemila Mills still expected their annual 10 per cent of the profits.[43]

Up to this point, Dunant seems to have 'made things work' – using methods that were perhaps not exactly standard, but which kept his stockholders happy enough until the next deadline. Recently, he had even started speculating heavily on the stock market. But each month saw him with less and less room to manoeuvre, and the purchase of the Felfela quarry looks very much like a double or nothing, a desperate gambler's final chip cast onto the table.

The emperor had left Algeria, the quarry was purchased. By June, Dunant was employed more usefully in Paris where his connections within the French Soldiers' Aid Society could help him acquire his much-coveted board-member position in the *Société Générale*. On 25th June 1865, his star seemed to be shining bright again when, for the second time in two months, the gaze of Napoleon III briefly rested on him once more. Oh, this was nothing at all like the 'special audience' he claims to have had in Algiers. Although his memoirs definitely mention a new 'special audience', this time at the Tuileries Palace, it was via delegation of the Aid Society committee – with the Duke de Fezensac, General Chabaud-

---

[43] Pous, *Dunant l'Algérien*, 124–6.

Latour, Théodore Vernes, Count Sérurier and a few others. It would
not do to mention his small worries to the emperor at this time – no,
not at all. The subject of the day was the 1867 Universal Exhibition
in Paris, which would include a prominent position for the French
Aid Society as well as other Red Cross societies from around the
world. Dunant was looking eagerly forward to the event, assured of
his success: if the pavilion was looking to honour someone, who
else might it honour if not him?

But an unexpected event tempered Dunant's pride that summer
in Paris. In July 1865, the newspaper *L'Opinion nationale* published
an open letter from the famous writer George Sand to a certain
Henri Arrault, which began thus:

> My dear friend, I congratulate you on the measure which has just
> been proposed in Geneva [. . .] concerning the neutrality of field
> hospitals. This is a great thing, a noble idea, and you are its
> source [. . .][44]

George Sand continued on to assert that the articles of the
International Convention adopted in Geneva were 'an almost literal
repetition' of the articles drafted by this Mr Arrault, and that it was
'strange that Mr Dunant of Geneva, who had the excellent wit to
make himself the champion' of his plan, had 'unhappily assumed
the initiative for himself'.

It goes without saying that the International Committee was
flabbergasted, and Dunant most of all. He published a long response
on 7th August in the same newspaper in which he claimed his good
faith: he did not know of Mr Arrault's publication, nor of that by
Dr Palasciano either, an Italian who came out shortly after Sand's
letter as saying that he, too, had been plagiarized.

After this episode, Dunant would tend to honour his overlooked
predecessors; but he still always considered himself to be the sole
founder, initiator and inventor of the principle of neutrality. At the
end of the summer of 1865, the Red Cross was not, however,
Dunant's priority – he needed to resell his Felfela quarry, and it
wasn't in Paris he would find a buyer.

---

[44] *L'opinion nationale*, 25 July 1865, cited by J. des Cilleuls, '*Un des précurseurs de
la Convention de Genève de 1864 : le pharmacien Henri Arrault*', *Revue d'Histoire
de la Pharmacie*, December 1948, 357.

Troubles ahead

The heaven-sent buyer of the Felfela quarry would be none other than Dunant himself, in part. It was already autumn in Geneva when the board of directors of a newly established financial company, the *Crédit Genevois*, listened to one of its members present a deal that was not to be missed.

The young bank had been founded two years earlier and its goal was to 'get Geneva directly involved in greater European business affairs and form one of the links in a chain of financial establishments currently monopolizing big business'.[45] In terms of big business, their first steps were a bit wheezy: fixed by their statutes at 25 million, the company's starting capital did not meet its required minimum. The board members all scrambled for various ways to artificially inflate their share prices and, at the same time, they launched into oil and railways, suffering considerable losses. Their record was pretty much on par, in terms of financial daring, with the entrepreneurial dealmaker they'd welcomed onto their board of directors and who was about to offer them an enticing bargain.

Dunant had not come into this hornets' nest by accident. At the time, the chair of the *Crédit Genevois* board of directors was the Count of Angeville, one of the first to support the creation of the Algerian Omnium. Neither he nor Dunant were one of the founding shareholders of the *Crédit Genevois*, but they both belonged to its board at the time they offered the other members the possibility of buying the Felfela quarry.

The terms of the purchase were simple: 'Mssrs d'Angeville, Dunant and Pictet make the following proposal to the board: Mssrs Dunant and Nick possess a marble quarry in Felfela (Algeria) which cost them 400,000 francs.'[46] The speculative interest of the deal, Dunant continued to explain, came from the imminent repurchase of the quarry by the Algerian Omnium, which would soon be established under the aegis of the *Société Générale Algérienne*. The Omnium would buy the quarry at 500,000 francs through a package of its own shares, leaving a profit of 100,000 francs to be

---

[45] Pous, *Dunant l'Algérien*, 134. We mainly follow Pous for the whole story of the *Crédit Genevois*.
[46] Ibid., 140.

divided by the *Crédit Genevois* board of directors – including him – and the actual owners of the quarry – himself and his associate Nick.

What splendid reserves of trust Dunant must have had in his circles to successfully sell something for 400,000 francs on the idea that it would be bought later by a company that hardly yet existed.[47] But Dunant was, in fact, incredibly famous in Geneva in the wake of the success of the 1863 Conference – he seemed to be so familiar with the greats of the world, all the way up to the emperor and his ministers, that, as the other swindled board members would later say, '[we] had every right to believe him capable of achieving just such a deal as the Felfela bargain.'[48]

Indeed, the other board members believed him so unreservedly that they agreed to reimburse Dunant before the end of the year for the 200,000 francs he claimed to have 'already paid' to buy the quarry.

Four hundred thousand francs as the sale price of the quarry? Two hundred thousand 'already paid'?

These figures were far from the 100,000 francs that Dunant and Nick had actually paid out several months earlier. But Dunant would later say that the first liar was Nick, who had largely inflated the actual sale price at the time he told Dunant of the deal.

As for the 400,000 francs cited to the board of directors, Dunant would later explain that this included the costs of significant construction work already undertaken for a road, a pier, buildings, a blacksmith, housing for the workers, etc. Although it might be possible to justify this estimation of the quarry's value, Dunant did lie about the original sale price. This was the lie that would prove fatal for him, along with the revelation that the Omnium was a far less real company than he had made it seem. At this moment, though, he still had good reason to believe that his utopias could become realities; he'd seen it happen. But maybe philanthropy and business were just too different to be played the same way. Dunant would soon learn, as we know, and it would cost him dearly.

---

[47] Or even 'did not exist', according to the verdict delivered on 17 August 1868, *Journal de Genève*, 23 August 1868; *Journal des Tribunaux Vaudois*, 35, 5 September 1868, 561.

[48] 'Answer of some administrators to a Memo about the *Crédit genevois*', cited by Pous, *Dunant l'Algérien*, 141.

For now, the clock was ticking. In light of the scenario he'd just handed the board of the *Crédit Genevois*, it was no longer just desirable but imperative that he be nominated to the board of the future *Société Générale Algérienne*, without which his own company would die before even being born. In the week following the board meeting at the *Crédit Genevois*, he couldn't just sit twiddling his thumbs in Geneva. He left for Paris, where everything would come into play. But the news that he picked up here and there in Paris panicked him more than anything. The hope he'd been harbouring since March was gradually turning into an unbearable anxiety.

He would think about it, then push the thought out of his head. But it would come back to worry him in the night. On the morning of the ninth day, he gave in. It was still cold in his room; this was 20th November 1865. He picked up his pen:

Dear General,
   I am currently in Paris and very busy with our Algerian affairs. I need to first tell you that all is going well. I've just received news of something that engages me to request your good will.[49]

The news was that the emperor, wanting to speed things up, was planning to establish Messrs Frémy and Talabot's large Algerian company within the next fifteen days.

'I have high hopes that I shall be included,' he continued, citing three names in support of his candidacy: Rothschild, Chabaud-Latour and Bartholony. But there were so many conspiracies! And the emperor had 'so many things in mind!'

The general probably didn't need to read to the end of the letter to guess where it was going:

And so I am writing to request you, my very dear sir, to be kind enough to write directly to the emperor for this matter so that HM might deem to mention my name to Mr Frémy as soon as possible. I believe that the entire future of our small Mons-Djemila Mills company will be directly impacted by my nomination to the board of the *Société Générale* established by Messrs Talabot and Frémy.

---

[49] Dunant to Dufour, 20 November 1865, BGE, Ms. Dufour 166, env. 8.

Once again Dufour did as requested: he wrote to the emperor in favour of his protégé. Although Dufour's letter has been lost, we have its reply: on 15th December, Napoleon III wrote that he was willing to think Mr Dunant 'could be very useful as a board member' within the future colonial business; but since, he hastily added, it was not up to him to hire all personnel, he only promised Dufour that he would speak to Mr Frémy 'at the first opportunity'.

The definitive verdict would take a long time to come and, when it did, it was without appeal. On 10th May 1866, Napoleon III sent General Dufour the second volume of his *Histoire de Jules César* (History of Julius Caesar), a work that he had been passionately dedicated to for some years. In the closing of the letter that accompanied it, like a dashed-off postscript, there was one phrase – the final blow: 'I have not forgotten your recommendation; nevertheless, I believe Mr Talabot little disposed to admit your friend into the business.'[50]

The sun rises in the East

Failures may produce one of two inverse effects in those who experience them. Some may lower their ambitions each time they fail, others shift their hopes to a future project even greater than the first. These kinds of desperate optimists, well known in casinos the world over, increase their wager as they continue to lose. Dunant, on the eve of his impending disaster, was clearly one of them.

The beginning of 1866 saw Dunant erecting a new establishment that made his Omnium look like a neighbourhood deli. It was a kind of Byzantine assemblage of the East India Company, a colonial enterprise, a political movement and a religious crusade, entirely focused on Palestine. The project was titled the *Société internationale universelle pour la Rénovation de l'Orient* (International Universal Society for the Invigoration of the East). Among its stated goals was helping pauper Jews move to Palestine, the restoration of the Holy

---

[50] Napoleon III to Dufour, 15 December 1865 and 10 May 1866, BGE, Ms. Dufour 166, env. 8. Henri Nick was luckier than Dunant as he would be hired later by the *Société Générale*, a bank co-founded by the same Paulin Talabot. See Humbert, *Failllite en Algérie*, 149ff.

Lands, the reconciliation of Arabs and Jews, but also the economic development of the region through massive investments, all of this behind the flame of His Majesty the Emperor Napoleon III, this 'genius of the century', this 'Imperial sun' who would 'light the way in all his splendour'. The eight-page brochure written by Henry Dunant involved the same mystical grandiloquence as his Restoration of the Empire of Charlemagne, which had been categorically refused by the emperor eight years earlier. But this time, it was a colonial plan with clear operating instructions, however difficult to achieve:

> To attain such a lofty goal and the success of something seemingly so difficult, one of the first conditions should be to make the East a neutral zone, through the creation of a great Eastern company placed under the patronage of the head of the French nation and endowed with a capital of 500 or 600 million, raised from the Jews scattered around the world and who possess immense riches, as well as from the great fortuned families of Europe and America.[51]

Beyond Zionist visions, there were financial goals: investors should be able to expect 'considerable and certainly far more lucrative results than those they are able to obtain in the west'.[52] When presenting Dunant's project in August 1866, the *Scattered Nation* showed no delusion about this forthcoming 'Eastern International Society': 'Although designed on so vast and comprehensive a scale, it appears to be a commercial undertaking, promoted chiefly with a view to material profit. We do not anticipate that the "resurrection of the East" will be attained by such means.'[53]

Of all his projects, the invigoration of the East would be both his most ambitious and his least successful. Perhaps Dunant had taken his audience's enthusiasm a little too personally the previous winter in Paris when he'd presented his work to the Universal Israelites

---

[51] *Société internationale universelle pour la Rénovation de l'Orient*, cited by Alexis François, *Aspects d'Henry Dunant* (Geneva: Georg, 1948), 45.
[52] *Société internationale universelle pour la Rénovation de l'Orient*, cited by Pous, *Dunant l'Algérien*, 130.
[53] 'Scheme for the Invigoration of the East', *The Scattered Nation*, 1 August 1866, C. Schwarz (ed.), vol. 1 (London: Morgan and Chase, 1866), 195–6.

Alliance. Indeed, no one came forward from among his new wealthy Jewish connections to support his colonial dream in Palestine. Ever tenacious, Dunant would take a long time to abandon his mirage; but this wouldn't be enough to save it.[54]

Several weeks later, rumours were circulating in Geneva about the Mons-Djemila Mills company's 'very difficult'[55] financial situation, so much so that Count Sautter de Beauregard, still head of the Geneva Company, instructed his on-site director to no longer deal with Henri Nick. As for Dunant, he seemed unaware of the emperor's response to his friend Dufour since he was still knocking at every possible door that might help him obtain a position within Frémy and Talabot's company, all while the shareholders of the *Crédit Genevois* were waiting for the repurchase of the Felfela quarry. This was when he would attempt a new pivot.

The summer of 1866 saw Dunant gathering his most faithful supporters and companions for a lightning-fast relaunch of the aborted Algerian Omnium, this time with a new structure and a new name. The statutes were registered in July and the company baptized on 18th September 1866, with a name seemingly chosen to create confusion with other existing entities: the new company would be called the *Compagnie Algérienne*. Dunant claimed the directorship, Nick was a member of the board, along with Dunant's brother Daniel and their uncle Daniel Colladon; the two accomplices of the *Crédit Genevois*, Alexandre Pictet and the Count d'Angeville; board members or shareholders of the Mons-Djemila Mills, Thomas Mac-Culloch, Colonel Pierre-Charles Trembley, Henri de Saussure; long-time friends, Théodore Necker and Ernest de Traz; and, finally, a few necessary notables, a professor, a lawyer and several committee members from the Genevan and Parisian Soldiers' Aid Societies.

What did all these men want from another company like this? Pretty much the same thing, but with varying degrees. To get their money back, save the Mons-Djemila Mills by seeing it absorbed into a healthier and larger company, keep Dunant from drowning and to avoid drowning with him, or, at the very least, avoid getting their feet wet.

---

[54] For a detailed account of Dunant's project in the East, see Jacques Pous, *Henry Dunant, colon affairiste en Algérie pionnier du sionisme* (Paris: L'Harmattan, 2020).
[55] Count Sautter de Beauregard, 30 May 1866, cited by Pous, *Dunant l'Algérien*, 129.

So that the new company could be established, the statutes set a
required capital fund of 'half of the 20,000 shares of the first
series'.[56] This minimum threshold would never be reached; nothing
could save Dunant and his mills – not the Algerian Omnium, not
the Invigoration of the East, and not his final desperate move, the
Compagnie Algérienne.

Prussian honours

Far too preoccupied by his financial woes, Dunant was barely
following the war that had erupted in June 1866 between Prussia
and Austria. But in September 1866, Queen Augusta of Prussia
invited Dunant to take part in the festivities given for the return of
her victorious troops.

Considering how prominent and emotional this episode is in
Dunant's memoirs,[57] his trip to Berlin granted him one of his life's
last real experiences of narcissistic joy. Chaperoned upon his arrival
by a high-powered guide, Count Otto de Stollberg-Wernigerode,
Dunant was immediately buoyed along by the elation of a city not
only paved in Prussian colours but also draped in the international
flag of wounded soldiers, 'his' flag. The weather was magnificent;
the Count led him quickly to the grand plaza of the castle, inviting
him to sit alongside the Knights Hospitaller next to the royal
pavilion. Everywhere he went, Dunant could see the red cross on its
white background floating in the sky above the rooftops, on the
arms of the knights seated beside him. Even the single voluntary aid
worker who suddenly appeared in the middle of the parade, limping
from a bullet taken while on mission in Bohemia, was wearing the
white and red armband, as were the two soldiers holding him up as
best they could. Dunant had tears in his eyes. For a few days he
could forget all about his mills and the Omnium, about Mr Frémy
and Mr Talabot, the dukes and the counts, his debts and accounts
– he was in Prussia, and Prussia was celebrating him while
celebrating its victorious troops.

---

[56] Art. 7, Title II of the '*Statuts de la Compagnie algérienne*', *Recueil authentique des
lois et actes du gouvernement de Genève*, vol. 52, 1866 (Geneva: Vaney, 1867), 330.
[57] Dunant, *Mémoires*, ch. 22; Dunant to his mother, 23 and 26 September 1866,
BGE, Paul Dunant Archives.

As if in a daydream, the honours followed one after the other. He was invited that first evening 'to a monstrous gala supper' at which he would have been seated at the royal table if he hadn't gone 'and made himself very small', as he tells us so charmingly, at the very back of the last room in a series of rooms. His chaperone found him there at the end of the evening to inform him that his place had been set in the room with the king and princes. From that moment on, the Count remained at his side, leading him to the palace reception and presenting him to the entire court, including the royal family who welcomed him with oohs and aahs! Only Bismarck, from his grand height of 1.88 metres, remained silent and withdrawn. He looked at him solidly – 'questioningly' as Dunant would say – as if the minister had been shocked to see so many honours heaped upon a man dressed 'in a simple black suit'. What extreme bliss for Dunant the commoner to be distinguished by kings! He sipped drunkenly from this experience for several days, perhaps aware this would never happen again.

Queen Augusta seemed more devoted than anyone else. Throughout the entire supper, she wore the red cross band, claiming she had kept it on for the entire war. Later that evening she summoned the philanthropist to a private audience, to tell him how much *A Memory of Solferino* had moved her. She'd handed the book to her husband, William I, who upon reading it had firmly decided to make 'this work a success'.

That evening when Dunant returned to his room at the Hotel Saint Petersburg, Unter den Linden, he was clutching a small alabaster statue representing the Archangel Michael, upon whose chest the queen had had a red cross painted. 'I would like you to place this on your working table, as a memory of me,' she'd said as he was leaving.

The next morning Dunant left for Potsdam, where the Dowager Queen Elizabeth, widow of King Frederick William IV, had invited him to visit the Sanssouci Palace. Dunant arrived late – indeed this was not the first time he'd made a royal personage wait, a confession that belies a recurring shame – but this didn't prevent his royal hostess from welcoming him warmly upon her return from a walk. Other visits followed with princes and countesses who all wanted to show their devotion to the Geneva Convention. Dunant left Prussia feeling that the most beautiful fruits of his labour were to be found in this region, and that the values most closely aligned with his own were also to be found here, rather than in the 'Holy Roman Empire Reconstructed' that he'd been courting, flattering, laying siege to for the last ten years.

The winter race

The Sadowa victory warmed Dunant with the last fires of his glory and his honourability. The months that followed would reveal a hunted man seeking any means of salvation. The tour began with Prince Jerome Napoleon, the emperor's cousin, who'd previously hosted Dunant at his lovely lakeside home near Geneva. Considering this imperial cousin's notorious fiasco as Minister of Algeria between 1858 and 1859, Dunant's approach could not be more inadequate, and inevitably led to failure: 'I keep myself very distant from any industrial business,' the prince responded on 13th November; 'and especially, you must understand, those in Algeria, since I was once in charge of managing this colony.' The rest of the letter makes it clear that Dunant solicited help both for his mills and for his board-member position: '[A]s for the rest, I do not know about all the other business in which you have an interest, and I have no influence on the company which you have spoken to me about.'[58]

The end of the year was approaching; Dunant was in hot water. The Felfela quarry had been sold to the *Crédit Genevois* and his board had given him the promised 200,000 francs, but in return, they had seen no repurchase offer from any kind of Algerian *Société, compagnie* or Omnium. The day after Christmas, the board of directors required the provisory delivery of 2,000 shares of the *Compagnie Algérienne*. The shares were definitely sent at the beginning of January 1867, even if everybody was aware that the company in question still only existed on paper at that point. Confidence in Dunant was slipping further every day, while the man himself stubbornly continued to chase after a seat on the board of his French rival, which he seemed to consider his only way out. Had he still not heard – or was he ignoring – the discouraging response the emperor had given Dufour several months earlier?

---

[58] Jérôme Napoléon to Dunant, 13 November 1866, BGE, Ms. fr. 2109, f. 292.

It wasn't enough that he'd already tried in vain via the general, it wasn't enough that he'd recently addressed the emperor's cousin Jerome, Dunant finally decided to strike his last match and write directly to the emperor himself. In a long letter[59] which betrayed his state of panic, he listed his past misfortunes to His Majesty, and reminded him of the 'warm reception' that he had granted him in Algiers. Relaying the facts in such a way as to make himself the victim, the chief executive of the newly founded *Compagnie Algérienne* dared to complain at having suffered from the 'simultaneous establishment of the *Société Générale Algérienne*', a little like the untimely appearance of an unfair competitor. Hence the need, quite logical according to Dunant, to prove to the public 'there was no antagonism between the two companies'. And what method did he devise to banish this unfortunate impression? To name Mr Dunant to the board of directors of Mr Frémy's *Société Algérienne*, as had been suggested by General Dufour to His Majesty, sometime before.

Again, he did not have to wait long for a response. By return mail, the emperor's office declared itself 'completely divested' of this matter, by virtue of the fact that it had promptly transmitted the request to Mr Frémy.[60]

After the *Account on the Regency in Tunis*, the *Restoration of the Empire of Charlemagne*, his *Mémorandum* on the Mons-Djemila Mills, *A Memory of Solferino*, the reprint of his *Notice* on slavery, and finally the *Invigoration of the East* – not to mention all intermediary correspondence – one might think His Majesty had probably had enough of Henry Dunant's postal assaults. But this would ignore the deaf stubbornness of a man who felt the threat of imminent bankruptcy. The Tuileries had literally just slammed the door in his face and yet he felt he'd been given some new hope. He unburdened himself to François Bartholony, the chief executive of the Orleans railway company to whom he had requested assistance and hospitality numerous times for his business affairs, as well as for the Soldiers' Aid Society. But was this man's counsel always wise? He was the one who'd suggested Dunant create his

---

[59] Dunant to Napoleon III, 21 January 1867, BGE, from Institut Henry Dunant Archives.

[60] The Emperor's Cabinet to Dunant, 25 January 1867, BGE, from Institut Henry Dunant Archives.

'small Algerian company', with strong French participation and, if not its headquarters in Paris, at least a Parisian branch office. Dunant had obediently followed these instructions. Right after the *Compagnie Algérienne* was created in Geneva, about ten French notables had been added. He now told Bartholony he was 'set up in Paris, with an office and an apartment on Rue de la Paix, 24'.[61] He even established a permanent vice director; what more could he do to win the favour of Mr Frémy and Mr Talabot?

'At this current time,' he wrote to Bartholony, 'I hope Mr Frémy will have no more bias against me.' He was still so full of hope! Eight days later, on 8th February, he wrote to him again, persistent in his blindness: 'Only you, my dear sir, can do something for me with Mr Frémy.' To hell with politeness, Dunant now laid all his cards on the table:

> [. . .] The question of money is henceforth secondary, this is now a question of credit and honour for me, and a question of honour, not only for myself, but also for my family. I need to be justified and to be held up in the world's opinion and in the consideration of my friends. I am now addressing myself to your goodwill so that you might render me this personal service. You are holding my future and my honour in your hands. I'm begging you to deal with this request in the way I am asking you [. . .] Please save, I beg you, a fellow countryman who trusts you and your generosity.[62]

The letter continues in the same tone; a third letter followed the next day. But it was already too late. Several days later, the game was up, there was nothing anyone could do.

The *Crédit Genevois* entered liquidation on 25th February 1867. It carried Dunant away in its wake.

---

[61] Dunant to Bartholony, 31 January 1867, BGE, from Institut Henry Dunant Archives.
[62] Dunant to Bartholony, 8 and 9 February 1867, BGE, from Institut Henry Dunant Archives.

The bankruptcy

On 21st February 1867, four days before the general meeting of the shareholders of the *Crédit Genevois*, an agreement was discreetly passed between its board members and Dunant, cancelling the engagement taken on the Felfela quarry. 'As a guarantee', the bank would keep the 2,000 titles of the *Compagnie Algérienne*, while waiting for Dunant to reimburse the money he'd already received, a little more than 200,000 francs since the deal in November 1865. As the board members had got into the unfortunate habit of borrowing from their own tellers, Dunant owed an additional 50,000 francs to the bank – his total debt was approximately 250,000 francs.

With a little luck, the affair might have ended there. Dunant was able to resell the Felfela quarry several months later, not to the fragile Algerian Omnium, as was initially promised, and not either to his ghostly *Compagnie Algérienne*, as alleged afterwards, but to Mr Frémy and Mr Talabot, who, for the first time, responded positively to an offer from Mr Henry Dunant. Naturally, the two Frenchmen would take advantage of the seller's distress to secure a deal at the lowest price. And so Dunant received about 100,000 francs, enabling him to pay back only half the sum he owed the bank, an outcome that embittered him until the end of his days. The Dunant family, however, was ready to sacrifice everything to spare Henry the shame of bankruptcy. Perhaps he would have been able to find the rest – if only he'd been given enough time.

But things started moving very quickly. The minutes of the general meeting of 25th February 1867 report that the shareholders asked Henry to explain 'his participation in an affair that had been highly criticized'[63] – indubitably the sale of the quarry. Dunant justified himself as well as he could, but it wasn't enough for the shareholders. They voted that same day to dissolve and liquidate the *Crédit Genevois*, the inevitable conclusion of a controversy that, although it may not have directly concerned Dunant, would remain tainted by his recklessness.

---

[63] Minutes of the General Assembly of *Le Crédit Genevois*, 25 February 1867, cited by François, *Aspects d'Henry Dunant*, 85.

Of everything that happened with the *Crédit Genevois*, the most embarrassing was that this was only the tip of the iceberg of Dunant's calamitous situation. If he could not reimburse the amounts he owed, it was because he was already up to his eyeballs in debt for the Mons-Djemila Mills, which was seriously floundering and had been for quite some time. The same year that he purchased the Felfela quarry, 1865, Dunant had jointly guaranteed the borrowing of 300,000 francs from the *Crédit Lyonnais* with his associate and friend Thomas Mac-Culloch. And yet it turns out that this amount was used to pay fictional dividends to the Mons-Djemila Mills shareholders, while waiting for the Akfadou forest to become lucrative and finally provide some actual profits.

The liquidation of the *Crédit Genevois* was like a bomb, its shock wave crumbling the already shaky foundations of the Mons-Djemila Mills. Just a few days later, a haggard Dunant appeared before its beleaguered board members, furious shareholders and inflexible moneylenders.

What could he do? Climb onto the gallows himself? Or run away, in secret, as fast and as far as he could, with his tail between his legs?

He would choose the latter.

Dunant, a friend of the kings of Prussia and Saxony, of the princes and marshals of France, the venerated founder of the Geneva Convention, the universal promoter of the Societies of the Red Cross, the inspired leader of the Young Men's Christian Association; Jean-Henri Dunant ran away from his home town in May of 1867, a day forever marked for an entire family, even an entire city, with an infamy as outsized as the glory it eclipsed.

Henry Dunant had just turned 39 years old when he fled Geneva. He would never return.[64]

---

[64] In an unpublished note, many years later, Dunant would claim that he hadn't planned on fleeing for good from Geneva in May 1867, but that he had first been retained in Paris for business negotiations concerning the Felfela quarry, and afterwards had no money to get himself home. BGE, 2116 G, f. 26v and 35.

7

The Fall (1867–9)

Escape to Paris

Did Dunant leave directly for Paris, as he suggests in his *Mémoires*, or did he first hide out in his family home La Chèvrerie, in Ain, France, just 60 kilometres from Geneva? The latter idea is irresistible because La Chèvrerie, an austere fortified house nestled against the hillside in the middle of the vineyards, protected from view but with a beautiful extended vista, seems to have been built for the very purpose of giving shelter to a man on the run. There is no proof for such a theory, however; Dunant's memoirs only mention that his brother gave him enough money for the trip to Paris, and that he spent several months in a deep depression. The historical record of his movements begins again in June 1867 when the liquidators of the *Crédit Genevois* arrived for him in Paris. They had him sign an agreement promising to reimburse his debts as soon as possible.

Around the same time, the Mons-Djemila Mills Company was taken over by some of its former shareholders; the company attempted to get back on its feet as best it could. The board of directors was not planning, though, to let their former director get off scot-free for the risks and irregularities he had committed. Henry was thus obliged, along with his brother Daniel, to renounce any receivables and any recourse, in exchange for their silence. Dunant's parents would also give up all rights and all shares in the Mons-Djemila Mills provided that Henry would be 'neither harassed nor pursued for the mismanagement that he had committed as board member, director or authorized proxy for the company'.[1] And so, in

---

[1] BGE, Ms. fr. 2116 G, f. 110v–111.

the hope of avoiding the shame of a trial or bankruptcy, the Dunant family abandoned all of its assets in Algeria, leaving behind more than 60,000 francs' worth of shares. Henry was completely ruined, his brother Daniel lost the majority of his assets, his friends saw their savings wiped out.

Henry's family would later obtain, with the assistance of the Mons-Djemila board of directors, a friendly settlement of the *Crédit Lyonnais* debt, as the company preferred to forgive some of it rather than seize assets in Algeria that they didn't know what to do with. Unfortunately, Dunant would not be able to reimburse the co-signer of that huge *Crédit Lyonnais* loan, his friend Thomas Mac-Culloch; the very mention of this name would burn him with shame whenever the subject of his bankruptcy came up.

But Mac-Culloch was not his only source of remorse, far from it. Dunant bore the responsibility for considerable losses of numerous friends who had been pulled into his deals, or from whom he had borrowed money, ranging from several thousand francs to more than 100,000. Unable to ever repay them, Dunant would be hounded by this for his entire life ... up until the moment when he would win a very substantial award. But by then, he would be so turned against Geneva, he would do anything to avoiding tossing it a single penny.

The Universal Exhibition

Although Genevan scorn may have sent him running in that spring of 1867, Paris seemed relatively free from rumours of the scandal. Dunant wrote to his friend and associate Henri de Saussure that he was quite convinced his 'moral position acquired in Europe by working in favour of wounded soldiers gave [him] an area of activity and some resources'.[2]

Resources, perhaps not, but activity, yes! The second Universal Exhibition had opened in Paris on 1st April and the Aid Societies were wholly invested in the event. Just beside the Krupp display with their 50-ton cannon was a 700-square-metre pavilion housing a kind of after-sales service, so to speak, for their neighbour

---

[2] Dunant to Saussure, 18 July 1867, BGE, Ms. fr. 2116 G, f. 131–2.

exhibitor – the objects, devices and inventions meant to provide aid for wounded soldiers. All the national Soldiers' Aid Societies had been invited to contribute to the collection; very quickly, the huge tent on loan from the French military was too small for the various stretchers, aid tents and other mobile medical units arriving from all corners of the world. Dunant, who had been interested in this adventure from the beginning – as early as January, he'd asked Moynier for 'some kind of rescue boat, as beautiful as possible'[3] – very quickly rediscovered his zeal as honorary vice chairman of the central committee for the French Aid Society. He happily accompanied Chairman Fezensac on his visits to the different ministers and friends of the emperor. Furthermore, he was named vice chairman of the commission in charge of the Aid Society pavilion at the fair, which brought him back with the dukes, counts and barons of the French Red Cross.[4] For the time being, nothing seemed to threaten his Parisian prestige.

But Gustave Moynier was taking notes. During his first visit to the Universal Exhibition, he must have been quite surprised to discover the garlanded bust of Henry Dunant set onto an arched cornice above the boats, stretchers and medical kits! For Moynier, this honour must have appeared even more misplaced because the scandal with the *Crédit Genevois* was still heating up. What would Genevan visitors to Paris think, discovering their notoriously bankrupted Dunant crowned in laurels? President Moynier's worries only increased in early June when he learned that one of the grand prizes of the fair was to be attributed to the International Committee of Geneva. In other circumstances he would have been delighted. But now he felt only the urgency of getting rid of the organization's black sheep. On 12th June, he wrote a first letter to the Swiss commissary of the fair, Mr Feer-Herzog, who was also one of the jury members. After his requisite gratitude, he announced he would not be able to come and accept the award himself and

---

[3] Dunant to Moynier, 17 January 1867, ACICR, A AF 20, 1-070.
[4] In the years that followed their founding, the regional or national Soldiers' Aid Societies were increasingly called 'Red Cross Societies' as demonstrated in the title of the journal launched in 1869 by the name of '*Bulletin international des Sociétés de la Croix-Rouge*' (International Bulletin of the Red Cross Societies). As we approach that time period, we do the same, making a distinction when necessary between a country's central committee and its various branches.

that 'in the absence of a special representative of the International Committee', he would be happy to have it sent to him through the mail. Then, attempting to outwit a man he knew wouldn't need to be asked twice to get up on a stage, he added conspiratorially:

> I must put you on guard, but in all confidentiality, against the *possible* intervention of Mr H. D. who has been secretary of the International Committee until now. We have very serious reasons for not wanting to be represented by this person. If, therefore, he offers himself to act in our name, I would be obliged to you to dissuade him, [which will] not be difficult, by simply mentioning that his presence is not needed.[5]

A second manoeuvre came two days later. Moynier wrote again, 'in the strictest confidence', to the treasurer of the fair commission to explain that the committee felt 'seriously that D. should not be included in any way and is no longer our representative, or authorized proxy, or even a colleague'.[6]

The cruelty of this initiative went far beyond even what Moynier could have imagined. Because the 'treasurer of the commission' to whom he was writing was none other than Dunant's former associate in the Algerian Omnium, Théodore Vernes, who had just been nominated to the position Dunant had so coveted: board member to Frémy and Talabot's *Société Algérienne*. If Dunant still had a tiny sliver of worth as a paper shuffler in Paris or clerk in Algeria, Moynier's insinuations despatched with this for good.

Nevertheless, it is easy to understand Moynier's precautions. While Dunant was ruthlessly speculating in Algeria and on the Paris stock market, he and Appia were toiling over a huge tome about war and charity.[7] Moynier was now promoting his book, sending it around to the European heads of state just as Dunant had done with *A Memory of Solferino*. Furthermore, he would be one of the vice chairmen at the Aid Society conferences taking place in Paris at the end of August in connection with the world's fair. This would involve

---

[5] Moynier to Feer-Herzog, 12 June 1867, ACICR, A AF 21, 04-002 (draft).

[6] Moynier to Théodore Vernes, 14 June 1867, ACICR, A AF 21, 04-004 (draft).

[7] G. Moynier and L. Appia, *La guerre et la Charité, Traité théorique et pratique de philanthropie appliquée aux armées en campagne* (Geneva-Paris: Cherbuliez, 1867).

nothing less than preparing for a potential revision of the Geneva Convention, offering Moynier, as president of the International Committee and 'guardian' of the Convention, a very prominent role. Looking ahead to these conferences, he had also written a small brochure on the neutrality of wounded military personnel that he was planning to distribute to all participants.

In short: at the very moment he was working flat out to establish himself as uncontested leader of the Work, Moynier couldn't risk it being discredited through the errors of his unpredictable and unwieldy secretary. But this was a difficult task indeed. In Paris, Dunant was untouchable; it would take a lot of scholarly articles, letters and scheming to knock him off his pedestal. Furthermore, he was on-site and as Moynier correctly feared, he had no intention of seeing himself deprived of the award ceremony on 1st July. 'I would not be unhappy to find myself at the ceremony with you and my foreign colleagues,'[8] Dunant wrote to the chief commissioner of the Aid Society delegates at the fair, Count Sérurier, with whom he still appeared to be on the best of terms. Did he want to retrieve the medal himself, or just hear the compliments? After his fall from grace, Dunant would play any card left in his hand.

Wounded sailors

Several days later, on 7th July, Dunant was summoned by Empress Eugénie herself. She'd heard a report about the sinking of an Italian battleship[9] that, with no rescue forthcoming, had led to the death of a thousand men in atrocious conditions. As a result, she wanted to see neutrality for wounded soldiers extended to sailors, and neutrality for field hospitals extended to equivalent naval structures – who better to discuss this with than the founder of the international work in favour of wounded soldiers?

Dunant listened to her respectfully, but he could hardly do anything, he said, to fulfil Her Majesty's request because his personal mission seemed to have ended. Surprised at the sudden modesty of

---

[8] Dunant to Sérurier, 29 June 1867, BGE, Ms. fr. 2116 G, f. 127v (handwritten copy by Dunant).
[9] The *Re d'Italia*, which was sunk during the Battle of Vis in 1866.

a man who had so relentlessly sought her husband's favour, the empress pointed her regal finger at him while loudly protesting: 'No, it must be you!'[10]

How much good this commanding finger must have done! What a refreshing salve for his wounded heart! Dunant promised to do everything in his power to get this question on the agenda of the August conferences. That very day he informed Count Sérurier of the empress's wishes. With moderate success: the conferences had already planned to address the question of 'wounded soldiers from armies of the land *and the sea*'.[11] Nonetheless, thirty years would pass before the Hague Convention would adapt the 1864 principles to maritime warfare.

Sometime after his audience with the empress, Queen Augusta of Prussia came on an official visit to Paris and learned of Dunant's misfortune. She sent Dr Loeffler to find him, which he eventually did, although with some difficulty, in his small lodgings: a tiny attic at the end of the Rue de Reuilly, very close to the current Place de la Nation. How embarrassing it must have been for Dunant to invite this man into his small apartment, the same man who had introduced him in Berlin to the royal family four years earlier, and who had bravely supported the idea of neutrality during the conference of October 1863! The gallant doctor knew all that had transpired; the rumours from Geneva had reached him quite directly, to inform him of everything. But he addressed Dunant with nothing but kindness:

> These rumours have very much troubled us, less against you than against the Genevans. And so the queen has expressly asked me to tell you that she still supports you, and that she is sorry not to be able to see you during her stay in Paris.[12]

Then, murmuring something in a low voice and tapping against his greatcoat, he drew out a thick envelope. 'This is just a beginning,'

---

[10] Maurice Dunant (ed.), *Les débuts de la Croix-Rouge en France*, 88.

[11] The actual name of these Conferences included the words 'land and maritime armies'.

[12] This exchange is based on letters from Loeffler to Dunant, 11 July 1867, BGE, Ms. 2109, f. 318, from Dunant to his mother, 9 January 1868, BGE Ms.fr.2115C, f. 9, and from Dunant's *Mémoires*, 234.

added the doctor as he offered a package containing 3,000 francs. 'I am working at court to restore you to a position of dignity, as you deserve.'

And so, from empress to queen to count to barons, Dunant could still consider himself, in that summer of 1867, as much the darling of the courts as he ever was. He also had several nice projects bubbling along, allowing him to think he might soon 'reconquer position and capital', reimburse his debt and wipe away its grubby traces. But in mid-August he received a devastating piece of news: his friend Thomas Mac-Culloch, the man who had co-signed his exorbitant loan from the *Crédit Lyonnais*, had unexpectedly died. He was not even 50 years old. This death filled Dunant with shame, as if it suddenly became unbearably clear how violently his financial troubles had affected his associates, shareholders and friends:

> It moves me greatly to think that this good, generous, loved and respected man died with the feeling that I was ungrateful and even maybe a dishonest man! [. . .] this is the cruellest of all my trials, and I am in despair.[13]

Usually at ease with his pen, he was literally paralyzed by the very thought of having to send his condolences to the widow: 'I do not dare,' he confided to his brother Pierre. Evidently, Mac-Culloch's death pulled back the curtains hanging over a reality he did not want to face – there was something irreparable in his bankruptcy, no matter his new projects, his illusions, his castles in the sky.

Two rivalries in one

The conference of the Aid Societies organized in Paris for the end of August 1867 played out beneath a double rivalry: first, between the two main founders of the Geneva Convention, and secondly, between Geneva and Paris.

To the likely astonishment of his former colleagues at the International Committee, the bankrupt man, the pariah, the man

---

[13] Dunant to his brother Pierre, 18 August 1867, BGE, Ms.fr. 2115C, f. 108, for this quote and the following.

banned from Geneva had managed to retain the trust and sympathy
of his Parisian friends, as was clear in the benevolent attentions of
Count Sérurier, chief of the Commission of Aid Society Delegates
and future president of the International Conferences.

'How are your affairs coming along?' Sérurier wrote to Dunant
over the summer. 'I'm very worried for you. You must absolutely
stay away, completely, from your compatriots. God wishes all to be
calm for our solemn reunion.'[14]

Alerted to Dunant's setbacks by Moynier, then by Théodore
Vernes who had been duly informed by Moynier, Sérurier had his
own reasons for taking Dunant's side: he was furious with Geneva.
As commissioner for the Aid Society exhibit at the Universal
Exhibition, he'd been expecting the French Committee would
receive the grand prize that the fair jury had just awarded the
International Committee of Geneva. Sérurier was enraged and
doing all he could to have the decision revoked; he directly argued
against Moynier, then had Vernes complain again, but there was
nothing to it: the great medal passed under his nose, the juries
preferring, as Moynier had correctly guessed, to 'give the medal not
to the exhibit, but to the idea that it represented'.[15]

To calm things down, Gustave Moynier could think of nothing
better than to suggest Count Sérurier retrieve the medal in his stead
on 1st July, by naming him 'the most dignified representative' of the
International Committee![16] Only the dreadful perspective of seeing
Dunant mount the podium can explain Moynier's inappropriate
proposal.

To the best of our knowledge no document reveals who did
receive the medal on that first day of July 1867.[17] But over the
course of the summer, from the tranquillity of his house near
Geneva, Moynier decided upon his most radical course yet.

---

[14] Sérurier to Dunant, [no day] August 1867, BGE Ms. fr. 2109, f. 327.

[15] Moynier to Vernes, 24 June 1867, ACICR, A AF A21, 04-006 (draft). The medal in
question went to all three men: Dunant, Moynier and Dufour. In all, approximately
sixty gold medals were distributed.

[16] Moynier to Sérurier, 27 June 1867, ACICR, A AF A21, 04-007 (draft).

[17] G. Moynier had suggested the General Commissioner of the Exhibition, Mr Feer-
Herzog, to send it to his own home in Ferney, near Geneva, which is probably what
happened. (Draft of a letter from) Moynier to Feer-Herzog, 12 June 1867, ACICR,
A AF A21, 04-002.

In June, he had asked Henry's brother Pierre Dunant to hand over the International Committee archives from the bankrupt man's home on the Rue du Puits-Saint-Pierre, which had served as committee headquarters. Since there was no 'looming danger' right then, as he wrote calmly to Théodore Vernes,[18] he hadn't thought it necessary to take measures other than 'confidentially' warn all of Paris of his secretary's disgrace.

But in August, Moynier changed his mind. Perhaps it was just too much to think of Dunant milling about with the official delegates at the upcoming international conferences. On 12th August he wrote to the conference president Sérurier to say that Dunant was 'so discredited he could no longer consent to sit with him in the conference "Bureau"'. Going further, he assured him of being 'the last to want to believe what was being said about Mr D.', but that he had had to face the facts, after being brought to make inquiries himself, and having put together 'a file of the most damning information'.[19] He then insisted to Sérurier that, before the meetings even began, the conference newsletter must include an exoneration of the International Committee with respect to the shameful rumours against one of its members.

On 16th August, having received a letter from an obviously refreshed Dunant, Moynier wrote a murderously polite reply: 'I'm happy to learn your financial affairs have improved', he assured him, claiming to be 'one of the people most sincerely hoping that you succeed in changing the current dispositions of public opinion towards you in Geneva.' He also enclosed a letter 'that the International Committee had long charged [him] to send': the letter invited Dunant to send his 'formal' resignation, all while thanking him for the 'services rendered' to the Committee.[20]

The affront of this 'thanks' was so much that Dunant didn't even protest. He replied immediately. The day before the conferences opened, 25th August 1867, he sent four lines resigning as secretary of the International Committee. In the end, what did this lowly title mean to him, and what did the Committee's lack of gratitude matter,

[18] Moynier to Vernes, 14 June 1867, ACICR, A AF A21, 04-004 (draft).
[19] Moynier to Sérurier, 12 August 1867, ACICR, A AF A21, 04-012 (draft).
[20] Moynier (for the ICRC) to Dunant, 15 August 1867 ACICR, A AF A21, 04-013 (draft), dated 16 August 1867, BGE, Archives Paul Dunant/IHD and Dunant's resignation, ACICR, A AF A21, 071.

when the entire world recognized him as the founder and promoter of the Red Cross!

The Paris Conferences

The five days of conferences opening the next morning must have witnessed some elaborate avoidance tactics. Since Dunant was not a member of the Bureau, at least Moynier would not have to sit directly beside him.

Settled in, Dunant kept his head high: 'I pretended not to see Mr Moynier,' he wrote to his mother at the end of the first day, 'and he did not come to me, so we did not see each other or meet each other.'[21]

Besides, Henry had other hands to shake: Count Ripalda, from Madrid, whom he'd met in Berlin in 1863; Charles Bowles, the American delegate to Geneva in 1864 who had since become a friend; Dr Loeffler, who 'was working actively' for him at the Prussian Court, and his colleague Dr Wendt; but also all his colleagues from the Central Committee in France, Count Sérurier, Dr Chenu, Colonel Hubert-Saladin and Théodore Vernes.[22]

Still doing well enough in social circles, Dunant was in a much weaker position when it came to the Red Cross. No longer representing the International Committee, he'd also lost his delegate status. In June, he had submitted a long treatise in favour of war prisoners to be discussed in the plenary conference, but although his report was read by Count Sérurier in front of the 3rd Section, it had not been selected as one of the debate subjects for the assembly. [23]

While the delegates took their places and Moynier, as a member of the Bureau, set himself up in his important position, Dunant found comfort in the sea of Red Cross armbands proudly adorning the arms of each delegate. It was now 9:00 a.m., the doors of 44,

---

[21] Dunant to his mother, 25 August 1867, BGE, Ms. fr. 2115 C, f. 7.
[22] The minutes of the *Conférences internationales des Sociétés de secours aux blessés militaires des armées de terre et de mer tenues à Paris en 1867* (Paris: Baillère, 1867) and Léonce de Cazenove, *La guerre et l'humanité au XIXe siècle* (Paris: A. de Vresse, 1869) are our main sources for the Paris Conferences.
[23] *Conférences internationales*, 56ff.; Cazenove, *La guerre et l'humanité*, 279–80.

Rue Bonaparte closed behind them, and President Sérurier laid out the rules of the game.

'It has been decided, gentlemen, that any member of the Conference may speak and discuss, but the right to vote will be reserved for the delegates, and, one exception, to Mr Dunant, promoter of the Work.'

'Excellent! Excellent!'[24] exclaimed several delegates, turning friendly faces to him. Dunant savoured this small honour like chocolate stolen from a sweet shop. Moynier may have already won, but the loser still had some stock with the public.

With the subject of war prisoners removed from the agenda for the day, Dunant began to simmer over the next conference proposal: the need to establish an international journal for the Aid Societies, and the best methods of publicizing their work to the general public.

The delegates began listing their bright ideas. Some proposed short publications or small brochures, others suggested articles to describe the doctrine 'simply and clearly'; some wanted an international newsletter, some preferred to develop the existing newspapers 'in Paris, Berlin and Brussels'.[25] Dunant must have been seething: were none of these talkative gentlemen aware of his skills in this area? No one appeared to remember that for the last four years he'd dedicated his evenings and nights to this, exactly this: 'short publications' and 'small brochures' ensuring the connection between the various societies, giving fresh news, marketing the work, promoting the cause. As early as 1863, he had proposed the launch of an International Committee periodical. But President Moynier, always cautious of his busy secretary's good ideas, hadn't jumped on this one. So Dunant had rolled up his sleeves on his own and kept up an extraordinary editorial drive, considering all his other work for the International Committee, the founding of the Genevan and then the French Red Cross, not to mention his Algerian mills. A first brochure had appeared under the name 'International and permanent societies', in 1863. Then came 'the Congress of Geneva', then 'the Congress and the Treaty of Geneva', then 'Fraternity on the Battlefield', then 'International Charity on Battlefields', all between 1863 and 1865. Every publication used the same ingredients in

---

[24] Conférences internationales, 18.
[25] Cazenove, La guerre et l'humanité, 281–2.

varying measure: large extracts from *A Memory of Solferino*; media articles praising *A Memory*, the International Committee of Geneva, the Congress of 1864 and the resulting Convention; the comments, opinions and compliments expressed by kings or military leaders, or more recent news from existing societies and the announcement of new ones, a list of up-to-date publications concerning the Work, and an increasing page count that inched towards 300 in the final editions. None of this was signed, but Henry Dunant was everywhere within and throughout these publications. As secretary, it was he who sent them out to the four corners of the world.

But he was now no longer secretary, and he had no voice in this conference discussion. Probably lost in his thoughts, Dunant was brusquely brought back into the room as the delegates began wrapping up the question. No one had asked his opinion as they trumpeted their 'novel' ideas – the very same methods Dunant had diligently employed for the past four years. Ultimately, the suggestion of an international newsletter was rejected. Dunant felt relieved. He would not have been able to handle someone else taking over this task.

In addition to the two men's rivalry was a rivalry between two societies. The representative from the Central French Committee at the Paris Conferences was a certain Count Breda, who could boast of being among the originators of the idea behind the Red Cross. In 1852, ten years before *A Memory of Solferino*, he'd published his *'Projet d'organisation des hospitaliers militaires'* (Project to organize military hospital staff) to improve the lot of wounded soldiers. During the first conference in 1863, he'd sent his text to the organizers, but they had not deemed it timely to act upon. Suffice to say that the success of the October 1863 and 1864 conferences must have strongly aggravated the Count's bitterness towards the Genevans who insisted they had invented everything. Furthermore, Breda had the noteworthy support of Henri Arrault, the other overlooked pioneer that George Sand had backed two years earlier. Throughout these conferences Breda was thus striving to introduce a notion of doubt regarding the legitimacy of the Geneva founders, in a fairly obvious attempt to shift the headquarters of the International Committee of Aid Societies to Paris. Ultimately disregarded by the delegates, the Count resigned angrily and with a roar, something which no doubt ensured the survival of the Red Cross: a transfer to Paris of the International Committee three years before the War of 1870 would have indeed been a risky operation.

While the Paris conferences did confirm the permanent establishment of the International Committee in Geneva, they did not put an end to the personal warfare between Dunant and Moynier. A week after the conferences were closed, a new letter from Moynier took note of Dunant's formal resignation as secretary, with a final and necessary thrust of the knife. 'To avoid any misunderstanding,' Moynier specified, he had to notify Dunant that his resignation as secretary also entailed his resignation as a member: '[S]ince your absence from Geneva prevents you from participating in our work, we are left with an empty position that we would like to fill.'[26] The break this time was final: even before the Committee took on its final name of the ICRC, the man universally known as the father of the Red Cross found himself excluded forever from the *Comité International de secours aux blessés*.

The misery of appearances

Once the Paris Conferences had ended, Dunant's memoirs tell us that he found himself 'in a state of sadness, desperation, deprivation and hunger that no one could imagine'.[27]

Gone were his days at the Hotel de Bade on the Boulevard des Italiens! 'I am well housed in a lodge located in a large garden which is very green right now and very pleasant when I return home from the noisy streets of Paris,'[28] he wrote to his mother with forced joy. Later, when he no longer needed to pretend, he would describe this oasis of calm and greenery as a sinister attic lost in the depths of the Saint-Antoine neighbourhood. He tried hard to never give anyone his address, not wanting anyone to see the place. The kilometres he had to walk each day to make his visits, his frugal meals, the rotten-smelling streams of waste running down the streets – all of this was nothing to Dunant compared to the daily suffering that hunched him little by little and shadowed his eyes. A misery that could not be hidden, of stained collars and wrists, of threadbare elbows, black

---

[26] Moynier to Dunant, 7 September 1867, BGE, from Archives Paul Dunant/IHD.

[27] Dunant, *Mémoires*, 234.

[28] Dunant to his mother, 5 August 1867, BGE, Ms. fr. 2115C, f. 15.

fabric turning grey, white shirts turning yellow, leather shoes cracked by bad weather and no hope of repair. This was his Achilles heel, his venial sin: Dunant had always taken care of his appearance, he'd never scrimped on the costs of his barber or his tailor, he enjoyed looking like the people he frequented, wearing what suited his friends the counts and marquis. When his misery fell upon him, he continued to move among the same society and set of friends as before, convinced he could only be saved by the ultra-chic circles of the French Red Cross. But how could he uphold the unbearable requirements of a society that might condemn you for a missing button? This 'misery in a dinner jacket'[29] was his perfect nightmare, a situation that had him inking his jacket collars and chalking his shirt cuffs. 'To see one's linens fall to ruin without being able to renew them' was for Dunant 'the cruellest' of all his misfortunes, especially 'if one wanted to be received in respectable homes in which the help would take it upon themselves to shut the door in your face if they found something amiss in your dress or sniffed a whiff of indigence'.[30]

His memoirs are vocal about this from the first to the last page: the pain of a social fall is intolerable. For fifteen years he had climbed continuously and quickly, with many successes: from the creation of the Geneva YMCA in 1852 to the ovation at the International Congress in Paris in 1855; from his first mission in Algeria to replace the wayward employee of Lullin & Sautter to prosperous owner of land, forests and mills; from solitary writer of A Memory of Solferino to internationally celebrated promoter of the Red Cross; and finally, more than anything, from a simple bourgeois citizen of Geneva to a friend of the aristocratic, military and financial elite of Europe.

And now, from one day to the next, he found himself relegated to the Mr Dunant who was not always able to pay his rent. Yes, he held onto – and would until his death – the title of honorary vice president of the French Soldiers' Aid Society. But what was a title worth when his dress or his beard no longer permitted him to frequent the society who might appreciate it?

---

[29] Dunant, Mémoires, 234.
[30] Ibid.

Return of the East

Dunant doesn't seem to have even considered finding a simple job to ensure his subsistence. Years later he would reflect upon this period and say that he 'would have swept the streets' if 'this might have enabled him to re-establish himself and repay his debts'.[31] But in light of their size, he could only envision being saved through extravagant projects. Which is why his efforts in 1867 were to remain in contact with the 'grand' world with a view on 'grand' business, even if this became a daily reminder of the unspeakable cruelty of his poverty.

Two projects kept him busy. The first renewed his fantasy of the invigoration of the East he'd been hoping for the year before. Also in Paris was banker Charles Bowles, a delegate to the 1864 conference who'd remained a loyal and generous friend to Dunant. The two men spoke business, and Bowles presented his friend to a Russian army officer named Papengouth. The trio formed a 'committee' to, once again, set up colonies in Palestine – with a view to make considerable profits, of course. This time the foundation was 'solid, straightforward, clear and precise', Henry wrote to his mother in June, like an item of great news: 'This is not like that horrible business in Algeria, where everything was always so difficult.'[32] The key to his future success was his role as an intermediary to purchase acres of the Promised Land at a low price ... and sell them on for a higher amount. His permanent role in the trio earned him not only a regular salary of 500 francs a month but, even better, an office at the Rue de la Paix that Bowles had originally offered him for the Algerian Omnium. This office would finally allow him to reintegrate into the real world.

By October 1867, however, the set-up had already changed. Bowles and his rich Russian officer were no longer in the running: in their place was a German Protestant sect intensely interested in the Palestine colony. The advertising widely distributed in European journals and signed by 'the founder and promoter of the Red Cross' had borne fruit.

---

[31] Dunant to his brother Pierre, undated [1892?], BGE, Ms. fr. 5206, f. 13–14.
[32] Dunant to his mother, 24 June 1867, BGE, Ms. fr. 2115C, f. 1.

The German Pietists of the Society of the Temple – farmers and craftsmen, mostly – weren't at all interested in making a profit; theirs was a vocation to restore the Holy Land by virtue of their faith, their crops and their labour. A discussion with Dunant convinced them that he could open doors for them. They entrusted him with their future, along with 2,500 francs 'for negotiations with the Sublime Porte'. The contract stipulated that the same sum must be provided to him once he had procured the desired authorizations. Dunant also promised to provide a large enough tract of cultivatable land for a fair price, as well as advocate with the Sublime Porte to obtain a semi-autonomous status for the Württemberg settlers, all in exchange for an annual 5,000-franc honorarium to come in the first year of the settlement.[33]

Dunant's ambitions for worldwide notoriety seemed to have returned in full force. In December 1867, he wrote to his mother that across Europe, in France, Spain, Germany, Belgium, England, the heads of state were rushing to patronize his work for repopulating Palestine. He had presented himself as the necessary intermediary because of his connections with the sultan (Palestine was under Turkish rule at the time). The only problem was that he had not yet approached the sultan ... and he would never get anything – not the land concessions, not the waterfalls, not the authorizations to build the hospices, farms or aqueducts that he'd promised his clients. Just like his Algerian windmills, his Palestinian colonies were nothing more than castles in the sky.

The Temple members must have been terribly disappointed, this return to the Holy Land being the living heart of their ideology.[34] But they weren't going to give up so easily. The movement's two leaders, Georg David Hardegg and Christoph Hoffmann, would set off on their own in August 1868 to plead their case with the sultan and would indeed get permission to set up a colony in Palestine. One family settled in Jaffa, another in the Haifa region, and there they would be joined by a few other families.

Strangely enough, his Württemberger friends from the Society of the Temple never withdrew their trust nor their friendship from Dunant, despite the total fiasco of his mediation with the sultan.

---

[33] The 'Council of the Temple' [Hardegg, certainly] to Dunant, 5 October 1867, BGE, Ms. fr. 2115 E.

[34] On the Society of the Temple, see Pous, *Henry Dunant colon affairiste*, ch. 8.

They did ask him to return his 2,500-franc advance but they gave him as much time as he needed to repay the additional 3,000 francs they had loaned him. They would even call him an 'honorary member' of the Temple, something which Dunant would never forget. It would take him years to renounce his dream of rejoining the colony of the Temple of Palestine, as if these Christian Zionists were the only true charitable friends he'd met during this dark period.

The Universal Library

Dunant's second project would last a little longer than his Palestine plan. Shortly after his arrival in Paris in 1867, he became connected with a man named Max Grazia, an Italian a few years older and engaged to a woman from Neuchâtel whose father, a fervent Bonapartist like Dunant, had connected the two men. Grazia lived just a few streets away, on the Boulevard Voltaire (then called the Boulevard du Prince-Eugène). Grazia began by assisting our exile in answering the constant barrage of administrative and legal letters that Dunant did not feel strong enough to answer himself.

But once he'd got some of his energy back, in the autumn of 1867, it was Grazia's turn to ask for help. The Italian was involved in a project Dunant could not resist, keen fan of universalism that he was: the progressive establishment of a library presenting the 'masterpieces of the human mind from all time periods and all countries', as the prospectus promised.

Grazia would look after the publication questions, but to give his library the prestige it deserved, Dunant's relationships within the *Institut de France* – many academics were also members of the Red Cross – might be very useful. And so Dunant leapt to it with the enthusiasm of a young man, excited as never before by Grazia's 100,000-franc promise on forecasted profits. On 16th January 1868, he wrote an extremely long letter to his mother with a detailed account of his sunny future. He listed the greatest names from the 126 visit cards he'd received for the New Year, including a prince, numerous ministers, generals and 'notable individuals of all kinds'. This letter was frothing with all the frustrated affection of a son missing his mother; in it he tells her about the cold water ablutions that prevent winter colds, the lovely fur-lined suit that kept him warm while the Saint-Michel fountain spewed ice and the horses

were all dropping like flies, and the lightning-fast progress of the
'marvellous business of the Universal Library' which would promise
him 100,000 francs without 'having to wait eight years'.[35]

The letter is long and tender because Dunant was feeling far
away. His tone becomes even more pressing in the following letter,
dated 31st January: 'Please take care of yourself, for all those who
love you, and for me who would so much like to kiss you.'[36]

Three days later, Nancy Dunant-Colladon passed away in
Geneva without her eldest son at her bedside. Henry wouldn't even
dare return to Geneva for her funeral, and would carry the weight
of her loss for the entire year: 'My sorrow,' he wrote to his brother
at the end of 1868, 'is as great today as it was eleven months ago.'[37]

His grief was in proportion to the affection binding these two
fragile beings, so similar in their temperamental ups and downs.
Dunant felt his exile more keenly than ever in the bottomless sorrow
he would have preferred to share with his father, brothers and
sisters, back in the family home in Geneva. His uncle Daniel's
presence in Paris was thus a huge comfort to him during this time.
In the evenings, the successful scholar would fetch Henry from his
office at the Rue de la Paix for supper, for the pleasure of a shared
meal but also to share memories of the deceased, the dear mother
and sister whom they both loved.

Paradoxically, Dunant's only consolation for his mother's death
arrived in August 1868, when the verdict of the *Crédit Genevois*
appeal appeared in the *Journal de Genève*.[38] Praise God a thousand
times that his mother was no longer able to read the headline in
bold with all the details and damning insinuations, the consummate
shame of her son. The previous autumn, the judges of the
Commercial Court had delivered a statement on 'the negligence,
lightness and incompetence' of the *Crédit Genevois* board of
directors, but hadn't condemned them for any heavy fault, thus
rejecting the shareholders' claim. But the latter had not let the
matter rest, and their appeal had been heard.

---

[35] Dunant to his mother, 16 January 1868, BGE, Ms. fr. 2115 C, f. 14.

[36] Ibid., f. 15.

[37] Dunant to his brother Pierre, 31 December 1868, BGE, Ms. fr. 2115 C, f. 110.

[38] The *Journal de Genève* of 23 August 1868 published the entire verdict from the
Civil Justice Court.

On Monday 17th August 1868, Geneva's Civil Justice Court, the highest court at the time, modified the initial verdict. It condemned the seven board directors for their 'grave error' during the Felfela quarry transaction. The Court focused particularly on one individual: 'Mr Dunant, who knowingly deceived his colleagues, should be held responsible for all the losses occasioned by this affair', while the six other board members 'should each be responsible for only one seventh of the loss', and could turn against their colleague for the sum they had to repay. And so the seller of the Felfela quarry found himself the scapegoat. In an unappealable verdict, Dunant suffered the disgrace of appearing to be the only one who 'knowingly deceived' his colleagues.

Dunant didn't even think of returning to Geneva for this trial. Completely discredited, he could not risk facing the disappointment, acrimony and scorn of his fellow citizens. Not then, not later. In fact, he decided to play dead for as long as his creditors kept away. For the forty-two years that remained of his life, he would never once return to Geneva, and, aside from his family, he would make sure never to cross paths with a Genevan again.

At the end of 1868, nonetheless, the *Bibliothèque internationale universelle* (International Universal Library) came into being. In December, the statutes were signed by several investors, including the 'wealthy family of Jackson Peugeot, from the Franche- Comté, owner of several steel mills'.[39] The project had clearly gone beyond the stage of well-intentioned committees. The Minister of Instruction, Victor Duruy, promised in writing to integrate the collection into all of France's imperial libraries.

Dunant enjoyed the project because of the close connections it necessitated with scholars, assembled into one of these prestigious boards Dunant was so fond of. He also enjoyed it because it gave him travel possibilities: that year he went to Bonn for an international congress on history. While there, he gave an idealistic speech on the goodness of a 'Museum of Nations' meant to 'multiply sympathetic connections' beyond political and linguistic borders and make peace simpler and more lasting on earth. All of this seemed so well established that he even involved his brother Daniel, his unlucky – or, rather, ruined – Algerian companion, in order to give him 'a

---

[39] Dunant to his brother Pierre, 31 December 1868, BGE Ms. 2115 C, f. 110.

position in the Library'.[40] The presses were launched. The first book
was printed. In the depths of his long night, Dunant believed he
could finally see something like the bright arc of the end of the
tunnel.

The last argument

Bankruptcy, shame, flight – despite all of this, Henry Dunant still
considered himself the man of the Red Cross and the institution as
his, even if he no longer held any formal powers or any rights. In
March 1869, he wrote a deferential letter to Conrad Kern, still the
plenipotentiary minister of Switzerland in France. He informed him
that the United States of Colombia wished to adhere to the Geneva
Convention, a request he was honoured to communicate to the
Swiss government. His friend Kern's response, received at his modest
lodgings on the Rue de Reuilly, gave him a clear indication of his
current position. If the minister of the United States of Colombia
wanted to have official communications regarding the Geneva
Convention, Dunant should kindly request him, wrote Kern, to
'address his correspondence directly to me in the name of his
government', as all other states had done before him. Since this was
an *official* matter, Kern emphasized, well then, he needed to receive
the request 'in an official capacity',[41] and not, he insinuated, from a
nobody.

As if this wasn't enough to put him back in his place, a final
confrontation played out with Moynier between April and May of
that year. While working at the Second International Conference of
the Red Cross in Berlin, Moynier wrote to Dunant requesting he
cease writing his correspondence on 'paper bearing the insignia of
the International Committee to which you have not been a member
for some time'.[42]

Dunant laboured over his reply. He made a first draft, slightly
whiny, that described all his misfortunes along with his efforts to
repair the wrongs he had caused. Then he rewrote a second letter,
much more dignified and resolute. He began by defending himself

---

[40] Ibid.
[41] Kern to Dunant, 11 March 1869, BGE, Ms. fr. 2109, f.353.
[42] Moynier to Dunant, 25 April 1869, BGE, Archives Paul Dunant/IHD.

against the accusation of misusing 'a letterhead to which I have a perfect right, as founder of the international Work'. He pointed out that his letterhead included neither the word Geneva, nor the International Committee, and that he had 'done enough in favour of aid to wounded soldiers for the right to place the Red Cross and the title of the work' on his mail:

> It seems you have jumped at the first chance to write so insultingly to your former colleague, as I believe you have already attempted to disparage him without any honourable motive towards those who have retained, despite his misfortunes and his faults, feelings of esteem and benevolence towards him. But this new aggression leaves me entirely indifferent.

Since he'd retained the support of his family and friends who'd suffered financial losses through him, he could play the stunned martyr in his final sentence, which he threw down like a glove:

> If, on the contrary, those to whom I owe nothing forget the due respect owed my current position, I give them the responsibility of their bad action. But one might be surprised that you have forgotten it, you, sir, who enjoy a position in the work that, you must admit, I very decidedly helped to give you.[43]

Upon his return from Berlin, Moynier responded to the stunned martyr as a surprised executioner: 'You bizarrely misinterpret my disposition and my conduct on your behalf, but it does not matter.' He then maintained, and it's understandable, that a stamp decorated with a red cross on a white background used by a former member of the International Committee might lead to confusion. The lawyer in him continued to retaliate: since Dunant did not appear 'disposed' to renounce his home-made seal, it was Moynier who would take care to 'disclaim any liability' in order to spare the International Committee 'from any new inconveniences'.[44]

This would not be their last battle. But it would be the final exchange between the two fathers of the Red Cross.

---

[43] Dunant to Moynier, 29 April 1869, ACICR, A AF 20,1-081.
[44] Moynier to Dunant, 29 May 1869, ACICR, A AF 16,1-181 (file AF 6,1.1 'France, mail sent').

8

Paris at War (1870–1)

In the name of celebrity

In the early months of 1870, Dunant could hardly have suspected that his tiny existence would soon be upended. Although none of his fabulous projects had yet to come into their own, he continued to believe that the Universal Library would soon send its series of masterpieces off into the world. The first two books were printed in April; Mr Grazia had been hard-nosed with his financial backers, threatening to break with them and put his entire business 'with someone else who wanted it' if they didn't advance more funds. This 'other person' was an 'immensely rich capitalist he had found,' Dunant wrote gleefully to his sister Marie, who would enable him, if negotiations went well, to take over the entire business. Of course, there were a few delays: the stipend for his brother Daniel, whom he'd brought over to help, was stopped two months earlier, as was Mr Grazia's, and everyone else's; despite the situation, Dunant had never been 'more delighted with its progress, with respect to his personal interests'.[1] What unshakeable optimism! Poor Daniel didn't have his older brother's patience. After waiting in vain for the project to become lucrative, he sent his wife and two daughters back to Geneva and then rushed off himself several weeks later, leaving Henry in Paris – mortified to have once again dragged Daniel into one of his fruitless adventures.

Daniel's departure also meant that on 12th June 1870, there was no one in the audience to applaud that bit louder when Henry

---

[1] Dunant to his sister Marie Dunant, 7 April 1870, BGE, Ms. fr. 2115 C, f. 25.

Dunant received a medal of honour from the *Société d'encouragement au bien* (Society for Encouraging Good), a charity founded eight years earlier by an admirer of Napoleon III, Honoré Arnoul. Placing a 'civic crown' on Dunant's head, in a gesture of 'public recognition', Arnoul claimed the honour was for the author of *A Memory of Solferino*, 'in the name of all families, in the name of all civilized nations, in the sacred name of humanity'.[2]

The ceremony took place at Paris's Cirque Napoléon,[3] which was filled to bursting for the event: six thousand people packed in to see a friend or loved one rewarded for some good deed – adoptions, caregiving, you name it. Dunant felt more keenly than ever the hasty removal of Daniel's family, the only audience members he would have enjoyed having at the event. But the smallpox epidemic raging through Paris consoled him; it would have been dangerous for the children. He was happily immunized by 'Dr Chéron's excellent vaccine, which has worked perfectly', as he wrote to his sister.[4]

Several weeks following this ceremony – was the timing a coincidence? – the very same Society for Encouraging Good began concentrating its activities on creating and managing aid clinics to assist army services. Had one of its prizewinners inspired the idea? The fact is that Dunant, crowned a 'benefactor of humanity' on the eve of a diplomatic crisis, was rediscovering the Red Cross persona he'd stashed away in his memories; and since he was never one to miss an opportunity, he wasted no time launching the 10th edition of *A Memory of Solferino* just when the first drumbeats of war began to resound nearby.

A leading role

At almost exactly the same time as *A Memory of Solferino* was republished with Lachaud in Paris, another work appeared entitled *Les victimes de la guerre et les progrès de la civilization* (War Victims and Civilization's Progress) by a certain Dr Chéron – of the

---

[2] Cited by M. Dunant (ed.), *Les débuts de la Croix-Rouge en France*, 120.
[3] Now Cirque d'Hiver.
[4] Dunant to his sister Marie Dunant, 24 June 1870, BGE, Ms. fr. 2115 C, f. 29.

aforementioned 'excellent vaccine'. Curiously, the typesetting in this book displays the very same small imperfections as the reprint of *A Memory*. Also intriguing, Dr Chéron's book looks very much like many of Dunant's other publications, in its structure as well as in its parts: a historic overview of aid to wounded soldiers, the role of Henry Dunant in the creation of the Red Cross and an extensive excerpt (eighty pages) of *A Memory of Solferino*. Even more remarkable was that Dr Chéron's historical section didn't mention the Committee of Five, nor the International Committee in Geneva, nor even the name of Gustave Moynier; it was exclusively focused on the author of *A Memory of Solferino*.[5]

Henry Dunant didn't ghostwrite for Dr Chéron; it was Dr Chéron who agreed to lend his name to Dunant. Since his exclusion from the International Committee, Dunant no longer had a regular publication schedule in which to supplement his propaganda for the Work as well as remind people of his role. This is exactly why he had asked his friend Chéron, with whom he was also in business, to literally lend him his authorship to help him find his way back into bookshops, and from there into the press and to the honours he deserved. This is the first time he would use this method; it would not be the last.

Dr Chéron's book appeared at the end of July 1870. The timing was perfect. War with Prussia had just broken out over an issue of succession. The Spanish throne was now vacant, Prince Léopold de Hohenzollern-Sigmaringen, cousin of King William I of Prussia, had presented himself as a candidate. France had immediately opposed this threat of a German encirclement. And so the prince agreed to remove his candidacy, but this wasn't enough for the hawks in France. They were demanding that William I, head of the Hohenzollern, definitively swear off the family's right to the Spanish throne, an idea quite displeasing to the king of Prussia. He confirmed his cousin's renunciation but added he 'had nothing further to say to the [French] ambassador'.[6]

Apprised of the events by his king, Chancellor Bismarck was swift to pour fuel on the fire: he had the despatch published in the

[5] These 'coincidences' were noted by André Durand in *'Un livre d'Henry Dunant écrit en collaboration avec le docteur Chéron'*, *Bulletin de la Société Henry Dunant*, 6 (Geneva: SHD, 1981), 1–9.
[6] Wellis, *Unification and Consolidation of Germany and Italy*, 158.

press, but heavily edited to make the Germans angry at French arrogance and the French affronted by the ill treatment of their ambassador. A successful manipulation.[7] Things quickly grew heated in Paris, mobilization was enthusiastically voted upon and war with Prussia was declared on 19th July, under the pressure of public opinion and with a feeling of resignation by Napoleon III, who was both politically and physically weakened.

The hostilities turned immediately to Prussia's advantage and to its allied German states. Dunant didn't even consider leaving Paris; amid the effervescence of the early war, he was discovering his vocation intact, renewed even, as if he were waking from a long slumber. Here he was again receiving letters addressed to the great founder of the Red Cross and being credited with both moral and operational authority.

On 20th July a priest wrote to Dunant, throwing the entirety of his annual holiday at Dunant's feet to help at whatever aid station Dunant wanted to send him. 'Give me some task. I will be at your service both day and night starting from today.' Better yet, he would also be arriving with full pockets. He explained that since it was the end of the school year, his students 'were giving up their prize money so that the 500 francs reserved for it could be dedicated to wounded French soldiers.'[8] How could one not weep when faced with such spontaneous generosity? But Dunant was focused more on the personal advantages that the dramatic events could offer him, as revealed in a letter to his sister Marie:

> Putting aside the question of how deplorable and anti-human this war is, it is the happiest thing that could have happened to me. I am able to step back into the limelight and it will be useful for me on all fronts. The newspapers are speaking about me more than ever again and we will see if the nasty people are disgraceful enough to speak badly of me at this moment.[9]

On 25th July, however, he wrote to Baron Brénier, a senator and one of the vice presidents of the French Red Cross, to ask him to turn the government's attention to the terms of the Geneva

---

[7] This diplomatic crisis is known as the episode of the Ems Despatch.

[8] Paulin Delafosse to Dunant, 20 July 1870, BGE, Ms. fr. 2110, f. 4.

[9] Dunant to his sister Marie, 31 July 1870, BGE, Ms. fr. 2115 C, f. 31.

Convention, ratified by France in September 1864. Obligingly, the baron questioned the government in front of the Senate Assembly but was told 'there was nothing to fault the organization of the army with respect to the care given to wounded, as on all other points of view'. As he spoke, the other senators sat playing with their paper cutters or chatting among themselves. When lamenting his failure to Dunant a few days later, he was still angry, still indignant: 'Ingrates! They silenced me!'[10]

Well, if the Senate wasn't interested, then it was time to work on the ministers. The president of the French Red Cross, the Count de Flavigny (who'd succeeded his father-in-law, the Duke de Fezensac) had already gone to see the Minister of War, who'd responded, annoyed, that to his knowledge France had not ratified the Geneva Convention. Discouraged, the count simply passed the baton to Dunant. Henry first addressed the Minister of the Interior but received no reply. As was his habit, he moved one level higher. On 16th August while a Napoleon III who could barely stay on his horse was leading his troops to the front, Dunant addressed the Regent Empress to draw 'her august interest to the convention of 1864' and to politely point out to Her Majesty that France was being maligned in the foreign press for its refusal to conform. At the same time, he suggested to General Trochu (whom he knew through the Red Cross) that a few cities near Paris, and in the Champagne and Lorraine regions, should be declared neutral to facilitate caring for wounded soldiers.

General Trochu said he was too busy right then to consider the request. And the empress was hardly more encouraging. She transferred Dunant's appeal back to the Minister of the Interior, who this time deigned to reply but without answering the question: he didn't even bother to mention the Geneva Convention.

The following evening Dunant wrote to his brother Pierre, painting a rosier picture than it really was. He boasted that the empress had listened to him so well that 'yesterday the army doctors started wearing the armband, and the troops will certainly be briefed on the Convention'.[11] If this was true, it didn't last long. In his memoirs, years later, Dunant complained that 'not a single

---

[10] Dunant, *Mémoires*, 238.
[11] Dunant to his brother Pierre, 21 August 1870, BGE, Ms. fr. 2110, f. 15.

official doctor from the armies of the East wore the sacred armband'
and that the official medical units 'were simply painted in grey',
bearing no other distinctive symbol.

'It seems they want (?) to allow the Prussians to walk straight up
to the walls of Paris,' an astonished Dunant wrote in the same letter.
'Maybe they will come. In any case, do not worry about me,' he
underlined. 'I will play a leading role. And the French press definitely
avenge me for any earlier indifference and also towards my
enemies.'[12]

No, Dunant had forgotten nothing. Quite the opposite.
Immediately after his bankruptcy, he'd sincerely wanted to reimburse
his debts. Yet over the last three years he'd become increasingly
convinced that the Genevans were persecuting him, in cahoots with
Paris's Protestants, only adding to his self-inflicted shame, misery
and sorrow. But now his time had come. Everything seemed possible
again. On 2nd September, the French Army was encircled at Sedan:
a hundred thousand men, including the emperor, were taken prisoner
by the Germans. While this upheaval would undermine the support
network upon which Dunant had constructed his entire life, the
ensuing conflict would provide him with the very role he'd been
longing for.

In the shelter of the cross

The German advance on Paris didn't deter Dunant from his lucrative
projects. The return of his 'leading role' bolstered his confidence
and the war was giving him all kinds of new ideas. With his new
friend Dr Chéron and a pharmacist named Sirech, he was now
involved in a new scheme: the manufacture of a revolutionary
bandage made of cotton pre-dipped in ferric chloride, which in
addition to its haemostatic virtues had many advantages in terms of
use and packaging. 'Everything is going well, we think we will have
enormous orders,' he wrote to his brother at the end of the summer.
'As soon as the war is over, I will be well positioned for a business
in lint (no one will know I'm involved), and also the business of the

---

[12] Ibid. This letter shows the first signs of Dunant's paranoia about a group of
indistinct 'enemies'.

library, which has fallen into my hands.'[13] His reputation as battlefield benefactor would surely suffer from being mixed up in a lucrative business of haemostatic bandages. For obvious reasons, he felt strongly about guarding his anonymity in a business that would very directly profit from his Red Cross network. 'I will manage to get all the committees to buy them,' he wrote his sister in another letter. 'Dr Chéron, who is never so optimistic, assures me that for my part in the business, my part alone, I could easily make 125,000 francs profit per year. For each tiny package that costs one franc, one quarter – 25 centimes – would come to me.'[14]

As usual, Dunant had no trouble reconciling his professional ambitions with his humanitarian aspirations, not just by preventing any mutual damage but also by making sure they benefited each other. The shame of the bankrupt businessman that still shadowed the humanitarian doesn't seem to have dissuaded him for one second from this twofold approach. The only lesson he'd learned was discretion: 'No one will know I'm involved.'[15]

The Universal Library was clearly less suited to a war economy than packages of compressed bandages. But again, Dunant gave his family the impression of imperturbable optimism. He said the business had 'fallen into his hands', that he was 'delighted' and would soon be reaping the profits – a done deal.

On Sunday 4th September, as he'd done every day since the launch of the bandage business, Dunant made his way to Dr Chéron's workshop, to lend a hand, of course, but also to enjoy the good meal Mrs Chéron served him both noon and night. Even given the price of a ticket on the horse-drawn omnibus, it was worth crossing the city instead of paying for lunch himself. As he liked to do when the weather was fine, Dunant was sitting on the top deck that day, when he suddenly witnessed the pillaging of shops bearing even vaguely German names to the joyful cries of surrounding crowds. Some groups were waving flags just a hundred metres from where he sat, while a furious mob broke into the Palais Bourbon, shouting, 'Down with the Empire!' The French Republic was declared.

[13] Dunant to his brother Pierre, 21 August 1870, BGE, Ms. fr. 2110, f. 15.
[14] Dunant to his sister Marie, 31 July 1870, BGE, Ms. fr. 2115 C, f. 31.
[15] Dunant to his brother Pierre, 21 August 1870, BGE, Ms. fr. 2110, f. 15.

Naturally, Dunant could only consider these events from his own perspective; his memoirs brush over the Republic while dedicating three pages to the escape of the empress, 'saved', he wrote with pride, 'by a devoted member of the Red Cross Society'.[16] During the 1867 Universal Exhibition, the pavilion of the Aid Societies had greatly benefited from its proximity to a spectacular collection of medical equipment brought over at great cost from the United States. The collector and patron of this pavilion was Dr Evans, a rich American dentist whom Dunant very much admired. What a delight to learn it was this man who'd saved the empress! This man who'd helped her to leave Paris. This man who'd brought her all the way to Deauville where Mrs Evans hid her in her hotel room until it was safe to cross the Channel. Once this fact became public knowledge, however, it would have the unfortunate effect of tightening the association, in the mindset of the times, between the French Red Cross and the fallen Empire.

As soon as the Third Republic was declared, Dunant was suddenly more assiduously courted by the aristocratic leaders of the French Red Cross. They were obviously unwilling to deal themselves with the parties who had precipitated the fall of the Empire; this made them suddenly more indulgent regarding the activism of a Genevan commoner, now potentially useful with the new Republican authorities. In such times, if he wouldn't fight, who would?

Dunant picked up his crusade exactly where he'd left it. His recent pleas to the empress had almost achieved their goal; he'd received a reply from the Regent's chamberlain that his proposals were to be submitted to the Council of Ministers when 'the Imperial catastrophe'[17] occurred. But a regime change would not stop him! With his usual relay-style approach, he first wrote to the wife of the new Minister of Instruction, Mrs Jules Simon, asking her to give three requests to her husband to present to the president of the government, Jules Trochu. This request was essentially a word-for-word repetition of what Dunant had pleaded with the empress: the armband for all military doctors and official nurses; the application of the Geneva Convention with respect to wounded soldiers; the

---

[16] Dunant, *Mémoires*, 245.
[17] At least in Dunant's eyes: to his sister Marie, 11 September 1870, Dunant, BGE, Ms. fr.2115 C, f. 33.

inclusion of the mobile guard and the national guard among the beneficiaries of the Convention; and finally, the neutrality of several surrounding cities. He boasted he could ensure that 'the Prussian enemies' would support this last request because of the 'international character' of his modest person 'recognized by all'.[18] Though it had been a while, he believed the Germans would welcome him as an old friend, and in this he was not wrong.

On Sunday 11th September, he obtained an audience with the third Jules in his relay race, Jules Favre, who promised to defend his proposals that very evening at the new Council of Ministers. For Dunant, the first battle was won. 'I am so happy,' he wrote to his sister that day. 'I cannot even express it; I am truly living, I am breathing freely, I am, in a word, reborn.'[19]

This time, his message hit its mark. The day after next, excerpts of the Geneva Convention were published in the *Journal Officiel*. In contrast to the indifference the document had inspired until now, the publication of Article 5 would release a staggering wave of enthusiasm:

> The presence of any wounded combatant receiving shelter and care in a house shall ensure its protection. An inhabitant who has given shelter to the wounded shall be exempted from billeting troops and from a portion of such war contributions as may be levied.[20]

Fifteen days earlier Parisians may not have had the slightest idea what the Geneva Convention might mean, but at the very least they quickly understood the advantages they might reap from it. The entire capital was soon covered in red crosses on white backgrounds. From one day to the next, they were everywhere, 'on arms, on hats, on the chests of many men, women and children, on the sides of cars and even on horse saddles,' wrote Dunant.[21] The Parisian population

---

[18] Dunant to his sister Marie, 11 September 1870, Dunant, BGE, Ms. fr.2115 C, f. 33.
[19] Ibid.
[20] Art. 5 of the 'Convention for the Amelioration of the Condition of the Wounded in Armies in the Field' as published in the *Journal officiel de la République française*, 13 September 1870, 1557.
[21] Dunant, *Mémoires*, 244.

was duly informed that the symbol exempted them from 'billeting' troops, so one out of every four houses suddenly bore a red cross – a generosity a bit too widespread not to be suspicious.

It is easy to imagine Dunant sighing as he crossed Paris in those days. Was his sacred Red Cross emblem a mere repellant for lice-infested fugitives, or a scarecrow to ward off the Prussian helmets? This was certainly not what he'd envisioned. But this touching portrait must be amended.

On that very same 11th September, the day of his interview with Minister Favre and even before the decree was published in the *Journal officiel*, Dunant had already abandoned his dark attic (or 'bungalow' or 'shack', depending on when he was speaking and to whom) and was living in two comfortable rooms in a hotel in the centre of Paris. Here he claimed to be 'much better, a thousand times better than the Rue de Reuilly'.[22] And what had brought about this much appreciated promotion? Like all of Paris, he, too, was putting the decree to his advantage: he was neither nurse, nor soldier, nor wounded, at least for now. But when he received an unexpected offer from the good-natured hotel manager of the Ville de Paris Hotel, he'd jumped at the chance to have his prestige recognized and move into nicer quarters in the capital's swankiest neighbourhood, a few dozen metres from the Élysée Palace.

A week later, in response to the shameless abuse of what was then commonly being called the 'Geneva cross', a new decree appeared: the Convention's flag was now reserved 'to those individuals making at least six proper beds available'.[23] But this was not enough to stop the cheaters, who would happily count a laundry basket as a bed. And so, on 24th September, a new measure was enacted: the symbol would only be authorized for a house which 'effectively hosted' wounded or sick soldiers, with no distinction between the two belligerent nations.[24] This meant that the hunt for a flag was over, but it was open season for wounded soldiers. Every great lady wanted to have her own wounded soldier to shield her from more damaging intrusions. Dunant must have been disheartened. But this was not the case. The couple that managed

---

[22] Dunant to his sister Marie, 11 September 1870, Dunant, BGE, Ms. fr. 2115 C, f. 33.
[23] *Journal officiel de la République française*, 21 September 1870, 1587.
[24] Ibid., 1053.

the hotel established a dispensary which, whether or not it was used, at least cleared his conscience. And since they were 'terribly afraid of Prussians,' Dunant wrote, the hotel managers 'spoiled him with all kinds of attentions.' On one evening the hotel maid brought him a sugar bowl and a bottle of orange water; on another, the manager had a daybed set up in his second room; and every evening he took tea with the masters of the house. 'And this, and that,' Dunant wrote to his sister, amused. In the end, 'excepting the sad circumstances of war from a humanitarian perspective, nothing happier could have happened to me personally [. . .] In a word, I am truly in the best conditions possible.'[25]

How had he come to be living in this nice hotel without the least bit of money to pay for the night? Either through the Protestant network or the Red Cross network, or both. His colleague Léonce de Cazenove, from Lyons, founding pillar and first historian of the French Red Cross Society, had been living in this very hotel before the siege; and the president of the Society, his new 'best' friend Maurice de Flavigny, lived on the same street and had been using the Ville de Paris Hotel as an annex for Society work for some time. Religious solidarity may also have been a factor. To his brother, Dunant described the hotel manager, a certain Mr Ribes, as 'a long-established southern Protestant of the Old Regime', who was 'very happy (or honoured if you like) to have the founder of the Red Cross and promoter of the Geneva Convention with him, and he does not want me to be without anything and he absolutely does not want me to pay'.[26] Used as a 'safeguard against the Prussians',[27] Dunant was becoming a red cross himself, an embodiment he might not have minded. The hotel manager had his female pensioners make a red cross flag and its Swiss inverse, asking Dunant to hang them both from his first-floor balcony, a move which granted Henry the establishment's two best rooms looking out over the small Ville- l'Évêque plaza.[28]

On 19th September Paris was encircled: although they were still at some distance from the city, the German armies now formed a continuous 100-kilometre cordon around the city. The siege of Paris had begun.

---

[25] Dunant to his sister Marie, 13 September 1870, Dunant, BGE, Ms. fr. 2115 C, f. 40.
[26] Dunant to his brother Pierre, 19 February 1871, BGE, Ms. fr. 2110, f. 40.
[27] Dunant, *Mémoires*, 258.
[28] Currently Place des Saussaies.

Crossed actions

Right from the beginning of the war, the 'Internationale' – as the French Red Cross Society was unfortunately called – had remained active.[29] It took charge of six large temporary hospitals and thirty-three dispensaries, as well as an office which provided information to some 40,000 families looking for their loved ones. Although Dunant only mentions the Aid Society, it obviously didn't have the monopoly on care for wounded during the Franco-Prussian war. However, Dunant does not seem to have registered anywhere at all as a volunteer, not in the Society outposts nor, it seems, in any of the other numerous improvised care centres which sprouted like mushrooms all over Paris. He sometimes accompanied President de Flavigny on his inspection tours of the 'official' medical units of the Red Cross, but it seems he was not inclined to don again the white suit he'd worn as the eager nurse of Castiglione. From now on he defended his status as initiator of the 1864 Convention along with the symbol of the red cross – this was plenty to keep him busy.

Through a curious inversion of fate, while Dunant was fighting tooth and nail to remind a series of ministers about the Geneva Convention, the official guardian of that same Geneva Convention, Gustave Moynier, was fighting for prisoners, a subject Dunant had supported in vain in 1864 and again in 1867, and which the rigorous lawyer had never before been keen to discuss. But the Franco-German war got him interested. Fifteen days after war was declared, with the characteristic efficiency of its president, the International Committee offered – without any mandate from its member countries – to ensure the exchange of correspondence between prisoners of war and their families and to facilitate sending money to detained soldiers: these were both points that Dunant had tried to argue for during the conferences of 1867. For efficiency's sake, these activities were centralized near the borders of the two warring countries, in an agency in Basel, but placed under the entire supervision of the International Committee in Geneva.

---

[29] The term 'Internationale' frequently designated the International Red Cross and its Francophone affiliates, but also the revolutionary socialist International Workingmen's Association, a confusion which would cause problems for Dunant, as we will see later.

What was Dunant's response to Moynier's successful advance into one of his own pet subjects? There is not a word in his memoirs or his correspondence. At this exact time, he was busy launching a new charity project with Baron Dutilh de la Tuque. The project was the *Association universelle de Prévoyance en faveur des citoyens sous les armes* (Universal Welfare Association for Citizens Bearing Arms), touted as an 'auxiliary to the Red Cross Aid Society'. Dunant took the presidency, Dutilh de la Tuque was vice president, and neither man could suspect the outlandish adventures awaiting them on the horizon. As usual, the rest of the committee included representatives from the nobility, several members of the Institut de France, two or three military men – and almost everyone nostalgic for the Empire.

Why did Dunant found a new association whose members came from the very same circles as the French Red Cross? Why did he give it the emblem of a white shield with the international red cross surrounded by two palm fronds, as if wanting to create confusion? And why did it make 'so much noise',[30] as Dunant himself commented? He doesn't say. We do know the association's background, however, as summarized in a small presentation text:

A soldier – that is a citizen bearing arms – is placed in special conditions; he has his own education, instructions and hygiene [. . .] To raise the moral and intellectual level of citizens called to serve, develop in them the taste for instruction [. . .] create libraries for their use and temperance societies [. . .] awaken and develop in him all that will elevate and ennoble his character; this is our goal.[31]

But the Welfare Association was also focused on the 'material side' of these conscripts. Without aspiring to substitute the military administration, 'the association would work towards the adoption of all recognized useful improvements' for their health and material situation.

---

[30] Dunant to his brother Pierre, 19 February 1871, BGE, Ms. fr. 2110, f. 41.
[31] *Suprême tentative de conciliation & de paix entre Versailles & Paris, faite par M. le baron Dutilh de La Tuque en mai 1871* (Paris: J. Dangon, 1906), 29–30.

On the one hand, the creation of a library and, on the other, 'useful improvements' of the health of soldiers . . . Quite coincidentally these two goals exactly matched Dunant's two commercial interests – the Universal Library, suited to the 'instruction of soldiers', and bandages, suited to 'improving the state of their health'.[32] We also know that the charity's headquarters were located at the Ville-l'Évêque plaza, in the 8th arrondissement, at Dunant's new address. Evidently, he was not only the founder but the general secretary, coordinator and the principal driving force.

It's again difficult to determine in which direction things moved between his lucrative activities and his humanitarian work. Without a universal vision, he would not be interested in a world library; without a humanitarian sensitivity, he would not be devoted to tending wounds. But ironically, without a bandage workshop or a universal library, perhaps the Welfare Association would never have been created. Ultimately, there is no shame in any of this: Dunant was poor, he needed something to live on and all he knew was how to establish prestigious committees around grand ideas. It would be wrong to look for a pure idealist in a beleaguered exile who needed to exploit any opportunities he could to survive.

Once again the right man for the right job, Dunant got his breath back, his self-confidence, his centre of gravity. He also gained a few pounds: 'I've put on weight these last three weeks,' he remarked to his sister on 5th October 'because I'm working in an area that suits me.' Beside the hotel was a 'well-provisioned' restaurant run by an American lady, where he received 'superior' treatment. He concluded lightly, 'Each day I congratulate myself for having stayed – if I'd left, I would have missed my greatest chance to reassert myself and recover from my personal disasters.'[33]

Throughout the entire siege, Dunant reported being busier than he could express. His Welfare Association had 100,000 copies printed of a fourteen-page 'Plea to Parisians', that Dunant probably wrote almost entirely himself and which exhorted the population to demonstrate their 'charity and respect towards the vanquished or

---

[32] Ibid.
[33] Dunant to his sister Marie, 5 October 1870, BGE Ms. fr. 2115 C, f. 45.

wounded enemy and the prisoner of war'.[34] The new committee voted upon the purchase of several thousand packages of bandages for wounded soldiers – an order readily sourced, no doubt about it, from the booming workshop on the Rue Taitbout run by Dunant, Chéron and the pharmacist Sirech.

Meanwhile, Moynier was moving his pawns forward on the prisoner-of-war issue. On 12th November, in Basel, the *Comité international de secours aux prisonniers de guerre* (The International Relief Committee for Prisoners of War) was founded. As if to confirm its connection to the Red Cross movement, the committee selected a green cross on a white background as their emblem. Its mission was to distribute not only aid and basic-need items to prisoners, but also the letters and money sent by their families.

Dunant must have been aware of Moynier's activism on the other side of the border. And yet on 17th October he boasted of a new initiative. Writing to his sister Marie, he explained: 'I have created a commission in favour of war prisoners, of which I am the chairman.'[35] In early December, he described to her the activities of the Welfare Association: 'Our mission is to help victims of war, to protect the prisoners of war of both nations, etc. etc.'[36] This was not just empty talk. Dunant very much did send a request to the French Minister of War to obtain authorization to visit German prisoners. But the response was swift and clear: 'In the present circumstances,' an officer from the Foreign Affairs Office replied, 'it is absolutely impossible to grant you such permission.'[37]

And so Moynier's Green Cross wouldn't have to face any unexpected competition from Paris. Whether he wanted to or not, Dunant remained exclusively linked to the protection of wounded soldiers rather than prisoners of war, and it was for the former that he was continually solicited, even earning some non-negligible profit at this time:

---

[34] Roger Durand, '*Les prisonniers de guerre aux temps héroïques*', *De l'utopie à la réalité* (Geneva: Société Henry Dunant, 1988), 251.

[35] Dunant to his sister Marie, 5 October 1870, BGE, Ms. fr. 2115 C, f. 46.

[36] Dunant to his sister Marie, 6 December 1870, BGE, Ms. fr. 2115 C, f. 51.

[37] General Le Flô to Dunant, BGE, Ms. fr. 2110, f. 33, translated in Yvonne de Pourtalès and Roger Durand, 'Henry Dunant, promoter of the 1874 Brussels Conference', IRRC, 167 (Geneva: ICRC, March 1975), 66.

One would never say that Paris is under siege. I am fairly often invited out to dine here and there, the Ladies of the dispensaries all court me in order to receive wounded, which are not difficult to find, then for this or that other thing.[38]

On 3rd December, for the first time since the war had begun, Dunant mentioned direct contact with the victims of the conflict:

The last few days have been marked by a mass of wounded being transported on boats along the Seine and carried through the streets. I take special care of the German and Prussian wounded and prisoners, and I get them all possible and desirable care.[39]

A merciless winter

When winter arrived – a harsh winter, as harsh as wartime winters can be – many Parisians grew concerned. As the mission of the Welfare Association was to look after the health and hygiene of citizens bearing arms, Dunant now created a 'Committee for Warm Clothing' to gather thousands of socks, vests, shirts and blankets for the soldiers at the front. An instant success: the salon at Mr Ribes's hotel, obligingly made available for the association to stock and sort clothing, was quickly overwhelmed. Dunant, who'd named himself commission president upon its creation, went on the hunt for a former imperial building that he readily obtained, and which was located opposite one of the wings of the Tuileries Palace, on the Rue de Rivoli.

It appears that warm clothing was Dunant's obsession during that wartime winter, but not just for soldiers. In his correspondence of that period, there is a recurrent regret, a remorse, even an obsession: Daniel Dunant's family had left their winter clothing in Paris when they'd gone home to Switzerland, discouraged, the previous spring. Since then, the war had prevented Daniel from returning to collect their things, and Henry was positively sick about

---

[38] Dunant to his sister Marie, 17 October 1870, BGE, Ms. fr. 2115 C, f. 46.
[39] Dunant to his sister Marie, 3 December 1870, BGE, Ms. fr. 2115 C, f. 50.

this. He certainly associated these trunks with the failure of the Universal Library and his brother's pitiful return to Geneva, ruined for a second time by his older brother's imaginary gold mines. In nearly every letter Dunant wrote to Pierre or Marie, he mentioned the 'winter things' he was unable to send to Daniel's family. 'It spoils all my joy for the recognition I am given, today, for what I've done,'[40] admitted the man whom Paris was welcoming again as a hero. Which is to say how deeply the problem preoccupied him.

Evidently, sending warm clothes to thousands of soldiers wasn't a consolation for having deprived his brother, sister-in-law and nieces of their own woollens. Did the episode cause a falling out? It seems unlike the spirit of his family, which remained loyal even in adversity. But the connection might have cooled. While he continued to write regularly to his sister Marie and his brother Pierre, there is no trace of even a single letter to Daniel. He mentioned once to Pierre, in February 1871, of having written to his younger brother about some new working opportunities ... but misfortune would meanwhile befall this poor young man, who's luck was no better than his brother Henry's.

In contrast to his brother, sister-in-law and nieces, to the soldiers under siege, and to the great majority of all of Paris, Dunant seemed not to suffer at all from the terrible cold that winter of 1870–1 – thanks to the good care of Mr and Mrs Ribes. He even rejoiced to his sister Marie that he'd 'never felt better' than in that beginning of the year, while frostbite and pneumonia were causing more damage among the French troops than the combat itself. Even the siege-induced famine was related in an anecdotal tone in his letters; apparently the price of rats had gone up to two or three francs while the exotic animals from the menageries and public gardens were being sacrificed for the wealthiest tables in Paris.

Did Dunant actually go hungry? He may have claimed so in his memoirs, but none of his correspondence at the time mentions this. Perhaps he described himself so cozily throughout the war to avoid alarming his family. He complained years later, in hindsight, with a general bitterness about the state of poverty in which his Parisian 'friends' had left him during all of this intensely busy but always pro

---

[40] Dunant to his sister Marie, 25 October 1870, BGE, Ms. fr. 2115 C, f. 47.

bono work for the Welfare Association. No matter how hard he was working to print pamphlets, buy bandages (from himself and his associates, but shhhh!), distribute them, collect warm clothing, sort and deliver it, there were never any financial gains. Even the thousands of bandages purchased by an enthusiastic Welfare Association and broadly disseminated to thankful soldiers still remained unpaid; yet he was very much counting on receiving his rightful commission, even if no one on the committee should know about it. And while all these noble and charitable individuals were pampering him and complimenting him, no one managed to thank him in a more tangible way. Years later, he was still quite bitter about this:

> For three and a half years, the entire Committee had pretended to ignore my impoverished state, and yet I spent those three and a half years in Paris, in utter destitution and abject poverty; and even at the moment the war started, no one bothered to offer me the slightest job in the association offices, which were brimming with people![41]

Dunant certainly hoped the end of the siege would bring his friends back down to earth, revealing to them what they owed him, both morally and materially. But reality very quickly erased such delusions. The members of the Welfare Association were indeed admirably loyal to the salons of the hotel at the Ville-l'Évêque plaza while there was no way of leaving Paris nor much else to do to kill time, but at the end of January 1871, the armistice with the Prussians was signed and the siege of Paris was lifted. Those same passionate volunteers, who had soundly voted for the 100,000 brochures, for the purchase of thousands of packages of bandages and for warm clothes to be sent to the front, disappeared into the woodwork one after the other, casually leaving a bill of some 8,000 francs. Here again, Dunant was still sore twenty years later:

> The members of the Welfare Association, so devoted during the siege, took advantage of its end and the ensuing chaos to leave me entirely responsible, and without a word disappeared, never to return. Yet they had been supportive. I was then completely

---

[41] Dunant, *Mémoires*, 262.

impoverished, having lost everything in 1867. The members of the Welfare Association were from various backgrounds; but all of them were moneyed; among them could be found very rich Parisian merchants. As for me, I had no personal profit to take from the association, and I ended up with all the trouble and the woes [. . .]. This was just another disaster to add to the previous one, which had lasted three and a half years. On top of the more poignant stresses, my reward was slander, and new enmities.[42]

A new friend

Since its founding in September 1870, the Welfare Association had evolved. At the beginning of 1871, Dunant gave over the presidency, content to remain an honorary president alongside President Amédée Thierry. A crowd of new and prestigious patronyms was promoted to the rank of 'vice president'. Dunant, who very much enjoyed impressing his family with his connections to upper-crust Parisians, listed them all one by one in a letter to Pierre, dated 5th February. At the top of the list was Count Raynald de Choiseul, whose name was now appearing for the first time in Dunant's correspondence; they had probably met in the context of their work with wounded soldiers. Long-standing members of the Red Cross Society such as Count Sérurier and Count de Beaufort were also cited as 'honorary members' of the association; two other counts were recruited as secretaries.

Just like its members, the name of the Welfare Association for Citizens Bearing Arms had also changed to suit certain events and the mood of its founder: it was sometimes the *Société universelle* (Universal Society) with or without a reference to citizens bearing arms, and then simply became the *Association universelle de prévoyance* (Universal Welfare Association) at the beginning of 1871.

The charity's kind souls may have remained blind to Dunant's poverty, but this didn't stop them from asking him for a variety of personal favours. In March 1871, Count de Flavigny asked Dunant

---

[42] Dunant, *Mémoires*, 260.

to intercede on behalf of two seriously wounded *francs-tireurs*.[43]
They had been treated at Fontainebleau in one of the medical units
run by the Aid Society, and the Prussians were threatening to shoot
them as soon as they were healed.

'Please go to Versailles to see the Prince of Pless. He directs the
German Red Cross, he will listen to you!'

Dunant attempted to dissuade de Flavigny, but to no avail; the
president of the French Red Cross felt it was his duty to rescue these
men, even if he wasn't planning to lead the operation himself.
Always anxious to please, Dunant accepted. But to do what de
Flavigny was asking of him, he had to first beg money off a rich
compatriot from Lausanne, a Mr Verdeil, whom he'd met during the
siege. De Flavigny seems to have overlooked the significant detail of
Dunant's poverty and the cost of the trip. In contrast, Verdeil was
more than generous. Dunant could first pay his debt to Miss Morton,
the charming American who'd so kindly been giving him food on
credit for the last three months at her small restaurant near la
Madeleine. Then he rushed to Versailles, managing with great effort
the inherent difficulties of crossing German lines. He acquired the
Prince of Pless's promise to spare the lives of the two wounded men,
then, unable to return to Paris that same evening, he had to stay at
the Prussian-filled Hotel des Réservoirs. And guess what happened
there? He chanced upon an old acquaintance, a member of the
Prussian Red Cross who invited him for coffee in a small open-air
tearoom. Unfortunately, this friendly old face also happened to be
Bismarck's first secretary … meaning that from then on, Dunant
would suspect the French took him for a Prussian spy.

This hapless reputation wouldn't prevent him, however, from
returning several times to Versailles. Sometime later, Count de
Choiseul, undoubtedly a fairly close friend, requested a similar
service, asking him to plead another case with the Prussians. This
time the goal was to prevent the occupiers from pillaging the
mansion of a former minister of Napoleon III, Eugène Rouher. Why
on earth would Dunant accept a mission like this and on behalf of
a man on the run he didn't even know? Did he simply enjoy being

---

[43] TN: during the Franco-Prussian war, a *franc-tireur* (French for 'free shooter') was
the name given to riflemen who were not a part of the regular military. They were a
kind of militia formed out of shooting clubs and military societies. The whole story
is told by Dunant in his *Mémoires*, 261–3.

around the Prussians who'd treated him so well? Was it to please
the young and charming count who'd asked him? He never explains
his reasons for agreeing to such a task.[44]

What were Dunant's true motivations for doing things? This is
one of his best-kept secrets. However incomprehensible it may have
been, he went to a lot of trouble to save the family souvenirs of this
Mr Rouher – who meant nothing to him. In the middle of the siege,
in the middle of the war, he crossed battle lines at night to get to the
villa where Bismarck was living at 14, Rue de Provence in Versailles.
While Bismarck's deep voice carried through from the next room,
Dunant managed an audience with his private secretary to explain
the situation.

The consequences would be swift. Leaving the villa's garden a
few minutes later, he became aware of 'shadowy figures'[45] that
vanished as soon as he walked past. According to his *Mémoires*,
these shadows would never leave him. He found them in Paris, in
Rome, then in London, in Alsace, and even in Stuttgart. They would
ruin his life until the day he died. And he dates them from this
moment in Versailles, says they then became 'omnipresent': from
this absurd excursion into the Prussian quarters to rescue the family
souvenirs of a deposed French minister. Dear Mr Dunant, what on
earth were you doing mixed up in this? His *Mémoires* tell us nothing.

His gratuitous risk-taking continued. Dunant would go yet again
on another mission. Several weeks later, the very same Raynald de
Choiseul, now a refugee in London like half of the Bonapartist clan,
convinced him to undertake a second favour which makes the first
look like a walk in the park. This time de Choiseul asked him to
retrieve a chest belonging to General de Galliffet that contained
letters from the Prince of Wales. The chest had fallen into the hands
of some Communards[46] who were getting ready to publish its
contents, carefully rearranged no doubt, a possibility quite terrifying
for the English court. Pressed in London by Empress Eugénie, de
Choiseul made his request. And again, Dunant succeeded. He did
not retrieve General Galliffet's chest himself, but thanks to the

---

[44] Dunant, *Mémoires*, 263–4.

[45] Ibid., 265.

[46] The Paris Commune (see next section) was a socialist revolutionary government
that took power in Paris between March and May 1871.

decisive and highly risky assistance of the grandson of Dutilh de la
Tuque, vice president of the Welfare Association, the publication of
the letters was postponed long enough that the problem literally
went up in smoke – the Communards themselves set fire to the
Ministry of Finance where the chest had been stored.[47]

Again, the same question arises: what pushed Dunant to take
such a risk, and even worse, to have others run such a risk, for a
general whom he didn't really respect? Alongside his account of the
events, his memoirs twice refer to General de Galliffet's ill treatment
of prisoners during the repression of the Commune. How could
Dunant not see the incongruity of his boundless – yet absurd and
paradoxical – devotion to the Prince of Wales, the exiled empress
and her faithful circle, as well as to their spokesman Raynald de
Choiseul? While his *Mémoires* detail the events, they say nothing on
their hidden causes.

The era's gossipmongers may give us a clue about this Raynald
de Choiseul to explain Dunant's unreasonable heroism. Strikingly
handsome, the 30-year-old was the youngest son of the Duke de
Choiseul-Praslin who'd made headlines at the end of the July
Monarchy. In 1847, he'd assassinated his wife and committed
suicide several days later. Raynald, the ninth and youngest child,
was only 8 years old when the tragedy occurred. But his early
celebrity never prevented him from enjoying the limelight. A fan of
the theatre and transvestitism, he was all the rage at a ball at the
Tuileries, as reported by Mrs Carette in her *Recollections of the
Court of the Tuileries*:

> One evening Comte Raynald de Choiseul turned all heads, and
> everyone was on the qui vive to discover who the witty, audacious
> woman was who so well concealed her identity beneath an elegant
> domino worn with the perfection of feminine grace, and who
> never betrayed by the slightest awkwardness that she belonged to
> the sterner sex. Even in the masked photograph which she freely
> distributed it was impossible to detect the deceit.[48]

---

[47] Dunant, *Mémoires*, 284–6.
[48] Madame Carette née Bouvet, *Recollections of the court of the Tuileries*, tr. from the
French by Elizabeth Phipps Train (New York: D. Appleton and Company, 1890), vol.
1, 216.

The photo can still be found among collectors, and the confusion is striking indeed. Several other documents of the era which mention him highlight a feather and a domino costume, a small pink taffeta parasol and a beauty to stun both young men and women alike. If Dunant's attraction to masculine societies, his anxious attachment to his mother, his lengthy celibacy and the absence of any recognized feminine liaison had not already raised a few questions over time, the extreme consideration he suddenly granted Raynald de Choiseul probably could. This Raynald may have 'supported [Henry] with a devotion far beyond all praise'[49] between 1870 and 1871, but he also had him do his bidding at incomparable risk to Dunant and others.

In his later writings, there is not a single mention of the Count de Choiseul, as if it was just a passing relationship. And while Dunant obsessively kept and organized his correspondence with a wide range of personalities, from the most renowned to the most humble, there is not a single letter from this count, nor a copy or mention of a letter that may have been addressed to him, yet they must have communicated during the count's stay in London, at the very least about the chest belonging to Galliffet. The Henry Dunant archives do not contain the slightest trace of Raynald de Choiseul, no matter how 'beyond all praise' he might have been devoted to Dunant.

The Paris Commune

Paris wasn't calmed by the lifting of the siege. Quite the opposite. Having bravely resisted the Prussians, the Parisians considered the armistice to be a shameful surrender. The election of the National Assembly on 8th February 1871 only deepened the divide between rural and clerical conservative France and the Republican capital with its penchant for 'red'. The new, largely monarchist assembly appointed an ageing Adolphe Thiers to the head of the government. It then took a series of unpopular measures, including the suppression of the small salary granted to the national guards during the siege. Yet a growing part of this National Guard was refusing the government's authority; the majority of its companies and battalions were collected into a Federation, soon rallied by the

---

[49] Dunant to his sister Marie, 15 March 1871, BGE Ms.fr.2115 C, f.56.

activists of the International Workingmen's Association. Originally united to defend the threatened Republic, this 'Federation' needed but a tiny spark to catch fire. Thiers, who had become worried at the increasing influence of the Federation and the power amassed by its 'Central Committee', sent government troops to Montmartre on the night of 17th March to fetch the canons of the National Guard. But by then both northern and western Parisians had chosen their side. The Commune ignited. Supported by a large portion of the population, the Central Committee established its headquarters at the city hall while Thiers crept away to Versailles, soon followed by 100,000 terrified Parisians.

These revolutionary tremors were certainly not comfortable for the very chic society to which Dunant's friends belonged. From one day to the next, both the Welfare Association and the Red Cross Society started bleeding members. Only the staunchest devotees remained in Paris, among which were the Count de Flavigny and his wife who decided, Dunant said, 'to remain faithful to their work and their position',[50] though their children and grandchildren had already left the city. And so at least the Welfare Association committee continued to meet, for better or worse, at Mr Ribes's hotel, where Dunant was still living despite the lift of the siege.

When the Commune took power over Paris, Dunant complained to his brother Pierre about the stubborn blindness of his committee whom he had been warning for weeks about an impending civil war. Only Raynald de Choiseul shared his opinion at that time. Starting with the first skirmishes, the latter had even enrolled as 'a simple nurse soldier'; and more recently, he'd got it into his head to offer himself as a 'voluntary prisoner' in Montmartre, the headquarters of the insurgents, a novel heroic whim that President de Flavigny had wisely prevented. Still, young Raynald paid voluntarily and actively with his person, doing exactly what Dunant would have done if he were ten years younger and 10,000 francs richer. He liked to see for himself what was happening and, like his friend Dunant, evaluated the situation exactly as it was – explosive.

On Thursday 23rd March the overly confident Association committee finally had to agree with its two forward-thinking

---

[50] Dunant, *Mémoires*, 269. This period of the Commune follows Dunant's *Mémoires*, ch. 24, 267–76, for all following quotations.

members: Paris was now in the hands of the insurgents. The remaining members of the Association instantly begged the commoner Dunant to go to the Central Committee of the National Guard, which would give way a few days later to the Commune Council.

Dunant agreed. On 24th March he went to see the new Parisian government. After exchanging a few jokes with a jovial National Guard member, he managed to find a sub-officer of a sub-officer who answered to his 'Monsieur' with a hearty 'Citizen!' In any case, they knew who he was, which was all Dunant had been hoping for. They assured him that both his work and his person were sacred, and they would not forget to seek his advice 'in a case of civil war'. Dunant left the meeting delighted and reported the event to Count de Flavigny, who also declared himself 'highly satisfied'.

Momentarily calmed by this diplomacy with the insurgents, the president of the Red Cross wouldn't remain so. On 14th April an increasingly nervous de Flavigny convoked the committee of the Red Cross to announce that 'Mr Cluseret from the Commune's War Commission had decided to disband the society'.

Was it really the Commune who'd required this? As diplomatic as ever, Dunant doesn't detail the series of events himself but simply cites the 'remarkable report' by Count de Beaufort, general secretary of the Society, on these 'dark times'. Meanwhile this 'remarkable' report makes it clear, in a remarkably convoluted way, that instead of 'disbanding itself' as de Flavigny had suggested – supposedly on order of the Commune – the Society felt it more appropriate to 'take leave' of its president as well as its vice president. In other words, if de Flavigny and Sérurier wanted to jump ship right when Paris was a tinderbox, good for them, but the boat wouldn't necessarily go down with them.

What happened next better explains de Flavigny's rush to disband the French Red Cross. Several days after the unfortunate meeting of 14th April, the count set off early and in a complete panic for Dunant's hotel. The head of the dispensary on the Champs-Élysées, Dr Chenu, a celebrity believed to be untouchable, had just been arrested by the new government, and several trustworthy friends were warning de Flavigny he was next on the list. His position as president of the Red Cross, a role which should have kept him out of harm's way, had just become decidedly harmful, clarifying his recent haste to step down.

'It was you who introduced me into the Society!' he said to Dunant, sweat beading his brow. 'I now rely on you to protect me from the consequences, in the circumstances in which we find ourselves. I'm taking refuge with you.'

Dunant was speechless at the injustice of this allegation. After having savoured the honours of his position, de Flavigny was holding him responsible for the dangers it now involved! He was careful, however, not to show his disappointment.

'You are welcome in my room. But the wisest thing to do is leave Paris as soon as possible, with Madame de Flavigny. I know several individuals in foreign embassies. I will go to see them and get you a passport from a friendly country.'

Dunant didn't knock on the door of a single embassy. He went directly to his friend Raynald de Choiseul, who was still 'bravely in Paris during these unfortunate days' (the young man would soon leave for London, and from there ask Dunant for the 'favour' of retrieving Galliffet's chest). Dunant tells us it was Raynald who 'immediately' obtained – without specifying how – two precious passports from the ambassador of Italy. Count and Countess de Flavigny were now Signor and Signora Flavigni.

He met the Countess a few hours later on the Rue d'Astorg. Hidden in the shadows of a cab, she was looking miserable; she'd aged twenty years since the last time he'd seen her. And so the daughter of the Duke de Fezensac put herself blindly into the hands of the founder of the Red Cross Society that her father had first presided over, followed by her husband. Who else could she trust in these uncertain times?

The cab drove all three of them to the Gare du Nord, the only way out of Paris and towards 'freedom'; for the newly baptized Flavigni, freedom meant heading towards the Prussian occupier, now far preferable company than their fellow citizens. The waiting room was bursting with France's nobility, all of whom were waiting for the next train in a petrified silence.

Dunant believed his work was done. He was ready to say goodbye to his charges when a well-known figure broke through the crowd, leaping upon him with an abruptness that unsettled the cowed stillness of the room.

'You didn't get me a passport!' shouted a pale and dishevelled Count Sérurier into the packed waiting room. Then he added, to the simultaneous consternation of Henry, the Count and the Countess:

'Tell Cluseret I'll return to Paris . . . if it's necessary, if he wants me to . . . yes, I will come back!'[51]

Cluseret. Cluseret? What was he talking about? Cluseret: the Commune's strongman, the reigning general, the absolute terror of every single person in that waiting room, the sworn enemy of both the Thiers government and the Prussians! Dunant had nothing to do with Cluseret, had never even met him. And yet here was Sérurier throwing the man's name in his face as if he were Dunant's cousin!

But suddenly there was a movement, yes, finally, the train was arriving, and it was time to board. The room emptied in the blink of an eye, Sérurier moving as quickly as the others, faster even than the de Flavignys, leaving the rest of his speech for better days. In less than five minutes Dunant stood alone in an empty train station, listening to the long wail of the train whistle. He turned on his heel to walk back to his hotel, avoiding the restless neighbourhoods as much as possible.

Peace negotiations

Although the Commune had pushed 90 per cent of the population of Paris's wealthy neighbourhoods to escape, it didn't change Dunant's daily life. His Swiss passport enabled him to enter and leave Paris as he liked, and he availed himself of this privilege. But he was constantly torn between two contradictory states of mind.

On the one hand, his letters to his family demonstrate a clear bias in favour of the Prussians, against the French, as well as in favour of Thiers' 'Versailles' against the insurgent Parisians. At the end of April 1871, he went to Compiègne, where he was received by the royal Prince Albert of Saxony, who 'could not have been more gracious'.[52] All of his correspondence at the time, like his *Mémoires,* betray his boundless admiration for the Germans, for the chivalry with which they conducted the war, for their irreproachable respect of the Geneva Convention and treatment of the wounded and prisoners. In contrast to this, 'the French and, above all, the Parisians got what they deserved, because they were nothing but selfish both

---

[51] Dunant, *Mémoires,* 269–70.
[52] Dunant to his sister Marie, 27 April 1871, BGE, Ms. fr. 2115 C, f. 59.

during the siege and before it. They deserve a tyrant and I would be
delighted to see it.'[53] In letter after letter he complained of 'Babylon',
the city of Paris whose inhabitants he now hated, since the only
Parisians worthy of his time had cut and run when the revolution
threatened.

At the same time, despite his partiality for the Prussians and his
prejudices against democrats of any kind, he continued to believe in
his saviour role. 'All the different parties now in France: the
Germans, Mr Thiers and the Orleanists, the imperialists, the Paris
Commune, its Central Committee and the Internationale and all the
rest, regard me as the sacred representative of humanity,' he wrote
to his sister in the same letter. Five days later, he sprang into action.
He confirmed to his sister that he'd suggested the three parties –
'Prussia, represented by the royal Prince of Saxony, France, by Mr
Thiers, and Paris, by the Commune – form an International
Committee with several plenipotentiary ministers, of which I would
be the president'.

What was this committee's purported goal? To remove some
300–400,000 women, children and elderly from Paris, and save
their lives in the process. 'They accepted,' he solemnly wrote, 'and
this is likely to take place soon.'

As always, his lofty humanitarian ambitions mingled with his
more personal worries. After his dream of sending 300,000 civilian
victims out of Paris, his letter continued, 'I will find a way to
carefully send Daniel's belongings out of the city, too.'[54] Although
he doesn't explain the connection between the two actions, his letter
demonstrates his lasting obsession that winter, just as painful as
ever.

Up until 20th May, the day before the Bloody Week that would
put an end to the Commune, Dunant was nevertheless convinced
his civilian 'rescue plan' could work. For some time, he even seemed
to be counting on aid from the English, who had suddenly taken a
decisive role. On 10th May, Dunant told his sister that 'the entire
English press' was discussing his rescue plan, or that it was going to,
while in Paris, the Welfare Association was leading negotiations,

---

[53] Ibid.
[54] Dunant to his sister Marie, 1st May 1871, BGE, Ms. fr. 2115 C, f. 61.

'meeting constantly and serving as a link',[55] he stated, between the different parties of the agreement.

England's interest can be better understood in what follows in the same letter, completed by Dunant two days later: 'Count de Choiseul, one of the vice presidents [of the Welfare Association] has left for London upon my invitation (he's the brother of the ambassador in Rome). And there, he will attract the interest of the English who will come to our aid.'[56] It all becomes clear now: Raynald de Choiseul was in England and it was he who would make some waves on the other side of the Channel, since no one in France was interested. On 12th May, a long article on Dunant appeared on page twelve of the *Times*. Thank you, Raynald.

Meanwhile in France, a decidedly courageous Baron Dutilh de la Tuque, one of the few remaining Welfare Association activists in Paris, was trying to achieve something everyone else before him – the mayors, the deputies, the Republican Union League – had failed to do: an armistice between Paris and Versailles, not for an evacuation, but a true peace agreement. Dutihl had managed to get close to three heads of Paris's Federated National Guard, who were willing to negotiate with the heads in Versailles.

Wishing to explain this miraculous opening to Thiers, Dutihl begged Dunant and his Swiss passport to accompany him to Versailles. But they couldn't have chosen a worse moment. This was 11th May, the very day the Communards pillaged Thiers's Parisian home – filled with treasures the aged connoisseur had spent his entire life passionately collecting. Furious, Thiers despatched the two peace messengers without hearing a word.

While Dunant continued to believe in his evacuation plan, Dutihl de la Tuque continued to believe in his plan for peace. He spent the next few days meeting the three Commune generals – then went to Versailles again, this time alone, for new peace talks with Thiers. But while he was travelling, the Commune's hawks, who'd learned of his secret negotiations with the three Federated chiefs, had them imprisoned along with the man who'd offered his home for the secret meetings. The latter's wife, in despair, raced to warn Dutihl de la Tuque's sister that her brother would also be imprisoned when he got off his train that evening at the Gare du Nord.

[55] Dunant to his sister Marie, 7–10 May 1871, BGE, Ms. fr. 2115 C, f. 63.
[56] Ibid.

There was only one chance left: Dunant and his Swiss passport. Only he could go to Saint-Denis in time to stop Dutihl from getting on the Paris-bound train. Luck would have it that Henry was at the Baron's sister's house when the tragic news arrived. Another person was also there, a Scotswoman with the pretty name of Miss Rose Murray (niece of a countess and heir of a duke, Dunant tells us in passing), who offered herself and her British passport as company, to make Dunant look more like a husband than a spy.

Dutihl de la Tuque was saved, *in extremis*. Henry and Miss Murray arrived in time to intercept his cab just before it entered the Saint-Denis train station. They explained the situation and urged him to return to Versailles . . . to wait for a better day.

That same evening, after Dutihl had recounted the event he'd just escaped, Thiers, quite moved, presented the Baron to the many individuals gathered in his reception hall, and publicly honoured him. While recognizing the 'absolute failure' of the peace efforts with the Federated army (which, truth be told, he didn't believe in any way), Thiers expressed his gratitude 'to Mr Dutihl de la Tuque and to Mr Henry Dunant who, assuredly, had risked his own life to save his friend's!'[57]

Yes, quite true. While Dutihl had risked his life for peace, Dunant had risked his life for a friend. The Red Cross founder's scope of action had narrowed during these difficult days in the history of Paris, losing a measure of its universality.

The Bloody Week

In the second half of May 1871, the Communards were feeling the desperation of their position and thus hardened their hold on the capital. They arrested anyone suspected of passing intelligence to the powers in Versailles and accelerated the pace of arbitrary executions.

With a calm that bordered on recklessness, Dunant returned to Paris after each of his exterior excursions, despite the pleas of his nearest and dearest. His memoirs later explain that this was because he could not do otherwise, an allusion to the precariousness of his

---

[57] Dunant, *Mémoires*, 283. For the whole story, see ch. 30, 277–83.

financial situation. But in his letters of the era, he said he was 'very well in Paris, despite the incessant and deafening bombardments'. The civil war hardly affected him, he claimed, infinitely less than the 'ten, twenty, thirty thousand men who'd perished in the great battles that winter. Since the French seem to enjoy fighting each other so much,' he concluded, disenchanted, 'then let them fight.'[58]

And so he was a first-hand witness to the last week of the Commune, the infamous Bloody Week.[59] On Sunday 21st May, he spent a quiet day with a friend in Enghien. That night, getting into the train to go home, he was shocked to see only women. Several of them came towards him: 'But, sir, you aren't going to Paris! You will be taken upon your arrival! Get off at the second-to-last stop, otherwise you will be arrested!' Once they arrived at the aforementioned station, they implored him again. But Dunant would not listen, and when the National Guards entered the wagon and meticulously searched it, his Swiss passport protected him against further investigation.

He reached his hotel without incident – the night was splendid and perfectly calm – went to bed and slept the deep sleep that follows a trip into the country. But around 4:00 a.m. an incredible racket sounded beneath his windows: drums were beating and the alarm was ringing out. Sometime later, Dunant saw two soldiers in red trousers on the roof of the opposite hotel, while others were climbing the facade along the gutters, like thieves. The men of Versailles had entered Paris; Thiers's regular army had assaulted the capital and the Communards.

At that very moment, cries rang out from the ground floor and someone knocked at his door. The owner asked him to come down: it seemed urgent. Below, a colonel from the regular army was explaining to Mr Ribes that they would have to tunnel through his hotel from the front wall to the back. Seeing Dunant arrive, the face of the owner brightened. He pulled him to the colonel: 'Here he is,' indicating Dunant, 'this is the promoter of the Geneva Convention, and he lives in my house. As a result, this building is sacred!'

Stepping away from a crowd of increasingly agitated individuals, Dunant and the colonel soon came to an understanding: the former

---

[58] Dunant to his sister Marie, 1 May 1871, BGE, Ms. fr. 2115 C, f. 61.
[59] Dunant, *Mémoires*, ch. 31, 287–307, for all the following quotations.

explained to the latter that behind this hotel sat a dozen other houses that would need breaking down, and which would lead them nowhere – in any case, not where they wanted to go. The colonel was eventually satisfied with the requisition of mattresses, to the great relief of the hotel owner.

For two entire days, Dunant watched the battles through his window. Fighting between the Federated men and the Versailles men, between the capital city's insurgents and the representatives of 'legal France', between the National Guard and Thiers's regular army, between one France and another France. His observation post was ideally situated: the small plaza in front of the hotel gave onto the Rue de Suresnes which the Federated men had closed on one end, and which the Versailles men then barricaded on the other with a mountain of piled-up mattresses.

Unable to go out onto the street, Henry had free full board at the hotel. He spent his hours reading Wilkie Collins's *The Woman in White*, with its thrilling story of requited love thwarted by all sorts of mean secondary characters. He barely raised his nose from its pages to watch the opposite building riddled with insurgent bullets. 'As if to punish me for being so calm,' he recounts with an equally unsettling placidness, 'a few of the bullets came whistling against the door of my room and the glass of the corridor [. . .] breaking several panes.'[60]

And the shooting? The fires? The summary executions, the bayonet massacres, the attacked dispensaries, the mistreated wounded? Dunant would only take measure of the horror later. As the days passed, his detachment slowly transformed into a cynicism born of disgust and despair. Without judgement or tears, Dunant extensively recounts this hellish week in his memoirs: 16-year-old children mercilessly executed, prisoners shaved to be more easily identified, or even beaten if they tripped or fell out of line. His chronicle certainly reflects his instinctive partialities: on the Commune side, these 'men of the people and their wives fight with rage, with the energy of desperation, faithful to their flag, the bloody flag, which they call the flag of liberty!' But things were hardly better on the other side: 'They are handed a merciless war,

---

[60] Ibid., 293.

implacable, a real war of extermination with all its horrors, let's call it what it is, because this is the truth.'[61]

Politically, Dunant didn't hide his support for the reconquering of Paris by the Versailles government and the restoration of a conservative regime: he had not the slightest sympathy for the ideology of the Paris Commune. But the beastliness of Thiers's regular troops and the inhumanity of their officers was still repulsive: 'Nothing but blood everywhere, nothing but horrors and hatred for the future, Mr Thiers could have avoided this, with a little more generosity, skill, and heart!' Years later, after detailing these eight days of such varying emotions, Dunant would finish with these simple words: 'A vast human slaughterhouse.'[62]

For Dunant the observer, this was, in the end, the only way to sum up the Commune. Out of a disgust for the insurgents' actual cause, or for its protagonists, or because he saw no honour in war, or maybe because the French Red Cross didn't ask him for anything heroic, he kept his distance from this civil war, as if its wounded, its prisoners, its hostages, persecutors and victims weren't his concern. Only the personal requests by certain individuals – for the *francs-tireurs*, then Rouher, Galliffet, Dutilh de la Tuque, the archbishop of Paris and a priest of the Madeleine – would engage him enough to undertake each risky attempt to contact either the Commune, the Prussians or the Versailles government. But no other ambitious rescue or intervention strategy tempted him, not with the Red Cross or elsewhere, except for his evacuation plan which had never been very credible, despite its praise in the British press. Even more curious, his *Mémoires* demonstrate his nearly cavalier detachment – more occupied with the rousing novel he was reading or a beautiful starry sky or the spectacular vision of Paris burning – as if to absolve himself of any implication in this painful chapter of French history. Dunant seems to want to place himself, *a posteriori*, not just above the fray, but away from it, actually outside it.

At a greater distance, in fact, than his contemporaries perceived. Even before the end of the Commune, Baron Dutilh de la Tuque, whom Dunant had saved, went to the trouble of trying to get Dunant a 'national reward' of 500,000 francs for services rendered. Dunant

---

[61] Ibid., 303.
[62] Ibid., 322.

was immediately worried Geneva would get wind of the plan, because his 'dogged enemies'[63] would do anything, he believed, to see it fail. But what would the Genevans have to gain in preventing a sum of money enabling him to repay his debts and wash away the disgrace that still tainted his name? He was probably worried the sum would be seized before he could put a finger on it, and that the lights would be once again trained on him and on his past, something he desperately wanted to avoid. He was in the midst of preparing his relaunch, and his honourability was more necessary than ever before.

Dutilh's sought-after reward would never be granted. A first failure in a long series. Dunant's dread of having to bring up his past translated into several missed occasions to repay his debts, yet he continued to bemoan their heavy burden. This contradiction began that autumn of 1871 and lasted until his death, condemning him to relentless remorse and a lingering stain on his reputation. But in 1871, he could only see the near future. The war was over, the Commune was squashed, he needed to re-establish his position on the international scene. And quickly.

---

[63] Dunant to his sister Marie, 1 May 1871, BGE, Ms. fr. 2115 C, f. 61.

9

The Philanthropist's Revival (1871–4)

The aftermath

The day after the Commune fell, the French ruling classes were in a state of shock. Not only because the Commune's ideals terrified them, but also because of the extensive support these ideals had found with the Parisian population.

Something needed to be done. A strong power needed to be rebuilt. France restored its chambers and a conservative, royalist government. The Commune was overthrown; it was time for the French to get back on their feet.

It was also time to repress the socialist influences on the people: the masses would need to be re-educated. Amid a crusade reminiscent of the Holy Alliance of 1815, the 'pure aristocrat' Dunant – as he readily called himself – found himself a new vocation.

The Welfare Association's founding text in 1870 had already advocated for the spiritual edification of citizens bearing arms. After the Commune, members felt this programme was more relevant than ever. It only needed to be adapted to a peacetime situation. Dunant got to work on exactly this in the second half of 1871.

At the time, he didn't appear to resent his former committee for saddling him with 8,000 francs of debt as thanks for his good and loyal services. No, he set off for a new tour with exactly the same people, coming from the very same universe of all his previous committees. And so in June 1871, the *Alliance universelle de l'ordre et de la civilisation* (Universal Alliance for Order and Civilization) was reborn from the ashes of the former Welfare Association. Such a pompous name and more than anything its 'universal' character bear the unmistakable signature of Henry Dunant.

The general idea is crystal clear in its first sentence: 'The principles of the Universal Alliance are the legitimate interests of religion, family, work and property.'[1]

The shock waves of the Commune can be felt throughout the association's political programme. What mattered was working to 'strengthen order' and 'conserve political peace and social peace'. To do this, they needed to 'improve the conditions of those less fortunate and undereducated' – in other words, to silence, from the top down, the red sirens of the International Workingmen's Association, enemy number one of this new Universal Alliance.

With committee members as conservative as its goals, the Alliance nevertheless stood firmly 'outside personal conflicts, as well as outside the political conflicts of parties and governments'. An important point given that Dunant was planning to use the Alliance to relaunch several of his previous hobby horses and a few new ones: a diplomatic convention on prisoners of war, since the Geneva Convention still only dealt with war wounded; a procedure of diplomatic arbitration to manage conflicts 'between civilized nations'; and an international code of human rights 'for civilized nations'. Furthermore, the Universal Alliance immediately announced its intention to establish individual chapters around the world. During the aftermath of the troubles of 1871, Dunant was visibly seeking to reposition himself at the centre of the humanitarian stage, and on all fronts at the same time.

A handwritten note found on a programme of the Universal Alliance indicates that Dunant wrote it himself, as well as the 'manifesto'[2] which would appear a year later. While all this suggests he was the linchpin of the movement, his name only rarely appears, as if he were waiting for proof of success before jumping out of the woodwork. He first preferred to keep himself in the shadows of the

---

[1] *Bulletin de l'Alliance universelle de l'ordre et de la civilisation, Recueil des documents publiés* (Paris: Aux Bureaux de l'Alliance, 1873), 2–4, for further quotations.
[2] This *Manifeste de l'Alliance universelle de l'ordre et de la civilisation* will be republished as an introduction to the minutes of the 1872 Congress (see further reference, n. 12 below), I–XII.

celebrities he'd plucked from his previous committees – from the French Red Cross, the Welfare Association, the Universal Library. This new Alliance included all the same faces from the former Orleanist-legitimist-Bonapartist nobility, army officers and academics, a distinguished assembly now enriched with a larger dose of the Catholic Church: an archbishop, five bishops and an archdeacon. The senator Amédée Thierry, Institut de France member, officiated as the first president. Alongside an admiral, a general, a colonel, three dukes, six viscounts, six barons, seventeen counts and several marquis sat some celebrities of the time: Elie de Beaumont, the lifelong secretary of the Academy of Sciences and former president of the Welfare Association; Ferdinand de Lesseps, Suez Canal engineer; and the economist Frédéric Passy, pacifist and future co-laureate of the Nobel Prize with Dunant. Henry wrote proudly to his sister Marie in March 1872:

> It is I who have assembled all these names, despite the ruthlessness of those to whom I've done only good, those who would do anything to see me fail. I mean the Protestants of Paris, it has to be said because it's true. [. . .] They lie shamelessly; during the siege, they gossiped widely that I was a Prussian spy; now they say I have become a papist and all the rest.[3]

Is this another sign of the persecutory delusions that would later perpetually haunt Dunant? At this point it is more a euphoric recklessness than a paranoid mania. Throughout the entire Commune siege, he'd continually flaunted his connections to the Germans, had crossed enemy lines twenty times and was then surprised to be suspected of harbouring German sympathies. It's also clear that his outreach to the upper Catholic clergy wasn't going undetected among the Parisian Protestant gentry. In August 1871, he had already written to the Bishop of Nancy; then to the Bishop of Nantes on 13th September. In February 1872 he requested an audience with the Bishop of Paris; on 27th February, he wrote to Monsignor Dupanloup to announce that he had modified the Alliance's statutes 'in the direction that will certainly please your

---

[3] Dunant to his sister Marie, 17 March 1872, BGE, Ms. fr. 2115 C, f. 71.

Greatness'. All this to then complain to his sister Marie that his
Protestant enemies were suspecting him of having become a papist!

But Paris's reformed souls were not Dunant's only antagonists.
Since the Commune, the man who claimed to work for 'the good
harmony between nations and individuals' had developed a number
of fierce hatreds, which he expanded upon freely in his private
correspondence, as we can see in the very same letter to his sister:

> Parisian bourgeoisie is so disgusting that I look forward to see it
> dealt a despot's iron hand. I hope to help there. The workers of
> Paris are much more worthy of interest – what I am saying may
> seem paradoxical, since the goal of my new Universal Alliance is
> to combat the International Workingmen's Association; but this
> is exactly true.[4]

This statement is perfectly clear on all subjects at once: on the
Alliance's real goal and on its new adversaries, as well as revealing
a significant change in Dunant's character, which had developed
a bitterness bordering on obsession. The Universal Alliance was
seemingly an outlet for his hatred – and the word is not too
strong – for the city he was constantly referring to as 'Babylon',
for its undisciplined bourgeoisie, for its insubordinate workers,
'Internationalized' or not, for its disorder and levity, not to mention
its numerous Protestants.

A new alliance

Throughout 1872, Dunant worked very hard to get the Alliance off
the ground. As well as charming the bishops, forming his committee,
sending out the first leaflets, setting the programme, writing the
manifesto and several newsletters, he also wanted to acquire worthy
patronage, whether Orleanist or Bonapartist. It seems he began
with Prince Louis Philippe d'Orléans.

The prince responded politely at first that he was obliged not to
enter into Dunant's 'league of order'. Dunant doesn't appear to
have let go so easily – discretion not being his strong point – because

---

[4] Ibid.

PLATE 1 *The house where Henry Dunant was born (rue Verdaine, Geneva), where Dunant later returned as a teenager for private lessons.*

PLATES 2–3 *Henry Dunant's parents, Jean-Jacques Dunant and Antoinette Dunant-Colladon.*

PLATE 4 *The founders of the YMCA (Paris 1855). Dunant is second (from left to right) on the second row, Maximilien Perrot is standing on the farthest right.*

PLATE 5 *Henry Dunant around the time he established his first business in Algeria.*

PLATE 6 *Emperor Napoleon III.*

PLATE 7 *The Pastori palace, in Castiglione, where Dunant is said to have stayed in June 1859. At the end of the street stands the Chiesa Maggiore.*

PLATE 8 *The manuscript of* A Memory of Solferino.

PLATE 9 *The members of the Committee of Five (from left to right and top to bottom: Louis Appia, Guillaume-Henri Dufour, Henry Dunant, Théodore Maunoir, Gustave Moynier).*

PLATE 10 *The Conference of 1864 (with Dunant's portrait hanging on the wall).*

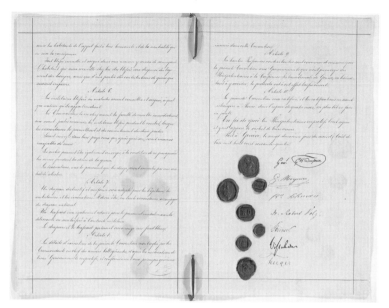

PLATE 11 *The Geneva Convention of 1864.*

PLATE 12 *Dr Jan Christiaan Basting, a strong supporter of Dunant's idea of neutrality in humanitarian aid.*

PLATE 13 *Queen Augusta of Prussia, wearing the Red Cross armband.*

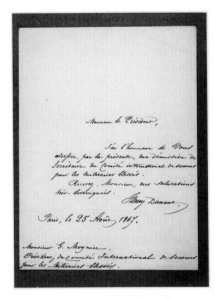

PLATE 14 *Henry Dunant's resignation from the ICRC, 1867.*

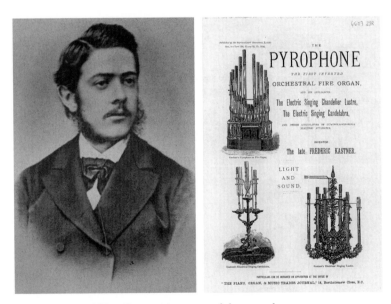

PLATE 15 *Frédéric Kastner, inventor of the pyrophone.*

PLATE 16 *Advertisement for the pyrophone. From Science Museum Group Collection. © The Board of Trustees of the Science Museum.*

PLATE 17 *The Paradies guest house in Heiden, Switzerland.*

PLATE 18 *The Lindelbühl guest house, in Trogen, Switzerland.*

PLATE 19 *The Heiden district hospital.*

PLATE 20 *Heiden district hospital's Chief Doctor, Hermann Altherr.*

PLATE 21 *Wilhelm Sonderegger (on the far right) with his wife and children.*

PLATE 22 *Dunant's membership to the Heiden section of the Red Cross.*

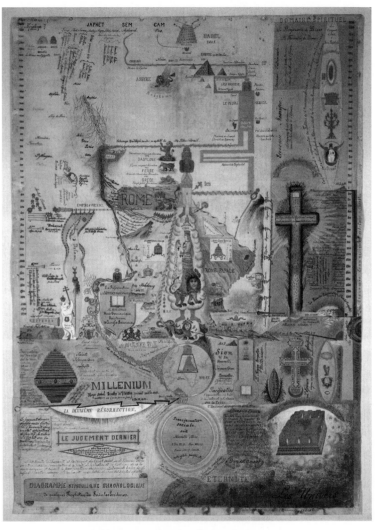

PLATE 23 *One of Dunant's famous diagrams.*

PLATE 24 *Johann Pfister, devoted secretary of the Winterthur Red Cross.*

PLATE 25 *The journalist Georg Baumberger.*

Über Land und Meer

№ 49.

74. Band.
Siebenunddreißigster Jahrgang.
Oktober 1894—1895.
Erscheint jeden Sonntag.

Deutsche Illustrirte Zeitung.

Preis vierteljährlich 3 Mark.
Mit Post-Aufschlag ℳ 3.50.

Redakteur:
Ernst Schubert in Stuttgart.

Henri Dunant,
der Begründer des „Roten Kreuzes".

Es war am 7. August dieses Jahres, als ich nach dem lieblichen Kurort Heiden im schweizerischen Kanton Appenzell fuhr. Es galt, einem Manne einen Besuch abzustatten, der — heute ein halb Verschollener und Vergessener — ein Werk schuf, das, selbst untödlich, auch seinem Schöpfer den Weiheluß der Unsterblichkeit auf die Stirn drückte: Henri Dunant. Der Weg zu ihm führte nicht in eines der zahlreichen comfortablen Hotels oder in eine der zierlichen Villen, die von behaglichem Menschendasein erzählen, sondern in das einfache Bezirkskrankenhaus, wo Dunant seit Jahren weniger als Patient, denn als Pfründner zu drei Franken Pensionspreis per Tag lebt. Eine Diakonissin führt mich in das Zimmer Nummer zwölf, die Wohnstätte des edlen Mannes. Es ist ein reinliches, lichthelles Zimmerchen mit zwei Fenstern. Ein Bett, ein Stehpult, zwischen beide eingeteilt ein Sofa mit verblaßtem Ueberzuge, und ein Schrank, zwei Stühle und ein Tisch bilden das ganze Mobiliar. Die Wände mit dem kalten Gipsanstrich muten eisig an. Kein Bild schmückt sie und kein liebendes Zeichen. Vorn über dem Tische hängt ein kleines Spiegelchen, wie man sie in Dienstbotenkammern findet, neben dem Bette ein Thermometer und an der Thür die „Hausordnung". Nun muß ich hier gleich beifügen, daß diese

Aermlichkeit nicht eine stumme Sprache des Vorwurfs an die Adresse der Anstaltsleitung führt. „Herr Doktor Altherr — der Anstaltsarzt — und die Diakonissinnen sind von den wenigen Freunden, die mir geblieben sind, die besten", sagte mir Herr Dunant. Er selbst begrüßte den Besucher auf das liebenswürdigste. Es ist eine prächtige Figur, dieser bald siebenzigjährige Herr, mit dem edlen, ausdrucksvollen Kopfe, dem

Nach einer photographischen Aufnahme von Otto Rietmann in St. Gallen.

Henri Dunant.

zart incarnirten Teint, der etwas Verklärtes im Farbenton hat, mit den silberweißen Haaren und dem silberweißen Barte. Die ganze Erscheinung hat etwas patriarchalisch Ehrwürdiges und doch wieder etwas Kavaliermäßiges in jeder Linie, in jeder Bewegung. Selbst im einfachen, braunen Schlafrode, aus dem Manchetten in tadelloser Weiße hervorragten, im schlichten Hauskäppchen, verleugnet sich des Mannes vornehme Abkunft und vornehmes Wesen nicht.

Diese Eindrücke verstärken sich, je länger man mit Herrn Dunant spricht. Er redet das Französisch der großen Welt; jeder Ausdruck ist gewählt, wo es paßt, fein und geistvoll pointirt; bald nimmt die Unterhaltung die Form liebenswürdiger Causerie an, bald einen hohen Selbstschwung und -flug, das letztere jedesmal, wenn er auf die Schöpfungen und ihren Ausbau zu reden kommt, denen er Leben und Vermögen opferte. Die modulationsfähige, welche, etwas hochliegende Stimme nimmt dann eine sonore, wuchtige Klangfarbe an, der Blick, der sonst lauter Güte zu strahlen scheint, leuchtet in machtvollem Funkeln auf und an den Rosenwurzeln zeigen sich jene Falten, die eine eiserne Energie verraten, und man begreift, daß dieser Mann eine Weltmission zu erfüllen im stande war. Und dabei ist er von kindlicher Bescheidenheit, von jener durchgeistigten Bescheidenheit, die das eigene Ich vor einer großen Lebensaufgabe und der Ergebenheit an sie vergißt. Wer ist Henri Dunant? Nun, zum Teil habe ich es schon verraten. Er ist der Schöpfer jenes gewaltigen völkerrechtlichen Vertrages, der unter

1895 (Bd. 74).

147

PLATE 27 *Bertha von Suttner, pacifist activist and friend of Alfred Nobel.*

PLATE 28 *Hans Daae, Norwegian military physician.*

PLATE 29 *One of the last pictures of Henry Dunant, taken by Maria Therese of Austria-Este (probably in 1902).*

PLATE 30 *Maria Therese of Austria-Este, posing as queen of Bavaria in 1913. According to Dunant, this lady resembled Léonie Kastner, for whom there is no known picture.*

a second, this time slightly annoyed letter from the prince arrived three weeks later: 'I can only repeat what I explained in my last letter,'[5] namely, his refusal to join the 'league of order' which surely refers to the newly reformed Alliance.

Dunant then went hunting for more familiar prey. In March, he sought patronage from the former emperor, still living in exile in Chislehurst in south London. The response is very like so many others he'd received from Napoleon III. Writing through his aide-de-camp, the emperor, though 'very touched' by Dunant's request, prayed him to understand 'the feelings which, in the current situation, prevented His Majesty from accepting'.[6] Was Dunant unaware of the deposed emperor's calamitous health? He was already suffering from the kidney stones that would kill him several months later. Or was he counting on the emperor's physical vulnerability to extract one last favour? The Alliance's numerous Bonapartists must have kept him up to date on the situation. But if they had, it didn't stop him.

If not the father, then the son! A few days later, Dunant sent a package to Chislehurst containing publications attesting to his own glory (the ones by his friends Chéron and Cazenove, respectively, among others), addressing them this time to the young prince, Louis-Napoléon, who thanked him by praising 'the man who'd given his name to one of the most interesting and useful works for humanity to date'.[7] Here was another compliment to stick in his next publication, but not the top-level support he needed. This time Dunant would have to do without.

This was in March of 1872. If we are to believe his correspondence, always more abundant when he was doing well, Dunant was clearly on the rebound. The final events of 1871 and the conclusion of the 'leading role' he'd enjoyed during the war must have sent him back into his darker prewar feelings for a few months. We have only one family letter from this entire period, dated November 1871, in which Dunant thanked his sister Marie for her recent mailing 'which has arrived well':[8] this was surely a sum of money posted to

---

[5] Louis Philippe d'Orléans to Dunant, 27 January and 19 February 1872, BGE, Ms. fr. 2110, 49 and 52.

[6] Count Davillier to Dunant, 27 March 1872, BGE, Ms. fr. 2115 C, f. 73.

[7] Count Clary to Dunant, 27 March 1872, BGE, Ms. fr. 2115 C, f. 76.

[8] Dunant to his sister Marie, 25 November 1871, BGE, Ms. fr. 2115 C, f. 70.

an indigent brother. His address was Rue Cambacérès, meaning the Ville de Paris hotel.

Thankful that his hotel had been saved from the Prussian battering ram, or simply out of compassion, Mr Ribes was still housing Dunant, but now in a small room on the uppermost floor. It is not hard to suppose that after the excitement of those wartime months, Henry had slipped into a depression that following autumn, only emerging in the first months of 1872.

After his hopeless search for princely patronage, the spring of 1872 saw Dunant entirely devoted to organizing the first congress of his Universal Alliance, which was planned for June in Paris. In charge of the agenda, he included all the questions he'd been focusing on for the last few years. Out of the limelight for half a decade, he was preparing for a grand re-entry onto the international institutional stage with subjects quite close to those dealt with by the International Committee in Geneva, perhaps hoping to overshadow it.

To raise his spirits even further, a flock of his faithful followers – Dutihl, de Flavigny, Sérurier, Cazenove, de Houdetot, etc. – was planning to launch a new funding drive for him. After the fiasco of the 500,000-franc 'national award' sought by Baron Dutihl de la Tuque the year before, they were being more subtle: to get around both his 'dogged enemies' and his Genevan creditors, the drive dreamed up by his French friends would be launched in England, without Paris and 'official' France knowing anything about it. Even the members of the French Red Cross – de Flavigny and Sérurier, for example – signed the support letter behind their committee's back to ensure no one got wind of the plan on the continent.

This new hope played a big part in Dunant's spectacular boost of morale that spring of 1872. The 'true founder' of the Red Cross believed in a fair return: 'When one thinks that Dr Chenu just received 11 million from an American as the founder of a society I founded,' he observed to his sister with an acidic irony, 'one wonders if the true founder might see justice done.'[9] Secret or not, the English project did reach the ears of the Central Committee of the French Red Cross. Not wanting to be left out, some members felt they, too,

---

[9] Dunant to his sister Marie, 12 May 1872, BGE, Ms. fr. 2115 C, f. 74. Dunant doesn't specify the currency of the 11 million.

should do something, either in the form of a 200,000-franc lump sum, or as a monthly stipend. Worst news ever! At first Dunant panicked, worried that rumours of any official support from France would reach Switzerland, and the money be immediately ogled by his creditors. The only way out would be to buy some time:

> If only in England I could get a similar sum or even less, I would let them do whatever they want in France, because then, I would have already been able to make arrangements with my creditors [. . .] once they would have received something and they could have appreciated my loyalty.[10]

The way in which Dunant equivocates with respect to his creditors – a behaviour he would take to his grave – seems to follow a regular pattern. Ideally, he saw himself reimbursing his debts just as he'd accrued them, through some fabulous business transaction so thoroughly enriching he could return the lost money to everyone in one go. It never seemed to occur to him he could reimburse such large sums little by little. This was why he never sought modest but regular employment. But even worse for him was the idea that an award honouring the founder of the Red Cross might be confiscated, as if an award of that nature would be meant entirely for his 'other' life, the celebrated humanitarian, not for the naive, unlucky businessman of those windmills in Algeria – as if the bank accounts of these two personas couldn't touch each other. This would remain his position until the end, and because that entrepreneur's account would never be full – not in one go, not in steady dribbles – his creditors would have to wait for him to die, or die themselves, in the hope of ever being reimbursed.

At the very beginning of June 1872, however, a glimmer of hope illuminated a small path forward. Henry's paternal uncle, David Dunant, had just died; his legacy included some tactful help for his two ruined nephews: 'I hope my entire family will approve of the bequests I've arranged for in these unfortunate circumstances, in order to guarantee a living to my two nephews Henry and Daniel.'[11]

---

[10] Dunant to his sister Marie, 23 June 1872, BGE, Ms. fr. 2115 C, f. 81.
[11] Cited by Roger Durand, 'Henry Dunant et sa famille', Bulletin de la Société Henry Dunant, 1 (Geneva: SHD, 1975), 10.

For Henry, this income would amount to 1,200 francs a year, just about three francs a day, which was enough to ensure lodging and simple board. But his creditors saw things differently: this was an inheritance corresponding to a gift of nearly 16,000 francs! It didn't take them long to respond. On 1st June, ten days after his uncle's death, three of the board members of the *Crédit Genevois* requisitioned the inheritance, as reimbursement for the share of Dunant's debts they'd had to pay themselves.

What to do? As if fate was working hard to smash his hopes as soon as they were formed, the news of the seizure came at the worst possible time – the day before the congress that was destined to turn everything around for him. Henry was worried sick. He couldn't allow himself to be distracted; the stress of the next five days would be considerable. There was no question of him going to defend himself in Geneva. Instead, and as usual, he put everything into his brother Pierre's hands – Pierre, de facto patriarch, the responsible doctor on whom everyone now relied. Could Pierre step in to combat the seizure? Yes, that would do it, Pierre would take care of everything, wouldn't he? On Monday 3rd June, Henry left his small room on the Rue Cambacérès for the headquarters of the Alliance, about 100 metres away on the Rue de Penthièvre. He swept everything else from his mind: Geneva, Uncle David, the scowling faces of his creditors. One thing and one thing only mattered: his Universal Alliance, his congress, the world.

The congress of 1872

The Alliance's first congress was held in Paris from 3rd to 8th June 1872. There were more than a thousand individuals involved across its many sessions: fourteen nations were represented by supporters who'd come in a private capacity. Clearly, Dunant had lost no measure of his skills in bringing people together, high-ranking people for that matter, at an event he'd dreamed up and put together himself. Considering how poor he was, the fact that he managed, seemingly on his own, to unite such a diverse and high-level assembly is a testament to his interpersonal skills, his charm and the power of his convictions. It's obvious that Henry Dunant's renown was not at all diminished in the France of the Third Republic.

The congress was split between two themes. Half of the questions were direct follow-ups to the trauma of France's civil war: they focused on domestic issues relating to the living conditions of workers and peasants, to re-establishing the family as society's fundamental institution, to the best methods of 'encouraging good'. Conference attendees debated the advantages of savings accounts, worker circles, pension and management funds, often taking Great Britain as the model to follow with their *saving-banks* and *friendly societies*. 'Elementary and technical' education was a top priority – 'for men and for women', and for the 'moral and intellectual improvement of the rural and working classes'. The fight against common-law couples and out-of-wedlock childbirth was thoughtfully entrusted to a group of ladies. There was a unanimous desire for the moral 'recovery' of France's 'disadvantaged'[12] classes, approached with the same paternalistic altruism as colonials supporting the development of indigenous populations.

But Dunant's focus now lay elsewhere. During the Paris conferences of 1867, he had unsuccessfully attempted to draw attention to the fate of war prisoners. His report had been left out of the subjects discussed in the plenary session which had focused solely – under Moynier's watchful eye – on amendments to the Geneva Convention on wounded soldiers. Had Dunant been harbouring his frustrations all this time? It seems so; the report he presented to the first congress of the Universal Alliance for Order and Civilization is essentially a word-for-word repetition of the text he'd prepared five years earlier.

The first session on international topics, presided by Amédée Thierry, focused on a 'project that may serve as a basis for a diplomatic agreement between the civilized powers, regarding prisoners of war'. Henry Dunant maintained his stance: he would not take centre stage. But he had duly instructed his friends. Loyal Dr Chéron was charged with situating the question as a natural extension of the Geneva Convention. Count de Houdetot, French Red Cross colleague and former member of the Welfare Association, was tasked with reading long extracts from Henry's 1867 report and dropping his name in as often as possible. Another faithful

---

[12] [No author], *Congrès de l'Alliance universelle de l'ordre et de la civilisation* (Paris: A. Pougin, 1872), 103–6, 131 ff.

friend, Henri Musson, launched into an extensive accolade of
Dunant as the pioneer of the war-prisoner question, just in case
anyone hadn't caught the hint yet: the man who'd done so much for
wounded soldiers was the only one able to do the same for the
unfortunate soldiers who had been taken prisoner.[13]

Of course, there was no mention of the Basel Agency and Moynier's
Green Cross, despite the fact that their work for war prisoners could
not be so easily dismissed. However, everything seemed to be running
as smoothly as it had for the Geneva Convention on wounded
soldiers. In the same way that the October 1863 conference had
concluded with *Resolutions* and *Wishes*, the Alliance congress would
produce a number of *Conclusions* that their presumed author, Henry
Dunant, planned to bring to an equally brilliant future. A 'permanent
international committee' (echoing the February 1863 Committee of
Five) was created to 'lead a way to a conference that would uniformly
resolve the fate of prisoners of war in civilized countries'.[14] This
committee, like the one for wounded soldiers, was charged with
writing a draft concordat on prisoners which would be discussed, as
the Geneva project was, by the delegates of all interested countries.
Dunant was the committee chairman.

Finally, again as they had for the Geneva Convention, the
congress was initially considering the French government to launch
the official invitation 'for a diplomatic convention'.[15] But Dunant
quickly changed his mind: on 23rd June 1872 he wrote to his sister
that he wanted to ask the Belgian government to host the conference,
a request which, according to him, had the Belgian king and the
country's major figures 'rubbing their hands together with glee'.[16]

The congress's second biggest theme was another of Dunant's
long-term obsessions: to prevent and avoid war, rather than labour to
heal its wounds. Dunant had been thinking of this for a long time.
Even before the horrors of the Commune, he had defended the idea

---

[13] Ibid., 13–45.

[14] Ibid., 45.

[15] *Bulletin de l'Alliance universelle*, 11.

[16] Dunant to his sister Marie, 23 June 1872, BGE, Ms. fr. 2115 C, f. 81. In the
hardcover Report of the Congress, the conclusions of the session on prisoners of war
would no longer mention the French government but the Belgian government
instead, 'as a Neutral State', to call upon for the Conference. *Congrès de l'Alliance
universelle*, 45.

of international arbitration within the Welfare Association, going so far as to dream up a procedure and a committee (chaired by the indispensable Raynald de Choiseul) for just this subject. Back in April 1871, the idea had gained enough ground to merit an article in the *Moniteur universel*, mentioning that the establishment 'of a grand, international jury to which all serious arguments leading to war might be referred' was a key ambition of the newly created association.

This meant that when international arbitration appeared on the agenda of the Universal Alliance congress, it wasn't a novel idea. But it seems the president named by the committee, the seductive Count de Choiseul, was no longer in the running. Although he was still listed in the conference papers as one of the numerous vice presidents, he didn't oversee any of the debates on arbitration and he hardly spoke. Had Dunant preferred to pad this particular congress with intellectual and moral heavyweights, instead of worldly celebrities? Indeed, he 'gave' the prisoners of war to Amédée Thierry, member of the Institut de France; he gave international arbitration to Félix Esquirou de Parieu, an early visionary of the European Union; the historical introduction was ensured by the general secretary of the *Société des amis de la paix* (Society of the Friends of Peace), Henri Bellaire. Among the speakers was also Frédéric Passy, founder of the *Ligue internationale et permanente de la paix* (International and Permanent League for Peace) and active promoter of arbitration as a means of resolving conflicts.

Although it did not end up convoking an international conference, the assembly did give the idea of international arbitration its first academic and intellectual sustenance, by 'organizing competitions and awards with a view to inducing scholars and legal experts to work on the drawing up of an international code'.[17]

English support

The success of the congress gave Dunant the comforting certainty that his Alliance was hitting the right note, and that it was viable. Several days after it finished, he wrote to Marie – the sister for whom he always saved his good news:

---

[17] Boissier, *From Solferino to Tsushima*, 287.

To think that it's me who created this entire Alliance by hiding
behind a curtain and running everything my way. I've been able
to cross unhindered through so many difficulties that everyone
here (and certainly important men) will swear only by me. Ah! If
they knew my fears, my torments, my anxieties, my sorrow and
my absolute poverty, no doubt they would consider me a man of
energy and know how far I can take the Alliance![18]

The cosmopolitan make-up of the congress facilitated the creation
of 'foreign chapters' of the Universal Alliance. Depending on their
respective interests, these different chapters would go on to focus
on various subjects. In France, which maintained the Alliance's
international headquarters, the chapter would continue along a
path shaped by its recent political events: managing the
'disadvantaged classes' and the country's return to morality,
prosperity and order. Meanwhile, the questions that interested
Dunant – prisoners of war and international arbitration – seemed
to be finding a more promising future in England. Dunant was also
quite distracted by the infamous funding drive that had been
launched for him in London. The petition had appeared in several
British newspapers the month before the congress, subtly merging
the financial difficulties of the work and the man:

> This important charitable work, in which Mr. Dunant took the
> initiative eleven years ago, has exhausted all his resources; and
> while so many victims of war have benefited by his labours, he
> himself has in promoting this work been reduced to a state of
> pecuniary difficulty.[19]

Dunant convinced himself the appeal needed the support of its
actual beneficiary. So he prepared to set off for England, where 'the

---

[18] Dunant to his sister Marie, 23 June 1872, BGE, Ms. fr. 2115 C, f. 81. Dunant
would remain 'behind the curtain' all the way. Among the hundreds of presidents,
vice presidents, founding and lifetime members named in the first pages of the official
Report of the Congress (*Congrès de l'Alliance universelle de l'ordre et de la
civilisation*), Dunant appears nowhere, not even as the president of the committee in
charge of organizing the next Conference for Prisoners of War.

[19] 'Monsieur Henry Dunant, To the Editor of the Medical Press and circular', *Medical
Press*, 29 May 1872, attached to Dunant's letter to his sister Marie, BGE, 23 June
1872, Ms. fr. 2115 C, f. 81.

people were highly disposed' towards him, as he explained to his sister at the end of June:

> [. . .] The way has been paved, the paths are laid down, the *Times* has committed to me, along with several other big English newspapers, the English have open hearts and open hands and if their pride is engaged, some 100,000 francs could be collected quickly if the business is well organized. God hopes it will be so.[20]

Who paved the way for him in England? Who rallied the British newspapers? Who 'agitated', to use Dr Maunoir's term, on behalf of Henry Dunant in England?

There is no way the English campaign for the founder of the Red Cross was spontaneously generated and not orchestrated by someone who'd been worrying over Henry's interests for several months. But who could it have been? Dunant is careful to keep us guessing. And if there's a name that comes to mind, there's no evidence that allows us to state it.

A proposal for prisoners

Dunant left for England in July 1872. The Franco-British fundraising was struggling, the press campaign in May seemed to have fallen like a soufflé and Dunant now felt no one but he could rally the British in his favour. As he made clear in his late-June letter to his sister: 'Only I can lead this campaign, I must go to England and I do not have the money to do so.'[21] Marie apparently relayed his message to the right party, because several days later 300 francs were sent by Pierre Dunant to finance the trip.

It wouldn't be hard to find a pretext for the journey. Probably at Dunant's own suggestion, a British philanthropic society, the National Association for the Promotion of Social Science, invited him to speak at a conference on 6th August in London – just the ticket to remind the English of his existence. Not only would

---

[20] Dunant to his sister Marie, BGE, 23 June 1872, Ms. fr. 2115 C, f. 81.
[21] Ibid.

Dunant promote himself as the founder of the Red Cross, he would address the society under the banner of his latest project: the Permanent International Committee for War Prisoners, a satellite of the Universal Alliance.

Delighted by the momentary financial comfort which Pierre's subsidy granted him, Henry moved into the St James Hotel near Piccadilly. He had received a surprising invitation (via Sir Henry Verney) from Florence Nightingale to spend a couple of days at Claydon. But just as he arrived in London, some news reached him from Geneva that knocked him flat: his sister-in-law Sophie, Daniel's wife, had just died of a puerperal fever after giving birth to the couple's third child.

'I cannot get over this sudden death,' he wrote to Pierre, 'I am thinking of it constantly. – I don't have the courage to write.'[22] He may have felt a little guilty, too, since his relationship with Daniel had perhaps suffered from the financial fiasco of the Universal Library[23] and the involuntary sequestering of the family's winter items in Passy, not to mention many open wounds from Algeria.

But Dunant could not just let himself go. In his own words: 'I must get over this in order to act.' He needed to convince the English to open their hearts, and thus their wallets. He needed to take advantage of the fact that his reputation was still intact on British soil, unaware that Moynier was already several steps ahead of him. As soon as he had learned of Dunant's travels, the president of the International Committee had sent a few select extracts from the *Crédit Genevois* verdict to several notable members of the English Red Cross, specifying that 'this affair created a scandal in Geneva', where Mr Dunant 'would not dare to show his face again'.[24] Henry Dunant, the brilliant communicator, had certainly met his match.

The invitation card for the 6th August conference referred to 'A proposal to regularize conditions for prisoners of war'. The

---

[22] Dunant to his brother Pierre, 10 August 1872, BGE, Ms. fr. 2110, f. 68. Dunant mentions Florence Nightingale's invitation in the same letter.

[23] Although unprofitable, the International Universal Library still existed. In 1872, several books were published in which Henry Dunant was still listed as a member of the editorial committee alongside Max Grazia, A. Pino, J. David and Frédéric Gustave Eichhoff.

[24] Boissier, *From Solferino to Tsushima*, 288.

conference took place at 3 p.m., at 1 Adam Street, and was presided over by Lord Elcho, a member of the British parliament.

After requisite praise of Florence Nightingale[25] and Charles Dickens, Henry Dunant, the speaker of the day, recalled the origins of the Geneva Convention and the very personal role he'd played during its preparatory tour in Germany, his support of sailors with Empress Eugénie in 1867 and his work during the Franco-Prussian war of 1870–1. After these 30-minute preliminaries, he launched into the subject of his conference: prisoners of war, who, he claimed, had been an interest of his since his very first publications, as well as during the Paris Conferences of 1867. He described at length the suffering of soldiers held as prisoners, as if he were familiar with some of it himself: hunger, cold, separation from their families ... He also mentioned their precarious status before finally winding around to his conclusion: the creation of national committees – similar to those that already existed to support wounded soldiers – and the organization of a preparatory conference uniting not only the delegates from these committees, but also government emissaries – similar to the model of the 1863 conference. Once these two steps were completed, 'one of the neutral states of Europe, Belgium, will probably take the initiative in sending an invitation to all civilized governments, and the object will be attained by ordinary diplomatic agency'.[26]

According to Dunant, his conference was a raging success. It had 'achieved its goal while giving me such great renown in England,' he wrote on 10th August to his brother Pierre, 'that I am beginning to hope ...' To hope what? That the struggling drive in his favour could be relaunched amid this shower of favourable public opinion. That the 'grand committee' and 'powerful patronage' which would soon be established for war prisoners would bring him luck and

---

[25] Dunant would send her the text of his conference, for which she thanked him on 4 September. She was more positive this time about the Red Cross than she had been in 1862, though she apologized for 'doing nothing more than offering her profound admiration'. She mentioned the death of her niece Emily Verney the day before as an excuse for her 'paltry note'. Nightingale to Dunant, 4 September 1872, handwritten copy by Dunant, BGE, Ms. fr. 2115 C, f. 82.

[26] Henry Dunant, *A proposal for introducing Uniformity into the Condition of Prisoners of War*, 2nd edn (London: Head, Hole & Co, 1872), quoted by R. Durand, *'Les prisonniers de guerre aux temps héroïques'*, 259.

'finally address my concerns', as he so modestly referred to his financial worries.

But above and beyond a success which, in his own words, 'exceeded all imaginable forecasts', his conference also soothed his heart. Several Swiss came to listen to him, and these were not just any Swiss. Among the listeners was the son-in-law of a lady he'd never been able to reimburse after borrowing from her in 1866; a Swiss pastor and a few members of his congregation, and all these good people 'enveloped him with expressions of their sympathy'. 'This made me happy,'[27] he confided to his brother in a British-style understatement; in the wake of the painful excommunication he'd experienced from his former Christian 'brothers and sisters', this olive branch offered by a few French-speaking Swiss Protestants probably gave him at least a few nights of restful sleep.

The conference of 6th August 1872 would most definitely rescue him. But not necessarily in the way he'd imagined. Not via his prisoners of war, whose fate was not likely to soon be improved, not via the 'grand Committee composed of Red Cross members', which Moynier had torpedoed for him, not via a relaunch of the funding drive buried by the British press,[28] and not via a few forgiving Pietists. No, he'd be saved by something he'd never even dreamed of.

Eve on Adam Street

On 6th August 1872, sitting in a conference room on Adam Street, was the first known 'Eve' of Dunant's bachelor life. Her name was Léonie Kastner. She was a few years older than Henry, she was a widow and she was accompanied by her son. While she was listening attentively to the man speaking at the podium, she may have noticed that it wasn't just his English that was poor. From that day forward, she would not let him out of her sight.

---

[27] Dunant to his brother Pierre, 10 August 1872, BGE, Ms. fr. 2110, f. 68.

[28] A letter from 1892 tells the end of the story of this English funding drive: two pounds sterling – offered by a single donor. 'That was all. Dr Gordon sent them to Baron Dutilh de la Tuque, who gave them to me minus the exchange commission, just enough to buy a black frock coat that I urgently needed to go to England.' (To Rudolf Müller, 11 September 1892).

Dunant's memoirs describe the encounter like this:

Mrs Kastner-Boursault[29] was encouraged to assist me by Emperor Napoleon III, who was still in exile and whom she had visited in Brighton with her son in August 1872. This lady witnessed on 6th August the lecture I gave, while Lord Elcho presided at the headquarters of the Social Science Association. This day dates the benevolent interest of this family towards me. Having been received with much kindness by the ex-emperor, for whom they profess a profound veneration, Napoleon asked them 'What is Dunant up to?' in a kindly way. He had read the 'lecture' given on 6th August.[30]

The beginning of Dunant's friendship with the Kastners thus began either at the London conference itself, or a little bit earlier, perhaps through some connection within the network of exiled Bonapartists.

When they came to greet him after his August conference, Dunant would have been particularly more solicitous, recognizing they were regular visitors to Chislehurst. He gave them a copy of his speech so they might pass it onto His Majesty on their next visit.

The Kastners kept their word. On 14th August, the former emperor's secretary signalled to Dunant that their mission had been accomplished: 'Sir, it is my honour to inform you that upon your recommendation, the emperor was happy to receive Mr Kastner who presented His Majesty your document regarding the conference you gave in London.'[31]

It's clear now why Dunant insists so much in his memoirs on the 'affability' and 'benevolence' with which the Kastners were received

---

[29] Léonie Kastner was the daughter of Jean-François Boursault (called Boursault-Malherbe), an actor who became rich through various industrial and commercial businesses; in 1820, when Léonie was born, second daughter of his second marriage, he was 69 years old. Léonie Boursault married her music teacher Jean-Georges Kastner, when she was 16 years old and he was 27. She became a widow in 1867.

[30] Dunant, *Mémoires*, 325. These same *Mémoires* date the beginning of Mrs Kastner's generosity at 'several months following the re-establishment of order in Paris', meaning in the framework of the Welfare Association, whose debts she gradually reimbursed (324–5). The memoirs seem to want to deliberately obscure the chronology of events on this chapter of Dunant's life, but there is no clue to indicate a particular relationship with the Kastners before this 'encounter in London' (327).

[31] Count Davillier to Dunant, 14 August 1872, BGE, Ms. fr. 2110, f. 69–70.

by Napoleon III: for Dunant, who could afford neither the trip to Chislehurst nor a new frock coat, the mother–son duo were his ambassadors to one of the men he most venerated but whom he no longer dared approach. Instead, he had to settle for basking in the emperor's glow from a distance.

Another element confirms that 'the Kastner era' had well and truly begun in that late summer of 1872. Until Dunant left for England, the headquarters of the Universal Alliance in Paris were located at the address of its secretary, the Duke de Feltre, on the Rue de Penthièvre. Once he'd returned from London, the Universal Alliance took up its lodgings at the Rue de Clichy, in one of the buildings belonging to Mrs Kastner. From that moment on, the fate of the Alliance and its main promoter would be inextricably and forever linked to Léonie Kastner and her son Frédéric.

Survival in London

No matter the exact circumstances of their first meeting, Mrs Kastner's support of the founder of the Red Cross doesn't appear to have begun immediately. Between August and September 1872, Dunant was racing about getting his conference text published and distributed as widely as possible. By this point, his London worries were the same as those he'd had in Paris: how would he survive? He managed on the hotel's small, frugal breakfast of tea and cold meats, which he could afford because of an additional 100 francs sent by his brother Pierre. When he wasn't invited anywhere for the rest of the day, the state of his finances meant he had to skip lunch and dinner. 'This situation lasted for fifteen days. No one suspected it,'[32] he would later admit.

As we've seen, Dunant's invitation for the August conference had come from the National Association for the Promotion of Social Science, who were also interested in the other subject he was promoting in the name of the Universal Alliance: international arbitration. By chance, the association was planning a large colloquium in September in Plymouth, including a discussion of the following: 'Can an International Court be created in order to

---

[32] Dunant, *Mémoires*, 326 n. 2.

prevent war, and if so, in what way?'[33] Obviously, Dunant had an answer at the ready that he would be delighted to present. But how could he get to Plymouth? And who would pay?

Which was when Dunant remembered the London Peace Society and its general secretary Henry Richard, a former pastor and long-time campaigner for peace, for international arbitration and against slavery – three causes all dear to Henry's heart. Richard received Dunant enthusiastically, encouraging him to attend the Plymouth colloquium; the Peace Society was well-endowed and would agree to cover some of his costs.

No need to tell Dunant twice. Gathering up the last of his savings, he left for Plymouth to give a lecture on 13th September 1872 in support of creating a high court of international arbitration. Just as he'd done for war prisoners, he opened with a long and metaphor-laden preamble reflecting on civilization's great progress. He offered the Geneva Convention as proof and a model of civilizing humanitarian thought. He eventually got around to his main point, describing his idea of the court of arbitration: a mediating body whose efficacy would become its moral authority. He reminded his audience it must not, in any case, become a tribunal, because governments and nations do not like being judged.

A heated current event bolstered Dunant's topic that day. Great Britain was eagerly awaiting a court decision soon to be delivered in Geneva regarding the US–Great Britain dispute over damages caused by the CSS *Alabama* during the American Civil War. The boat, which had been commissioned and armed in England by a Confederate agent on behalf of the Confederate States Navy, had engendered heavy losses for the northern fleet, before being sunk during a naval combat. The US government was pursuing claims against Great Britain and the situation required a neutral arbiter.

The court of arbitration was being held in Geneva at exactly the same time as the Plymouth congress; the decision was to arrive the day after Dunant's presentation. Not a favourable coincidence in the end since the English were ultimately found liable for 15.5 million dollars in damages to the United States! But as luck would have it the decision hadn't yet arrived when the British public were

---

[33] André Durand, 'L'idée de paix dans la pensée d'Henry Dunant', De l'utopie à la réalité, 362.

listening to our Genevan expand on the benefits of arbitration: for at least a few hours, the situation worked in his favour.

Indeed, the conference was a great success. His customary praise of Napoleon III, which he most certainly didn't forget to mention to His Majesty, earned him, for the first and only time, a small note signed by the sovereign himself: 'Thank you, sir,' the emperor wrote on 20th September, 'for your flattering words during the Plymouth congress, and I congratulate you for your generous efforts on behalf of a humanitarian cause.'[34] The newspapers were also filled with praise and included detailed summaries. *The Globe and Traveller*, *The Western Daily Mercury* printed long extracts from Dunant's report, calling it one of the most important contributions to the congress.

Dunant would have more fully enjoyed his success if he hadn't had to savour it on an empty stomach. The Peace Society had deemed it unnecessary to advance the money to him, so he was as hungry in Devon as he'd been for the last two weeks in London. As the conference was concluding, he very nearly fainted and needed to briefly hand his text to John Morley, his neighbour at the podium.

Although struggling, Dunant remained in Plymouth. From there he wrote to his sister Marie on 4th October, as usual presenting everything as sunnily as possible. But however pretty a picture he painted, his depressive mood was shouting out from the page. He hated the English climate, he'd not yet recovered from the death of his sister-in-law Sophie, he was hoping for some kind of 'under-the-table' work from the Peace Society but didn't know how to get it – he was at the end of his tether. After a freezing return trip to London in October 'in damp weather in an awful train, nearly unable to know what to do and ill dressed for the humidity and the cold',[35] he fell gravely ill. The doctor diagnosed a serious jaundice which Dunant would later claim nearly killed him. He blamed his illness on the 'anxiety, poverty, cold and lack of food'[36] he'd been enduring

---

[34] Napoléon III to Dunant, 20 September 1862, BGE, Ms. fr. 2110, f. 80a (handwritten copy by Dunant). A fac simile of Napoleon's handwritten letter is in Bernard Gagnebin and Marc Gazay (eds), *Encounter with Henry Dunant* (Geneva: Georg, 1963).

[35] Dunant to his sister Marie, 4 October 1872, BGE, Ms. fr. 2115 C, f. 82; Dunant to Müller, 21 March 1896, BGE, Ms. fr. 5202, f. 13.

[36] Dunant, *Mémoires*, 325–6, for this quote and the following one.

for the past few months. In other words, on the hardship of his situation, which he could no longer stand. Neither morally, nor physically.

'But, this is when the Kastner family, returning from Brighton after visiting Napoleon III, demonstrated their admirable benevolence and devotion,' Dunant modestly recorded in his *Mémoires* twenty-five years later. Was it Bonapartist solidarity, during these years of deception and exile? Was it a maternal intuition of his suffering? Was it burgeoning love? In the autumn of 1872, at the very moment he needed it most, an elegant silhouette, a friendly face, a kind of fairy godmother appeared at the door of his guest house – there was no more question of a hotel – with her son. Léonie Kastner took pity upon this thin, sick, miserable man whom the former emperor of France had asked about. Not accepting no for an answer, she handed him 500 francs and convinced him to leave a London that suited him so poorly. Her son Frédéric would stay with him for the trip, to help him and take care of his expenses; a single cabin was reserved right away on the boat from Dover to Calais. For his lodgings in Paris, well, they would take care of that when needed.[37]

Without exactly knowing why, Dunant trusted her. He hardly knew who she was: the daughter of a former actor turned successful businessman, and the recent widow of a renowned composer from Alsace. No matter who she was, for the first time in weeks, Dunant was feeling better. At the end of the autumn of 1872, he left for Paris with Frédéric Kastner.

Parisian parenthesis

Between the end of 1872 and the summer of 1873, Dunant has left us few traces. It seems he remained with the Kastners: this is perhaps the only explanation for the sudden gap in his correspondence.

The small group set themselves up in Paris. For a variety of reasons, Mrs Kastner kept her adult son on a very tight leash. Her first son had died before the age of 5. Twenty years later, she had argued with her second son, Albert, when he'd married his younger

---

[37] Dunant to Rudolf Müller, 21 March 1896, BGE, Ms. fr. 5202, f. 13.

brother's maid, an older woman with whom he'd had a child in 1865.[38] Frédéric was all she had left, a third son she'd given birth to late in life and coddled like a mother hen with her chick.

As for Frédéric, he wasn't one to turn his nose up at the numerous temptations a city like Paris could offer a young man, excesses his mother paid for without batting an eyelash. It is quite possible she saw Henry Dunant as a model gentleman who might counter the absence of a father and an older brother's bad example. This may be one of the reasons behind the kindness she so quickly offered him when they first met in London, as well as the family-like connection the trio rapidly developed.

Accepting Mrs Kastner's request, Dunant soon became a mentor for Frédéric, helping him manufacture his first 'pyrophone', a musical instrument born of lengthy and sophisticated research into acoustics. Because not only did Frédéric Kastner have his composer father's gift for music, he also had a head for physics: before he was 20, he had discovered a system of producing stable sounds through gas flames circulating in glass tubes, an invention known as 'singing flames'. Dunant, who'd never given any hint of an interest in music until then, was interested enough in the family to jump into this new business with his very own brand of enthusiasm. He encouraged Frédéric to create an actual prototype, and then supervised its manufacture, something the young man 'could not have done on his own'.[39] Their collaboration in Paris lasted between the autumn of 1872 and March 1873, during which time the Universal Alliance for Order and Civilization changed its address to 43 Rue de Clichy.

---

[38] The dispute between Mrs Kastner and her second son seems to have lasted until Mrs Kastner's death, if we believe the monumental biography of her husband J.-G. Kastner by Hermann Ludwig, certainly written upon her request and with her active collaboration. Ludwig gives the couple only two sons: Georges, born in 1838 and deceased as a child, and Frédéric, born in 1852 (Ludwig, II, 219; III, 179). Following Ludwig, the biographer of Jean-François Boursault, Ernest Lebègue, repeats the error (Lebègue, 260). Erased from the family chronicle, Albert Kastner did, however, play a pivotal role in Dunant's life; he was credited with a significant portion of the persecutions (especially on behalf of the Jesuits) which he and Mrs Kastner were subject to between 1872 and 1887 (letters to Rudolf Müller, 3 June 1892, and to Maurice Dunant [1894?]).

[39] Dunant to his niece Adrienne Dunant (daughter of his brother Daniel), 29 June 1885, published *in extenso* in R. Durand, '*Flash sur une année obscure*', *Bulletin de la Société Henry Dunant*, 8 (Geneva: SHD, 1983), 6–17.

This building was part of the Kastner-Boursault family's significant property legacy. The ground floor included a vast apartment between the courtyard and the garden, fully furnished, that Mrs Kastner offered not only to the Universal Alliance but also to its founder, who enjoyed use of a large bedroom and a dining room. In the course of these changes, Frédéric Kastner became the archivist of the Alliance's French chapter, deepening the connections between Dunant and the Kastners even further.

If we believe Henry's later-recorded commentary, Léonie didn't just provide a beautiful apartment to the Universal Alliance, she also covered most of the association's costs between 1872 and 1876 and gave its founder a level of comfort he no longer dared aspire to. In addition to the rooms so graciously offered, she had what Henry would later describe as a 'far too luxurious'[40] lunch sent to him every day from a fancy Parisian caterer.

What motivated such generosity? A passionate belief in the Alliance's goals? A romantic passion between a 52-year-old widow and a 44-year-old ruined bachelor, both of whose fates had been ruined in 1867, one through bankruptcy, the other through grief?

Many years later, Dunant summarized the deep-seated cause of her immense goodness. By fostering the existence of the Universal Alliance, 'she'd hoped to settle her son, give him a goal, good connections, make him useful'.[41] The very reason Frédéric was named archivist and then secretary. The very reason she treated the Alliance's main proponent so favourably and why she certainly asked him, in return, to keep an eye on her son. But what could poor Henry do with a younger man whose interests were so diametrically opposed to his own? It was a lost cause from the start.

Twenty years later, Dunant tells us that this overwhelming maternal benevolence 'did not save the unfortunate boy. He lost himself via a mistress who befuddled him and via drunkenness.'[42] However, while trying to save her son from misfortune, she managed to save Dunant from misery.

---

[40] Dunant to Rudolf Müller, 26 November 1892, BGE, Ms. fr. 5201, f. 162.
[41] Dunant to Rudolf Müller, undated 'various notes' (probably November 1892), Ms. fr. 5201, f. 162.
[42] Ibid.

It's likely Dunant remained in Paris through the spring of 1873. If January had brought him to England, his memoirs would not have omitted the emperor's funeral in a small church in Chislehurst on 15th January, with the hundreds of French citizens who had crossed the Channel to pay their last respects. But the registry doesn't list his name among the attendees of Napoleon's funeral, although Frédéric Kastner, his mother Mrs George Kastner, Raynald de Choiseul and, strangely enough considering his age, a certain 'Dufour' are all included.[43]

In Paris, and now freed of any anxieties about room and board, Dunant dedicated himself to his Work. Haunted by the eviction he'd experienced in 1867, he was careful to have himself named 'life-long secretary' of the French chapter of the Alliance, and Honorary International Secretary for Life of the English chapter. Better safe than sorry. It was most likely Dunant who wrote most of the newsletters and publications published by the various Alliance chapters, with titles that must have sent Moynier's head spinning, like L'Étendard de la Croix Rouge (The Banner of the Red Cross) or, more simply, The Red Cross!

Most of his energy remained focused on the war-prisoner issue. Another Alliance member was equally fervent about this cause: Count de Houdetot, whom he knew through the French Red Cross Committee. The Count seconded Dunant with passion and efficiency. Just as he had done for the Geneva conference of 1864, Dunant was again seeking France's patronage (he had obviously abandoned the Belgian track for the moment). On 7th March 1873, completely unconcerned that Mr Thiers may have had other things to keep him busy (he would resign two months later), Dunant calmly wrote to the president of the French Republic, requesting his support. A reply came swiftly. Barthélémy Saint-Hilaire, whom Dunant knew well from the Welfare Association, delivered the usual response, which was that the head of state could not 'declare himself protector of any work in particular',[44] no matter how highly he considered the initiative. He also suggested sending his request along to the Minister of Foreign Affairs.

---

[43] Fernand Giraudeau, La mort et les funérailles de Napoléon III (Paris: Amyot, 1873), 57, 58 and 61 ; L'Ordre de Paris, 465 and 466, 17 and 18 January 1873.
[44] Saint-Hilaire to Dunant, 9 March 1873, BGE, Ms. fr. 2110, f. 84.

Here again a familiar face. The Count de Rémusat was a member of the Alliance whom Dunant had entreated when he was mounting his rescue plan of Paris's civilians during the Commune's worst excesses. De Houdetot and Dunant travelled to Versailles on 26th March 1873 to explain to the minister why it was necessary to organize an international congress to 'uniformly resolve the fate of war prisoners in civilized countries'.[45] He maintained the parallel with the Geneva Convention, its 'preparatory' conference of 1863, and the then-emperor's support, finally announcing the congress date as if it were a done deal: 2nd June 1873, in Paris.

No matter how urgent this request was made to appear – first in writing, then in person – the response was rather vague. On 7th April a letter from Rémusat arrived, filled with much encouragement but no guarantees of any kind. Our two philanthropists accepted defeat: France would be of no help and their plans for the congress on 2nd June were scuppered.

A letter from Persia

Dunant then turned to London, where he found some reassurance. First, the war-prisoner issue had been launched there the year before following his successful presentation at the Social Science Association. In June 1873, London's prestigious private club, the Athenaeum, which has seen the likes of Darwin, Thackeray and Dickens within its walls, invited him to stay for a month in its solemn white building at 107 Pall Mall – which boasted comfortable parlours, a vast library, as well as several bedrooms for renowned guests like himself. What else could he possibly want?

For some obscure reason, Dunant didn't respond to the Athenaeum's invitation. He was definitely in England at the end of June, but neither Pall nor Mall figured at the top of his letters. Instead we have the quaint Flodden Road, in Camberwell, where he'd already stayed after returning from Plymouth and which seemed to suit him well. He was lodging with an 'excellent family,'

---

[45] De Houdetot had also written to Rémusat, no date, BGE, Ms. fr. 2110, f. 182. For more details about the numerous steps of this initiative, see R. Durand, 'Les prisonniers de guerre aux temps héroïques', and Harouel, Genève-Paris 1863–1918, 458 ff.

he wrote to Marie, in the welcome quiet of the English countryside, his main expense being the train journey from Camberwell to get to 'Victoria station in the heart of London and to proper society'.[46]

Did he go to London hoping to relaunch his war-prisoner convention, or was he attempting to relaunch it in England because he happened to be there? His correspondence tells us that a certain Pastor Marzials, based in London, had entreated him 'not to lose any time coming to England'. Marzials was an old acquaintance; in 1864, he and a group of evangelicals had worked diligently to have *A Memory of Solferino* translated into English, a project Dunant hadn't followed with his usual tenacity. At the time he'd been busy untangling the future Red Cross from its Protestant foundations; this may explain his reticence towards Pastor Marzials, who was John Wesley's translator and so quite connected to the Pietist milieu. But his previous hesitations were now, ten years later, nowhere in sight. When he'd returned from Plymouth the previous year, ill and depressed, it was Pastor Marzials who gave him over to the good care of Mrs Coombes and the greenery, the flowers and birdsong of Flodden Road. And this year again Dunant was counting on the devoted pastor to provide the connections he very much needed in London.

'Unfortunately,' he wrote to his sister in the same letter, 'poor Pastor Marzials, of the French church in London, who knows so many people and is completely English, has just fallen ill right as I am beginning my introductions to London Society, and he is still unwell!' Several days later, quite directly: 'Mr Marzials is much better, and I am counting on him.'[47]

Until the indispensable Pastor Marzials was better, however, Dunant had to manage on his own. And it seems he did quite well. In less than two weeks in England – and he'd spent the first week 'a little unwell' – he'd achieved a feat he couldn't have dreamed of even in his most secret hopes. 'At his request',[48] the Shah of Persia had accepted the Geneva Convention.

That is to say, Mr Gustave Moynier would need to recognize Mr Henry Dunant, pariah of the International Committee, for Persia's signing of 'his' Convention. The founder of the Red Cross even had the delightful pleasure of carrying the Shah's acceptance

[46] Dunant to his sister Marie, 1 July 1873, BGE, Ms. fr. 2115 C, f. 85.
[47] Dunant to his sister Marie, no date, [July 1873], BGE, Ms. fr. 2115 C, f. 87.
[48] Dunant to his sister Marie, 1 July 1873, BGE, Ms. fr. 2115 C, f. 84.

to the general Swiss Council in London so that it could be sent to
Berne. The very idea of ruining Moynier's day was certainly enough
to brighten his stay in England. Indeed, several days later, the Shah
of Persia was in Geneva and the Committee saw first-hand how its
former secretary had one-upped them. Moynier's reply to Federal
Councillor Schenk, the next day, betrays his anger:

> . . . in the event, the result we were seeking has been achieved,
> and that is assuredly the main thing, but the International
> Committee is very anxious to avoid any misunderstanding about
> the capacity of Mr Dunant and not to let it be thought that he
> was acting as its official representative [. . .] For the honour of
> the Red Cross, we ourselves feel very strongly that it should not
> be served by individuals with tarnished reputations.[49]

Moynier didn't wait long to enact his revenge. In October, Conrad
Kern, the Swiss minister in Paris, invalidated Dunant's opening with
Persia: since the document had been delivered by 'someone without
official title or mandate',[50] Kern explained to his superiors, it could
not be taken into account. Persia had to repeat the procedure all
over again . . . most likely cursing Dunant in the process.

And meanwhile, Dunant had begun dreaming of a diplomatic
position in Persia! What kind of distress must he have been in to
even imagine moving to Persia at the age of 45? He, a man unsettled
by plain English food, a man who lived entirely *for* and *by* his social
networks, a man already suffering from the distance to his family!
His distress was immense indeed. 'Should I do this?' he asked gentle
Marie, to whom he did not usually ask for advice:

> The uncertainty of my future in France is so vast, and I hate the
> French so much that this high position in Persia, if I might get it,
> would be useful and perhaps enable me to rebuild my fortune.[51]

---

[49] Moynier to Federal Councillor Schenk, 2 July 1873, Swiss Federal Archives (BGE
copy), cited by Boissier, *From Solferino to Tsoushima*, 278. Boissier's translation has
softened Moynier's last words (*individualités tarées*) which in French means
something closer to 'demented' or 'defective' individuals.

[50] Conrad Kern to the president of the Swiss Confederation, 18 October 1873, Swiss
Federal Archives, E2E1000/44/309*.

[51] Dunant to his sister Marie, 1 July 1873, BGE, Ms. fr. 2115 C, f. 84.

And here lay the crux of the matter, his constant and constantly deceptive obsession: to rebuild himself. To rebuild anywhere, in any way possible, in bandages, in books, in diplomacy or in charity. To rebuild himself as he should have been, as he should have never stopped being: a person for whom money didn't matter, because there was always enough of it.

Did Marie still believe what her brother told her, in letter after letter, about his impending prosperity, in other words the clearing of his name? Dunant was most optimistic when he wrote to her, embroidering his fortunes and his imminent ability to reimburse his debts. Marie Dunant, who never married, never changed her name nor had a family of her own to divert her social ambitions, may have been particularly sensitive about her brother's honour. This is probably why Dunant's letters to Marie are consistently marked by an optimism and more than anything by an obsession with the 'profits' to be had from his most noble occupations. Contrary to his brother Pierre, to whom he truthfully poured out his soul, Henry always wrote to his youngest sister to reassure her, which explains why he so often transformed lofty causes into opportunities for money, fortune or useful connections of some kind. But who was the most gullible between these two, the brother or the sister? Their letters don't tell.

That year, however, London worked hard to win him over. Mrs Coombes, Dunant's landlady who managed a boarding school for young girls, 'did all she could to please him, as did her young ladies'. The lovely English lawns, the sunshine, the sounds of the countryside reminded him of La Monnaie 'thirty years ago', and all of this warmed his heart. And above all, 'it seems to me my path is to be found in England.'[52] What caused this sudden reversal?

The Shah of Persia adhering to the Geneva Convention had made enough noise in London that Henry no longer needed to go to Persia himself; England, meanwhile, had become very sympathetic to him and his project, and was considering to invite the world's powers to a preparatory conference in view of a 'London Convention on war prisoners'. 'Naturally, I will be the soul of this committee; with well-compensated tasks.' And that wasn't all. The idea of a

---

[52] Dunant to his sister Marie, no date but surely later in July 1873, BGE, Ms. fr. 2115 C, f. 86–7.

'sanitary museum' was slowly taking root; he would obviously oversee the entire business for which he needed to write to all of Europe, etc. – he could already see the rest. 'In short, I believe I have won over England.'[53]

Pastor Marzials, now up and well, seems to have kept his promise regarding social introductions. Before the end of July, Mr Henry Dunant found himself ushered into the world of the 'powerful, rich and influential' aristocracy, 'who are truly reliable and sympathetic'.[54] He strongly believed he would now convince London (after Paris, then Brussels, then Paris again) to host the prisoners-of-war conference. This delusion gained ground in September when the Lord Mayor of London offered his support, agreeing to become the treasurer of the 'Dunant Fund'. As Dunant explained to his sister, the goal of this fund was to 'ensure the success of the convention for war prisoners' and create his much-desired sanitary museum. It went without saying that these coffers would grant him the means to live so he might dedicate himself to his work, 'and in a much higher level than I could have done on the continent'.

Another happy result of his English visit was that Dunant learned the English Red Cross wanted to remain 'only English, with nothing to do' with the International Committee in Geneva: 'I'm delighted about it,'[55] he wrote to his sister.

The Brighton Conference

On 15th September 1873, Henry Dunant stood speaking to a room filled with distinguished philanthropists, all gathered beneath the ornate ceilings of the exotic Royal Pavilion of Brighton, George IV's former summer palace. The topic of the day was the convention for war prisoners, a subject in which our orator had become more and more comfortable.

Taking his audience by surprise, he made a strong opening, and one likely to delight the English: 'A great threat of social dissolution

---

[53] Ibid.
[54] Dunant to Pierre Dunant, 21 July, 1873, BGE, Ms. fr. 2110, f. 90.
[55] Dunant to his sister Marie, 5 September 1873, BGE, Ms. fr. 2115 C, f. 88.

is currently threatening the continent.' But fortunately, he went on, along with England wisdom, there are genius institutions like the Red Cross offering diplomatic solutions to the problems of our time. Which was why, together, they and he, he and they, Dunant continued to his flattered audience, would find a solution to the suffering and vulnerability of prisoners of war. A society had already been created in London, he said, of which the mayor here is the treasurer. 'Many Lords and Members of Parliament, as well as other distinguished people, have given their patronage and taken a strong interest in the matter.'[56]

The goal of this society, as we already know, would be to lobby Queen Victoria's government to convoke a diplomatic conference in London that would lay the foundations for an international agreement – replicating the proven model of the Red Cross. Dunant must have wondered why things were not moving as swiftly as they had for the Geneva Convention.

With a century and a half of hindsight, we can see how that first success of 1864 was a complete miracle and not likely to be repeated. Transforming a proposal made at the end of a book by a quasi-unknown man into an international treaty ratified by the major powers of the era in just two and a half years? It's a feat almost as miraculous as the multiplication of the loaves and fishes. Unfortunately, Dunant could not help measuring his ambitions against this improbable success. Since he'd already achieved the impossible, the impossible was always within reach.

But the world had changed. And so had he. His hair was thinning, his former vanity softening, and settled around his eyes were the worry lines of a man who fretted over what the next day might bring. Six years of resentment, misery, misfortune and confusion between his humanitarian ambitions and his financial worries had clouded his face and his ideas. While Moynier back in Geneva was happily uniting his legal skills and his charitable aspirations, collaborating to set up the Institute of International Law, Dunant was struggling more desperately than ever to reconcile the visionary and the businessman. In a lesser way, he was unable to simply combine his future projects with his daily needs. Confiding to his

---

[56] R. Durand, '*Les prisonniers de guerre aux temps héroïques*', 262. This article quotes excerpts of Dunant's conference in English.

sister in October 1873, he pretended he still believed all of this was possible, but with a certain restraint:

> If the Prisoner's Society is established as I hope and its headquarters set solidly in London, I will have a permanent and well-paid position as acting committee secretary; this is exactly what I would like, but it does not stop me from continuing to look in all other directions, in vain.[57]

Dunant would remain in London long enough to accept that nothing was happening. For an unknown reason – perhaps a falling out with the Kastners – he decided not to return to France unless something urgent came up. Well, this something urgent presented itself at the end of the year. On 24th November 1873, in Geneva, following a new appeal with the court of justice to seize his uncle David's inheritance, Dunant's creditors were conclusively denied. This meant he could finally make use of the small living his uncle had provided. On 4th December 1873, Henry was in Paris, Rue Ménard, to sign the contract stipulating the instalments he would receive: 600 francs twice a year, in December and in June.

The reason certainly justified the trip, but he would pay dearly for it. On 31st December, he wrote a heartbreaking letter to his sister Marie:

> Even though I do not speak of it, it sometimes seems to me impossible to endure the chagrin caused in part by my own error, in part by the meanness of others, in part by unfortunate circumstances: but soon, resignation, sent by God, seizes me, and with this feeling the certainty that I will get out of my troubles [...] How much I would love to be able to embrace you tomorrow for New Year's Day, my dear Marie, and Papa, and Anna, and Daniel, whose so recent sorrow breaks my heart, and Pierre, and his children.[58]

This letter was written from the Rue Cambacères, where the gallant Mr Ribes, whom Dunant had dragged into the Alliance, had offered

---

[57] Dunant to his sister Marie, 31 October 1873, BGE, Ms. fr. 2115 C, f. 90.
[58] Dunant to his sister Marie, 31 December 1873, BGE, Ms. fr. 2115 C, f. 92.

a free room to his former guest. But why wasn't he at the Rue de Clichy? Where were his friends the Kastners? Dunant spent a sad New Year of 1873 all alone, depressed, thinking only of returning to London as quickly as possible. The French political situation, however, had never been more favourable for him. Since May, France was under the authority of the so-called 'Moral Order' government formed by President Mac-Mahon and headed by Albert de Broglie, both old acquaintances. The values guiding their work were perfectly in line with the Universal Alliance. But Dunant was now out of step. The tasks had been divvied up in a way Dunant never explains, and it was now Count de Houdetot leading the French effort for prisoners of war. And besides, the file was momentarily at pause: after a new request to the French government to take charge and convoke a conference, the Minister of Foreign Affairs, Louis Decazes, had just sent his definitive refusal to grant the Alliance 'the support, even indirect, of the French government'. And so, by early 1874, the prisoners-of-war issue had been stalled on both sides of the Channel, and most likely Dunant's relationship with Léonie Kastner as well. Two good reasons to return immediately to England.

The battle of the prisoners

Following France's refusal to get involved, the Alliance's commission for war prisoners would follow a well-proven model. Just as the Genevan Society of Public Welfare had in 1863, the Universal Alliance of Order and Civilization would independently convoke a preparatory congress hoping for a future convention on the protection of prisoners of war. The congress was set for 4th May 1874; it would be held in Paris, but at the headquarters of the *Société pour l'amélioration du sort des prisonniers de guerre* (Society for Improving the Fate of War Prisoners) – which is what it was now called, after changing its name at least three times.[59] A few clamours of protest immediately arose against the choice of France

---

[59] For the preparation of the Brussels Conference, see Yvonne de Pourtalès and Roger Durand, 'Henry Dunant, promoter of the 1874 Brussels Conference', *IRCR*, 167 (Geneva: ICRC, March 1975), 61–85, and R. Durand, '*Les prisonniers de guerre aux temps héroïques*', 264–97.

(the Franco-Prussian war was still fresh in people's minds), which incited de Houdetot to 'insist again that Dunant find a way to convoke the conference in London'.[60] But Dunant could do nothing more: it was now clear that the English government was not interested either.

Between February and March, the Rue de Clichy was busy with meeting after meeting; an International Executive Committee was established with Frédéric Kastner and Henri Musson working in relay as secretary. Musson was a pillar of the Alliance and an expert on the subject. In February, the draft agreement was written – exactly as a draft agreement had been written in 1863. In March, the various governments were approached – exactly as Dunant had done by visiting Berlin, Dresden, Vienna, Munich, Stuttgart and Karlsruhe. But this time, Dunant wasn't directly involved in the preparatory work. He may have been named 'international secretary' of the 'International Executive Committee' of the 'Society for Improving the Fate of War Prisoners', but it was *in absentia*. He was in London and he didn't budge.

Something was keeping him there. Between January and July 1874, Count de Houdetot repeatedly asked him to come to Paris; he needed to share his worries, share in the decision-making and letter-writing. But Dunant would not be moved: he remained in London as if some sort of secret connection was binding him to the island or, more likely, as if a few demons were keeping him from going to France, even for a few days. But who, or what, could it be? He would never give his reasons, not to his Parisian colleagues, not to his family in Geneva.

Instead of participating in the excitement at the Rue de Clichy, Dunant 'agitated' in London, and from London. As only he knew how, he assembled an honorary committee comprised of the English gentry, no matter what level of engagement was promised – as this pleasant note from the Duke of Wellington implies: 'I have no objection to be a Patron, as you say, "entièrement honorifique" of your society'![61] In addition to the English delegates, Paris also gave Dunant the responsibility of ensuring the German states would participate, just as he had done so well in 1863. It took him only a

---

[60] De Houdetot to Dunant, 4 February 1874, Ms. fr. 2110, f. 123.
[61] Wellington to Dunant, 12 March 1874, BGE, Ms. fr. 2110, f. 189.

few days to enlist the support of Austria, Bavaria and Saxony. On 28th March Paris sent the invitations for the 4th May congress. Everything seemed to be rolling smoothly.

Three weeks later a first bump in the road appeared when Paris decided to delay the congress by fifteen days. De Houdetot explained to Dunant, who was still on the other side of the Channel, that Germany and Russia had requested more time to prepare. Unfortunately, the press campaign also wasn't achieving what they'd hoped it would: the *Figaro* and the *Débats*, undertaken by Frédéric Kastner, had both promised an article, but nothing had yet appeared.

Over the next few days it became clear that the Russian-imposed delay was the best possible news. The Russians wanted to integrate the war-prisoner question into a vast international agreement on the customs and practices of war. Through this governmental intervention, the members of the executive committee could now begin to dream of a success as great as 1864, with an iteration of the Geneva Convention on war prisoners and under the auspices of the Universal Alliance.

Dunant, who had been feeling extremely discouraged (de Houdetot, a week earlier, was sad to find him 'unhappy and suffering'), was bolstered by the news and began to write his sister again in early May:

> I'm happy to be able to give you some good news. The emperor of Russia has taken the war-prisoner issue in hand and under his special patronage. The president, whom I selected, Mr de Houdetot (who is not 'a Moynier'), is going on the third of this month to Stuttgart to meet the emperor [. . .] He will be for this work on prisoners what Napoleon III was for the Geneva Convention.

And as always in his letters to Marie, humanitarian concerns were followed by financial concerns: 'Mr de Houdetot is perfectly decided, after the success of requesting Russia and England and the other governments in Europe and in America to give me some proof of recognition.*' At the bottom of the letter, Dunant clarified his asterisk: '*These proofs of recognition are the fashion in England, very often reaching several 100,000 francs.'[62]

---

[62] Dunant to his sister Marie, 1 May 1874, BGE, Ms. fr. 2115 C, f. 100.

The Russian offensive

Their disenchantment with the Russian friendship would be progressive, but relentless. President de Houdetot and Russian Ambassador Orlov met twice at the end of April 1874. Confidence reigned; the two men knew each other. Orlov was an honorary president of the French Red Cross, in itself a kind of guarantee. Also, de Houdetot didn't immediately detect the trap, not in Orlov's proposition to defer the Paris congress, nor in his idea to merge the Alliance's project into the Russian project, nor in his plan to move the congress from Paris to Brussels.

Things started to become clearer when, on 29th April, Russia sent 'its' invitations for 'its' conference, which had been set for 27th July in Brussels. However, Russia did organize a new audience with the Alliance, this time between de Houdetot and the Russian Minister for Foreign Affairs, Prince Gortchakov. The two men met in Stuttgart in early May, and the chancellor made short work of de Houdetot. He convinced him to cancel his 'preparatory' conference in Paris, ensuring him the Alliance would have a seat at the Brussels conference table and that his war-prisoner project would be presented there alongside that from the Russian cabinet. De Houdetot left the meeting on cloud nine: 'Our work is done, my dear sir,'[63] he wrote to Dunant immediately.

But Dunant didn't answer, he kept silent. He must have suspected something was amiss. And he was right.

The first warning was that in the preparatory dossier addressed to the hosting Belgian government, Russia had 'forgotten' to insert the Alliance's project beside its own 'for an international convention concerning the laws and customs of war'. Next, Russia 'forgot' to send its project to the Alliance, just as it would 'forget' to send it to Switzerland and to the International Committee in Geneva, despite the fact that amendments and additions to the Geneva Convention were an integral part.

Finally, as the conference date drew near, Russia seemed to slowly 'forget' about the existence of the Universal Alliance and their Society for Improving the Fate of War Prisoners. They were accordingly less and less interested in speaking with Count de Houdetot.

---

[63] De Houdetot to Dunant [between 5 and 12] May 1874, BGE, Ms. fr. 2110, f. 166.

In terms of invited guests, things weren't looking any better. France declared that it didn't like the initiative 'of private individuals in such serious questions',[64] as if to emphasize that the minor miracle of the Geneva Convention, organized and implemented by 'private individuals', would not occur again. Only Russia taking charge of the situation would have them rethink their position. Scepticism in Berne came from other quarters. Since Dunant continued to remain in London, Count de Houdetot went to see Minister Kern in Paris to convince him to participate in the conference organized by his committee. Yet, here is what Kern wrote to the Swiss president on 3rd May:

I have noticed that the name of Mr Dunant is listed among the members of the executive committee as international secretary, and even as a representative of Switzerland in this committee. I allowed myself to tell Mr de Houdetot that, while not debating the merits of Mr Dunant in terms of the initiative of the Geneva Convention, I could imagine that certain facts, only partly known to me, had probably decreased the trust Mr Dunant was previously granted [. . .] I could see that Mr de Houdetot knew nothing about Mr Dunant, though Dunant was clearly inspiring his actions.[65]

The Genevans were also growing anxious. The most upsetting point was not that Henry Dunant was the 'instigator' of the affair, as Moynier highlighted to his colleagues at the International Committee. The Russian initiative was the problem, with its draft agreement looking to sweep all war rights into a single conference, and absorb, if necessary, the Geneva Convention. Moynier, who didn't necessarily oppose a reconsideration of the Geneva Convention, rightly felt this wasn't the best moment and that the context of the Brussels meeting wasn't optimal. If the conference delegates absolutely wanted to discuss certain articles of the Convention, that was fine, but this discussion should be separate from the Russian project, at the very

---

[64] Response from the Minister of Foreign Affairs Louis Decazes to Conrad Kern, cited by Kern in the next letter.
[65] Conrad Kern to Karl Schenk, then president of the Swiss Confederation, 3 May 1874, Swiss Federal Archives, E2#1000/44#333*.

least to save the Geneva Convention from sinking if the Russian project began to take on water.

In this Moynier demonstrated excellent foresight. Since he could not prevent the Brussels conference from being held, he would instead simply explain the situation to the various national Red Cross committees. These committees could then request their respective governments to instruct the delegates not to allow the Geneva Convention to be overwritten or absorbed. He didn't just find the right arguments; he also employed the right strategy and would indeed save the Geneva Convention.

Alas, the Universal Alliance showed itself far less skilled in retaliation. June passed, then July, and with each passing day the executive committee was confronted with the worst-case scenario: contrary to the promises of the ambassador and the Russian minister, neither the Alliance nor the committee of the Society for Improving the Fate of War Prisoners received an official invitation to the conference. The committee members were distraught. Refusing to accept such a betrayal, they went ahead and designated a Brussels delegation: President de Houdetot, Henry Dunant and Henry Musson, accompanied by the indispensable Frédéric Kastner, the youngster of the team.

Several days before the conference, however, de Houdetot grew angry. He'd been working on this conference for six months, he'd spent his personal funds to advance the committee's costs, so much so that he claimed he'd run dry. He could not and did not want to spend another penny to get to Brussels. The English chapter of the Alliance had promised it would contribute funding but was now stubbornly refusing to advance even the tiniest sum for the war-prisoner cause, all while blatantly scheming to get credit for the conference's success. To top it all off, the Russians had reneged on all their promises. This was too much, and de Houdetot made it a point of honour not to set foot in Brussels:

> Fortunately, dear sir, you will be in Brussels to support a project whose proposals must be adopted in the interests of humanity; with Mr Musson who also knows this question well, you will be a powerful team.[66]

---

[66] De Houdetot to Dunant, 17 July 1874, BGE, Ms. fr. 2110, f. 162.

Had de Houdetot been unsettled by Minister Kern's revelations regarding Dunant's discredited reputation in Geneva? It's not impossible. Contrary to his president, however, Dunant did not intend to abandon his prisoners, his draft convention, his conference, nor his trip to Brussels. God knows he understood de Houdetot's disgust, having endured exactly the same thing with the feckless Welfare Association that went up in smoke at the end of the siege of Paris. 'I can only sympathize with you,' he swiftly replied to de Houdetot, 'having been myself the first victim.' Nevertheless 'I am anxious to leave,' he continued as a kind of excuse, and as soon as 'possibility of travel appeared, I rushed to take it, hoping to rest there and meet with you.'[67]

And so Dunant packed his bags at the end of July 1874 and left for Brussels, via Douvres. On 26th July 1874, the night before the diplomatic conference opened, he presented himself at the Hotel de Flandre, a comfortable establishment in central Brussels. As he followed the bellboy through the hallways, he realized this change of air was what he desperately needed.

---

[67] Dunant to de Houdetot, 26 July 1874, BGE, Ms. fr. 2110, f. 172.

10

Last Attempts (1874–6)

Reunion in Brussels

In 1874, Henry Dunant now had enough to live upon – frugally. His annuity from Uncle David gave him 100 francs a month; another 100 was added fairly regularly by his brother or sister in the form of a bill affectionately slipped inside the fold of their letters. Not enough to cover the costs of a hotel, neither in London nor in Paris, where he usually stayed in friends' of friends' establishments. He had no employment worthy of the name that would have enabled the luxury of casual travel abroad. So who financed his trip to Brussels? And who offered him a room in a nice hotel, when even the certainly wealthier Count de Houdetot couldn't afford it?

Quite curiously, Dunant has provided three different explanations. To de Houdetot, he claimed he had come to Brussels 'charged with a special mission by the Society of Palestine'.[1] To Rudolf Müller, twenty-five years later, he would say his trip was paid for by the London Peace Society, but then two months after that he told Bertha von Suttner his travel costs had been paid by the British and Foreign Anti-Slavery Society, who had asked him 'to present the Congress with a request regarding the abolition of the Slave Trade'.[2]

Coming from Dunant, these differing accounts are highly suspicious. As a general rule, his claims tend to correlate. Except

---

[1] Dunant to de Houdetot, 26 July 1874, BGE, Ms. fr. 2110, f. 73 (draft).
[2] Dunant to Rudolf Müller, 8 March 1899, BGE, Ms. fr. 5203, f. 131–2, and to Bertha von Suttner, 18 May 1899, UN Historical Collections, Suttner-Fried Collection (BGE copy).

when they are all false, or only partly true. Not one of these three
humanitarian associations would have had any plausible reason to
pay him for an entire month on his own in Brussels; it is possible,
however, that each of them would have had an interest in seeing
him there.

But a fourth reason most definitely encouraged him to come to
Brussels. He knew that Frédéric Kastner was there, meaning his
mother was likely in the vicinity.

Dunant never specifies how the encounter came about. He
presented it to his sister in the most neutral way possible, not as a
coincidence, nor as a rendezvous: 'I ran into the Kastner family here
at the hotel in Brussels,' he told Marie who, strangely, must have been
hearing of the duo for the first time because Dunant judged it
necessary to explain who they were: 'Mrs Kastner is the widow of the
Institute member of the same name, and the daughter of the banker
Boursault, whom the street in Paris is named after. They are extremely
rich, they live in a large suite and they have asked me to lunch and
dine with them every day. They are from the Alliance in Paris.'[3]

Was Brussels the site of a simple reunion, or a reconciliation?
During his last season in London, Dunant had written very little to
his family, something that usually indicated depression or illness. In
July, he'd admitted to Count de Houdetot how much he wanted to
leave London, repeating three times in the same letter how he was
looking forward to seeing 'Mr Musson and Mr Kastner' again.[4] This
may all confirm that he'd stayed on in London not by choice but as
the result of a sentimental cooling off. However, once settled at the
Hotel de Flandre, everyone was delighted to see each other. Beyond
taking all their meals together, Léonie seems to have met Dunant's
smallest needs like a doting husband might coddle an expectant
wife: 'They have gone out of their way for me with so much
friendliness and Mrs Kastner is so good that it's really wonderful for
me,' he continued in his letter to Marie. 'If I mention something I like
or that some favourite meal of mine could not be found in London,
I am certain to see it appear the next day at the table.'[5] But Dunant
hadn't travelled only to charm. Eleven years earlier a certain Berlin

---

[3] Dunant to his sister Marie, 10 August 1874, BGE, Ms. fr. 2115 C, f. 95.
[4] Dunant to de Houdetot, 26 July 1874, BGE, Ms. fr. 2110, f. 173 (draft).
[5] Dunant to his sister Marie, 10 August 1874, BGE, Ms. fr. 2115 C, f. 95.

Statistics Congress had taught him that no matter the subject, and no matter whether he was a part of it or not, an international conference was an occasion to cross paths with well-placed dignitaries, military men and ministers who would be useful for all sorts of business. He was also in Brussels in support of his three causes: war prisoners; the invigoration of Palestine for the Alliance; and the fight against the slave trade for the Anti-Slavery Society.

His first issue with the prisoners of war would keep him much less busy than he'd hoped. The conference was only just beginning when our delegate from the international executive committee of the Society for Improving the Fate of War Prisoners realized he would not have an official seat at the table. In the plenary session on 27th July, the diplomatic assembly had decided it would only allow debating from 'the official delegates of the governments who had received an invitation from the Imperial Russian government and who had accepted the invitation, but not any of the delegates from the private societies, nor from individuals who were members or even experts'.[6] Henry Dunant was not a delegate from any government. He'd attempted to receive accreditation from Great Britain just before leaving but Lord Derby, the Minister of Foreign Affairs, had not seen him. And neither he nor the 'private society' he might represent had been extended a personal invitation from the imperial government of Russia.

This wasn't the only slight. The Alliance's project was listed nowhere, since the Russians had definitively removed it from the list of working documents. In the end, the Russian chancellor's third solemn promise to de Houdetot, given at their Stuttgart meeting, was worth no more than the first two: he'd given his word that both Asian and American countries would be welcomed at the same level as the Europeans. Yet, to his great consternation, de Houdetot learned that the delegate from El Salvador had essentially had the door closed in his face.

Desperate, enraged and legitimately disgusted, the Count bombarded Dunant with letters. Henry, however, handled the sequence of Russian insults with an astonishing calm. How on earth

---

[6] *Actes de la Conférence de Bruxelles*, cited by R. Durand, '*Les prisonniers de guerre aux temps héroïques*', 282.

could he be so lighthearted in the face of such an obvious disregard for the Alliance's efforts?

It appears that for the very first time in a long while, Dunant was enjoying life and quite happy to savour the feeling. 'In all respects I am extremely happy to be in Brussels,' he wrote to Marie during his stay, congratulating himself for 'the change of air' the Belgian capital afforded him, and which was 'so much better than the London smog'. Not to mention the warmth he'd been missing during the years away from his family; he was quite content throughout that summer of 1874 to enjoy a bit of pampering. 'The Kastner family is always excellent for me. They order a profusion of peaches and grapes for me, and I lunch with them every day.'[7]

How long had it been since he'd eaten peaches? Henry Dunant would later become a vegetarian, and Mrs Kastner's careful attentions must have satisfied his delicate tastes. But if Léonie's affection – or love – wasn't enough to explain Henry's excellent moods, two other reasons might explain his serenity, despite the diplomatic disappointments of his trip. The first is one we are now familiar with; he was naturally prone to seasonal mood variations, his dark periods coinciding with the gloomy winter season, his good humour returning with the sun. The second, perhaps more important reason, is that even without a seat at the conference, he could act just as usefully on the sidelines. Notably, in the account he provided his sister, he did not take the trouble to specify that his society had been excluded from speaking.

'There is still a month left of the Congress, and slowly the Russian project has returned to purely humanitarian questions,' he explained on 10th August in the tone of an accredited expert. 'Today, the work is guaranteed; but fortunately very different from the Russian's primitive project.' And in an even more specific way, on 27th August: 'The Congress will finish this week. I have been fighting Russia because Russia wants to regulate war, by making it seem that war is both normal and perpetual for humanity, while I, with the Society of War Prisoners (like the Red Cross Society) would like to decrease the inevitable horrors of war.'[8] *I* fought Russia? Sure, of

---

[7] Dunant to his sister Marie, 10 and 27 August 1874, BGE, Ms. fr. 2115 C, f. 94–5 and 96–7.
[8] Ibid.

course. But only behind the scenes. Not that his sister needed that little detail.

Double cross

For about ten years, Dunant had been corresponding with the secretary of the Red Cross in Brussels, a certain Van Holsbeek unloved by Geneva but 'who has always remained [my] friend and resisted Mr Moynier,'[9] he wrote to Marie. However, this Dr Van Holsbeek had the ear and the trust of the Belgian delegation at the Congress and was working closely with them. Immediately after arriving in Brussels, Dunant had approached him as an ally because he represented the best possible connection to a conference he'd technically been excluded from.

But there was another reason to sidle up to the Belgian Red Cross. Dunant managed to convince Secretary Van Holsbeek to form a Belgian chapter of the Universal Alliance and, even better, to get it to merge with the very official and national Red Cross Society! The deed was accomplished during Dunant's first two weeks in Brussels, delighting him even further when Van Holsbeek told him how the events had made waves all the way to Geneva: 'Mr Moynier is furious.' Of course he was. Of course, the president of the International Committee would be enraged to see one of 'his' Red Cross societies join ranks with one of Dunant's latest projects – the so-called Universal Alliance with its hazy goals and wild, unknowable ramifications.

To confuse things even further – because nothing seemed to make him happier than maintaining ambiguity – Dunant had another idea: a joint newsletter from the Belgian Red Cross and the new Belgian chapter of the Alliance. Dunant wrote the entire first issue, as he boasted to his sister when he joyfully sent her a copy. The title of the newsletter? *The Red Cross*. And why wouldn't he use it? Wasn't this the emblem of the Universal Alliance, as much as it was for the aid societies? Yes, indeed, plenty for Moynier to be furious about.

[9] Ibid., f. 94.

Dunant was also planning to benefit from the conference in Brussels and the presence of its delegates to get the 'International Society of Palestine' moving again, a project headed by the Universal Alliance and founded upon premises that still resound today:

> Palestine is certainly the place where national, political and religious rivalries come together with all their requirements, it is where they may lead, if we are not careful, to deplorable conflicts.[10]

Through this society, the Universal Alliance reinvigorated Dunant's old dream of an active, international and multi-confessional colonization of Palestine, the very cause he had worked towards in his first years in Paris, between 1865 and 1870, and that he had attempted to resuscitate during the first Alliance congress in 1872. At the time, the French chapter had not been very enthusiastic, but the English chapter had shown its support in its own newsletters starting from 1873. This encouragement spurred Dunant on to relaunch the subject. According to its usual procedure, the Alliance would suggest a new diplomatic conference to the 'civilized powers'. The purpose would be to make Palestine a neutral state, thus ensuring the peaceful coexistence of the different populations as well as enabling Western capitalists free investment possibilities without Turkey messing anything up. In Brussels, Dunant attempted to approach delegates from any seemingly interested countries:

> The *Times* mentioned in its telegraph reports that I'd arrived in Brussels, which helps prepare for the success of the Alliance's second work, the project from the International Society of Palestine [. . .] The English and the Jews in England look very favourably upon the success of this work, and in which there will be many advantages for me.[11]

Dunant's third focus in Brussels was his work to combat the slave trade, which despite international regulations was still operating in

---

[10] *La Croix Rouge, Bulletin belge de l'Alliance universelle, Revue de la Charité internationale sur les champs de bataille et en temps de paix,* 3: 3 (September 1874), 55.

[11] Dunant to his sister Marie, 10 August 1874, BGE, Ms. fr. 2115 C, f. 94.

several African countries. This project returned Dunant to an issue he'd felt strongly about even before Solferino, as we saw in the 1857 publication of his *Account of the Regency in Tunis* and its extensive diatribe against slavery in America. His work with the Alliance now inspired him to revisit the question. In its name, therefore, and with his deep knowledge of the subject, Dunant wrote a memo detailing the countries where slavery was still in practice in defiance of the Vienna Declaration and the Verona Resolutions. But this time, he wasn't planning to do everything himself. He got in touch with the very powerful British and Foreign Anti-Slavery Society, emphasizing the advantages of joining up with the Universal Alliance to organize a 'semi-diplomatic' conference to challenge the ongoing slave trade. He then bombarded the good Reverend Millard, society secretary, with a mountain of newspaper clippings and other material proofs of the Alliance's international credibility, hoping to win his trust and secure the society's collaboration.[12]

Millard duly submitted the question to his committee, who found the conference idea interesting enough to encourage Henry Dunant to probe the governments currently gathered in Brussels on the idea. Even better: the Anti-Slavery Society sent him a check for 25 pounds – quite a sum at the time – so that he might continue on to Berlin to sound out the Germans as well on the question of an international conference. There is nothing to prove, however, not in any correspondence, nor in the London archives of the Anti-Slavery Society, that Dunant actually went to Berlin. But he was careful to specify upon his return to London that he hadn't spent the 25 pounds. It's entirely possible that, for once, he was quite happy where he was and didn't want to leave Brussels.

No matter how enjoyable his stay, as the conference debates wound towards their conclusions, Dunant's visit in Belgium was also reaching its end. On the war-prisoner issue alone, the delegates had adopted no less than twelve articles ensuring their protection and equality of treatment as recommended by Henry Dunant in 1867. Moynier, who was following the debates from Geneva, could also consider himself a winner: the Geneva Convention remained safe, even strengthened by the proceedings in Brussels.

---

[12] On Dunant and the Anti-Slavery Society, see Johannes H. Rombach, 'Henry Dunant and the Anti-Slavery Society', *De l'utopie à la réalité*, 345–52.

Ultimately, the diplomatic meeting the Alliance had called for had indeed resulted in an international declaration, requiring only ratification. The Alliance certainly didn't receive its fair share of the glory, now that Russia had monopolized its initiative, but at least its name had become known on the diplomatic circuit. And when Dunant returned to London in October 1874, it was with the firm belief that the Brussels conference had launched the Universal Alliance, loaded with all his pet subjects, onto the international scene. All that remained was to await the fruits of his labour. And to forget, for a time, the sweet flavour of peaches and grapes.

The slave trade

In general, when Mrs Kastner was nearby, fewer letters made their way home to Henry's family.[13] There is no record of how Dunant spent his time between the end of August 1874, when the Brussels conference ended, and when he first appeared in London at the beginning of October. Perhaps a holiday? If so, it was a short one. On 15th October, the English chapter of the Universal Alliance met to listen to Honorary Secretary Henry Dunant's report on the recent congress in Brussels. The speaker of the day did not mince his words regarding the unworthy tactics of the Russians, more focused on their own interests than the humanitarian views endorsed by the Alliance. Russia's imperialistic manoeuvrings had turned several powers against it, who were now hesitant to support a law of war so clearly marked with the seal of a single great power.

Dunant was right to be worried. On 20th January 1875, Lord Derby officially notified Russia that Great Britain would not ratify the Brussels Convention. Following this defection, the other countries would not sign. The work of an entire summer simply fell apart, and along with it the nearly year-long endeavours of the Universal Alliance in favour of war prisoners. The subject was effectively closed for Dunant and would remain so for a long time.

But Dunant had another subject up his sleeve. The British and Foreign Anti-Slavery Society had shown him some interest, and he

---

[13] We do not actually know whether Dunant wrote less when he was with Mrs Kastner, or if the letters speaking about her were systematically destroyed, an equally plausible hypothesis.

would certainly not let the opportunity pass him by. In the same way that he stood before the Alliance to drum up support for war prisoners, Dunant wanted to go in person to the Anti-Slavery Society 'to give an account of his success on the continent'[14] regarding the fight against the slave trade. Indeed, the Reverend Benjamin Millard was expecting nothing less: since the day the 25-pound cheque had left London for Brussels, neither he nor any other member of the society had received the slightest news from Dunant. It was time he showed his face.

But instead of news from his trip, he gave them mostly fresh ideas. Dunant's final project was a vast international conference that would – under the aegis of the Universal Alliance, of course – be simultaneously dedicated to all his obsessions at once: the slave trade, Palestine, international arbitration, etc. The conference would take place in June 1875, Italy and Germany were already signed up, he assured his English friends, and 'all the other states would surely pledge themselves'.[15]

The English Anti-Slavery Society probably hesitated somewhat, seeing their theme drowned in a flood of other subjects. On 4th November Dunant changed tactics: he suggested that Millard create an international committee within the Alliance solely dedicated to the fight against slavery as well as convoke a special conference on the slave trade. He also suggested moving the conference date forward, so it could take place earlier in January or February 1875. Did Dunant also sense the Society's frustration with the intrusive Alliance? Quite possibly, since we know that several days later Dunant offered reassurances on this very point: 'Let me make this very clear: the British and Foreign Anti-Slavery Society will head this, we are nothing but the arms that will be directed entirely by the head.'[16] Nonetheless, he encouraged Reverend Millard and his friends to get moving if they really wanted to have the conference in early 1875. And he used an argument that was surprising coming from him:

---

[14] Rombach, 'Henry Dunant and the Anti-Slavery Society', 347.
[15] Dunant to Millard, 24 October 1874, Oxford Rhodes House Library, Brit. Emp. 518 C42/146 (BGE copy).
[16] Dunant to Millard, 17 November 1874, Oxford Rhodes House Library, Brit. Emp. 518 C42/151 (BGE copy).

I have influence at the moment, yes; but if we wait another seven months, I cannot predict whether I will still be as influential, owing to the instability of humanitarian causes and because of the worrying state of the continent.[17]

Eventually they all agreed: the conference was set for 1st February 1875, and Dunant took the trouble to widely distribute information on the subject. Then he left for Paris at the beginning of December, just as he had done in 1873 – almost certainly to collect his annuity from Uncle David. But he continued to work for the conference using a method that was now his speciality. From his experience with *A Memory of Solferino*, he'd learned and remembered a valuable lesson: emotion moves mountains faster than even the most rational arguments. He now asked the Anti-Slavery Society to pull from its archives 'a certain number of true and indisputable facts on the horrors of the slave trade and its continued practice in various countries'.[18] These intentionally horrible examples could be used as arguments in the small pamphlet he was writing to convince the governments to send representation to the 'semi-diplomatic' conference the following February.

But why didn't anything work as it had ten years before? Expected in London on 6th January for a very important meeting of the Anti-Slavery Society, he sent word to his colleagues on the 4th excusing his absence due to an 'indisposition produced by extremely cold weather' that prevented him from leaving Paris. Tensions began to rise among the English. On the 18th, Dunant had finally returned to England, but he still hadn't finished the pamphlet he'd said he was preparing in Paris. The document was essential for reminding the invited guests and, more urgently, needed in preparation for the meeting that had been miraculously obtained with Lord Derby. But nothing was moving forward. The Anti-Slavery Society grew seriously impatient: with only two weeks until the conference, what was Dunant doing?

---

[17] Ibid.
[18] Dunant to Millard, 4 January 1875, Oxford Rhodes House Library, Brit. Emp. 518 C42/153 (BGE copy).

The conference took place, or rather a kind of conference that looked nothing like what Dunant had hoped for. Overall, it brought together a Portuguese diplomat and five gentlemen without titles from various countries. The Alliance continued, however, to hope that other delegates would show up and a new session might be held. Dunant, increasingly nervous, sent reminders to all chapters of the Alliance, asking them to insist that the conference being held in London 'was international and that it would remain in session until the moment when, in one way or another, it obtained its listed desiderata'.[19]

This was obviously Dunant's last manoeuvre to keep his conference from becoming a complete fiasco and, at the same time, to safeguard himself a job as secretary in case the conference became a permanent body. But Reverend Millard's society had little use for the letters of support from the Universal Alliance, signed by Frédéric Kastner or Dr Van Holsbeek, thus clearly sponsored by Dunant. The committee of the Anti-Slavery Society had already drawn its own conclusions. During the general meeting of 5th March, the society acknowledged the conference's pitiful success and stated they did not see a reason to prolong the operation. The society wrote to Dunant the same day to inform him of its decision and it added a phrase which was probably meant to soften the accusing nature of the letter, but which had the opposite effect:

> Such being the case, and there appearing to exist at the present time and in other quarters a disinclination in the British public to unite in international conferences on the part of several of the European powers, this committee deems it undesirable to pursue the line of action this far attempted as a joint international Anti-slavery Committee.[20]

This last sentence must have felt like a death sentence to Dunant. What else was he good at except putting conferences together? What else had he done, over the last ten years, other than attempt to unite diplomats around a table? And the worst was that they

---

[19] Villars and Kastner (from the French chapter of the Alliance) to Dunant (certainly on his request), 23 February 1875, BGE, Ms. fr. 2110, f. 207.

[20] The ASS Secretary to Dunant, 6 March 1875, Oxford Rhodes House Library, Brit. Emp. 518 C42/162 (BGE copy).

were right: public sentiment was no longer interested in seeing hostile governments seated together. But what did he have left?

Dunant wrote to Millard the same day. With a handwriting that belies his rage, filled with underlinings, reminders of the correctness of his views and a list of England's numerous faults. To then conclude: 'As a result, we must continue the conference meetings.'[21] Poor Benjamin Millard didn't need this. He was gravely ill and had only a few more months to live. But he probably detected the depth of his correspondent's wound. Unfortunately, he could do nothing for him. Dunant needed to find something else. Without Millard, and maybe outside of London where the sails of international ambitions had lost their wind. In the East, perhaps. Yes, of course. In the East.

Palestine

The International Society of Palestine looked very much like all the other projects Dunant had been promoting over the last decade: impervious to any number of trials and tribulations, the society crossed through both hell and high water, dissolutions and resurrections, relegations to the scrap heap and reconstructions. It manifested multiple avatars and a variety of different names, with numerous vice chairmen, dozens of titled satellite personas and always, always, a life-long honorary chairman named Henry Dunant.

Since the 'International Universal Society for the Invigoration of the East' in 1866, Dunant's interest for the East had always included several parallel ambitions, but they were prioritized differently depending on the moments of his life. Over the years his dream had involved a religious utopia – the reconstruction of the Temple and a return to the authentic faith of biblical times; a political utopia – the international neutrality of the region; a financial utopia – the lucrative development of a prosperous region if properly exploited; and finally, at the end of his life, a completely personal utopia – a place to perhaps escape from his enemies or their hounds.

---

[21] Dunant to Millard, 6 March 1875, Oxford Rhodes House Library, Brit. Emp. 518 C42/157 (BGE copy).

During the Brussels conference, Henry had already advanced several pawns to attract international attention to Palestine and its possible neutral status. But first the war-prisoner and then the anti-slavery issue had delayed the relaunch of the project which emerges, in hindsight, as his last chance of rescue in early 1875. Since the English Alliance had a Palestine Society amid its various commissions, well then, it must be revived.

Dunant got in touch with his old friends from the Society of the Temple, the Württemberg Christians who had relocated to the Jaffa region between 1868 and 1870, after having waited in vain for the enormous subsidies Dunant's Society for the Invigoration of the East had promised them. A sustained correspondence was now re-established with Christoph Hoffmann, saint among saints energized by a faith in God big enough to perform miracles and a trust in Dunant which bordered on devotion. At the end of April, Hoffmann wrote a long letter of thanks, which shows that Dunant had most definitely attempted to connect his Temple friends with the English Alliance's Palestine Society:

> We were extremely touched to learn that the London committee decided to introduce English Christians to the Temple's colonies [. . .] Now that the Universal Alliance has named us honorary members and correspondents, it is our duty to send them news from time to time on our work.[22]

Probably around the same time, Dunant wrote to his sister Marie, who had not received any news for quite some time, telling her that he was now 'the secretary of certain associations which might become very powerful, and which are even already becoming so. They involve a vast enterprise of railway lines across all of Palestine, Syria and the Euphrates Valley, all the way to the Persian Gulf and crossing through Baghdad. Naturally,' Dunant adds without considering the painful echoes of Algeria this might elicit in his sister, 'the company will receive vast land concessions, and is destined to make what could be considerable profits,'[23] etc.

---

[22] Hoffmann to Dunant, 23 April 1875, BGE, Ms. fr. 2115 E, f. 60.
[23] Dunant to his sister Marie, no date, BGE, Ms. fr. 2115 C, f. 102.

With help from the Germans of Palestine, Dunant was designing
a funding drive meant to cover the various and necessary investments
of a potential new colonization scheme. In November, Christoph
Hoffmann submitted a list of priorities to the 'Members of the
Palestine Society of London' that included: farming and industrial
establishments like mills; the acquisition of land well positioned vis-
à-vis waterways; sustainable forest exploitation; increased capital
for existing industries; road construction; and, finally, increased
cattle for farming.[24]

Vast concessions, mills, waterways, forests, roads and cattle – didn't
this ring a bell? Wasn't Dunant at all wary of racing headlong towards
the same mirages which, ten years earlier, had destroyed both his
family's and his own fortune, his reputation, dignity, work, happiness
and future? Of course, now the approach was completely different:
'Since gold and silver belong to the Lord,' as Hoffmann formulated in
awkward French, 'we cannot do like oriental moneylenders and offer
large per cents'.[25] But despite this Christian approach, the obstacles
were the same. And Dunant knew this very well.

In December 1875, Christoph Hoffmann wrote specifically to his
'dear brother in Jesus Christ' a magnificent letter in which he
emptied his heart. He admitted to Dunant that this colonization
project, as laudable as it was, could not work, neither for Syria nor
for Palestine:

> I cannot in all good consciousness encourage the English in
> general to immigrate as colonists to Syria. I know well enough
> the difficulties and dangers to which one is exposed in colonizing
> this blessed and cursed country [. . .] I have no doubt that the
> Turkish ambassador gave you only the most beautiful promises,
> but do not forget the only thing the Turkish government can do
> in the current situation – to lie shamelessly and boldly.[26]

Without even realizing it, had Hoffmann sealed the project's fate
here? Dunant's Palestinian and Syrian adventures would die before

---

[24] Hoffmann to the Palestine Society in London, 27 November 1875, BGE, Ms. fr.
2115 E, f. 71.
[25] Ibid.
[26] Hoffmann to Dunant, 31 December 1875, BGE, Ms. fr. 2115 E, f. 79.

they were even born. With this triple failure – the prisoners of war, the conference on slavery and the invigoration of Palestine – the Universal Alliance had played its last hand. This time Dunant folded his cards and left the game.

The pyrophone

Since his Brussels trip of 1874, not a single letter sent from London by Mr Henry Dunant had hailed from the address of his guest house on Flodden Road, in Camberwell. Only the very official '41, Pall Mall' – the address of the headquarters of the English chapter of the Universal Alliance.

And for good reason. Like Melville's Bartleby the Scrivener, Dunant slept at his desk, or beside it, or on top of it, in an airless and dark room the Alliance made available to him. How did he earn his living? His philanthropic activities cost him much more than they brought in – something he was happy to tell anyone – because the English chapter of the Alliance was too stingy to defray his costs.

On the other hand, he was still helping Mrs Kastner with *her* life's work – the advancement of her son Frédéric and his pyrophone. It was she, and no one else, who enabled him during his months in London to survive on a cup of cocoa in the morning with two croissants, and a cutlet with a piece of cheese at lunch *or* at supper.[27] Mrs Kastner didn't shower him in gold, no, but she looked after his well-being, in return for the completion of tasks which enabled both of them to keep up the appearances of their strange relationship.

Frédéric had first presented his invention on 17th March 1873 to the Academy of Sciences in Paris, thanks to Dunant's help and encouragement over the previous winter, and several months later the pyrophone was presented in Vienna; it seems Dunant did not attend either event. It was only once his relationship had deepened with the Kastner family, after their reunion in Brussels, that Henry's devotion to the celebrity of Mrs Kastner's son returned and even grew, hampered only by his various committee work. Might it have

---

[27] Many details of Dunant's daily life during these years come from his steady correspondence with his friend Rudolf Müller while he was in Heiden, after 1887.

been the pyrophone which had distracted the 'secretary of the Anti-Slavery Committee' from his immediate tasks and provoked the frustrations of his slave-trade-fighting partners in early 1875? This is more than probable. On 13th January 1875, only just returned from Paris and immersed in preparations for the unfortunate conference of 1st February, Dunant had been responsible for a demonstration of the pyrophone at the British Association for the Advancement of Science, at a talk given by the physicist John Tyndall. A month later, in an even more precarious personal situation (by now the Anti-Slavery Society's opinion of him was souring once and for all), he was invited to present the pyrophone himself at the London Society of Arts, with a scholarly and detailed text on the musical and philosophical virtues of the instrument.[28]

But there's more. Dunant also got it into his head to go beyond playing for the curious onlooker, but to look for potential manufacturers and buyers. Success came a year later, in April 1876, when the pyrophone was admitted to the Scientific Exhibit of the South Kensington Museum, in London.[29] 'Very serious offers',[30] according to Dunant, were in view for the acquisition of the English patent. New instruments were being constructed for the British market, since the three existing models were in Paris.

Henry recounted all of this to his brother Pierre, and he obviously knew his subject like the back of his hand. He seemed to be managing the production and promotion as well as the distribution of Frédéric's invention. Later, hoping to justify his commercial services to Mrs Kastner as well as cover for having so freely benefited from her fortune, he claimed it was 'completely natural, after Mrs Kastner-Boursault's immense generosity' that he'd dedicated himself to her son's invention 'with an absolute devotion, and with success, throughout the four or five years that followed our meeting in London'.[31] In reality, however, everything indicates that in the spring of 1876, he didn't have much else to do with his time.

---

[28] Dunant, *Mémoires*, 328. About the 'pyrophone', see *La Nature, Revue des Sciences*, 36 (7 February 1874), 145–6 (based on Kastner's presentation in Paris); Félix Christ, 'Le pyrophone', *Bulletin de la Société Henry Dunant*, 8 (Geneva: SHD, 1983), 1–3.
[29] As of 1899 this becomes the Victoria and Albert Museum, in South Kensington.
[30] Dunant to his brother Pierre, 24 April 1876, BGE, Ms. fr. 2115 C, f. 112.
[31] Dunant, *Mémoires*, 323.

In August 1876, Count Sérurier, one of the last French Red Cross Parisians who'd continued to support Dunant in all of his projects and who called him a 'dear colleague' as a point of honour, slipped him a note in passing:

Dear Sir, and dear colleague,
     I happened upon an appeal in the newspapers for a Committee for the Christians of the East, I went for more information and learned this committee originated with you.[32]

The last of a seemingly infinite list, this committee would be the final manifestation of Henry Dunant's philanthropic creations.

Something had broken. For more than ten years, not a single one of his projects had reached its conclusion. His optimism, his resistance, even his resilience was exhausted. From now on he would dedicate his remaining energy to his friends, to those who had carried him for the last two years, helping him keep his head above water.

In September 1876, an envelope appeared in the letterbox at 41, Pall Mall from the British Museum of London. On a small preprinted card, the museum librarian presented his compliments to 'Mr. Henry Dunant' (these words written by hand) and confirmed reception of 'his letter' and 'the books that accompanied it'. Then, in the name of the museum, the librarian offered the abovementioned Henry Dunant, as well as a Mrs and Mr Frédéric Kastner, his gratitude for their respective donations.[33]

What was this about? Henry Dunant's various publications, no doubt: his report on the slave trade, his last text on the pyrophone. Léonie and Frédéric Kastner had perhaps also included several works by their deceased husband and father, the composer George Kastner. The details do not matter: Henry Dunant, with or without the Kastners, left England in May 1876. A chapter of his life had come to an end. In front of him stretched a blank page of uncertainty and rootlessness.

---

[32] Sérurier to Dunant, 28 August 1876, BGE, Ms. fr. 2115 A, f. 78.
[33] The Principal Librarian of the British Museum to Henry Dunant, 28 September 1876, BGE, Ms 2110, f. 212.

11

The Miseries of Wandering (1876–87)

Zigzagging

At the age of 48 and in a fragile state – nervous for his future, worried about his deteriorating health and achingly homesick – Dunant finally decided to break his nine-year exile and return to Switzerland to see his family. He was not planning to show his face in Geneva, not on his life; but his sister Anna and her husband, the pastor Ernest Vaucher, had moved four years earlier to a large house near Lausanne, where Mrs Vaucher felt a bit lonely and was often moping about. So Henry rang at this door in August 1876. Several family members made the 60-kilometre journey from Geneva to visit him, tears of sorrow mingling with tears of joy at their reunions. The weeks flew by as he avoided thinking about his looming future.

This was a welcome haven, but it could not last forever. He was aware he had become an unwieldy guest. Not only was he developing the habits of a fussy old bachelor, but he now travelled with an incredible mountain of 'stuff': archives, journal clippings, documents, brochures, manuscripts and, more than anything, stacks and stacks of his correspondence, all tied up with old ribbons. He was frequently ill, and a painful eczema on his right hand (which he attributed to the hepatitis he'd contracted in Plymouth) prevented him from making himself useful.

Also, the lake view from his sister's home, all that water stretching back towards Geneva, only added to his stress. He was living in a permanent terror that he might chance upon someone he knew while strolling in the vineyards or along the lake. And so, one morning as he walked in the gardens and noted the first rust-coloured tinge of the leaves, Dunant knew it was time to think of leaving. He went into his room, started to write a few letters, carefully arranged his files into small boxes and folded his meagre wardrobe into his travel bag. The next morning, he was gone.

Early October saw him returned to Paris where his room and offices were waiting for him at the Rue de Clichy. But his heart was no longer in it. The Alliance was stumbling along, and Frédéric Kastner had, for some time now, been vaguely hostile in a way that made Dunant fear he might also be undermining him vis-à-vis his mother. For the time being, Léonie was acting as if nothing was amiss. But it was she who suggested Henry leave Paris.

They spent the end of the year together in Strasbourg. Alsatian by marriage, Mrs Kastner owned a few lovely homes in the region. She also stood apart from a good portion of her fellow citizens by approving of the area's new owners. She certainly didn't shout her preferences from the rooftops, but when Bismarck reclaimed Alsace and Lorraine from the French in 1871, she didn't find it all that troublesome. Now that the Empire had fallen, the widow Kastner wasn't feeling quite so at home in Republican, anti-clerical France, but neither was she at ease among devout nostalgic aristocrats. Although a baptized Catholic, she hadn't set foot in a church since her first communion, and her husband, who had first studied for the Protestant ministry before becoming a musician, had further separated her from Rome. In 1871, she certainly didn't mind seeing Alsace as part of an authoritarian, well-organized and Protestant empire.

Her travel companion followed her convictions as closely as he followed her European itinerary. In early 1877, they spent four months on the North Sea coast, near Holland. Spring brought them back to Alsace, near Strasbourg, but on the other side of the Rhine river, in the village of Kehl where Mrs Kastner had another one of her many homes.

Each time they approached the cities where Léonie's social circle was more closely connected to her family or married background, Henry noticed she grew nervous and on edge. Finally, one evening, he brought her to admit that her son Frédéric was suspicious of Dunant's motives. He did not need to hear more; they both decided to take some distance from one another, at least in areas where they were known and might be seen together. Which meant that Dunant had to leave.

Portcullis

For the last ten years, Dunant's hopes and dreams had, one after the other, all fallen apart. Just the thought of the capital cities he'd visited where so many kings and queens had spoken to him as an equal now brought a single image to his mind: a portcullis crashing to the ground at his feet, barring his way. Every Genevan child is raised with the epic tale of the 'Escalade', detailing the moment when the duchy of Savoy attempted to take the city one night in 1602, and Geneva bravely kept the invader at bay. Among the many courageous acts of that night, the 'dropping of the portcullis' in just the nick of time was one of its greatest moments, so much so that all of the city's tiniest citizens can describe that fortified gate with the detail of a medieval scholar. This was the portcullis Henry could hear dropping each time his mind had dared to think of Geneva over the last ten years, but now it seemed to have fallen between him and Paris, London and Brussels as well. The Universal Alliance had lost its credibility on the international scene. It could no longer help him move into any other European capital.

There were rumours as well. Mrs Kastner said she would not heed them. But he could not expose her to her son's disdain by exposing the two of them to gossip. The difference in their age and fortune meant that, surely, he was only after her money. It was time for him to run away again. If only he could find an address not too far from Strasbourg, not too far from Switzerland. Léonie advised him to locate a city where he could rely on the friendship of trustworthy individuals. Not many places fitted the bill. In fact, there was only one. In Germany, in the Baden-Württemberg.

Sometime in 1877,[1] Dunant arrived in Stuttgart with a bag and with baggage. He went directly to the Hasenbergsteige, a pleasant

---

[1] In later notes, Dunant remembers having arrived in Stuttgart in 1876, from where he 'went on with some tasks for Mrs Kastner'. But in another document listing his travels, the first mention of Stuttgart is specified as July 1877. BGE, Ms. fr. 5202, f. 7, f. 11–14, and Ms. fr. 2102, item 11.

street running along the forest at the base of one of the city's hills. At no. 7, an elderly man walked out of a nice little white house to open the gate for him. They shook hands for a long time. At the entrance was a pewter plaque engraved with the words, 'Rev Dr E. R. Wagner'.[2]

A delegate at the Geneva Conference of 1863, Ernst Rudolf Wagner was the first German translator of *A Memory of Solferino*. Henry considered him a dear friend and they had never lost touch. When he'd recently written to him with a request, the pastor had replied immediately; there was no hint of hesitation in either his handwriting or his phrasing. Yes, the house was big enough to welcome a long-stay guest. Yes, he and his wife Ida would happily make two rooms available for him so he could bring all his stuff. Yes, the rent would be symbolic.

From this day forward and for the next ten years, Stuttgart would be Henry's home base, no matter how long or often he might travel and stay elsewhere.

The promised land

Could Dunant finally settle down? Six months after he arrived, Pastor Wagner died. Suddenly, Dunant could hear the rumbling doom of his portcullis crashing down again. Just when he thought he finally had an address! What would he do? Where would he go?

For some time, a crazy idea had been brewing in his mind. Since moving to Stuttgart, he'd renewed his friendship with Adolf Graeter, member of the Society of the Temple with which he had collaborated in Paris in 1867 and had tried to help again from London, two or three years earlier, via Christoph Hoffmann. This was the same Graeter who had showed such remarkable generosity in Paris by lending Dunant, then deep in misery, a 2,500-franc advance he frankly didn't deserve since his negotiations with the sultan had come to nothing. But Adolf Graeter was goodness incarnate. And when Dunant moved to Stuttgart, alone and frail, he accepted dinner invitations from the Graeters – who lived very close to the

---

[2] For this part, see Hans Amann, *Henry Dunant und Stuttgart* (Stuttgart: Deutsches Rotes Kreuz, Kreisverband Stuttgart, 2000).

Wagners – a little more often than discretion might advise. It was on one of those evenings together, listening to Graeter tell stories of his friends in Palestine and Syria, that Henry began to dream again of the Holy Land. Wasn't it a place for unfortunate souls like him, who gave their fate entirely into God's hands? Of course, the stories of daily life in the Holy Land would have discouraged anyone else. But what wouldn't Dunant do to escape the endless gossip, to be rid of enemies and spies, to get away from the maliciousness he felt closing in all the time?

The idea went far enough in his mind that he obtained a visa: his passport bears the seal of the Ottoman consulate, dated September 1878. But he never put his plan into action. After the death of her husband, Mrs Wagner offered to move Dunant into a large room on the second floor of the house, a favour inspired perhaps as much by charity or respect for the friend of her deceased spouse as by the indescribable mess Dunant had piled up at their home, for want of anywhere else to store the successive layers of his various lives. The portcullis remained open for now, for a few more months or years, for however long Mrs Wagner had left to live or however long her patience endured.

Losing Dr Wagner and his impeccable French was a more difficult hardship than Dunant might have imagined. Away from his family and friends, exiled among a population he could barely understand, and now he'd lost one of his dearest friends as well as a person for whom his former glory as Red Cross founder had still counted for something. How could he handle living in Stuttgart, even for only a few months a year, without ever coming face to face with someone who saw him as he wanted to be seen – the Henry Dunant of 1863. If Pastor Wagner was gone, who else might see him for who he once was?

The meeting on the hill

In the summer of 1877, a few months before his friend Wagner's death, Dunant set off for a walk up the Hasenberg Hill. The path leading up from the Wagners' home was easy: a little steep at first, then rising in a series of gentle switchbacks, all the way to the top of one of the many tree-topped hills surrounding and freshening the city. At the Hasenberg summit was a small rectangular terrace, a

perfect destination for a morning walk. At that time of day, there
was no one else. Standing so high above the world just then, Henry
would have felt his exile with a sharper pang than usual. And then
a sound made him look around: someone else had stepped onto the
terrace, nodding towards Dunant.

The two men now stood side by side, watching the view that
gently quivered with the rising temperature. Dunant had enough
time to notice his companion was a young man. Without even
thinking he heard himself say, 'Schön Wetter 'eute!'[3]

The young man turned towards him, smiling, and ... alleluia,
answered Dunant in a French that promised the possibility of a real
conversation.

Thirty years of travelling in German-speaking countries wouldn't
do any good: Dunant would never be comfortable in German, and
really only enjoyed discussing in French. Rudolf Müller – this is the
young man's name – was probably amazed at how much his
companion spoke as they wound their way back down the path
towards the city. The Wagner home was only a few steps from his
own, and the walk lasted no more than twenty minutes; but this
was enough for Dunant to tell his life story – or, enough of it, at
least, to inflame the younger man's curiosity. In the following weeks,
their relationship would deepen through visits, walks and letters,
and even through a several-day excursion to Liechtenstein and
Urlach. These weeks witnessed the birth of the friendship that
would become Dunant's strongest emotional connection for the
next thirty years of his life.

A journey to Italy

Henry Dunant left for Italy with Léonie Kastner in September 1877.
The detailed summary of his journey, discovered in his papers after
his death, indicate they went from Menaggio, near Lugano, on to
Venice, Florence and Livorno. They arrived in Rome towards the
end of the year and first visited, unsurprisingly, the German
ambassador on 27th December. On New Year's Day 1878, from the

---

[3] 'Lovely weather, today!' Quoted by Willy Heudtlass, *J. Henry Dunant, Gründer des
Roten Kreuz, Urheber der Genfer Konvention: eine Biographie in Dokumenten*
(Stuttgart: Kohlhammer Verlag, 1962), 111.

Hotel Bellevue on the Pincian Hill, Henry sent a letter to his new
friend Rudolf, describing how Rome had not only modernized since
becoming Italy's capital city, but that it had also done away with its
'horrible, detestable, false and anti-Christian papal yoke'. Despite
the many seminarians 'of all flavours' and as many priests 'looking
to keep the people in ignorance',[4] neither species was yet able to
spoil Henry's excellent disposition, which was fully delighted at the
mild climate, the blooming roses and the city's grandiose ruins.
Leaving his letter half-finished for several days, he took it up again
to tell Rudolf with exclamation marks about the nearly simultaneous
death of King Victor-Emmanuel[5] and Pope Pius IX. For someone
who'd been a first-hand witness to the Italian wars, the jocular tone
of his announcement was more befitting an amorous tourist than a
clerk on business, and far less like the companion of an 'elderly and
infirm lady', as he would later claim to his nephew.[6] Henry may not
have mentioned Léonie Kastner to Rudolf, but her perfume lingers
between the lines.

Their Roman holiday lasted for at least three months, about
which we know very little. At what point did things go wrong for
the two travellers? In his memoirs, Dunant's account has many
holes, and his correspondence reveals hardly much more. But the
two sources agree that Rome was the place where he and Mrs
Kastner were first subject to what Henry calls their 'molestations',
which would continue for a good ten years. Their enemies were so
unremitting that what should have been a pleasure trip became an
actual hell: Dunant lost his appetite, and his stomach would remain
disturbed until his death.

But who were these foes, and why were they after the pair? There
are several types of enemies, all chasing them for different reasons.
The oldest were the French, including certain affluent individuals
who'd accused Dunant of being a Prussian spy during the Franco-
German war of 1870–1. Six years later, the 'agents' of these same

---

[4] Dunant to Müller, 1 January 1878, BGE, Ms. fr. 5201, f. 3–4.
[5] In his *Mémoires*, Dunant mentions having attended – closely or at a distance? – the
king's funeral, having caught a glimpse of Prussia's crown prince Frederick. However,
there is no mention of this to Rudolf.
[6] Dunant to Maurice Dunant (likely March 1894), BGE, Ms. fr. 2115 C, f. 163–4. He
claims in this letter he was offered the trip: 'She wanted to take care of all the costs,
and since this was quite correct, I agreed. What might be extraordinary about that?'

people were still now at his heels, tracking both Kastner and Dunant even more fiercely since Dunant had never hidden his sympathies for Prussia and Mrs Kastner had jumped at the chance to take German citizenship in 1871, an act that added a handful of Alsatians to the horde of their persecutors.

But, as mentioned earlier, there was also the catastrophic confusion between the French Red Cross and the International Workingmen's Association (the famous 'First International'), both known colloquially as the 'International'. During the Paris Commune, Dunant was referred to as 'one of the main leaders of the International'; his memoirs tell us that he believed he remained under permanent surveillance as an anarchist, nihilist, as a 'radical red'. French president Thiers had boasted in 1871 that mere affiliation with the International was a crime, thus placing the guilty party 'under police surveillance for the rest of their life'.[7] Whether correctly or not, Dunant considered himself to be a victim of this police harassment, which lasted well after the fall of the Empire.

Products of the *Kulturkampf*[8] of their time, Henry Dunant and Léonie Kastner had also developed a general aversion for the Roman Catholic Church and, by extension, for the Latin world – the French, the Papists, the Jesuits and other ultramontanes whom they credited with Europe's misfortunes. Convinced from the moment they arrived in Rome that they were being spied on and hounded, Dunant decided to vent his spleen by taking notes which, he later claimed, 'he did not ever intend to print',[9] even if he wasn't usually a hobbyist writer of any kind.

Their return trip saw them stopping in Lugano, in the Swiss canton of Ticino. Unfortunately, their enemies were lying in wait. Worse, they had done some groundwork by warning the staff of the hotel that an 'odious rogue' was soon to arrive: an inheritance stealer, a fortune hunter, a former Communard, a nihilist. Various strange incidents began to take place, angering Henry so much that

---

[7] Parliamentary inquest regarding the insurrection of 18 March 1871, cited by Dunant in his *Mémoires*, 270–1.
[8] The late-nineteenth-century struggle between the Roman Catholic Church and the German government over various civic issues related to education, marriage, etc. The German word 'Kulturkampf' has spread to other countries faced with the same opposition between religious and secular powers.
[9] Dunant, *Mémoires*, 331.

he decided, with Léonie, to get their revenge once and for all. Instead of leaving his Roman notes safely at the bottom of his suitcase, he made the disastrous decision to publish them, which he immediately did in Lugano, and which he would regret forever. Published as *Jésuites et Français* (Jesuits and French) by 'A Swiss citizen', Dunant spent eighty-eight pages randomly denouncing the political manoeuvres of the Jesuits, France's centralizing obsession, the despotic tendencies of the French and all manner of dangers threatening any European country subject to Catholicism's papal interference. Alas, it wasn't even a passing whim on his part; he would then further develop these ideas, with even more violence, in *La Conspiration Noire et la Société Parisienne* (The Black Conspiracy and Parisian Society), which he would at least be wise enough not to publish. He should have done the same for 'Jesuits and French'. But no! He let Mrs Kastner look for a printer willing to publish such polemical writing. Not only did she find one, she paid the entire bill and didn't stop its author from sending a copy to the German ambassador in Rome.

These travels would have dramatic consequences: they would enhance Dunant's feelings of persecution, whether real or imaginary, that would hound him until he died. 'I am pursued everywhere by the hatred and cruelty of the Alsat[ians], the Fr[ench] and the Ultra[montanes] – separately and sometimes all at once,'[10] he would tell his young friend Rudolf when he returned to Stuttgart in the summer of 1878. These Catholic enemies would soon be joined by the 'Calvinist fanatics' who, instead of cancelling out the first, only increased Dunant's pathological mistrust of all Christian regions. What a lot of enemies for only one man!

The end of a story

The first victim of Henry Dunant's Roman vacation was Léonie Kastner. Even if their relationship was never formalized in any way – Dunant always denied they had been lovers – Mrs Kastner had nevertheless fulfilled the emotional, if not social role of companion. Once they began to believe they were being watched, their first

---

[10] Dunant to Müller, 28 [July?] 1878, BGE, Ms. fr. 5201, f. 9–10.

pretence was to take some distance from each other: 'We were tactful not to bring harm to one another: so we've decided to stop seeing each other.'[11] From this point on there would be nothing between them but a sustained correspondence – presumably destroyed later – and a visit or two in their respective locations. In 1879, Henry accepted an invitation to see her in Heidelberg, north of Stuttgart; then in 1880, she went to visit him in Baden, Switzerland where he was staying at the time upon her infinite generosity. Even though they no longer shared each other's company, Léonie Kastner continued to request his services up until 1887, giving him ad hoc work which she generously remunerated in an ad hoc manner: 'I was tasked with all sorts of small jobs, [. . .] but I didn't receive any specific compensation, no fixed sums, I never received a salary,' he painstakingly explains in his memoirs. Since Mrs Kastner's money came 'so irregularly', Dunant claims he was sometimes strapped for the cash to pay Mrs Wagner's small rent. But aside from the duties requested and handsomely rewarded, there was also affection, love, or at least the memory of love: 'Mrs K. knew that the weight of my sorrow was heavy,' he continued in his justifying tone, 'and in her goodness, she wanted me, more than anything, to be distracted and breathe pure air.' Which explained Léonie Kastner's regular advances of money, even if they came with strict restrictions regarding their use, as Dunant would explain years later to Rudolf Müller: 'She always stipulated that such and such a sum was for such and such an object. She wanted me to go to Seewis, or to the Schinznach baths, or to Heiden, or to Warmbrunn, etc.'[12] Though financed by his benefactor, the numerous 'healing journeys' Henry took between 1878 and 1887 were no doubt solo trips, that is, entirely dedicated to his ailing hand, his intestines and his nerves – Henry Dunant's faithful new companions.

Somatic disaster

One does not need to be a psychologist to see a connection between Henry Dunant's illnesses – stomach troubles and eczema, mainly –

---

[11] *Mémoires*, 332–5 (this citation and the ones that follow).
[12] Dunant to Rudolf Müller, 21 March 1896, BGE, Ms. fr. 5202, f. 11–14.

and a constant foul mood caused by his supposed persecutions. The second victim of his Italian travels, his health would never recover from the relentless delusions of spying, surveillance, thefts and plots that he believed were constantly awaiting him, delusions which increased with the quite legitimate fear that no one would believe him. Bad luck or symptom? The eczema on his right hand bothered him so much he was sometimes unable to write for several days at a time. This means that the activity on which he hung his identity – he still called himself a man of letters – the task he spent six to ten hours on each day, was compromised by the psychosomatic effects of a decidedly disastrous trip to Rome. No less disastrous, his 'Roman paranoia' was now overwhelming all of his correspondence. This begins in early July 1878, right after he returned home from Italy through Ticino: Dunant is convinced that his letter to Rudolf, a humble schoolteacher with no connection yet to any affluent circles, will be opened, intercepted or stolen. This fear would only increase, and to such a degree he began enacting very complicated precautions: multiple layers of wax, borrowed names, intermediary addresses, rerouting his letters to a general delivery address, etc. Postal procedure instructions often filled up half of the letters he was sending out, in the hope of outwitting the Machiavellian meddling of his enemies. Young Rudolf Müller must have known the Stuttgart post office better than his own front parlour after six months of complying with instructions like these:

> I am writing this short note [from Trieste] to give you news of my health, and to ask whether you could be so kind as to take this letter for Geneva to the Stuttgart post office, with an international stamp, no need to send it via registered mail. Please send the other letter from Stuttgart, via registered mail [. . .] Both letters are included. If the heat has left bits of white paper on the seals for the letter to Baden, please remove them with water, or alcohol, without ruining the seals.[13]

Paternalistic, tyrannical, affectionate and concerned: the fifty initial letters to Rudolf Müller – between 1878 and 1884 – reveal a Henry Dunant we've not yet encountered. This is certainly due to the intensity

---

[13] Dunant to Rudolf Müller, 5 September 1878, BGE, Ms. fr. 5201, f. 11–12.

of their friendship, likely a first for Dunant, and the simultaneous aggravation of his persecution complex. Combined together, though totally independent of one another, these two changes in Dunant's personality bring out a much more affectionate man than seen before, but a demanding affection, even dictatorial, for big things as well as small details. On 31st December 1878, a year and a half after they met, Henry Dunant sent a gift to Müller with the following note:

> My dear child[14]
> I hope you will wear this small item every day in your room, which is called a 'fireside' because it is worn at home.
> You must button it all the way up to the top, every day. For ever,
> Yours very affectionate Paul

Paul and Timothy were the nicknames Henry had recently given them, in reference to the friendship between the Apostle Paul and his disciple and 'well-loved child',[15] and also probably to throw off the 'spies'. The 'fireside' garment in the letter is a testament to the rare intimacy that had been established in just eighteen months between two men who were not related, nor lovers, but who had chosen each other as father and son.

What could this mutual affection be based on? Before 1885, Dunant had no thought of returning to the international scene, thus excluding the possibility of a self-serving friendship to pave the way for the devoted biographer role he would later bestow on his young friend. We have no way of knowing what they discussed in person, but their correspondence at least indicates that they hardly touched upon any worldly or existential questions, despite the fact that, at the time, Dunant was writing on a variety of subjects: religious issues, historical problems, scientific discoveries, as well as his usual copious notes and statistics on the main European powers. No, the letters from Henry to Rudolf were mostly focused on the health of one or the other, related advice, anticipation of a future visit, worries

---

[14] Both the opening and closing of this note to Müller ('My dear child', 'For ever, Yours very affectionate') were written in English by Dunant. We have maintained his spacing and spelling.

[15] Second Epistle from Paul to Timothy 1.1–2.

over sneezes or postal delays and, finally, the endless traps of his enemies. It's worth noting that the first ten years of their friendship were marked by Dunant's frequent visits to thermal baths and spa towns, which meant he had a keen interest in medical questions, quite typical of experienced spa tourists. He consistently reported on his own health in detail before spending the same amount of energy asking after the ever-fragile health of his young friend. We do not know what Rudolf suffered from exactly. But any hint of breathing trouble was enough to send the older man into a panic and brought forth advice worthy of a queen mother afraid for the continuation of her line. It seems that Rudolf gave Henry Dunant a relationship that made him useful, or at least the feeling of being useful, and at the very moment when Mrs Kastner was slowly vanishing from his life.

As 1879 ran its course, Dunant's paternal feelings strengthened and deepened. During the eight months that he spent in Stuttgart, their proximity enabled the older gentleman to request a visit from his younger friend every day.

A last trip to London

Why can Dunant never stay put? By the end of August 1879, he was off again. His itinerary was quite literally 'hand-made': his ailing right hand sent him from spa town to spa town on a quest for new treatments, just like any self-respecting chronically ill individual. By September he was testing the thermal baths of Badenweiler, near Basel, whose hot water springs had been famous already with the Romans. After a cure of three weeks, Dunant spent several days crossing Switzerland, from west to east, arriving on 30th September, in Heidelberg, Germany, where Mrs Kastner was staying. A long time had passed since they'd last seen each other. Dunant had turned 50 the year before while Léonie was inching dangerously close to the decade above. What did they say to one another? Ever close-lipped about their relationship, Dunant has left us nothing about this meeting – doubtless a poignant one – but the following: 'The last time I was able to see her, *at her invitation*, was during the summer of 1879 in Heidelberg.'[16]

---

[16] Dunant, *Mémoires*, 322.

After Heidelberg, Dunant continued on to England, passing
through Amsterdam on the way. He wrote to Rudolf that he'd been
followed all the way to the Netherlands by 'these villains', so much
so that he'd had to make numerous detours to escape their evil
traps. Things only got worse in England: three letters and a trunk
filled with clothing and personal effects were stolen, 'just to obtain
[his] address'.[17] His postal instructions now became mind-blowingly
complicated; the further he travelled, the more international the
plots became, his suspicions extending to the servants of the houses
where he happened to be staying. He was so affected he eventually
fell sick; holed away near London at Mrs Coombes's, his kind host
at Flodden Road, he remained in his room for three months without
once stepping outside.

The only thing he had to look forward to was an impending visit
from Rudolf, who was then in Paris. The exchange of letters shows
Dunant counting down the weeks that separated them. Their
relationship had intensified; they now used the informal form of
address with one another (the very familiar French *tu*), and 'dear
friend' had definitively become 'my dear child'. The concerns were
more vigorously made, the advice more intimate and the tone now
seemed to whisper promises:

> My dear child,
>   It is I who felt such great happiness when receiving your good
> letter [. . .] I advise you to be very careful because of the cold and
> damp, and the doctor was very right [. . .] It is also good to work
> as much as possible and to apply yourself; but do not make
> yourself ill by working, because that will help nothing, quite the
> contrary. On everything you mentioned, you know of course that
> I am sure; and that I would never doubt it – and be assured it is
> the same on my side.[18]

During his first months at Flodden Road, Dunant spent most of his
time treating his ailments and looking forward to the arrival of his
'dear child'. On 7th January 1880: 'I am still not well [. . .] I am
taking all kinds of purgative and appetizing remedies; it disgusts me

---

[17] Dunant to Müller, 2 December 1879, BGE, Ms. fr. 5201, f. 30–1.
[18] Dunant to Müller, no date [probably February] 1880, BGE, Ms. fr. 5201, f. 33–4.

in the end. However, I am hoping, if it pleases God, to be well for your visit.'

On 4th March: 'Only about eight weeks remaining now; I am very happy. DV[19] you will arrive and spend a fortnight here to rest a little and then you will leave directly, is that right? First of all, it won't be wasted time, far from it. You will give me these fifteen days, it's necessary to help you find your way in this desert. Because it is very different than in P[aris].'

On 1st April; 'I'm counting and recounting the ten weeks since the 20th of February! And I now see it's only five weeks left, isn't it?'[20]

As Rudolf's visit drew near, Henry was feeling better indeed. In March, he even went for a week to the sea for some fresh air after so many weeks of being cooped up inside, catching 'a small cold' in the process. But now he just needed to hold on; he could hardly wait, he sent Rudolf a one-page reminder on how to get to Flodden Road, desperate for him to come as soon as he'd arrived in England.

However, almost as if joy was no longer a part of his emotional repertoire, he fell sick as soon as his friend arrived, spiralling down into a depression so heavy he could not hide it from his visitor. He could only apologize.

Saturday morning: 'PS You must *never* pay attention to my sorrows and dark moods (*blue devils*).'[21]

Thursday: 'I am such sad company, so little agreeable, and I require much indulgence to be forgiven for my nervous state – which should be ignored, as I've said and will continue to say. I was better this week; but being irritated and frustrated beyond all hope, this kills in the end; – the others see nothing, and this is what happened when leaving the restaurant the other day. I see and hear too much; and while the others see nothing and hear nothing, *they* already managed to antagonize me.'[22]

His persecutory delusions had reached new heights. His enemies were everywhere. He no longer signed his letters Paul; it was too

[19] Dunant used the abbreviation common in the language of the Revival, DV, for *Deo Volente*, 'God willing'.
[20] Dunant to Müller, 7 January, 4 March, 1 April 1880, Ms. fr. 5201, f. 37–8; 42–4; 45–7.
[21] Dunant to Müller, no date, BGE, Ms. fr. 5201, f. 67–8. The parenthesis 'blue devils' is in English.
[22] Dunant to Müller, no date, BGE, Ms. fr. 5201, f. 72–3.

compromising. Now his letters closed with the name of an old English ancestor, Hilditch, to throw off the spies from a nearby 'papist convent', or Mrs Coombes's domestics, or the 'young ladies' of the nearby boarding school: 'I do not go out, I lunch and sup alone, and I work quietly in my room.'[23] While Rudolf was in England, Dunant constantly requested his company – envisioning outings for concerts and conferences, for walks in the parks or off to see the Crystal Palace for a flower exhibit. But could he actually go out? These months in London were marked by a series of uninterrupted illnesses, black moods, 'sad dispositions' and 'general ill health'. He tells us his brother even came to see him. He doesn't specify which one, but it's almost certainly the doctor since Daniel was too busy taking care of little Georges, a recent gift of his second marriage. Dr Pierre Dunant would have easily seen what Dunant could no longer hide: during this extended stay in London, Henry's mental health was starting to fall apart.

The blue devils

Why did Dunant stay for nearly an entire year in London, from early October 1879 to the beginning of August 1880? What did he actually do aside from watch over his own health and worry over Rudolf's? Why did he lock himself away in a city that persecuted him so, among people spying on him all day long, constantly breathing a fog that made him ill, without employment or any friends? Except for the fact that just before leaving he visited Mrs Kastner – perhaps to receive instructions – there are no other clues to indicate whether the point of this London stay, unlike the next one, was to promote the pyrophone. Dunant was sick for three quarters of the time, and he enjoyed Rudolf's company for the last three months only. Had Dunant crossed the Channel as early as October 1879 because his young friend had initially planned to arrive that same winter in England? It's anyone's guess.

Henry left London on 2nd August 1880, returning via Rotterdam, the Rhine, Heidelberg and Stuttgart, which he only passed through: with Pastor Wagner deceased and Rudolf still in London, why

---

[23] Dunant to Müller, 4 March 1880, BGE, Ms. fr. 5201, f. 42–4.

would he make a stop? He went directly to Baden, in western Switzerland, to return to his spa tourist life.

His good humour returned immediately. Although his hand did not improve in the slightest, he was convinced the baths were helping and that the location was especially healthful: 'The good *Swiss* air, and the country itself is just what I need, along with the sunshine,' he wrote to Rudolf upon arrival. 'And just in time, because I was falling into a depression in London.'[24] With a curious precision, Dunant reports in his memoirs that during this period he dined three times with Mrs Kastner: twice in Aargau (in Baden and in Brugg), and once on the Uetliberg, just above Lake Zurich. 'I have not seen her since,' he added, 'because she has not invited me again.'[25]

Had his foes vanished into thin air? Not at all. They were still lying in wait behind the fountains, in the hotels and on the mountains:

> The healthy air here has a marvellous effect on me and has improved my appetite, all of this together has given me more strength – which enables me to better stand all that reaches my ears from the French, of whom there are many, and they have not lost time in condemning me in every way. They waited for my brother to leave to begin their serious persecution, no matter that it remains 'underground'.[26]

What a coincidence that his enemies waited for his visitors to leave, cropping up only once he was alone. This letter, written on 24th August from Baden, was addressed to Rudolf, who was still in England. But by the 28th, Dunant was already worried sick: 'I have not received any reply to my letter which posted last Monday. I think it must have been *stolen*, and I beg you to send me a few lines immediately, by *registered* mail to Baden, in Aargau, Switzerland, to tell me what's happening.' He finished his letter with a serious: 'I am well now. Your affectionate H.'[27] As it happened, Rudolf's reply

---

[24] Dunant to Müller, 24 August 1880, BGE, Ms. fr. 5201, f. 76–7.
[25] Dunant, *Mémoires*, 332. The dates of any final meeting between Mrs Kastner and Dunant are a little contradictory.
[26] Dunant to Müller, 24 August 1880, BGE, Ms. fr. 5201, f. 76. 'Underground' is in English.
[27] Ibid., f.78.

arrived the next day, proving an enviable postal speed of five days between Aargau and London and back. But Henry's panic attacks had lost all rationality, even when he was feeling well enough to say so. His paranoia was all-consuming and now completely independent of his general state. His blue devils had set up house for good.

A divided Europe

By this point, Dunant's Europe was divided into two subcontinents along the very lines of the *Kulturkampf*. With a cultural bias in favour of the Protestant countries, Dunant couldn't stand southerners, and Rudolf's next move gave him the perfect opportunity to run them down. Wanting to perfect his language skills, his German friend switched from English to Italian and found a job as a tutor for a Neapolitan family for most of 1881. Rudolf's young charge was unbearable, though, which could only have delighted Henry. The latter began spoon-feeding pedagogical advice to Rudolf, recommending he 'not worry too much that he [the student] took no interest in anything – poor basic education, laziness and natural indolence are often found in the south, so very different from the Germanic and Anglo-Saxon temperament.' The letter continued on to stretch this charming assessment from Naples all the way to France, and even to 'the entire Levant and the south'.[28] Closer to Christmas, Rudolf's staying on in Naples provided Dunant a new chance to claim that southern people were worth 'nothing, nothing at all', given how he closed his year-end letter: 'Is the *réveillon,* such a stupid and gluttonous French custom for the day before Christmas, widely spread in Italy as well?'[29]

Worse than the Italians, the French and Alsatians topped his list of offenders. In 1882, when Henry was spending two weeks in Schinznach, another spa town in the mostly Catholic canton of Aargau, the presence of fifty French and Alsatians tourists upset him so much that he ended up leaving the baths, even though he avowed they were doing him a world of good. He hid away in Seewis, where the hotel harboured only 'Swiss and Germans and Dutch', which made him feel 'serene' again:

---

[28] Dunant to Müller, 25 June 1881, BGE, Ms. fr. 5201, f. 86–7.
[29] Dunant to Müller, 26 December 1881, BGE, Ms. fr. 5201, f. 94–5.

The country is completely Protestant and I am not tormented as I was in Schinznach, where the papist domestics let the ultramontane Alsatians, who hate me, as you know, into my room, open my trunks, etc. – When I was passing through Zurich, they thought it amusing to tell the porters not to give me my trunk! I had to take it and carry it myself![30]

However safe he felt in Seewis, these unbelievable ambushes kept Henry locked in his room for fifteen days. He confessed he ate nothing, nor did he write to anyone out of fear that his letters would be stolen. To make things worse, his paranoia was continuously fed by intense writing, as he attempted to weave theories out of his hallucinatory observations and fantasies. His notebooks from this period contain two manuscripts which directly outline the racial ideas he had been developing, informally, in his letters to Rudolf. Dunant spends nearly a hundred pages denigrating 'France as it is', and more generally the moral decay of the 'Latin races', while exalting, in comparison, English and German views on the family and the virtues of a healthy education.[31] The same Manichean vision was already blossoming in his religious pamphlet, 'The Black Conspiracy and Parisian Society'.[32] Did Dunant try – in vain – to have these published, or did he cautiously relegate them to his desk drawer, having learned his lesson from his 'Jesuits and French'? At any rate, there is no record of a publisher's interest. Fortunately, indeed – at least for a future Nobel Peace Prize candidate.

Between 1882 and 1885, Dunant kept up his travels at a rapid clip, seeking cures, baths and fresh air for his hand and his nerves, all the while avoiding Catholic regions like the plague. But nothing could ward off the lone source of his misfortunes, which he would find wherever he went: the hordes of invisible enemies that inhabited his mind.

---

[30] Dunant to Müller, 7 to 12 August 1882, BGE, Ms. fr. 5201, f. 96–7.

[31] *Allemagne, Angleterre*' (Germany, England) and *'La France telle qu'elle est, comparée à l'Angleterre et à l'Allemagne'* (France as it is, compared to England and to Germany), BGE, Ms. Fr. 4503, Cahiers 1 and 3.

[32] Henry Dunant, *'La Conspiration noire et la société parisienne'*, 1881, BGE, Ms. fr. 4509, Cahier 9.

The man with the white beard

Whether real or imaginary, his persecutors got the better of him on
one thing, and not a tiny one: the worldly, well-turned-out man, the
devoted admirer of Léonie Kastner, the dandy that his 1877 passport
reveals as tall with dark brown hair, a high forehead and well-
proportioned nose[33] was nowhere to be found five years later.
During his nervous illness in the summer of 1882 in Seewis, Dunant
let his beard grow out and it was as white as snow. At the end of the
summer, he decided to keep it, as if resigned to turn his back on his
earlier life and give way to another man: a slightly manic, slightly
lunatic, eccentric old bachelor, living within the memories of a
glorious past. On his way back to Stuttgart in September 1882,
preparing to see Rudolf for a few hours in Ulm, he warned his
friend: 'You will hardly recognize me with my white beard.'[34]

So in 1882, one man died and another took his place. The Henry
Dunant known by the European courts was no longer. He had lost
the awesome power of his confidence. He had lost his illusions. He
had lost his oldest friends. He had lost the woman of his life. He
had even lost the memory of his happiness. Even his friendship with
Rudolf, the apple of his eye, seemed threatened. For some reason,
their correspondence had begun to grow thin. Dunant, who was
most responsible for the silence between them, tried first to place
the blame on his hand:

Seewis, 19 September 1884.
My very dear friend,
    My hand has prevented me from writing you for months; it is
very sick, and I am taking advantage of the first moment in which
I can write a few lines in pencil to tell you that I only received
your communication very late, right when both my arm and
hand were quite ailing, and I was also unwell. Last year, I stayed
nine or ten months in Switzerland [. . .] Finally I only spent a few
weeks in Stuttgart.

Nothing but excuses! But what was the nature of the 'communication'
that had Dunant apologizing for his months-long silence (including
during a visit to Stuttgart)? The rest of the letter explains:

---

[33] BGE, Ms. fr. 2102, item 4.
[34] Dunant to Müller, 29 September 1882, BGE, Ms. fr. 5201, f. 99.

> You must not be in doubt, I hope, on my kindly interest regarding the news of your marriage; but I was unable to write and I wanted to tell you myself how delighted I am. – Please excuse me, my illness consumes me and prevents me from writing longer.[35]

Henry quickly finished his letter with the usual congratulations, closing with the words *meilleurs souvenirs* – an expression most aptly rendered as 'best regards'. In the fifty-five letters appearing before this one, he had never once sent his simple 'regards'. Kind wishes, much devotion, plenty of affection, 'a thousand friendly thoughts', anything and everything except these impartial *meilleurs souvenirs*. What had happened?

Yes, Rudolf was getting married. And Henry was not coping. He went to ground, went silent and, when he could no longer avoid answering, he was as awkward as possible. From 1884, through no fault or wish of his own, Rudolf Müller was put on hold from Dunant's life for about two or three years. The elderly gentleman didn't attend his younger friend's wedding, nor did he seem in a hurry to make the acquaintance of his new wife; Mrs Müller only met Dunant for the first time in the summer of 1887. And after that meeting, Dunant would radically change his tone towards the man he had once called 'his dear child'. Significantly, from one day to the next, he would stop using the French familiar *tu* when addressing Rudolf.

After testing the waters of Aargau, the Grisons, Bavaria, the grand duchy of Baden and even Silesia in hopes of healing his right hand, Henry Dunant discovered a certain Dr Koestlin who, at the end of 1884, convinced him that drinking iodine would cure him. This treatment kept him for six consecutive months in Stuttgart, for a change, leaving only twice for a short visit to Ehingen-Donau, at Christmas and at Easter, to visit the family of his friend Ernst Neuffer, an architect he'd met at the Wagners' and one of the rare Pietists he continued to see.[36] Then in April 1885, he left for London

---

[35] Dunant to Müller, 19 September 1884, BGE, Ms. fr. 5201, f. 105–7.

[36] In his correspondence with Ernst Neuffer, Dunant continued to use the forms of address specific to evangelical circles, like 'Dear Brother in Christ'. According to Hans Amann, this Ernst Neuffer, whose architect work meant he was proficient in drawing and calligraphy, may have contributed to Dunant's graphic diagrams (cf. Chapter 12), which are extensively discussed in their letters. Hans Amann, *'Diagramme symbolique chronologique'*, *Bulletin de la Société Henry Dunant*, 21 (Geneva: SHD, 2003), 35–46.

on one last assignment for his dear friend Léonie, who, from a distance, was still keeping a close watch.

The only plausible motive for Dunant to agree to return to London, a place which suited him so poorly, must have been the hope of earning a little money. In his *Mémoires*, he is constantly explaining that he was 'employed' by Mrs Kastner during this last visit, 'with various tasks related to her pyrophone'.[37] The pyrophone had indeed become Léonie's after Frédéric's premature death in April 1882. According to several obituaries, he had died from excessive work, a deep languor or a disfunction of his nervous system,[38] but Dunant believed that Frédéric had succumbed to the same sorrow that would eventually take his mother – a persistent persecution by the Jesuits. The truth is that since the death of her beloved son, Mrs Kastner had hidden herself away in her house in Kehl, fully dedicated to preserving the memory of the dual geniuses of her husband and her youngest son. Which was why she'd asked Dunant to take as much time as needed in London, at her cost, to get the pyrophone placed in a museum.

Just as he had in 1880, Henry began to fall ill as soon as he arrived in England. With the same symptoms and for the same reasons: 'as a result of these continued persecutions by the French', he declared himself victim of a 'very serious indisposition of the liver and nerves',[39] which had him bedridden for three months at Flodden Road. So we must believe that all the arrangements had most probably been made prior to his arrival because in May the pyrophone was exhibited at the International Inventions Exhibition in South Kensington, not as a musical instrument but as a scientific object. Dunant himself wrote a small report on the late Frédéric Kastner's inventions, covering the various models of the pyrophone, his musical chandeliers and other singing lamps.

And what was he doing the rest of the time? This is much less clear, just like his previous stay. Mrs Kastner had advised him to exercise as much as possible by exploring the outskirts of London,

[37] Dunant, *Mémoires*, 335.

[38] *Journal d'Alsace*, 12 April 1881; Charles Staehling, *Histoire contemporaine de Strasbourg et de l'Alsace* (Nice: Gauthier, 1884), xii; Wilfrid de Fonvielle, *Georges Eugène Frédéric Kastner* (Paris: 1882), 9.

[39] Dunant to Müller, 30 December 1885, BGE, Ms. fr. 5201, f. 110–11.

'which are charming'. She also asked him, 'knowing his taste for charity', to make donations and alms in her name. And so he used his long walks to make offerings to various London institutions and to distribute, 'at no cost', he specifies, cheap pamphlets against drunkenness – another matter that connected him to Gustave Moynier, the eternal warrior against alcoholism.[40] His memoirs are silent, however, about a curious affair he mentioned to his brother fifteen years later. In this version of his stay, it wasn't just 'the French', he claimed, but also some Genevans who slandered him so mercilessly that he lost the support of 'very powerful individuals who had been interested in him'.[41] Graver still, because of this he 'missed out on some business' that would have given him 50,000 francs 'by Mrs Kastner's volition', he specified enigmatically, 'regarding her pyrophone [. . .] A first success might well have led to a second!' He'd been saying this for ten years. After slumbering for some time, his hope of reimbursing his creditors now raised its sleepy head for a few weeks, just long enough to be swept away by his enemies.

In a different letter, he would tell his nephew what had tormented him so much during his time in London. A few months before his arrival, a scandal had erupted in Paris: Albert Kastner, Léonie's oldest son – the one she'd disinherited – and his wife had argued so violently that the wife had tried to throw herself out the window; their son – now about 20 years old – then attacked his father with a knife. This rousing episode sent rumours flying, mutating as they winged their way across the English Channel. By the time they hit London, poor Henry was declared the dark hero of the entire affair, since the so-called Mrs Kastner had been confused with her mother-in-law, and the husband with Dunant. 'This story, this slander was passed among London's most devout, and it was the Swiss who were my greatest slanderers and my cruellest enemies.'[42]

We do not know which of the two, Léonie or Henry, was most destroyed by this new scandal, but neither one would ever get over it. Dunant left London at the end of June 1887, never to return. Several months later, in January 1888, Leonie Kastner-Boursault died in Kehl. No one in her family thought to alert Henry Dunant

[40] Dunant, *Mémoires*, 335.
[41] Dunant to Pierre Dunant, (likely 1892), BGE, Ms. fr. 5206, 12–13.
[42] Dunant to Maurice Dunant (likely March 1894), BGE, Ms. fr. 2115 C, f. 165.

– least of all Albert Kastner, who had always hated him. And so her most loyal friend, her companion, her accomplice in adversity, the most respectful suitor of the last fifteen years of her life would learn of her death from Mrs Wagner's daughter, as if she were just a casual acquaintance.

12

The Last Station (1887–92)

The Paradies

Leaving England in the early summer of 1887, Dunant took stock of his situation. Rudolf was married, Mrs Wagner had died while he was away, Stuttgart held no more interest for him. But he was 60 years old, he no longer had the physical or mental strength to keep wandering between London, Amsterdam and Stuttgart, between Seewis, Baden and Warmbrunn. And besides, without Mrs Kastner's generosity, how could he afford his travels?

It was time to find a permanent address, to finally answer a question grown very thin through such frequent asking: where to now?

Among the many spa towns he'd visited, there was one that might meet his complicated penniless aristocrat requirements: a slightly cosmopolitan environment but far from any urban smog, decent comfort on a small budget, fresh air and possible treatments for his ailing hand, his poor stomach and his weary nerves. A final and non-negotiable necessity to ensure the stability of his health was the absence of any Pietist or papal influences. He'd come across this unlikely place for the first time in July 1881. He'd revisited it between October and December that same year and, despite the less favourable season at the time of his stay, found himself very well there, felt the air was 'excellent' and appreciated (surprise surprise) the perfect peacefulness of this 'entirely Protestant' region.[1]

---

[1] Dunant to Müller, 10 November 1881, BGE, Ms. fr. 5201, f. 91–2, as well as the following citation.

The place was none other than one of the spa towns most appreciated by Stuttgart's citizens, a Swiss village named Heiden, 'in the beautiful canton of Appenzell with views across the Bodensee and all the way up to the Souabe Alps!', as he described it in the same letter to Rudolf. It wasn't truly a rural village; it was more an elegant township reconstructed in the Biedermeier style following a terrible fire some fifty years earlier. The location was also renowned for its fresh air, its whey cure,[2] its small cog-wheel train linking it through the city of Rorschach to the international railway network. Alongside the town's Swiss clientele, its dozen or so hotels brimmed with guests from Russia, Germany, France, America, Poland, England, Italy and Holland. It was a place for walking in the hills overlooking Lake Constance, for guessing which towns one could see on the opposite shore – Langenargen to the left, Wasserburg directly across, Lindau a bit to the right with its island visible when the weather was fine, and Austria all the way to the right – it was a place for strolling between the Moorish columns of the Kursaal Hall before sitting down at any of the little tables with their Persian-motif tablecloths, arranged in charming disarray across the gravel lanes of the park in the shade of tall fir trees. The village had a telephone switchboard, an exceptional privilege for the era. It was not Paris or London, but it was not in the sticks either. An elderly socialite could imagine retiring there without too much nostalgia.

Won over by its charms, Dunant had returned there for another three months in the spring of 1882. Over the next few years, the pain in his right hand sometimes had him preferring the baths of Schinznach or the stone treatment in Seewis, but he kept Heiden on his mental map, filing it away in a special place with considerations for his future.

But that future was now knocking at the door; it was time to put his suitcases on the shelf. The late Mrs Wagner's children hadn't offered to renew the advantageous contract that had enabled him to remain on the Hasenbergsteige. So he just passed through Stuttgart on his return from England in the summer of 1887, and set his

---

[2] Whey is the watery part of the milk left over after the curd has been formed. In the nineteenth century, milk and whey cures were extremely popular, especially in Swiss spa towns – and afterward abroad – as they were supposed to cure tuberculosis, gout or skin and intestinal disorders. Spa establishments with their own cattle production were a widespread phenomenon.

compass directly for Heiden where the modest sum of 2.80 francs a day granted him a room at the Paradies guest house, an establishment recommended to him by some of the local gentry. By chance, the advice was good: the guest house may not have topped any list of luxury hotels, but it suited him in all respects.

Close to the station on the outskirts of town, the Paradies had two buildings and a much larger garden than the city-centre hotels, with a stream at the bottom of the garden providing a lovely background music. The view from its rooms could not rival that of the town's heights, which surveyed a generous two thirds of Lake Constance, but the guest house did look out over several green pastures dotted with the lighter spots of grazing animals. The food was quite delicious and the society amiable: two 'very nice' Prussian women, a mother and her two daughters from Frankfurt, the widow of a pastor from the Grisons and her little 9-year-old son. What a welcome refuge after the London smog![3]

Thanks to an introduction by some friends from the region, Dunant was pampered by the hotel owners and their two daughters, a very respectable family of the Free Church of Berne. Each passing day saw Henry feeling more restored, with an increasing appetite and the unexpected pleasure of conversation in the garden with a neighbour who spoke French! These small blessings would have him feeling very well at his 'Paradise', if only his hand could be healed. Mrs Stäheli, the hotel owner, spent a month praising Heiden's new hospital and its chief physician, a certain Dr Altherr, whom she pressed Dunant to consult. Henry gave in and let him come, without any clue that this agreement would put an end to his wandering for the rest of his life.

A famous patient

Dr Altherr was the director of the Heiden district hospital, a vast building on the southern flank of the coomb that crossed the village, directly across from the promenade where the town's healthy citizens would stroll along in their frock coats and bustled dresses, admiring

---

[3] Dunant to Henri and Hélène Vaucher (children of his sister Anna), 16 September 1887, BGE, from Institut Henry Dunant Archives.

the sparkling water of Lake Constance. Instead of strolling, the good doctor spent his days diagnosing, writing prescriptions, wrapping bandages; he was just about 40 and was the hospital's first doctor, which meant he had a clientele about as mixed as it could be, ranging from a poor farmer gored by his cow to a baron with hay fever. And so he would have had no idea who he was examining that July afternoon, just a distinguished-looking older man who complained, in French, of eczema on his finger. The doctor responded in kind in a hesitant French, but which, as Henry detected, had a decidedly solid foundation. The conversation continued and, after a few exchanges, Hermann Altherr was stunned to realize he was in the presence of the founder of the Red Cross.

This was unbelievable: his astonishment turned to excitement as he walked quickly up the Chemin du Paradis to reach Heiden's main thoroughfare, which, along with the Kursaal Hall, was the spa town's central meeting point. On this tree-lined street sat the Hotel Freihof, the very establishment that had made Heiden famous for its whey cures. Dr Altherr stepped inside like he owned the place – which, in fact, he almost did. His wife was in the hallway speaking to a Dutch couple, explaining how the whey cure worked at the nearby treatment centre. The doctor gently motioned for her to join him in their rooms.

Dr Altherr's wife (née Simond) was originally from Chamonix in France and had inherited several buildings in Heiden from her mother, including the Hotel Freihof, one of the town's most chic, international establishments. Once she'd heard her husband's story about the founder of the Red Cross, she immediately said: 'Ask him to take his meals here! He'll enjoy the company and be able to speak French!' Dr Altherr very quickly passed the invitation along to his patient, who was visibly delighted.[4] Heiden certainly had some unsuspected resources!

However, summer was winding down. Heiden's altitude was perfect for avoiding the heat of the plateau in the warm months, but Dunant was afraid of the coming cold. Perhaps Seewis, in the Grisons, would be better for him for the winter? He headed off at

---

[4] Hermann Altherr, 'Henri Dunant's *Letzte Jahre*', first published in *Das Rote Kreuz*, May 1828, reprinted in R. Durand (ed.), *Dunant und die Ostschweiz* (Geneva: SHD, 1992), 44–53.

the end of August, looking for somewhere to hibernate. But temperature wasn't his only enticement: Rudolf Müller would be in the Grisons with his young wife, whom Dunant had not yet met. This time their geographical proximity made it impossible to defer the meeting once again. Dunant told Rudolf of his intention to spend a day in Seewis to look for a guest house and also, 'in part', he mentioned rather inelegantly, to meet his friend's wife.

What was this encounter like for Dunant? Our only clue is Dunant's polished commentary to Rudolf, once he'd returned to Heiden:

> I was very happy to make the acquaintance of Mrs Müller, and please tell her so when you write to her. I was enchanted to go for a lovely walk, and to have several conversations with her.

On Mrs Müller's side, however, a single afternoon in the company of the great man was probably more than enough time to whet her curiosity, as Dunant correctly guessed:

> Please be so good as to explain to her, and to excuse my apparent indiscretion at that very moment [Mrs Müller had mentioned a future occasion to see each other], in the middle of so many people, some of whom, although not enemies, were also not friends [. . .] I would like to see the mountains and take walks with you; but before – remember that I am followed everywhere I go, and my enemies are relentless about damaging me everywhere and upsetting me.[5]

And so an easy day trip to Seewis was enough to awaken all his former demons. Was this what finally settled it? A few weeks after returning to Heiden, he made up his mind: 'I am planning,' he wrote to his nephew, 'to stay here.'[6]

---

[5] Dunant to Müller, 27 or 28 August 1887, BGE, Ms. fr. 5201, f. 112–15.
[6] Dunant to Henri Vaucher, 16 September 1887, Coll. J.-J. Vaucher, BGE, from Institut Henry Dunant Archives.

The French circle

No need to send a second invitation to Henry Dunant to take his meals at the Freihof. First, Mrs Altherr's hotel was of a higher standing than the Paradies, and, just as the doctor had boasted, the establishment indeed enjoyed a very upscale clientele – at that very moment it included a Russian prince, a Parisian couple and a ship owner. How could Dunant resist? Even more enticing was Mrs Altherr-Simond's francophone background. As we know, Dunant's pitiful German restricted him to such a point that he preferred a few trivial exchanges over the garden hedge with Mrs Küng-Krüsi to an elevated discussion with a learned scholar in which he might not understand half of it. So when Dr Altherr suggested he come looking for a more familiar language and company, Dunant accepted with the same joy he might feel upon discovering an orchid in a field of potatoes. The situation suited him so well that, at the end of the high season, when the Hotel Freihof emptied of its guests, Dunant moved in for the winter, with his trunks and his manias. He'd definitely been invited, yes, but perhaps, judging from what the doctor would later reflect, the Altherrs might not have guessed just how generous their offer would become:

> Mr Dunant was almost completely vegetarian [. . .] He would happily eat fish, which made things quite expensive for my wife and I who shared meals with him. [. . .] Since we were almost completely alone in our hotel during the off season, and since we did not have any other guests, Mr Dunant helped us write our flyers in French.[7]

In early 1888, this is what Henry Dunant's future in Heiden looked like: a calm retirement spent between the Paradies guest house in the summer, and the Freihof in the winter; a small society centred around Dr Altherr, his wife, a few passing guests at the Freihof and Mrs Küng on the other side of the hedge in the Paradies garden. From time to time this circle was widened by visits from his nephews, with or without their children, and Rudolf Müller once or twice a year. What else might he look forward to, now that Léonie Kastner had passed away?

---

[7] Altherr, 'Henri Dunant's *Letzte Jahre*', 47.

It had been eight years since he'd last seen her. Following her quasi-official funeral in Alsace, she had been inhumed beside her son Frédéric in their family mausoleum at the Saint-Gall cemetery in Strasbourg. Dunant could not think of it without a heavy heart. Léonie, buried without him even being told, and only a few hours away from Heiden! This sorrow would soon be compounded by a new obsession – that he'd been deprived of a considerable inheritance.

We know that Wagner's daughter gave Henry the news that fateful spring, after she'd read of the event in a local newspaper. Henry was in Stuttgart to collect his last trunks before the Wagner home was sold. Elise Wagner hadn't only passed along the surprising news of Léonie's death, she'd also let it slip that Mrs Kastner had left a million francs to the Baden-Baden baths. A million francs!

Once his astonishment had passed, he made up his mind: 'There are odious undertakings behind this!' he wrote to Rudolf. How could Mrs Kastner leave a million francs to the Baden-Baden baths and nothing to her financially distressed friend? She had promised him several pieces of art, but he'd seen nothing of them, not even the small bronze she'd always said would be his! There was no doubt: 'Someone must have stolen her will.'[8] Dunant would not let the idea go, even if Mrs Kastner had settled her affairs as carefully as possible. The aforementioned will, written in 1880 right when she and Dunant had parted company, was mainly focused on a gift of 55,000 francs to the Institut de France in memory of her husband's work and her son's inventions. Seven years later, Dunant still wanted to know the exact circumstances of her death. He asked a mutual friend to request some information from Baron Larrey, an old friend of the Kastner family. But the baron had nothing to offer, nothing about the circumstances of her death nor what might have been in her will. Only one thing was certain: Dunant would not inherit a single penny from the Kastner-Boursault fortune.

An apocalyptic hobby

Cognizant of his fragile mental health, over the last ten years Henry had been developing a pastime that could distract him when his dark

---

[8] Dunant to Müller, 23 March 1896, BGE, Ms. fr. 5202, f. 23–4.

ideas came banging at the door; he turned to a task that focused his
mind as well as his hand. These were large-scale drawings depicting
a complicated mixture of various writings, symbolic drawings,
cartouches, crosses, strangely shaped monuments and terrifying
animals, all composed into an artful spatial arrangement that called
the viewer to follow a specific path.

He called them 'diagrams', and the goal of these curious drawings
was to translate in the most imagistic and intelligent way possible
– at least in Dunant's mind – the prophecies of the Bible. Henry was
very proud of them and willingly showed them to his visitors or
even asked them to contribute. One of his first diagrams was begun
back in England, during the time Rudolf came to see him at Flodden
Road. While staying at the Paradies guest house, he continued
working on it and was content to discuss it with the numerous
Darbyists, Wesleyists and other sectarian Protestants who frequented
Mr and Mrs Stäheli's guest house. In that summer of 1889, a young
married couple turned out to be willing partners for theological
debates around his latest diagram. Mrs and Mr Clibborn-Booth
were no less than the daughter and son-in-law of the founder of the
Salvation Army, a charity they intended to introduce into France
and Switzerland. 'Colonel' Clibborn-Booth – according to the
military terminology the movement had adopted – knew his Bible
like the back of his hand and, unlike some, was not put off by the
amazing imbroglio of calligraphies and symbols covering the
immense piece of paper laid out across Dunant's floor. Nothing kept
these two men from the pleasure of a debate. 'You're a mystic!'[9]
Dunant exclaimed one day in response to Colonel Clibborn's
liberties with biblical interpretation. They would often continue
their conversation in the guest house's small reading room once the
newspapers had been folded up for the day. Dunant loved to hear
stories of spectacular 'conversions' – the Colonel had a raft of them
– a reminder of the good old days of the YMCA.

But beyond their didactic virtues, and beyond their value as a
subject of conversation, Dunant's diagrams were also a personal
blessing in the way they kept him busy in his solitude. For anyone

---

[9] Henri Vaucher to his future wife Julia Schaffroth (during a visit to his uncle in
Heiden), 26 August 1889, published in 'Un nouvel éclairage sur l'"ermite de
Heiden"', Bulletin de la Société Henry Dunant, 16 (Geneva: SHD, 1992–3), 7–13.

who might be tempted to try the exercise themselves, he wrote in a small explicative text:

> [...] accomplished in a prayer-like mindset and Christian modesty, this work will endow him with wisdom in the Scriptures, will be a source of light, will interest, captivate and may become, with God's blessing, a way of growing strong in one's faith, of solace when knocked down, a consolation in trials, adversity or isolation [...] Finally, it can contribute to taking a step away from this world and this terrible century, so as to live in a more intimate communion with the Saviour, while waiting and looking towards his second coming.[10]

Religious practice seemed to have vanished from his life in recent years, as he'd been so angry with anything connected to a church, in any form whatsoever. But the Bible truly remained for him, and more than ever, his first and only way of interpreting the world. His diagrams were the visual expression of the same biblical prophecies Pastor Gaussen used to explain when he was a teenager, and that he now recreated using his own historical and political interpretations from the books of Genesis, Revelation and Daniel. In his view, every single one of the world's greatest historical moments, both past and future, were proclaimed in the Old Testament, and his diagrams were a way to illustrate their chronology up to the final reckoning, the so-called 'red revolution' that, according to Dunant, would ruin humanity forever.

It must be said he wasn't living in optimistic times. Alongside his apocalyptic diagrams, Dunant was preparing a new work he wanted to call *L'Avenir sanglant* (The Bloody Future). The defender of wounded soldiers was beginning a foray into another combat, upstream in a way – against war itself, against the army and over-armament, and against nationalism. The texts Dunant worked on between 1889 and 1897 laid out the increasingly clear edges of a universalist anti-militarism, a far cry from the fatalistic resignation in *A Memory of Solferino* that had claimed that 'the hopes and

---

[10] Cited by Roger Durand, '*Diagrammes symboliques chronologiques de quelques prophéties des saintes Écritures*', *Bulletin de la Société Henry Dunant*, 7 (Geneva: SHD, 1982), 10–11. On the diagrams, also see Heudtlass, *J. Henry Dunant*, 92–7.

aspirations of the Society of Friends of the Peace must be abandoned'.[11] What was happening? Had the zeitgeist reached all the way to his Appenzell hideaway, enticing him away from his usual conservatism and prompting a re-evaluation of the world's most sacred institutions?

Indeed, 1889 saw the publication of *Die Waffen nieder!*,[12] a novel by Austrian aristocrat Bertha von Suttner; its passionate plea against war and the army was making great waves in intellectual circles. If he had not yet read it, he had grasped its message: repairing the damage from war was no longer enough. At a time when 'the European continent, from the Pyrenees to Mount Ural, is shining with the bayonets of more than twenty-two million soldiers',[13] as Dunant denounced in *The Bloody Future*, there was no other prediction to make, alas, than civilization's imminent return to barbarianism. Page after page, Dunant feverishly filled his brown and blue notebooks with hurried script, underlinings and crossings out, as if he needed to express every last one of these beliefs that preoccupied him by day and kept him awake at night. Write, write, write – while there was still time.

And what about the past? His cursed past? In the *Mémoires* he began compiling around this same period, Dunant returned to the misfortunes his family had suffered through his bankruptcy, twenty-two years before. The wound had not yet healed in 1889, and his pen poured out the events of 1867 with the same feelings of injustice and the same bitterness from ten or fifteen years prior. Recent literary news certainly played a part in this painful return to the past. The academic Maxime Du Camp had just published a history of the French Red Cross in which he declared that the Italian Ferdinand Palasciano, by virtue of his 1861 motion in favour of neutrality for wounded soldiers, was in fact the true architect of the Geneva Convention.[14]

---

[11] Dunant, *A Memory of Solferino*, 116.
[12] The French translation, *Bas les Armes!* came out in 1889 and the English translation *Lay Down Your Arms!* appeared in 1902.
[13] '*L'avenir sanglant, Un déluge de sang, Guerre Générale*', 1, BGE, Ms. fr. 4557, f. 10–11; cf. Henry Dunant, *L'avenir sanglant* (Geneva: Institut Henry-Dunant and L'Âge d'Homme, 1969), 191.
[14] Maxime du Camp, *La Croix-Rouge de France* (Paris: Hachette, 1889), 73.

Dunant pouted, frothed, sputtered angrily: but what could he do from his little Paradies guest house, lost in the middle of green fields in the middle-of-nowhere Switzerland? The peace he claimed to have found in Heiden didn't seem to have any effect on the touchiest areas of his memory. And the approaching winter only increased his distress: Dunant knew how much his demons loved the cold and the encroaching night. Mrs Stäheli now lit the lamps in the salon at 5:00 p.m., and the emptying house meant that footsteps echoed. Dunant would have been happy to pack up his things and leave . . . if only he had somewhere to go.

The schoolteacher

When the spa tourists and holidaymakers left Heiden and gave the village back to its year-long residents, there was obviously no one around with whom to share a bit of French conversation. As reclusive as he'd become, Henry still yearned to communicate with others, no matter how trivial or serious the chat. Which was why he was grateful for any newcomer who might turn up. One day on the street in Heiden, he was approached by a young man with a round, open face and light eyes, both in contrast to his large, policeman-like moustache. He could speak only basic French, but it was enough for Dunant to take an interest.

Wilhelm Sonderegger was the new teacher at Heiden's primary school. He'd just moved over from the neighbouring valley and set himself up a few months earlier with his wife and son on the Rue des Bains, in a house like a Swiss cuckoo clock, decorated with all sorts of crosses and shields. Contrary to much of the rest of Heiden, this particular neighbourhood had been spared by the 1838 fire and still conserved several Appenzeller-style homes, as opposed to the Biedermeier architecture everywhere else. The Sondereggers owned their home and were very proud of it, nesting like a pair of turtledoves. Their house was also big enough that they could use their basement to set up and display the object of their shared passion: a huge papier-mâché model of the region, that Wilhelm invited Dunant to come and see whenever he liked.

And here it began. Exactly as he had done with Rudolf Müller, Dunant exhibited a friendship so attentive it was initially disconcerting for its beneficiaries, but simultaneously flattering when they realized who they were dealing with. As Mrs Sonderegger would say later:

> The first time that Dunant came to our home, I felt a deep respect for him, such that I had never felt for anyone else before. This feeling would strengthen as we got to know each other more, because despite the poverty of his exterior, he radiated a goodness of mind, love and distinction.[15]

This first visit set them off into a very intense relationship, which saw Henry walking nearly every day to the top of the Rue des Bains, buttonholing Mrs Sonderegger while both of them stood waiting for the schoolmaster to come home. 'I just have to hint at something, and your husband understands me,'[16] he said one day to the courageous young woman, who was probably beginning to find their distinguished visitor a little invasive. It must be said she was blessed each year with a new baby, something which might have relegated their illustrious guest to the background. But this never stopped Dunant from visiting whenever and however long he pleased; he often stayed late into the night, soliloquizing on his past misfortunes or the world's impending misfortunes even when Wilhelm Sonderegger still had to prepare his lessons for the next day or write an article for the *Appenzeller Anzeiger*, for which he was a regular contributor. But the schoolteacher found himself further enmeshed by the new translator role offered by Dunant. Our Red Cross founder had gotten it into his head to return publicly to his past exploits rather than continue obsessing over them in private or complaining to Mrs Sonderegger. What began with requests for the occasional translation during visits soon led to the couriering of various papers to their home with requests to be done 'as soon as possible', with a casualness that bordered on disdain:

> I've received the attached letter from Dr Altherr, which you would be generous enough to translate for me. I can't even try to uncode his chicken scratch because German script is so annoying

---

[15] As remembered by Susanna Sonderegger, published in the newspaper *Du*, 8 August 1942, cited by Hans Amann, *Wilhelm Sonderegger – die rechte Hand Henry Dunants* (Heiden: Henry-Dunant-Museum, 1999), 13.
[16] Amann, *Wilhelm Sonderegger*, 15.

for me. I ask you to send me, as soon as possible, an idea of what
he's written.[17]

All this he did, aware that he was abusing the good graces of a new
friend: 'I very much enjoy writing you every day, but I fear I am
ultimately a bother to you.'[18]

But what was the cause of this sudden excitement? Nothing less
than the imminent founding of the Heiden branch of the Red Cross
by Wilhelm Sonderegger and Henry Dunant. After more than twenty
years of banishment (his last engagement as a member was in 1871
in Paris) this would offer him an official relationship with the Red
Cross again. Bolstered by the youth and enthusiasm of his new
admirer, Dunant orchestrated everything. During the first assembly
of the foundation, which was held in February 1890 in one of the
town's hotels, he agreed to speak publicly, something he had not
done for years and which he would not do again. Nevertheless, this
new branch was his brainchild: he wrote the statutes and formed the
committee. Convinced that 'it was through the Ladies one had to
start, because they alone know and can do the propaganda work',[19]
he selected most of the members from among the spouses of Heiden's
notable families. Wilhelm Sonderegger would become 'corresponding
secretary', the same title Henry Dunant originally had in the YMCA
and then later at the Red Cross. Dunant himself bestowed this title
on his new friend: his handwriting is recognizable in the list of
functions attributed to the different members, and it's the only title
written in French. The first letter he would have him write was to the
president of the Swiss Red Cross, Dr Staehelin, proof of Dunant's
desire to be welcomed back into the Red Cross universe.

Homage from Reims

Even so, Heiden had some French competition for Dunant's
attention in early 1890. In January, he received a letter from

---

[17] Dunant to Wilhelm Sonderegger, no date (likely after September 1890), from René
Sonderegger, *Jean Henry Dunant Revolutionär* (Zurich: Reso Verlag AG, 1935), 101.
All letters from Dunant to Sonderegger come from this book.
[18] Amann, *Wilhelm Sonderegger*, 15.
[19] Dunant to Sonderegger, no date (likely early 1892), 118.

Ferdinand Lambert, secretary of the Reims Red Cross, asking him
how to get a copy of *A Memory of Solferino*, apparently unfindable,
he claimed, in 'Reims and Paris bookshops'. With a slightly strange
emphasis, Lambert finishes his letter with a convoluted dictum: 'A
good master doesn't reject the questioning disciples keen to spread
his doctrine!'[20] Words to warm Dunant's heart, certainly, but also
reawaken his dreams of ultimate posterity. What was this news?
Customers lamenting that *A Memory of Solferino* was no longer
available in bookshops?[21] Why not capitalize on Reims's goodwill
with a new French edition?

This was the vein in which he replied to Mr Lambert, who then
answered by return post more fervent and devoted than ever. The
Reims secretary of the French Aid Society for Wounded Soldiers (in
France this was still the official name of the Red Cross) was
definitely in favour of launching a popular edition of *A Memory*,
popular because, he went on, 'indeed it must be a book read by
everyone – retailers, artisans, workers, farmers';[22] this project
seemed so settled that Lambert was already promising to personally
deliver a copy to Dunant in Heiden. The letter is addressed to 'Dear
and Venerated Master', a title the Reims secretary would maintain
throughout their entire correspondence.

The following letter indicates the Reims project was even more
promising than it first seemed: a doctor named Colleville was set to
present a history of the Red Cross to the Academy of Reims. This
would provide the 'occasion, in a certain milieu, to correct the error
involuntarily propagated by Mr Maxime Du Camp', who was
guilty of, as we've seen, designating Dr Palasciano the 'founder' of
the Red Cross. Second, it was important the section on Dunant be
'well done in Mr Colleville's work, since the newspapers would
reprint it'.[23]

Bullseye! Dunant raced to the post office to send an entire box
filled with copies of the irrefutable proof of his paternity of the Red

---

[20] Ferdinand Lambert to Dunant, 16 January 1890, BGE, Ms. fr. 2111, f. 3.
[21] In April 1890, the president of the Central Committee of the Swiss Red Cross, Dr
Staehelin, also complained that *A Memory* could not be found in Swiss bookshops;
indeed he used the copy he'd had to borrow from Mr Moynier! Dr A. Staehelin to
Dunant, 25 April 1890, BGE, Ms. fr. 2111, f. 23.
[22] Ferdinand Lambert to Dunant, 16 January 1890, BGE, Ms. fr. 2111, f. 3.
[23] Ferdinand Lambert to Dunant, 12 March 1890, BGE, Ms. fr. 2111, f. 13.

Cross, along with an outraged note emphasizing how much it hurt him that once again his role was being questioned.

At some point that summer, Dr Colleville – who'd given his presentation to the Academy of Reims in June – sent Dunant the small printed summary text along with a letter of thanks to the man who'd inspired his talk: 'My greatest reward would be that all those who have known your good deeds be reminded of your name deep in their hearts.'[24]

For Dunant, 1890 represented the first phase of his rehabilitation. Following his return to Red Cross circles in February through the Heiden branch, in June Reims would pave a much broader path as it could eventually lead to a new French edition of *A Memory of Solferino*.

The agenda of the next decade was now set: Henry Dunant would return to the place he deserved. And this comeback was in great part due to Dr Colleville of Reims, whose pivotal role he acknowledged well before the following events would confirm it: 'You have thrown a ray of sunlight over the end of my life,' Dunant writes to him the same year, 'piercing the thickening shadows, and its warmth did me good while those who could have and should have done, did not. They never understood me.'[25] Dunant's intuition was correct, as it always was when not blurred by resentment – the turnaround of 1890 indeed broke a hole through his shadows; though he could not yet guess how far it would take him.

Exile to Trogen

Dunant kept it from his mind throughout the summer of 1890. He didn't even mention it to his family; the very thought of it was enough to awaken his fear of rootlessness, of never knowing where to go. But there was no more putting it off: he now had to make a decision.

The Paradies guest house was going to close. Mr and Mrs Stäheli were planning to take over an unassuming guest house, the

---

[24] Dr G. Colleville to Dunant, 15 September 1890, BGE, Ms. fr. 2111, f. 24.
[25] Dunant to Dr Colleville, 28 December 1890, French Red Cross Archives, BGE copy.

Lindenbühl, about 10 kilometres from Heiden near the small town of Trogen, where they counted on relocating their most faithful clients.

Did Dunant have a choice? Once the news had broken, he began to secretly hope for a year-long invitation from the charming Mrs Altherr. No dupe, she pulled the rug out from under his feet by offering to house him just during the move, from the end of September to the middle of October, thus excluding the possibility of permanent residence at the comfortable Freihof – something which would have involved the financial sacrifice of one of their hotel rooms, not to mention taking on the burden of such a delicate client's preference for fish, vegetables and seasonal fruits. In the end, Dunant was forced to accept the inevitable: he would follow the Stähelis to Trogen.

After three years in Heiden, the piles of paperwork, prospectuses, various writings and newspaper cuttings in Henry's room had doubled. Impossible to move all this! There was only one thing to do: Dunant would transport fifteen boxes to the Sonderegger's home. Mrs Sonderegger had just given birth to her fourth child a week earlier, but this didn't seem to bother Dunant. With the brutish authority he now assumed when dealing with the schoolmaster, he requested Wilhelm house his troublesome boxes as long as necessary.

The move to Trogen took place in October. The most loyal of the loyal were there: Dr Altherr had come to an understanding with Wilhelm Sonderegger to share the work of transporting their friend's belongings. Dunant was blatantly dragging his feet: the end of the year was approaching, the quickening shadows darkening his mood in kind. On the evening of the move, Dunant stood watching Dr Altherr's wagon disappear down the hillside with the feeling that he was being deported.

He spent a year and a half at the Lindenbühl, with varying states of mental health. He kept himself afloat for the first few months by writing. He continued writing *The Bloody Future*, for which he requested help from his friend Rudolf Müller. With an obvious autobiographical projection, he was hoping to dedicate a chapter to persecuted geniuses: Kepler, who'd died in misery; Dryden, starved to death; Mozart, ruined; Gutenberg, unjustly imprisoned, etc. There was no more paternal intimacy flowing from Paul to Timothy, but the older autodidact still had plenty of respect and affection for a young man as educated as Rudolf Müller. Dunant wasn't yet thinking of him as a future biographer, of course; the tone of his request was that of a researcher approaching a foreign colleague, equal to equal. 'I'm writing to solicit your erudition and your grace, my dear Friend [. . .] I think you must have all of this in mind and that it would be easy for you, without too much research taking up too much of your time – Thank you in advance.'[26]

What a contrast to his tone with Sonderegger! Considering the parallel with his own early role in the YMCA and the nascent Red Cross, the 'corresponding secretary' title Dunant gave Sonderegger in the Heiden Red Cross is like a slip of the tongue giving away the true nature of their connection. Since the enthusiastic letters from Reims, Dunant was dreaming of his possible worldwide rehabilitation as the founder of the Red Cross. But he no longer had the physical energy needed to accomplish such a feat. Sonderegger may have appeared to him not only as 'correspondent' for the Heiden branch and not only as a docile personal secretary, but perhaps as a clone of himself who would willingly and without compensation provide the energy he needed right at that very moment. Like an echo of his own past, this curious 'correspondent' title shows how Dunant saw himself in his new friend Sonderegger, and all the expectations attached to it.

Expectations which Sonderegger accepted.

A consenting slave

The exceptional charisma that Dunant exerted over his entourage can be understood simply by listing the number of individuals who offered him their unconditional, even irrational, devotion without any familial or emotional connection to him. Why would Wilhelm Sonderegger – a responsible, healthy and strong-minded man – consent to be treated in such a way? Why would he put up with, ostensibly without mutiny, Dunant's orders, summons, sermons, reprimands, tantrums, threats and indignations? 'For the good' of Heiden's Red Cross, then later 'for the good' of eastern Switzerland's Red Cross, and apparently 'for the good' of the very martyr himself, Dunant would have Sonderegger perform an extraordinary amount

---

[26] Dunant to Müller, (no day) March 1891, BGE, Ms. fr. 5201, f. 118–19.

of work to further Henry's own notoriety. The first onslaughts began immediately after the arrival of a copy of the small *Historique de la Croix-Rouge* (History of the Red Cross) from Reims, in which Colleville had given him a tribute. Over the following weeks, Dunant suggested Sonderegger should write to a big Zurich-based publisher, Orell Füssli, to press for the reissuing of *A Memory* in German. His plan was all set out, Sonderegger just needed to follow it. With no rest for poor Wilhelm, Dunant assailed him with orders, barely concealed as advice, to put together the Heiden branch report, to format his brochure, to compose the history of the Red Cross and, above all, to transform the brochure version of Colleville's report into a real book. 'You would do it better than him using what has been done in various European countries. Finally, your book should be bought in Zurich, Basel, Bern, Lucerne [followed by a list of fifteen other cities in Switzerland and Germany]. We must not count on Heiden.'[27]

Dunant's clear conscience came out of the conviction that he was liberating Sonderegger from the regional barriers of his small horizon. In January 1891, in a letter containing an endless list of things Sonderegger should do and people he should see, his mentor insisted: 'Do not forget anything, and please allow me to remind you to set aside this narrow-minded, foolish and petty village mindset.'[28] Was Sonderegger himself part of this narrow, village mindset? While not stated blatantly, this is certainly implied.

Victims do sometimes fall in love with their captors. Well, in this case, the persecuted man courted his tyrant. Even in the wake of steady harassment, Wilhelm Sonderegger offered Dunant, as a birthday gift on 8th May 1891, to stay at his home 'for the summer or forever'[29] rather than languish at the Lindenbühl. How did the schoolteacher manage to get his wife – currently pregnant with her fifth child – to swallow this bit of news? The documents tell us nothing, of course. And Dunant didn't even bother to reply to Sonderegger's sacrificial generosity. Not a word at first, then he pretended to be grateful but was actually dithering, then silence again. This went on for months.

---

[27] Dunant to Sonderegger, no date (likely after October 1890), 105.
[28] Dunant to Sonderegger, 16 January 1891, 108.
[29] Quoted by Dunant in his (non-)answer to Sonderegger, 11 December 1891, 109.

As his second Lindenbühl winter was settling in, however, Dunant had only one idea in mind: escape the Stäheli's guest house with its countryside ambience, clanging church bells, blinding solitude, with its sorry little hillsides out his window, its distance to the neighbouring town and, worse yet, its distance to his friends in Heiden. When he went to Trogen to mail any urgent post, the neighbouring farmers could hear him stumbling along, grumbling in French along the hilly treacherous path. The children laughed and scampered away at the sight of this white-bearded Santa Claus. No, he'd had enough of the dogs barking, their yaps echoing between the valleys, he'd had enough of his difficult nights, the darkness pressing in, suffocating, the silence in which he waited, desperate, for his next breath to come easy. But also, no, thank you, to living with the Sondereggers, to spend the day amid the 'horrible gibberish' of Swiss German and the constant clucking of a brood of children. No, thank you, indeed. It was more than he could bear: he was unable to accept the schoolmaster's offer, despite the mounting pressure to leave the Lindenbühl at the first chance.

In December he finally plucked up his courage to respond to the Sondereggers' now six-month-old invitation. 'It was extremely kind of you; but how could you expect me to answer – just then, right away, in the heat of the moment – without any explanation, without us having spoken of it before?' What follows is a litany of reproaches about the way in which the offer had been made, and of various tiny incidents to justify his hesitations: 'Forgive me for speaking frankly to you, dear Mr Sonderegger, but you must admit none of it was very engaging (even if I was touched by your offer).'[30]

His decision is still not clear by the end of the letter; Dunant finished it promising to answer upon his next visit to Heiden, 'upon the next fine day'. Not an imminent deadline, indeed, as it was mid-December. He would write to him a few more times, always in the same critical, scathing and superior tone. Until February, when an event brought a new twist to an already tumultuous friendship.

---

[30] Dunant in his (non-)answer to Sonderegger, 11 December 1891, 109.

The siege of Rome

In February 1892, Dunant learned that an international conference
of Red Cross Societies would take place the following April in
Rome. Of course, he didn't imagine going himself. But in his
delusional projection onto the young correspondent of the Heiden
branch, he had the idea of sending Wilhelm Sonderegger, as if this
ambassador would bring him closer by proxy into the world he'd
been excluded from. He hardly had a chance to close the newspaper
with the announcement before he was at his table:

Dear Mr Sonderegger,
   Next April 21 in Rome will be the opening of the Fifth
International Conference of the Societies of the Red Cross.
   Wouldn't you like to go to Rome for this? You would represent
the Ladies' Society of Heiden. It seems to me these ladies could
definitely delegate you and pay for your trip. [. . .] I'm sure you
would be granted leave to do this. [. . .] This is a unique occasion;
do not let it pass you by, it would be very unfortunate.[31]

We do not have Sonderegger's reply, but he appears to have gone
along with Dunant, who then sent him a series of letters detailing
a methodical battle plan. Wilhem only needed to publish an
announcement about the Rome conference in Heiden's local
newspaper. And then Dunant would take this article from Trogen
into Heiden to raise a collection with the ladies of the area and get
enough money for the trip. But Wilhelm dilly-dallied. The
announcement didn't appear. Dunant felt his plans were being
thwarted. Time was passing and the conference was approaching,
for goodness' sake! And so day after day, the Lindenbühl hermit
scolded the schoolteacher in an increasingly authoritarian tone and
with increasingly cruel reproaches which betrayed a sickly confusion
between his own priorities – those of a forgotten founder of the Red
Cross – and those of the modest 'correspondent' of the local Heiden
branch. 'One cannot be more of an enemy to one's own interest
than you are in these circumstances!' he wrote to him on 3rd March

---

[31] Dunant to Sonderegger, 4 February 1892, 119.

1892. And then the next day: 'Have you now finally understood my letter? I am doing all of this for you, for you alone.'[32]

By mid-March it was settled, Sonderegger would go to Rome. Now Dunant's tone began to soften and his flattery recommenced, all the more necessary because he feared his pawn was now subject to the influence of his entourage, apparently attempting to put Wilhelm on his guard against the tyrannical old man:

> You are a distinguished, educated man with elevated ideas, you are not like all of your selfish, obtuse democrats, stuck in their bourgeois foolishness, always imagining that when an aristocrat like me makes an idea or advice or something it is nothing but a personal consideration! – I think more highly of you – And you have well proven for many things that you are not like these people. You have too much mind; it is to broaden this mind that I would like for you to go to Rome.[33]

And the next day again:

> It isn't only because I think this would interest you to go to Rome that I am doing what I do to help you go: but also – ungrateful as you are – because I believe that it would be useful for you, later, for your future and the well-being of your family.[34]

Did Dunant believe what he said? Could he imagine for a second that Wilhelm Sonderegger, devoted corresponding secretary of the Ladies' Society of Heiden, would even slightly benefit from this prestigious reunion of delegates from the national Red Cross Societies? But he didn't let up; at the end of March he attempted to make his friend feel guilty for not following his instructions to the letter, even though writing his complaints gave Dunant 'a swollen thumb for eight days, and the fatigue of running to the post office'.[35]

But his machinations were all in vain: the ladies of Heiden, who did not at all see the usefulness of sending their children's schoolmaster

---

[32] Dunant to Sonderegger, 3 and 4 March 1892, 121–2.

[33] Dunant to Sonderegger, 15 March 1892, 122–3.

[34] Ibid., 124.

[35] Dunant to Sonderegger, 25 March 1892, 128.

for a stroll around Rome, cut the collection short. Without enough funds, but also perhaps without a strong enough conviction of the personal advantage he would take from the adventure, Wilhem would not attend.

At the Lindenbühl, nothing was left of winter but some piles of dirty snow along the edges of the road leading to Trogen. Dunant watched anxiously for any signs of spring in the leaves of the trees: the guest house's clients would soon return, and the managers would then be asking him politely, like they had the year before, to move out of the more luxurious room he was graciously given in winter and into his tiny room upstairs. But he hated the attic on the third floor, it was too high and had no air and no view, and so this year he decided to make a more radical move. In mid-April, without having actually refused the Sondereggers' offer, he wrote to Dr Altherr asking if he might be willing to take him for the summer at the Heiden hospital.

On 30th April, Dr Altherr picked Henry up at the Lindenbühl to drive him into Heiden. It is not impossible that the doctor, who knew his patient well, had already guessed he wouldn't be bringing him back in September; but Dunant simply sent word to his friends that he was moving to Heiden for the summer, that he found it 'more economical and better than at the Lindenbühl' and that he was 'surrounded by care and respect'.[36]

Painful paradox

Dunant's calm would not last. Where could he ever be happy? Just three months into his hospital stay he was already wondering if he'd made the right decision. First of all, the Lindenbühl was quieter. 'My lodgings are nicer, materially speaking,' he wrote to his brother Pierre, 'but the hospital is hell because of all the neighbouring cabarets and the road they're building beneath my windows, not to mention the cries and the yells.' Of course, Dunant wasn't unaware of his own particular sensitivity: 'None of this is very important,' he added, 'but they become more serious because of my constant state of irritation.' He was even regretting – over a year later! – that he

---

[36] Dunant to Müller, 12 May 1892, BGE, Ms. fr. 5201, f. 145.

hadn't accepted Sonderegger's offer, with its two rooms, 'his lovely little wife and four pretty children'[37] (there were actually five, Dunant must have missed the arrival of the last one). The three eldest had even come to see him that morning at the hospital. How could he resist little Emma, with her beautiful eyes and her intelligent grace? Dunant was exceedingly moved. That same day, he wrote a much more affectionate letter to Wilhelm that broke with the pouting silence he'd been radiating since his protégé's Roman defection.

But other places were now competing with Heiden. A very friendly letter came to him from the Red Cross in Winterthur. Its secretary, Johann Pfister, who'd come across an article by Rudolf Müller in the Ulm *Tagblatt,* had called for a meeting of his own section to think of ways to support this great man who had been so unjustly forgotten. With incredible tact, the first thing these total strangers did was send him a gift for the anniversary of the Battle of Solferino in June, along with the very words he needed to read: 'Wherever the essence and the goal of the Red Cross are claimed, your name carries the highest glory.' The gift was equally delightful – Bertha von Suttner's novel *Die Waffen nieder!* that had made so many waves since its publication three years earlier. Wasn't this touching? There was nothing like a well-phrased compliment to have him thinking the grass might be greener elsewhere: 'Perhaps this would be a place for me,' he wrote in the same letter to his brother about Winterthur. And not stopping there, he also signalled to Pierre another possible escape route: 'Reims continues to show me great interest. If it had happened earlier, I certainly would have moved to Reims.' Evidently, on 22nd July 1892, Heiden was getting on his nerves.

But there was something else bothering him. An ordeal he'd previously experienced in Paris. Then in London. Then in Brussels. An ordeal that neither his intelligence, nor his ethics or conscience had ever managed to successfully resolve. In the summer of 1892, Dunant sensed the sharp teeth of his creditors again, yapping at the heels of a new financial promise.

A first alarm bell had not worried him too much; just unnerved him. Sonderegger, the fool, wanting perhaps to be forgiven for not going to the Rome Congress, had thought it wise to send a petition

---

[37] Dunant to his brother Pierre, 22 July 1892, BGE, Ms. fr. 2115 C, f. 117.

to the delegates, in the name of the Ladies' Society of Heiden and without Dunant's knowledge, asking for some financial assistance in his favour. 'This was terribly hurtful, and made me so upset. Naturally, they received no reply. But what a stupid thing!' Dunant wrote to his brother in July.

Henry felt more than betrayed: humiliated. And with more sincerity than he'd ever before displayed, his letter to Pierre explains the torments, dilemmas and the real suffering he experienced, ironically, at the very thought of a financial compensation for the work that was nevertheless so deserving of this in his eyes:

> It would be different if it were a question of simply accepting it; but asking for it, when it's for me alone, disgusts me beyond all expression [. . .] I had so much hope to one day be able to repay my creditors, I would have accomplished the impossible. But now when a bit of bread and a bit of milk are enough for me, it's very heavy.[38]

The deep depression he fell into during his stay in London in 1872 had been the first symptom of this contradictory pain which would poison the second half of his life. At the very moment he seemed to be becoming famous again, he could hear his creditors looming. And so it started again, in Heiden, where he'd considered himself safe from his demons: signs of interest were showing in his favour in Berne and in Winterthur, and not to mention Reims. Of course, he had something to do with this rekindling of public opinion! Hadn't he been the one to encourage Sonderegger to establish a Red Cross in Heiden? And the Swiss Red Cross – hadn't he acted first, asking Sonderegger to write to Dr Staehelin, the president? And wasn't it upon his written request that Rudolf sent a query to the Ulm newspaper, eventually leading to interest from Winterthur and its charming secretary, Johann Pfister? Of course, of course. But since it was too late, much too late to make his fortune, and since only a fortune could erase his debts, any material assistance received at this point must in no way appear like a personal enrichment that might then be taken from him! If public opinion were returning in his favour, and if it brought some financial resources, how could it

[38] Ibid.

not bring his enemies, creditors and persecutors rushing after him again?

'They might send me 300 francs,' he said again to Pierre regarding a request he was encouraged to make with the Swiss Red Cross: 'If I die next year,' he mused with a painful lucidity, 'this request I am being asked to make will become history.'[39] And a little later to Rudolf, 'In any event, I do not want to ask or receive, and I will return the money as an insult if it is sent to me.'[40]

His line would be clear from this point on. Yes to money as long as he didn't have to ask for it – accept, yes, beg, never, this was his mantra. And money, yes, as long as it wasn't for him but for his writing, his publications, his version of the facts – meaning for his name, his notoriety, his role in the Work. His only goal now: the publication meant to restore his name as the sole founder of the Red Cross, as he confided to his friend Müller:

> It is through this publication that I am most consoled, nothing else matters. I have been too hurt. And I have but a single desire, that I may be left to die in peace, since I was kept from earning my living and being able to repay my debts.[41]

The rupture

Starting in 1892, the tome meant to re-establish Dunant's paternity of the Red Cross became his only lasting obsession, his only reason for living. But with each passing day, he grew increasingly convinced that Sonderegger wasn't up to the task. In September, he asked Rudolf to revise the translation of *A Memory of Solferino* that Wilhelm claimed he'd already finished in part. Müller accepted immediately, delighting Henry who wrote immediately to his brother that the news had 'relieved him of one large worry because Mr Sonderegger was only a schoolteacher while Professor Müller

---

[39] Ibid.
[40] Dunant to Müller, 22-23 August 1892 (wrongly dated 1893 at) BGE, Ms. fr. 5201, f. 200.
[41] Ibid.

was a distinguished philologist'.[42] At the same time, the Berlin Red Cross was sending 2,000 marks to finance the publication, adding to the generous and decidedly friendly offer from the Winterthur branch to oversee the entire project. Dunant's morale momentarily shot up like an arrow.

Obsessed with re-establishing his own version of the facts, Dunant was now set on writing a solid historical introduction to *A Memory* designed to explain the origin of the Work himself; Muller would not only translate it but *sign* it as well. Dunant summarized the arrangement on 11th September in a way to remind him, without stating it explicitly, that he was the ghostwriter but Müller the official author: 'Everything now relies on you, dear friend; I must finish my book and send it to you.' The same game of smoke and mirrors he had played with Sonderegger was now set up with Müller, but in a fundamentally different manner. With 'simple schoolteacher' Sonderegger, Dunant had been compensating for his poor health and bad German by using a docile, energetic, German-speaking assistant. With 'distinguished philologist' Müller, Dunant was expecting the critical and supportive eye of a friend more equipped than he to transform his disordered memories into a proper, rigorous and well-structured German book. After thinking on it, he would happily confer everything to his friend Rudolf – not only the translation of the introduction, but also the translation of the entire *Memory of Solferino* Sonderegger had already been working on. But how to get rid of Sonderegger without humiliating him outright?

As always with Dunant it's difficult to untangle his unconscious motives, the reasons he believes are true, the justifications he offers and the memories he later retains. Between September and November 1892, he began to move further away from Sonderegger and closer to Müller: he was clearly choosing the Ulm professor over the Heiden schoolteacher, hoping for an ambitious German edition rather than a modest local one, seeking the greater world

---

[42] Dunant to his brother Pierre, 19–21 September 1892, BGE, Ms. fr. 2115 C, f. 114. Dunant had apparently never spoken to his family about Rudolf Müller, who was mentioned for the first time to Pierre in July 1892 as 'a professor in Ulm' who was translating *A Memory*.

and rejecting his little corner of it. In October, his impatience started to increase. He insisted Wilhelm Sonderegger return his written notebooks and the various books he'd leant him for his translation of *A Memory*. The schoolteacher took his sweet time and a package only arrived from the Rue des Bains at the end of November. As always, it was the hospital's head nurse, deaconess Elise Bolliger, who climbed the two flights of stairs to deliver them.

'Mr Sonderegger has insisted I give these to you in person,' Sister Elise said to Dunant as she handed over the package.

'Doesn't he want to see me?'

'No, he said he was in a hurry.'

Poor Sonderegger! Since the foolishness of his clandestine petition to the Rome delegates, he seemed afraid of visiting Dunant in person; for several months at that point they'd been corresponding only by letter.

What a relief and a joy to have his documents back in his possession: his precious handwritten notebooks, Dr Wagner's now hard-to-find German translation, the two other translations of *A Memory* he'd leant to Wilhelm. Opening a thin envelope slipped among these materials, his shock must have been immense – Wilhelm Sonderegger's manuscript was four pages long. Four pages for what was supposed to be a new German translation of *A Memory of Solferino*. And Sonderegger had claimed he'd been working on it for nearly two years!

'Four pages! That's it! And it's not like it was difficult because there are already three other translations!' An hour later Dunant was still thundering about his room, tapping on the books still half-unwrapped. Dr Altherr, whom he had called immediately, was silently looking through the pages while Dunant raged on: 'All it needed was some pruning and transitions, or maybe change a word from time to time, shorten a phrase here and there. And look at this!'

Dr Altherr finished the last page and slipped it behind the first three. He sighed and handed them back.

'Is it at least well-written?' Dunant asked with a stubborn face.

With an apologetic smile, the doctor replied: 'I would not say this is the work of a man of letters.'

Dr Altherr was not a fan of Wilhelm Sonderegger. He had always been wary of him. As soon as the very first glimmers of a connection had formed between his illustrious patient and the young teacher, Altherr had been warning Dunant about him. His next hand was easy. 'I would simply advise you to no longer speak of this translation to Mr Sonderegger.'

Once the doctor was gone, Dunant wrote to Rudolf Müller with a full report, including the doctor's final sentence. 'We thought to ask for your advice,' Dunant wrote carefully, using the plural as if he'd just stepped out of a council of elders. 'We believe it would be better to put the whole thing in your hands.'[43]

Dunant followed Dr Altherr's advice to the letter, but he fired Sonderegger in his own way. We have only the story as related by Susanna Sonderegger.[44] Apparently, after he received the package, Dunant complained that a page was missing from one of the notebooks he'd leant. When the schoolteacher insisted the page was not in his possession, Dunant never once again spoke to him; not *once* in the twelve years they lived 100 metres from one another. At some point, Dunant was obliged to receive Sonderegger, who'd been asked to accompany a professor from Basel on a visit. The old hermit simply greeted him with a slight bow but did not say a word.

According to his wife, Wilhelm Sonderegger would remain very hurt by this rupture, all the more so because he'd never received a single explanation. But did he really need one? Dunant had always been cruel, arrogant and dictatorial in reply to Sonderegger's fawning and submissiveness. The schoolteacher did nothing but personally pay for the general disdain Dunant now held towards the citizens of Heiden, a region he considered much too democratic, 'encrusted and tangled up in obsolete and absurd laws you cannot imagine', a people of 'drunk and vulgar radicals', 'stupid and mean, insolent and brutal, lazy and loud',[45] etc. Dunant's list of charming adjectives for the Heiden population is long and repetitive. Sonderegger was simply a scapegoat for the aristocratic delusions of a bourgeois exiled to an area he increasingly detested each year, no matter that its inhabitants were his fellow countrymen.

[43] Dunant to Müller, 26 November 1892 BGE, Ms. fr. 5201, f.159–62, for the whole story.
[44] Amann, *Wilhelm Sonderegger*, 28–32.
[45] Dunant to Müller, 26 November 1892, BGE, Ms. fr. 5201, f. 162.

Starting from November 1892, Rudolf Müller became the only confidant, translator, historian and panegyrist for the founder of the Red Cross. Was he aware when he accepted Henry's mission that he was embarking on a five-year adventure? He may not have known this for sure, but he must have suspected it. Because he knew Henry Dunant better than anyone else.

13

Stepping Out into the World (1893–6)

Nostalgia for activism

Once done with *The Bloody Future* – a text he would never have printed – Dunant was now focusing the bulk of his time on his *Histoire des origines de la Croix-Rouge* (History of the Origins of the Red Cross);[1] what had begun as a mere introduction to the German edition of *A Memory of Solferino* had now evolved into a wide-ranging text intended as a follow-up publication to the translation, and signed by Professor Müller. Each month saw a package of papers and documents travelling between Heiden and Ulm. In May 1893, the new translation of *A Memory* seemed almost ready; Dunant only needed to finish the history, which he was writing in French to be translated by Rudolf Müller. 'They are waiting impatiently for it in Winterthur and in Berlin, but they will wait,' he declared with the aplomb of an author convinced of his due. Both the Berlin Red Cross with its 2,000 marks for the printing and the Winterthur Red Cross with its offer to coordinate the publication would have to bide their time: two years later, Dunant was still rewriting his account, adding new details, going all the way back to the Middle Ages to assert his family's honour – as if this might interest his future readers. Because Dunant was not writing

---

[1] The original French chapters of this *History* are what comprise chs 2 to 10 of the *Mémoires* edited by B. Gagnebin, cf. ch. 1, n. 9.

to entertain or instruct. No, he was writing to recover his work and clear his name.

Writing had never been enough, though, to fill his life. He needed to launch ideas; this was his talent and his passion. This was also his biggest connection to the greater world, which he was not planning to give up simply because he happened to be tucked away in a hospital in Heiden. Wounded soldiers at one time, France's morals at another, then conflict resolution through arbitration, prisoners of war and Christian colonies in Palestine – he had worked on them all. Now that the Heiden branch of the Red Cross was founded, what committee might he create next?

Two or three years before, Dunant had reconnected with his friend Jean-Jacques Bourcart, a manufacturer and committed philanthropist from Alsace whom he'd met in Strasbourg in 1866 while there to create its Red Cross. Bourcart had invited Dunant to his home in Guebwiller at the time, and since then, bearing the utmost respect for Dunant, had tried with great difficulty not to lose sight of him. When he'd learned of Dunant's misfortunes in 1867, he had lobbied Emperor Napoleon III who had made him a remarkable promise: if Dunant's friends managed to come up with half of the amount due his creditors, His Majesty would reimburse the other half. Bourcart spent years trying to find Dunant but letters kept being returned; he'd never been able to avail himself of the sovereign's extraordinary offer because he'd been unable to locate the interested party. Bourcart subsequently bankrupted himself and moved to Zurich with his large family. But he never forgot Dunant, and as soon as he learned the man had retired to Appenzell, he sent a letter right away.

Upon rediscovering the father, Dunant then discovered the daughter – Sara Bourcart, an intelligent 26-year-old with whom he began to correspond in early 1893. We are missing the first letters, which makes it impossible to know how their conversation originally began. But it appears that Dunant initiated the exchange, which was centred on a single question: the role of women in society and in the world.

A decidedly surprising interest in a man for whom women had remained so often on the sidelines throughout his entire life, except for his mother and the unforgettable Léonie Kastner. Like many others, he had certainly been marked by well-known figures such as

Harriet Beecher Stowe[2] or Florence Nightingale; Valérie de Gasparin had usefully relayed his appeal in 1859, and the queens and princesses with whom he crossed paths gave him decisive support. Still, looking at his private life, his engagements and his correspondence, it is clear that aside from a few anecdotal exceptions, women didn't have much influence on him, nor did he have any particular concern for them. So why then, in 1893, did his curiosity alight upon the social role of women?

It would be futile to look in Dunant's writings, before the 1890s, for the slightest inclination towards equality between the sexes, no more than between men, classes or populations. Equality being a republican and democratic virtue par excellence, it didn't figure among the values he championed so fiercely. Dunant came to this quite late, and through a strict moral vision – that of Agénor de Gasparin, whom Dunant cited at length in his *Bloody Future:*

> However uncomfortable, let us look again and not give ourselves a pass, while some of our fellow humans buckle beneath the weight of an impossible situation.
>
> Equality's march forward is not yet finished. Equality which has, along its way, squashed slavery, servitude, feudal hierarchy, the tyrannies of the *Ancien Régime*, will crush industrial pauperism beneath its feet. And once it has done that, equality will keep marching on. What is so admirable in its marching is that it will never stop.[3]

Despite Dunant's unreserved co-opting of Gasparin's text, equality wasn't the founding philosophical principle of his feminism. In June 1859, the women of Castiglione had impressed him with their devotion to the wounded. Well directed, they could have done

---

[2] *Uncle Tom's Cabin* (1852) by Harriet Beecher Stowe made a strong impression on young Henry Dunant, who wrote in his *Mémoires* that he met the author when she came to Geneva in 1853; because of her prodigious voluntary aid on the Crimean battlefields in 1855, Florence Nightingale remained a reference for Dunant, despite her more than sceptical reception of *A Memory of Solferino* (cf. Ch. 4 above).

[3] Agénor de Gasparin cited in '*Cri des déshérités*', part of *L'Avenir sanglant* (The Bloody Future, written or reworked until 1892 in any case), handwritten manuscript no.6b, BGE, Ms. fr. 4564, f. 49.

marvellous things: 'What was needed was not only weak and ignorant women there, but, with them and beside them, kindly and experienced men, capable, firm, already organized.'[4] In the Red Cross Societies, he also appreciated help from the ladies, restricted of course to a group kept separate from the men's committees, either for preparing aid material and making bandages, like in Geneva in 1864, or to carry out propaganda work, like in Heiden in 1890.

When the Universal Alliance was founded in 1872, women were admitted as donor members (at the top of which was the very generous Mrs Kastner, whose exclusion would have been regrettable); however, they were not among the active members, nor did they figure among the plethora of presidents, vice presidents and honorary members of various commissions. Nevertheless, the Alliance did have a group of 'patron ladies', who were charged with a commission 'specially reserved for women' to accomplish the praiseworthy goal of combating out-of-wedlock relationships, 'scourge of contemporary society and one of the causes of physical and moral decadence in the deprived classes'.[5]

Twenty years later, Dunant hadn't changed his opinion, nor had the world changed: women remained the consolers of misfortune, they were the givers of love, the family glue and conservative society's finest pillars.[6] But this mission took on new value in view of the serious lawlessness threatening the world. While so meticulously tracing out the prophets' predictions into his diagrams, Dunant had come to believe that humanity was rushing headlong towards the 'great Tribulation' foretold in the Apocalypse. In the coming anarchy and massive carnage, women would have a major role of resistance: they would counteract the cult of Power half the world ascribed to, since they were naturally endowed with mercy, love and virtue. Such an immense task required preparation: this was the reason behind the *Ligue internationale pour la défense de la famille* (International League for the Defence of the Family) that Dunant wanted to initiate with the help of his younger accomplice Sara Bourcart.

---

[4] Dunant, *A Memory of Solferino*, 121–2.
[5] *'Dames patronesses de l'Alliance'*, *Bulletin de l'Alliance universelle*, 15.
[6] On Dunant's 'feminism', see R. Durand, *'Henry Dunant féministe'*, *Bulletin de la Société Henry Dunant*, 2 (Geneva: SHD, 1977), 10–29.

Feminism by correspondence

What role did Dunant play in the International League project? Certainly, the main one. Sara Bourcart seems to have written a few bits of text – more down to earth than Dunant's eccentric writings – but she served as secretary with commendable patience in consideration of the person she had to work with. 'After having studied your brochure on the League for the Defence of the Family,' she wrote to him in her first known letter, in March 1893, 'I am inclined to accept your proposal as secretary, but only *provisionally*, since I am not completely sure I can fulfil the tasks involved to your full satisfaction.'[7]

This could only encourage Dunant to leap into his role as mentor, and with a young lady this time! Step by step, from letter to letter, Dunant painstakingly instructed his student on what to do and which method to apply, the very method he'd been spending his last twenty years perfecting.

First recommendation: 'When one joins something,' he wrote in April 1893, in response to her unfortunate adverb, 'one should not, you must agree, signal the moment in which one will defect, therefore any word of "provisionally" is not acceptable.'[8]

Yes, Sara, be warned that working with our well-seasoned activist will not be a walk in the park. Second bit of advice: patience is the greatest virtue. 'Do not imagine this project will fall in line like dominoes.' For if there is resistance – and there seemed to be in Zurich as soon as Sara Bourcart attempted to sound out the ladies of her entourage – then, well, do not be discouraged, just wait it out: 'We will let the entire business sleep for seven or eight months.'

It seems, however, that the entire business was born of a misunderstanding. In light of Sara Bourcart's first reports, Dunant imagined a tidal wave was swelling amid Zurich's fairer sex in favour of a philanthropic alliance of women and that it would be child's play to mobilize and then unite them into an organization. But Sara Bourcart had to quickly temper his enthusiasm; her first visit with a willing woman was nothing but an uninterrupted series

---

[7] Sara Bourcart to Dunant, 26 March 1893, Ms. fr. 2115 B, f. 27.
[8] Dunant to Sara Bourcart, 11 April 1893, BGE, Ms. fr. 4613, f. 13–14, for this citation and the three following.

of objections. With the tactical suppleness that made up a part of his genius, Dunant immediately changed tack: 'I made a mistake; I believed you were a large group of young women already fired up and full of zeal,' he admitted to Sara, then described how they would need to begin again with 'three, or four, no need for many more, and then proceed more modestly.'

Third rule: visit instead of write, explain in person instead of publish anonymously, take one's time. If there was written material, it only needed to be given 'one by one, to people you are speaking with, without frightening them'.[9]

Fourth rule: only speak to those who might be interested in the cause. 'If there are no favourably disposed individuals, nothing can be done.'

And finally, alpha and omega of any Dunantian initiative, fundamental law of the Art of the Committee, a principle he'd been repeating to anyone willing to work with him for the last thirty years: 'We need to proceed aristocratically.'[10] 'To proceed aristocratically' meant, for Dunant, that the tip of the iceberg of a burgeoning committee had to *shine* in order to attract influential individuals to the cause, as well as subsidies – the crux of any combat. Dunant also felt that having an aristocratic organization signified independence and rapid decision-making, in stark contrast to what he saw as the paralyzing weight of the democratic process. At the same time, the movement wouldn't require a strong centralization: in this Dunant was the faithful child of Swiss federalism. One aspect of the Red Cross he had consistently stood for was the autonomy of its numerous branches and committees. This had been his vision even in the early days of the YMCA; he recycled it for the Aid Societies, and he would apply the same for his International League. Yes, they still needed to establish a world headquarters in Zurich, since it was all beginning there; yes, they would need a permanent and international committee. But beyond a strict coordinating role for this founding body, the League would essentially operate on a regional scale with committees sponsored by their nearest female sovereign:

---

[9] Dunant to Sara Bourcart, no date (addition to a letter of 11 April 1893), BGE, Ms. fr. 4613, f. 41, for this quote and the following one.

[10] Dunant to Maurice Dunant, 9 January 1895, BGE, Ms. fr. 2115 A, f. 11.

It must be stated clearly: the League has no centralized authority, but an International Congress that will meet every three years for all decision-making. And each country is free – and organizes itself as it likes.[11]

Throughout all of 1893, Sara Bourcart took her correspondence course in the Art of the Committee – from foundational principles to practical details. In September, she announced she would visit her professor master along with a young lady named Pauline Gendre, a friend who shared her philanthropic ambitions. Dunant was ostensibly delighted by their visit, as proven by his disappointment when he learned, three days later, that Miss Bourcart was indisposed and needed to delay the encounter. The meeting finally took place in early October, Dunant welcoming them to what he called, with some exaggeration, his 'modest shed'[12] at the Heiden hospital.

Did these two young women understand how much the Red Cross founder had honoured them by accepting their visit? A man who soon wouldn't bat an eyelash at sending the Swiss president packing? 'Your visit was much too short, even if you were kind enough to give me all your time in Heiden,' [13] he wrote after they'd gone. Then followed a summary of their discussions, in which he seemed to have convinced Sara Bourcart to take on the title of 'President-Secretary of the Initiative Committee in Zurich', while Pauline Gendre would be responsible for founding the committees of Basel, Neuchâtel, The Hague and Utrecht. 'A provisory committee needs only three people,' he emphasized, inoculating them against any future discouragement, before continuing, 'The path will become clear as you march down it, but you must march!'[14]

What energy, what kick, what incredible enthusiasm was still effervescing in this ailing 65-year-old! Yet he was in his element; he knew the rulebook of a president-secretary like the back of his hand, he'd written it himself and he fervently believed this new

---

[11] Dunant to Sara Bourcart, no date (addition to a letter of 11 April 1893), BGE, Ms. fr. 4613, f, 41v.

[12] Dunant to Sara Bourcart, 26 September 1893, BGE, Ms. fr. 4613, f. 16.

[13] Dunant to Sara Bourcart, 4 October 1893, BGE, Ms. fr. 4613, f. 25-7.

[14] Dunant to Sara Bourcart, [5 or 6] October 1893, BGE, Ms. fr. 4613, f. 20-3, and the following as well.

work would earn the patronage of Europe's crowned heads, thanks
to his infallible know-how:

> I intentionally placed the sovereigns at the beginning of the
> Statutes, that I have the honour of sending you; I also intentionally
> included a small word of praise for the monarchies [. . .] I place
> much importance in this.

Nothing would change this man. He knew his world; he used it as
he could: 'I will take care of the other twenty-nine 'founding-
correspondents', he wrote calmly to Sara Bourcart, who was having
trouble finding the first three: 'They will come out at the right time
and place.' Allocating tasks would also be done according to a
proven recipe: 'The vice presidents of the definitive Grand
Committee are active members; the honorary vice presidents are
princesses, duchesses or individuals with considerable weight, but
inactive members.' [15]

Did his insistence on the crème de la crème make Sara Bourcart
uncomfortable? According to Dunant himself, Sara's father had lost
his fortune supporting worker participation in company
management. It's very clear the young woman was not fixated on
the aristocracy. What she wanted was guarantee of a minimum
revenue for women, certainly an excellent idea but completely
utopic in the eyes of Dunant, and, even worse, one that carried a
whiff of socialism: 'If it's for both man and woman, I understand
the idea, but the conservatives and radicals will not understand it
and will always label those who ask for it as "socialists".' [16]

It wasn't, however, these small ideological disagreements that got
the best of Dunant and Sara Bourcart's appealing project. It would
be something more banal and predictable. Despite the expansive
advice provided by their mentor in Heiden, the two young women
grew discouraged by the difficulty of the job. Already back in
October, Pauline Gendre had written from Utrecht to tell Dunant
that her efforts 'had not been crowned with brilliant results'.[17] She
mentioned as well that 'Sara Bourcart had not yet formed her group

---

[15] Dunant to Sara Bourcart, [5 or 6] October 1893, BGE, Ms. fr. 4613, f. 20–3.
[16] Dunant to Sara Bourcart, 4 October 1893, BGE, Ms. fr. 4613, f. 26v.
[17] Pauline Gendre to Dunant, 23 October 1893, BGE, Ms. fr. 2111, f. 52.

in Zurich', a delay which Sara would confirm several weeks later when admitting to Dunant that the founding manifesto had yet to be printed.

The idea was vast, generous, universal: too much, probably. Before the end of the year that saw its birth, the project for the International League of Women for the Defence of the Family fell apart. Dunant did not abandon feminism, or his vision of it, however, because he held it as the most direct and surest road to pacifism. But he would wait two more years before getting back in the saddle.

A bombardment

When the members of the Winterthur Red Cross had learned in the spring of 1892 that their illustrious founder was living a few kilometres away in near poverty, they'd asked for more information from Dr Altherr, who confirmed: 'He wakes every day and works constantly for the Red Cross, whether through his many tasks of correspondence or through new projects.' The chief physician also judged it wise to warn them of Dunant's temperament: 'Sometimes he is a little excited and sensitive, especially if one comes to speak with him of his bitter fate and his disappointments. We cannot get him to leave his room. And so he lives like a hermit at the hospital.'[18] This was enough to melt some hearts at the Winterthur section, who then placed the well-being of the great man on its list of priority work, not only through funding – a collection was rapidly organized – but also through sustained moral support.

Most likely inspired by its secretary Johann Pfister, the various interventions by the Winterthur section were, when viewed *a posteriori*, increasingly appropriate. As mentioned earlier, the first package sent to Heiden had contained *Die Waffen nieder!* by Bertha von Suttner – very well chosen, in light of what followed. Next, they immediately fulfilled Dunant's wish to become an honorary branch member, a tribute no one had given him for more than twenty years. After the initial and fruitful collection for financial support in 1892,

---

[18] Cited in Emanuel Dejung (ed.), *Die zweite Wende im Leben Henry Dunants 1892–1897*, 294th Neujahrsblatt der Stadtbibliothek Winterthur (Winterthur: Ziegler & Co, 1963), 48–9.

the one in 1893 didn't do so well, nor did the following ones. Pfister then turned his attention to another kind of assistance, one that his thoughtful sensitivity rightfully perceived was the most important for Dunant: help with his publications and, through them, his rehabilitation.

When Dunant suggested to Pfister, sometime in 1893, to publish a small 'overview' of Red Cross activity around the world in the next annual report from the Winterthur branch, Pfister kindly welcomed the proposal. Dunant, not a man for making empty promises, set himself to this task in the beginning of 1894. There was no question of him writing the text himself as it would be in German, but he sent any and all documentation he deemed useful to Mr Pfister, including a five-page letter every two days, if not every day, accompanied by a mountain of documents from all sources, all eras, all formats, in all languages, and he did this with the perfect awareness, as he did with Sonderegger, that he was pushing his luck. As disagreeable and dictatorial as he'd been with Sonderegger, he was as charming and apologetic in equal measure with Johann Pfister, even joking: 'It is not in vain one is secretary of the Red Cross; there are moments one must expect to be bombarded. This is your case, and I beg your pardon, because for now I'm the enemy and bombarding you with an onslaught of letters.' And then six weeks later, on 31st March: 'I beg your pardon for assassinating you with letters, in the midst of your numerous occupations.'[19]

This harassment would bear fruit. Finally, in May 1894, the annual report of the Winterthur Red Cross appeared, much thicker than usual and for good reason: of the forty-five pages comprising the report, twenty-eight were dedicated to Dunant's contribution, and which would later be published separately as well. 'Your "bombardments" were not murderous,' Pfister wrote to him when their shared work was published, 'but it's true they were sometimes so numerous that more than once I thought I might lose heart.'[20]

His foot now firmly in the door, Dunant would continue to write for the Red Cross. The chief editor of the national newsletter, Dr

---

[19] Dunant to Pfister, 5 February and 31 March 1894, *Die zweite Wende im Leben Henry Dunants*, 91, 105. The following letters between Dunant and Johannes Pfister come from this book.
[20] Pfister to Dunant, 16 May 1894, *Die zweite Wende*, 109.

Mürset, gave him page space as often as Dunant wished.[21] Needing no encouragement, the promoter of the Work regularly took advantage of this newspaper so obligingly placed at his disposal.

While some local branches of the Red Cross were slowly becoming aware of the existence of its founder, this resurrection went mostly unnoticed elsewhere. Not only was the Work itself little known outside of Geneva, but also no one suspected that the man who'd set it in motion thirty years earlier was still alive. Zurich would launch the first rescue flare, and the fallout would be stupendous.

Making waves

On 17th May 1895, a double-page article dedicated to 'Henry Dunant and the Geneva Conference of the Red Cross' appeared in the Zurich newspaper *Zürcherische Freitagszeitung*. Its instigator was Pauline Gendre; despite giving up on the League for the Defence of the Family project two years earlier, she was still, and would remain, an unconditional admirer of Dunant. While visiting eastern Switzerland, she became acquainted with the editor of the aforementioned newspaper, Samuel Zurlinden, whom she managed to convince that Dunant's rediscovery was a 'scoop'. Zurlinden immediately went looking for some information from a few other members of Dunant's entourage: Jean-Jacques Bourcart now living in Zurich, and his banker Hermann Scholder-Develay who had recently become friends with Dunant. Both men heartily encouraged the journalist to make a visit to the flamboyant founder of the Red Cross.

Curiously, Dunant didn't mention Zurlinden's visit to anyone at the time. It was not until August 1895, when defending himself against the idea that he'd sponsored the article, that he admitted he had not been able to refuse 'helpful individuals' who came to see him looking 'to become acquainted with authentic documents', including 'for example, the editor of the *Freitagszeitung* and others'.[22]

---

[21] Correspondence from Dr Mürset to Dunant, 1895–1896, BGE, Ms. fr. 2115/A and B.

[22] To Major Schenker, secretary of the Swiss Red Cross, 18 August 1895, BGE, Ms. fr. 2111, f. 88.

None of these three protagonists could have imagined the unlikely chain of events which would occur after the article appeared. By June, Jean-Jacques Bourcart wrote to Dunant: 'neither Mr Scholder, nor Mr Zurlinden, nor [him]self, are considering reprinting the *Freitagszeitung* article'. They were right, it was no longer necessary: the flood doors were open, the deluge was now unstoppable.

Even Dunant could not have predicted the height of the tidal wave. As he'd always done – for the YMCA, for Algeria, for the Red Cross, for the Universal Alliance – now that his project was a Red Cross comeback, he diligently sent the *Freitagszeitung* article to the necessary people. The president of the Swiss Red Cross, Dr Staehelin, thanked him immediately and added his own praise to those from the journal:

> While all those who work with the Red Cross know your name, it is not everyone who knows what it took in work, in passion and energy, to arrive where you have. The article and its contents do you justice.[23]

Indeed, the *Freitagszeitung* helped Dunant make a gigantic step forward, propelling his name beyond the milieu of the Red Cross. Several regional dailies reprinted the Zurich weekly's article word for word, some summarized it, others expanded on it, including a newspaper from St Gallen which took the affair even further. On 26th July, *Die Ostschweiz* published an article, or rather an unsigned call to arms, pompously titled, 'A Duty of Honour for all Peoples and Governments'. It began with a long summary of the genesis and role of *A Memory of Solferino*, included a reminder of the Geneva Convention and the honours which momentarily were bestowed on its principal artisan, and then a lofty appeal:

> Shouldn't we blush with shame and confusion, if History will one day say of our era that it let languish, let vanish into the amnesia of a great silence, the great man who gave it one of the most beneficial and greatest institutions of international law, the man who gave our century, with its red cross on a white

[23] Dr Staehelin to Dunant, 19 May 1895, BGE, Ms. fr. 2111, f. 79.

background, a new symbol of universal peace? No, we cannot wish this! We do not have the right to wish this.

Inspired by the press, the article also appealed back to the press in its final word:

> That the press of all countries and all parties proclaim a resounding appeal, an appeal that is for all hearts of all governments and all peoples a pressing invitation. That the red cross on a white background come to brighten the twilight of the life of the one who made it an immortal gift to our century.[24]

Who wrote the article? It doesn't matter. Dunant immediately sent a note to the editor of the newspaper, who replied by return post with a touching letter, asking permission to come and see him. His name was Georg Baumberger. He was 40 years old. He was the head of a conservative Catholic newspaper yet still held a few progressive ideas. He had already understood when he mailed his reply on 2nd August 1895 that the rediscovery of the founder of the Red Cross deserved more than a few small articles in a few regional Swiss-German newspapers in the middle of summer. No, a man like Henry Dunant deserved something else. Something bigger. Something worldwide.

On 7th August 1895, the editor-in-chief of the *Ostschweiz* showed up at the district hospital of Heiden in Appenzell. Dunant had been watching for his arrival, but Baumberger couldn't know this. The shutters on the second floor were always two thirds closed, and Dunant hid like a child whenever he thought someone from the road might be able to see him watching. All of Heiden knew he was there and would happily look up when passing by the building; and so he rarely dared peek out from his window. But what would a journalist from St Gallen know about this? Dunant watched him arrive at the top of the Werdstrasse with his small spectacles, his curly hair and a kind of schoolchild's backpack bursting with

---

[24] *'Eine Ehrenpflicht der Völker und Regierungen'*, *Die Ostschweiz*, 26 July 1895. This article is reprinted *in extenso* in Roger Durand, Arthur Bärtsch and Grégoire Müller (eds), *Georg Baumberger, Die Ostschweiz, Henry Dunant'* (St Gallen and Geneva: SHD, Geneva and St-Gallen Red Cross, 1993), 30–4; all sources related to Georg Baumberger's campaign are taken from this publication.

papers. He came alone. Dunant was certainly relieved. As he waited
for the Sister Superior's familiar knocks at his door, was he excited?
How much was he looking forward to this visit?

Baumberger made him repeat the information several times:
since moving to Heiden in 1892, Baumberger was only the third
visitor to whom Dunant had shown the original copies kept in the
enormous trunk settled at the base of his bed. Who were the first
two? Not counting Sonderegger, it was likely Müller and Zurlinden.
Pfister had been bombarded through the mail; he'd never met
Dunant and would never meet him. After so many years of feeling
so constantly subject to his enemies' dark dealings, our old hermit
had become quite wary. And so Baumberger had the exceptional
privilege of his trust. When he wanted to interrupt the interview, for
fear he was tiring him, Dunant was offended: 'But no! I only receive
very few visitors, and I only want to receive very few – and definitely
not any prying eyes.'[25]

They spoke for six hours. Baumberger allowed him to speak, a
rare virtue among journalists, and he listened to him. He admired
the distinction of his French and his manners; the depth of his views
when speaking of his work and its developments; the iron will on
Dunant's face when he recalled his travels in 1863 to garner support
from the European nations. Dunant knew to provide picturesque
anecdotes as well as explain his great principles and great actions.
He embellished upon his moods a little: 'In my entire life,' he assured
him, with respect to the Commune, 'I have never been as depressed
as I was during that period: I was a witness to horrible things.'[26]
This may have been true the day he said it to Baumberger, but this
wasn't exactly how he relayed things to his sister at the time. But
what did these variations matter to posterity?

The evening had fallen when Dunant accompanied Baumberger
to the door of his room. Earlier, when leading the journalist to the
second floor, Sister Elise had mentioned how little Dunant ventured
into even the hallway. Opening his door again now, the old man's
fearful attitude confirmed the nurse's words; he checked there was

---

[25] Georg Baumberger, *'Besuch bei Henry Dunant'* (My visit to Henry Dunant), *Die Ostschweiz*, 10 September 1895, in *Georg Baumberger, Die Ostschweiz*, 37.
[26] Georg Baumberger, *'Dunant bei der Commune'* (Dunant during the Commune), *Die Ostschweiz*, 20 September 1895, in *Georg Baumberger, Die Ostschweiz*, 69.

no one on the landing before letting his visitor step forward, as if Baumberger was at risk of being devoured by some wild animal hiding in the stairwell. Shaking hands with his visitor, Dunant summarized the documents he needed to send him the next day. Despite the visible fatigue on his face, Baumberger had no doubt he would do it, would even spend the night putting them together. A current of understanding had passed between the two men, the article was done – he just needed to write it.

Baumberger left the district hospital of Heiden as he had arrived – observed. Before turning right towards the train station, he turned around and waved. Dunant could not stop himself from responding from behind his half-closed shutters. Why deny it? That day a miracle had occurred. For six entire hours, Dunant had not heard a peep from the 'peasants' in the streets.

Beyond the seas

From the 8th to the 14th of August Dunant would give a thick envelope to Sister Elise every day to be taken to the post office beside the train station. This was not exactly next door, so Dunant always had to insist a little, especially because the head nurse had other things to do. But she was the only one the prodigious letter writer trusted, and so she agreed. There could be no delay; Georg Baumberger was leaving for vacation on 17th August and he intended to turn in his series of articles before he left. He had to receive everything he needed in time.

Over these few days, Dunant wrote and wrote and wrote, until he was exhausted. Baumberger had asked him, he explained to Müller on 13th August, 'to summarize the Work'.[27] In truth, Dunant didn't need much encouragement; he was more worried Baumberger would be disheartened by the mass of documents arriving for him each day. It would be his pleasure to personally lead him through the labyrinth, offering his own version of the facts, just as he'd done until now, word for word, with Rudolf Müller.

---

[27] Dunant to Müller, 13 August 1895, BGE, Ms. fr. 5201, f. 260.

In parallel to the series of ten articles he was going to publish in his own newspaper, Baumberger had been assigned by a large German magazine, *Über Land und Meer* (Beyond the Lands and Seas), to write an article on Dunant, in reply to the call which had appeared in July in *Die Ostschweiz*. The magazine would also send a photographer to Heiden a few days later. His name was Otto Rietmann, and he was from St Gallen. He had Dunant sit down in front of a black sheet he'd spread over the room to hide the furniture, trunks and other objects which might lessen the solemnity of the portrait. Then he placed a white box at a certain angle to the window, to intensify the light. This all took a lot of time and seemed very long to Dunant, for something quite small. But OK, what was needed was needed; an illustrated magazine required photos. Dunant did not remove his Austrian dressing gown, nor his velour cap. Fortunately, he was not asked to smile. He was much too tired for that.

On 16th August, although Baumberger's articles had yet to appear, there were already a few ripples of interest. The first letter arrived from his brother Pierre. The envelope contained a second letter Dunant had to read twice, because he simply could not believe his eyes.

Dear Sir,
[As a] follow-up to various articles that have appeared in several journals, particularly in German-speaking Switzerland, articles related to the actual position of Mr Dr Henri Dunant, initiator and creator of the Red Cross association, whom these articles indicate is languishing miserably away in a small village in the Canton of Appenzell, the State council has asked me to request from you any information you might have on the position of this citizen.
Chancellor of the Republic and Canton of Geneva.[28]

Letter in hand, Dunant dropped into his armchair. Geneva! After thirty years of exile, now his city was worried about the fate of its prodigal child!

---

[28] Chancellor of Geneva to Pierre Dunant, 16 August 1895, BGE, Ms. fr. 2111, f. 84.

A second surprise came two days later. The secretary of the Swiss Red Cross sent him an article that had appeared in an Aargau newspaper, his name printed in big letters. It was a new appeal to the government and to the Federal Chambers in favour of the hermit of Heiden. These calls for support were now coming from so many different places, no one knew where to start. Henry's brother, the doctor Pierre Dunant, decided to ask the Swiss Red Cross to centralize the gifts; clearly Henry's family, still traumatized by the bankruptcy of 1867, wanted to avoid managing them themselves. President Staehelin answered him, not without humour:

> It appears that a real mania has occurred right now, both in Germany and in Switzerland; everyone wants to take care of Mr H. Dunant, and imagines that he is in the deepest and saddest misery [. . .] It goes without saying that we are completely ready to receive and administer the gifts addressed to us with this intention, as we have done for the last three years, by this I mean since the moment it was decided to give subsidies to the founder of the Red Cross as a form of recognition.[29]

At what point did Dunant mastermind this entire operation? When looking at the details, it all seems to have been a simple chain of random events. Some friends in Zurich incited the *Freitagszeitung* to do something, that article then prompted the *Ostschweiz* to make its own call, which then had Baumberger setting off to visit Dunant, a visit which led him to the first page of the *Über Land und Meer*. But if we look at things from a greater distance, Dunant was smart enough to understand his name could only be cleared in Switzerland by carefully avoiding Geneva, and that the only way to regain the favours of the Red Cross would be to approach them via a road his enemies wouldn't be watching out for: via the tiny branch in Heiden, Appenzell. This enabled him to attract the attention and then the sympathy of the president of the Swiss Central Committee, going over the heads of the Genevans and the International Committee of the Red Cross, sidestepping everyone who'd been barring his way for a quarter of a century. While this may not have been premeditated in any way, Dunant played the best hand possible

---

[29] Dr Staehelin to Dunant, 20 August 1895, BGE, Ms. fr. 2111, f. 87.

of his exile. Yet again, his extraordinary sense of opportunity had
worked its magic where least expected.

The benefits of fresh air

Amid all this hubbub about the founder of the Red Cross, the
announcement of a forthcoming new history of the movement's
origins took on a new meaning. At first, the arrangements remained
as they were: it was still agreed with Mr Pfister that the Winterthur
section would coordinate the publication that Müller and Dunant
were preparing. But as soon as the Dunant 'situation' had moved
beyond the small charity milieu to interest the international press,
the Swiss Red Cross wanted to be involved. In June, the secretary of
the Central Committee, Major Schenker, showed up in Heiden after
reading about Dunant in the *Freitagszeitung* – none of it was new
information to him, but it had suddenly become freshly urgent by
reappearing so broadly in the press.

Adamant, he declared that 'the Swiss Red Cross must patron and
publish this new edition!'

'But the Winterthur section is already committed,' replied
Dunant, 'and it seems a little delicate to me . . .'

'I will take care of it!' interrupted Dr Schenker, empowered by
his Central Committee status.[30]

Let them arrange it between themselves after all, Dunant would
have thought once Major Schenker was gone. Indeed, he was less
worried at that point about his publisher than about his translator,
Rudolf, who had been struggling with a cough since January. The
letter he'd received that morning had only upset him further; Henry
still couldn't bear to know Rudolf was unwell. Out poured Dunant's
maternal instinct, only quieting once he'd inundated his protégé, a
nearly 40-year-old man, with grandmotherly cures and sundry
advice.

A little background: the previous year, Rudolf's house in Ulm
had undergone repairs that had very much unsettled him. Then in
January, after being named professor in Stuttgart, he and his entire

---

[30] According to a letter to Müller, 29 July/13 August 1895, BGE, Ms. fr. 5201,
f. 259–60.

family, including an infant, had moved into an empty apartment. 'This is likely what has caused your illness,' our self-taught gentleman elucidated to the university professor. 'You were very attentive to everyone else, but you didn't take care of yourself.'[31]

There was no discussion. Rudolf must immediately go to see Professor L***, escape to the mountains during the heatwave and find a substitute for school during the month of July; 'because you must do something right away, and this "something" is not medicine, but fresh air, in good conditions, and rest, taking great care to avoid the cold'. Also the following treatments, 'certainly a little annoying for a man', but nevertheless necessary, such as a cotton plaster on the chest ('in Switzerland the package bears a large red cross,' Dunant boasted), and at the first perspiration a smaller plaster must be exchanged immediately, all which must be done in a warm room, obviously. He also needed a thick woollen vest, which could be exchanged for a light white cloth when the weather was very hot, placed directly on the skin, with the point at the back and crossed over the chest. A camphor pomade, evening and morning, would be very good; camphor cigarettes might also be useful, not to mention boiled milk which was then cooled with Ems water. Etcetera: there are four pages in this same vein. 'I wish I could be in Stuttgart to care for you,' Henry declared to Rudolf at the end of his letter, momentarily forgetting that his 'dear child' had a wife presumably better placed than he to fulfil this noble office.

Nevertheless, Dunant was happy to learn that Müller would spend the entire summer in the mountains, away from the stifling heat of that summer of 1895. On his way home in September, he stopped in to see him. Together, the two men would finalize the publication plan for their history of the Red Cross, the media frenzy around the founder having somewhat rushed the projected schedule. Without explicitly deciding to push the Winterthur branch aside, they had agreed in September to leave all options open, in particular on the German side.

The long article that appeared in the *Ostschweiz* at the end of July had already whet the appetites of the publishers; but the front-page article with its gigantic photo of Dunant in the German

---

[31] Dunant to Müller, 4 June 1895, BGE, Ms. fr. 5201, f. 257–8, for this citation and those that follow.

monthly *Über Land und Meer* on 6th September 1895, followed by a flood of shorter articles by the same author, in ten consecutive issues of the *Ostschweiz* between the 10th and the 20th, unleashed an actual battle between various suitors for the right to republish *A Memory of Solferino*. After twenty years of oblivion, it suddenly needed to be published yesterday! The end of October saw the contenders lining up: the Samaritans of Zurich, who wanted to print 30,000 copies and sell them for fifteen centimes each; the Red Cross of Winterthur, who still believed itself solely responsible for the new edition enhanced by Dunant and Müller; Dr Schenker, from the Central Committee of the Swiss Red Cross, who wanted to knock Winterthur out of the whole business; the Red Cross of Berne, who had just announced they would print 5,000 copies for their grand annual bazaar in November; and finally, a bookshop in Aargau where Dunant had sent his manuscript five years earlier in the timid hope of a French re-edition, and who had done nothing at the time but were now suddenly on the scene, pretending that *A Memory* was already being printed, in French and in German!

'I am now embarrassed by an abundance of offers,' Dunant wrote to Müller in October. The 30,000 copies from Zurich were tempting; but Aargau was promising a French version; and how could he disappoint Winterthur, after all that Johann Pfister had done for him? 'I do not know what to do!'[32] Dunant wailed.

What he did know perfectly well, however, was that after being featured on the front page of one of the largest weekly German papers, a small local rehabilitation wouldn't be enough for him. Impressed by the snowball effect of the May article in the *Freitagzeitung*, he would have liked the ball to continue its course into Europe: now he wanted an article, as big as possible, in one of the big Berlin papers. Did Müller know someone who might be able to arrange that? And also, dear friend, might you know someone at the *Mercure de Souabe*? Or the *Beobachter* in Württemberg? Or at any other newspaper in Stuttgart?

As if he was coming out of a hunger strike, Henry Dunant was suddenly insatiable. He wanted more and more: now that the match had struck, he was ready to fan the flames.

---

[32] Dunant to Müller, 8 October 1895, BGE, Ms. fr. 6201, f. 264.

The price of copies

The renewed interest for *A Memory* evidently delighted Dunant, who had been waiting for this moment for the last twenty years. But it also made him considerably nervous and agitated, for at least two reasons.

The first, a material concern, requires a bit of imagination from today's perspective. Up until the end of the nineteenth century, the price of paper was high enough to trouble a tight budget; secondly, the only way to duplicate manuscripts and printed documents was by carefully copying them out by hand. So we must understand that when Dunant was sending, every week or every month, his personal archives, letters, books often out of print, and, most importantly, pages to be translated for the new history of the Red Cross, these were often his only copies and therefore priceless. Dunant's obsession in preserving all traces, every moment of his life, provides his biographers with the precious gift of his vast correspondence, thanks to the copies he often made of his letters and his own first drafts. But his eczema afflicted his most necessary instrument, his right hand! Writing was so painful and such an effort that he had not forced himself to copy everything he'd sent to Müller in preparation for the forthcoming book. Therefore, the sheer amount of correspondence that this book generated, going back and forth between Heiden and Stuttgart, was a daily stress for Dunant.

At his end, Müller was as sparing with paper as his era dictated. Once he'd finished his translation of *A Memory of Solferino*, he didn't think it necessary to begin a new notebook to open his narrative on the origins of the Red Cross. Unfortunate man! He would never hear the end of this. Since Henry was now being courted by a handful of editors, he was bristling with impatience to get *A Memory* out on its own. But how could he do this when the manuscript of the new translation was sharing space with the one they were still working on, and there was no way to separate them and give the first half to one of their suitors?

For the first time, Dunant was very close to reprimanding Müller. 'I regret you did not take the notebook for each chapter, as I did, and as I thought you would do,' he wrote calmly on 8th October. He returned to the question two weeks later: 'I've come to ask you if you would be good enough to recopy on one side of the paper the beginning of chapter two.' Then a week later, unable to wait any longer:

> My dear friend, I have decided to spend the money for a double of your German translation of my book. This copy is necessary because of the machinations of certain enemies who would be delighted to steal your notebooks and mine.[33]

And there we are. After a remarkably long hiatus, Dunant's enemies sneaked up on him again that summer of 1895. This was the second cause of Dunant's extreme nervousness, directly linked to the first. Inevitably, all the noise around his person and, worse yet, the indiscretions regarding the new history of the Red Cross had brought his enemies to the front door. 'In Geneva, it seems they are terribly afraid to see my memoirs published,'[34] Dunant wrote in November to Müller. But what could they do to stop its publication except intercept the pages in transit between Heiden and Stuttgart? Since each page was an original copy, nothing would be so simple as seizing a package in order to delay, disrupt or even prevent a possibly unsettling publication! On this point, Dunant's worries were not quite as paranoid as they may appear: the theft, loss or delay of a manuscript was a catastrophe which we are unable to fully appreciate from our computerized era.

To complicate things further, Dunant's and Müller's correspondence had to cross a border. Dunant believed that passing through customs involved numerous dangers; removal, confiscation or delays. Of course, as we might expect, the Rorschach customs depot was the worst of all; following various real or made-up misadventures, he had convinced himself of a permanent plot organized especially against him. In response, he'd dreamed up all manner of contortions to avoid the problem, either by sending manuscripts to Zurich or by asking Dr Altherr to fetch packages in person in Rorschach to prevent the customs agents, who, in Dunant's mind, were all in his enemies' pay, from opening them.

---

[33] Dunant to Müller, 9 November 1895, BGE, Ms. fr. 5201, f. 267.
[34] Ibid., f. 268.

We may be able to date the beginning of Dunant's rehabilitation to the autumn of 1895, but we must also acknowledge the return of his demons during the same period. In November, he announced to his brother Pierre that a committee had been founded in Zurich 'to fight against his enemies'.[35] His agitation increased from week to week, tracking the exact curve of his popularity. Did he have any actual concrete evidence of these enemies, as he was claiming, or was he simply adding two and two together? As he summarized to Rudolf:

> Since the editor of the *Freitagzeitung* in Zurich spoke of *Mémoires*, they are looking to cruelly prevent its publication, confusing the *Mémoires* with your work on the origins of the Red Cross. Be on the lookout for any eventuality. Be careful with your manuscripts and do not lend them to anyone.[36]

His enemies were not only motivated by a fear of his revelations, but by their jealousy: Moynier 'and his cabal', or Moynier 'and his clique', as Dunant liked to call his former colleagues, would be profoundly irritated by 'the justice served to the founder', and Moynier was 'even more furious,' Dunant asserted, 'since he'd spent twenty-nine years getting used to thinking of himself as the founder of everything.' And so they had begun to 'molest' Dunant again, but silently this time: 'My enemies dare say nothing; this is why they are increasingly duplicitous.'[37] Silence was now even more suspicious than open slander. How would he ever regain his peace of mind?

Ghost from the past

Since September, Dunant had been thinking very seriously of leaving Heiden. Up until that point he had reserved his comments about his neighbours for his nearest and dearest, but he'd recently begun shouting to anyone who might listen that he could no longer stand the Appenzell people, their vulgarity, their foolishness, their conservatism, their narrow-mindedness, their alcoholism and an

---

[35] Dunant to his brother Pierre, 7 September 1895, BGE, Ms. fr. 2115 A, f. 21.
[36] Dunant to Müller, 14 February 1896, BGE, Ms. fr. 5202, f. 3.
[37] Dunant to Müller, 29 February 1896, BGE, Ms. fr. 5202, f. 6.

entire litany of other regularly updated complaints. He first thought
he would move to Stuttgart, but Rudolf's last visit had discouraged
him: 'He does not live on a very lively street,'[38] he wrote to his
brother, and so he gave up the idea and was now looking towards
Zurich, where he had a small circle of friends. As usual, several
individuals began pounding the pavement for him. Dr Schenker,
secretary of the Swiss Red Cross, and Hermann Scholder-Develay,
the banker and friend of Jean-Jacques Bourcart, went on the hunt
to find him a 'pleasant and peaceful' guest house in Zurich 'or
nearby', in the words of the preferences listed by the interested
party. Bourcart even said he was ready to lodge him at his own
home while he waited to find something more definitive.

On 10th September, Scholder found the perfect thing: 'The house
is very well located, above the Polytechnicum. It is very agreeable
for living. There is sun all day, and some greenery, and a view over
the city and the mountains. You could still choose the rooms which
suit you, which are very large and comfortable.'[39] But suddenly
Dunant hesitated. What first appeared like an emergency exit now
seemed like an unscalable mountain. While recognizing that
Scholder and Schenker had been very thoughtful, he suddenly felt
up against a wall, which stressed him horribly: how could he leave
Heiden for Zurich 'without even knowing the conditions', without
knowing if he would like the location and if he could stay there?
'I don't even have the right clothing,'[40] he added to Müller, as if
this imminent return to a city made him abruptly aware that he
had been living in a dressing gown for five years. In short, he
procrastinated as long as he could, as if something were paralyzing
him. He made it known to Schenker and Bourcart that he could not
decide, leaving the two men with the task of informing Mr Scholder-
Develay themselves of Dunant's about-turn.

What had happened? In that autumn of 1895, all of Dunant's
correspondence began to display a worried agitation, manifested
through an endless rumination upon all injustices and misfortunes
suffered. A letter from his friend Bourcart, dated 3rd November,

---

[38] Dunant to his brother Pierre, 10 September 1895, BGE, Ms. fr. 2115 A, f. 27.
[39] Dunant quotes Scholder's letter to his brother Pierre, 11 September 1895, BGE,
Ms. fr. 2115 A, f. 30.
[40] Dunant to Müller, 10 November 1895, BGE, Ms. fr. 5201, f. 269.

attests that Dunant's obsessions had grandly resurfaced and with them an endless spiral of self-justification.

> You cannot take it badly that anyone would think or say you had financial misfortunes and that thereafter you are reproached of improper things. You never defended yourself against your slanderers [. . .] You have never informed your friends of everything that happened, cards in hand, so that they may stand up against the slander. As a result, they cannot force your enemies to prove their whisperings. That is a fact you must take responsibility for.

Take responsibility for? Bourcart obviously didn't know his friend very well! But, to his credit, he did tell him something no one else had dared say until now. He continued with the same honesty:

> It is clear you would have been better off dying in 1867; but God had probably destined you for some other cross.[41]

Dunant's return to grace had him feeling the icy blade of his enemies at his throat. But it was only in November that the damage to his psychological health began to show. 'I continue to be molested,' he wrote on 9th November. And the next day, in another letter to his confidant Rudolf, he listed 'jealousies between people who were very interested in him',[42] speaking about his friends who were looking for a house in Zurich for him; and then he was off – on all that he'd suffered ten, twenty, thirty years earlier at the hands of Moynier and his wife's family. Several days later, on 1st December, Bourcart sent him a curious letter detailing Napoleon III's promise from 1867 to pay off the second half of his debts if his friends could pay the first half.[43] The letter was evidently a reply to an explicit request from Dunant, who wished to understand the exact circumstances of this episode, as if he were preparing a new file for his defence, or to go on the attack.

His successes amassed and his distresses increased. On 15th December, Dunant told Müller how he'd been praised to the high

---

[41] Bourcart to Dunant, 3 November 1895, BGE, Ms. fr. 2115 N 1, f. 26.
[42] Dunant to Müller, 9 and 10 November 1895, BGE, Ms. fr. 5201, 267 and 269.
[43] Bourcart to Dunant, 1 December 1895, BGE, Ms. fr. 2111, f. 109.

heavens at the Berne Red Cross bazaar, then invited to St Gallen
where he would be fetched 'in a good car' and accompanied there
and back, etc. 'I am not sending you the multitude of newspapers
that are talking about me; that would be useless; but everyone is
calling me the *Begründer de la Genfer C(onvention). & Rote
Kreuz*.[44] The Genevan Calvinists, partisans of Mr M., have not
dared move.'[45]

In January 1896 he was at his peak state of alert:

> 'Mr Moynier's cabal (Moynier who the Bavarian newspaper
> calls the father of the C[onvention]) have not disarmed; they are
> looking to hinder the efforts of my friends, of those who wish me
> well. The small triumph in Berne seems to have exasperated
> them.'[46]

The full story came out in March. Dunant does not specify whether
he had just learned the facts or whether he decided only at that
point to tell Rudolf. But he had learned through Jean-Jacques
Bourcart that in the autumn someone had gone to Zurich 'looking
to damage him in that city as much as he could'. One of this
someone's many shenanigans was to visit Mr Zurlinden, editor-in-
chief of the *Freitagzeitung* whose May 1895 article on Dunant had
unleashed the media tidal wave in his favour. He made sure to give
Zurlinden all the details about Dunant's past financial woes. By
chance, one of Dunant's supporters, Scholder, happened to be in
Zurlinden's office that day. After having carefully listened to the
'mean man's' smears, he then raced to Berne to the main offices of
the Red Cross to defend Dunant's fame. And what did 'this idiot
Scholder' do? He began, Dunant wrote on in a rage, 'by detailing to
them all the slander Mr Perrot had on me. This Perrot is one of

---

[44] 'Founder of the Geneva Convention and the Red Cross.' The distinction between
founder and promoter remains, even today, an ongoing controversy in the history of
the Red Cross, according to the role attributed to Henry Dunant, and, respectively,
to his colleagues of the founding Committee. Evidently Dunant absolutely preferred
the term *founder* for the Red Cross, but he accepted promoter for the Geneva
Convention.
[45] Dunant to Müller, 15 December 1895, Ms. fr. 5201, f. 272–3.
[46] Dunant to Müller, 29 January 1896, Ms. fr. 5202, f. 1.

Moynier's cousins; and when Moynier doesn't act directly, he launches his lieutenant Perrot.'[47]

Yes, indeed, Perrot. Maximilien Perrot. A ghost from the past. Moynier's 'lieutenant' was none other than the first president of the Young Men's Christian Association of Geneva, the same timid and sickly man Dunant had dragged into the Thursday meetings and who had developed such a taste for the cause that he'd ended up being offended by Dunant's prominence.

Life offers such strange recurrences! The rivalry between Dunant and Perrot during his YMCA years had forecast what would happen ten years later with Moynier, after the founding of the Red Cross. And now, Dunant was discovering the very same Perrot alongside Moynier, his sword at the ready, still just as jealous and bitter towards the 'true' founder of the Geneva YMCA.

In telling the story to Rudolf, Dunant was so upset that he, in turn, levelled his worst accusations against this phantom-like enemy who'd stepped out of the shadows after twenty-eight years. But 'now that he [was] unmasked' as a merciless enemy and 'the most perfect Pharisee that could be found', this Perrot could be the hidden cause of the worst trials of Dunant's entire life. Who had turned the English Calvinists against him between 1885 and 1887? Who had peddled an unlikely story of fraud about him at the same time? Who had spread the rumour that Mrs Kastner was a former actress, and a number of other 'undignified things'? Had Perrot and his clique chased him with their villainy all the way from London to Stuttgart? Dunant was now ascribing all his misfortunes to him.

Pandora's box was open. Mixed in, higgledy-piggledy, in letter after letter, amid last-minute corrections for the manuscript of *The Origins of the Red Cross*, Dunant included a catalogue of memories; the Universal Exhibition of 1867, the French who let him die of hunger in Paris, his marriage to Mrs Kastner prevented, the argument with her son Frédéric, his luggage searched at Dr Wagner's in Stuttgart, the failure of the patent sale of the pyrophone in London, spies in customs houses and train stations, all these catastrophes had been brought on through the malice of his long-

---

[47] Dunant to Müller, 23 March 1895, BGE, Ms. fr. 5202, f. 20-4, for this citation and the following one.

term enemies: the Pietist Calvinists, the Evangelical Alliance, the YMCA, all the 'fanatical' Protestants. Perrot's visit to Zurich rekindled the sparks of his hate, which had been simmering beneath the surface all the time.

A late conversion

Between 1885 and 1895, Dunant's enemies had changed sides. Following his stay in Paris and under the influence of Mrs Kastner, even just catching sight of a Jesuit would ruin his day. Another enemy, also through solidarity with Mrs Kastner, were the French patriots still appalled by the humiliation of 1870 and the loss of Alsace-Lorraine. Dunant's connection to so many reigning families and German political leaders, as much as Mrs Kastner's choice to become German in 1871, had made the couple suspicious in the eyes of the Thiers government and other nostalgic French. In the spa towns in Switzerland and Germany he faithfully frequented during the 1880s, happening upon anyone with Parisian or Alsatian-inflected French in the streets was enough to send Dunant to bed for two weeks. For ten years he felt continually spied on, pursued and tormented. But this army of enemies had now stepped aside to give way to an older troop of acquaintances: the Genevan Protestants who hadn't vanished at all, who'd just been waiting in the shadows for the right time to recommence torturing their favourite victim. That time had come.

Dunant did not place his two types of enemies on the same level. The French patriots and their spies were the anonymous foot soldiers of an ideology, harassing any figure they considered against them. But the Protestants were attacking Dunant himself: the initiator of the YMCA, the promoter of the Red Cross and the Geneva Convention, the founder of the French Red Cross, the bankrupt man and debtor who 'knowingly misled his colleagues'.

They were not motivated by a religious or ideological conviction but, more vulgarly, by jealousy: Dunant *must not be allowed* to return to centre stage. He was over, finished, dead. And yet, was he?

Now that he could see them reappearing in the distance, Dunant was convinced they had always been there. His turnabout would be 180 degrees. 'We must call upon the Catholics as much as possible,' Dunant wrote to Müller on 14th February. 'I now have the proof, the ultra-Calvinists, the Pietist *Junglingsvereine:*[48] these are Mr M[oynier]'s cabal.'[49]

The episode with 'lieutenant' Perrot was not the only reason for this radical reversal. Sometime in February 1896, Müller had had to give a conference in Stuttgart in connection with the book he was supposedly writing (and in reality translating) on the origins of the Red Cross. 'When speaking of me,' Dunant recommended, 'do not forget to mention the recent sympathies of the Catholic prelates, Monsignor Freppel, bishop of Angers; – and in Paris; and Abbey Broyé of Reims, with Cardinal Langénieux, as well as the former support of the archbishop of Paris, of the bishop of Orleans Dupanloup, etc.' He must have felt very strongly about this because he returned to the subject at least four times.

The Red Cross had been marked from its inception with a Protestant seal that Dunant now felt only hindered its development. In a letter to his nephew Maurice, he complained of the trouble he'd had at the beginning to 'make the Catholics understand that the work was universal'.[50] Because he was now winding his way back into the Red Cross on a road that avoided Geneva, it also meant taking ad vantage of an opportunity to escape the curse of an overly Protestant connotation. While rewriting the history of the Red Cross that winter of 1895–6, he would attempt to 'unReform' the institution.

Small donations and grand appeals

Beginning from the autumn of 1895, the various schemes of material support for our poor Heiden hermit had been fighting at the door. Dunant himself didn't really seem to be following everything between the gifts of the Red Cross in Berlin, an allowance from the Swiss Red Cross and collections coming from various other branches; a number of funds were given to Dr Altherr, some were deposited in a Heiden bank, others sent directly to Winterthur for the book publication fund. On principle, however, Dunant refused

---

[48] The German YMCAs.

[49] Dunant to Müller, 14 February 1896, BGE, Ms. fr. 5202, f. 4.

[50] Dunant to Maurice Dunant, 15 January 1895, BGE, Ms. fr. 2115 A, f. 14.

to touch any of this money he considered barely good enough to pay for a few pages of his next publication. The idea that he might be considered greedy or, worse yet, that he might siphon funds due his creditors continued to paralyze him. In contrast, he was childishly delighted to receive actual gifts, especially from people he had never met. From Zurich he received as much paper and envelopes as he could use, children sent him chocolates, a pot of honey came in from Lucerne, several ladies brought him jams, a woman from Bienne sent him a box of mandarins, a Bernese lady offered pears from her garden, another family gave him cheeses, and an older gentleman from Leipzig sent him a handmade engraving to decorate his room. The most touching basket was sent to him by some ladies in Berne following the 'small triumph' of the Red Cross bazaar that had been organized in his honour by one of his most faithful and most efficient propagandists, Dr Jordy, president of the Samaritans of Berne. Fulfilling a wish list he'd given to Jordy, the basket contained everything he'd asked for: a complete tea service with a spirit burner, 'very simple, the old fashioned way', as he had specified; a good lamp, some toiletries, as well as a superb red azalea and some delicious Bernese spiced breads decorated in marzipan with the city's arms beside the Red Cross emblem.

His friends weren't sitting around doing nothing either. On 25th February 1896, Rudolf Müller was in Germany giving a conference for the fifteenth anniversary of the war of 1870–1 and the related activities of the Red Cross; his talk included an extensive homage to his friend. The text of his report was published in the local paper that happened to be seen by an old acquaintance of Dunant, Dr Graeter, the former treasurer of the Society of the Temple with whom he had reconnected upon moving to Stuttgart in 1877. Twenty years later had not changed the good chemist: faithful, generous and an unconditional friend to Dunant. He was still in Stuttgart and was still a perfume products merchant. Overjoyed to rediscover his old friend, Graeter wrote immediately to Müller to suggest the launch of a support committee. Rudolf, aware of his friend's wariness, mentioned it first to Henry.

But since the beginning of the year, Dunant had been in a full relapse. The constant tension between the pleasure of being honoured and the fear of his enemies had put his nerves through the wringer. What was more, there was no one in Heiden for him to complain to: Dr Altherr had been in Paris for a month at his only daughter's bedside, who was dying of typhus. Dunant was stuck alone going over and over his misfortunes or lamenting them in letter after letter to his only confidant, his surrogate son, his friend Rudolf. However much Müller might be aware of Dunant's changing psychological state, he had no idea how the man would take Adolf Graeter's proposal.

It must have landed on a good day. 'I welcome Mr Graeter's proposal with deep gratitude,'[51] Dunant responded on 21st March. But the good man must be warned about the villainy of the Genevans, he advised Müller, who would certainly throw their spanners in the works ... And then Dunant was off on four pages of bitter memories, from his jaundice of 1872 to the pyrophone of 1876. Dunant mainly wanted Müller to forewarn Graeter of the most hurtful slander which ultimately compromised his supporters' generosity: 'Today my enemies are saying: "When he is given money, well, he uses it so badly!"' It was important that Mr Graeter understood that all this was nothing but slander and gossip. He returned two days later with another instruction: Graeter must also be advised that no Pietist Protestants should be allowed on the committee; they could sabotage the whole thing.

The constitutive assembly of the Dunant Foundation took place in March 1896: to Dunant's great satisfaction, Müller had made the entire assembly weep upon hearing the list of misfortunes suffered by their hero. 'You have done well,' Dunant enthused; 'this will prevent the defections which may occur if anyone hears the lies from my enemies in Geneva.'[52]

A Dunant Foundation would, at last, enable a step up from cute little donations arriving from all and sundry in favour of something more significant. Similar schemes were appearing in other countries as well: it seems that Germany was ready to offer him a pension, and Russia had been sending him congratulatory telegrams for the past few days as the St Petersburg Red Cross wanted to grant him a monthly stipend, only waiting for final approval from the empress. In Vienna, Bertha von Suttner had made a call for a Dunant subsidy in her monthly newspaper *Die Waffen Nieder!* Finally, finally, the greats of the world were waking up.

---

[51] Dunant to Müller, 21 March 1895, BGE, Ms. fr. 5202, f. 11–14, for this citation and the following one.
[52] Dunant to Müller, 21 April 1896, BGE, Ms. fr. 5202, f. 33.

What about Switzerland in all of this? Switzerland didn't know what to do. Indignant letters were streaming into the federal government, shocked that the great man's own country hadn't raised a finger to help him. The *Union des femmes de France* (Union of French Women), which was part of the French Red Cross, was the first to open fire. In January 1896, it asked the Foreign Affairs Office in Berne for 'specific information' on Mr Dunant, following upon an article indicating the 'deep misery' in which he was 'reduced to spend his final days in hospital'.[53] The government, which had no desire to irritate the International Committee of the Red Cross, jewel of Switzerland in the eyes of the world, was horribly torn. It first asked for advice from the chief medical officer of the army, Colonel Ziegler, who told them exactly what they wanted to hear: 'It is preferable to leave Mr Dunant to live happily in peace. His past contains certain obscure elements that are not up to me to clarify, and so it is better not spoken about.'[54] But was the military the best judge of Dunant? Evidently in disarray, the federal authorities then asked for advice from some Genevan lawyers, who confirmed Colonel Ziegler's opinion. 'Officially, it is preferable to allow Mr Dunant to continue to live peacefully in the retirement he has chosen,' while citing the same rationale: despite what everyone said, and the Union of French Women in particular, his fortune had not been sacrificed to the Work but 'had been lost in business with no humanitarian purpose'. And so, it was best 'not to bring attention to his name, to let silence fall around him'. [55]

The Federal Council would maintain this stance: officially, it would do nothing. But it did make a gesture. At the end of May 1896, the president of the Swiss Confederation travelled to Heiden, not to visit the *founder*, because the word had been struck from federal vocabulary, but to visit the *promoter* of the Red Cross and the Geneva Convention. He went as a show of his personal respect

---

[53] A. Le Fort-Malgaigne (vice president of the *Union des Femmes de France*) to the President of the Swiss Department of Foreign Affairs, 24 January 1896, Swiss Federal Archives, E2001A#1000/45#581*: Nr. 561.

[54] Swiss Military Department (unreadable signature) to the Swiss Department of Foreign Affairs, (no readable date), Swiss Federal Archives, E2001A#1000/45#581*: Nr. 561.

[55] Odier, Renaud & Gautier, lawyers, to the President of the Swiss Confederation, 6 February 1896, Swiss Federal Archives, E2001A#1000/45#581*: Nr. 561.

since there would be no federal recognition. Dunant pretended that he was sleeping. Had he got word of the Federal Council's dithering? Most likely not. But the pressure was becoming too much; he was now wary of everyone, including Rudolf, including Bourcart, not to mention Scholder-Develay whom he, in his own words, 'had sent packing'.[56] His anxiety gave the Moynier–Perrot clan a power a hundred times more than what it could possibly have been in reality; on a bad day he could detect their malice in the skin that formed on his morning glass of warm milk. His letters were now increasingly unhinged, shifting from a few rational statements to long outpourings of acrimony and spite. All his friends understood that Henry Dunant was not well, all except for one.

The Episcopal operation

On 4th April 1896, Dunant wrote a letter he flagged as 'personal' to the journalist Georg Baumberger, to whom he owed a large part of his international rehabilitation. With his most bombastic tone, he articulated a wish he considered 'would be more precious than anything currently under discussion':

> Here is the wish: the smallest sign of benevolence from the Supreme Pontiff, the smallest mark of goodwill from His Holiness, a line from His august and most venerated Hand, or the slightest thing from the Holy Father, would fill me with joy and gratitude.[57]

The Voltarian Léonie Kastner must have been turning in her grave! A sign from the Pope! What next? But she could rest quietly a little longer: Dunant held onto his letter for some time, leaving it on his table to mature.

Baumberger passed through at the end of April. He was returning from Geneva to discuss his latest idea, in which Dunant immediately recognized the Satanism of his enemies: he suggested having a chalet built for him in Heiden! Dunant's reaction was unexpected: in a

---

[56] Dunant to Müller, 23 March 1895, BGE, Ms. fr. 5202, f. 20.
[57] Dunant to Georg Baumberger, 4 April 1896, League of Red Cross Societies (copy of Institut Henry Dunant/ BGE). This letter is also quoted *in extenso* in Cornel Dora, '*Bischof Augustinus Egger von St. Gallen*', *Henri Dunant und die Ostschweiz*, 123–4.

booming laugh, he reminded Mr Baumberger how much he absolutely hated the place.

Once this joke was over, the second subject of conversation focused on the medal that was to be engraved in Nuremburg with the effigy of *Joannes Henricus Dunant, Promotor Conventionis Genevensis, Fundator Opris Crucis Rubrae*. Some convoluted Latin which perfectly set the tone for the third item on the agenda that day – Dunant's papal advances.

'I wasn't sure whether to send it to you, not knowing if . . .'

'Send it to me tomorrow, my dear Dunant,' the editor-in-chief of the region's main Catholic daily replied. 'It would be a pleasure to do what is in my power for you.'[58]

And indeed, the next day, Dunant sent Baumberger his request to the Holy Father. A small note accompanied the letter, lauding their mutual idea to 'show the great and beautiful part' that the Catholic prelates had taken within the Work.

The whole business moved quickly. That very week, Georg Baumberger went to see the bishop of St Gallen, Monsignor Egger, who immediately turned to Cardinal Rampolla, confirming that, although Dunant was a Protestant, he was a 'man of good feelings'. His Eminence kept the ball rolling and then, on 25th May, Dunant received a lovely smiling photograph of Pope Leo XIII, with a handwritten signature and a Latin phrase, also handwritten: *FIAT PAX IN VIRTUTE DEUS.*[59]

Two days later, Dunant wrote to Müller:

> I cannot tell you how pleased I was; because suddenly the entire Catholic world is on my side. This is quite a checkmate for Mr Moynier, who will not get over it, given it receives the right publicity.[60]

The Pope might have been smiling a bit less in his photo if he'd known why it had been requested.

---

[58] Dunant reports the whole conversation to Müller, 15 and 18 May 1896, BGE, Ms. fr. 5202, f. 41–3, 44–9.

[59] There are different existing translations for this Latin sentence. Rothkopf suggests 'By thy power, let there be peace, O God.' (Carol Zeman Rothkopf, *Jean Henri Dunant, Father of the Red Cross*, F. Watts, 1969), 133.

[60] Dunant to Müller, 28 May 1896, BGE, Ms. fr. 5202, f. 52.

14

Rewriting History (1895–6)

A new pen pal

On 25th May 1896, the day Dunant received the Pope's autographed photo, he wrote to Austria to announce the news: 'I am putting everything aside in order to inform you, Madam, of an event that fills me with joy, that is extremely important to me. I wanted you to be the *very first* to know.'[1]

His correspondent's name was Bertha von Suttner. Countess by birth, baroness by marriage, pacifist by vocation, she had become an overnight sensation in 1889 with her anti-war novel *Die Waffen nieder!* whose heroine Martha experiences the horrors of war and outspokenly reveals its absurdity. After reading her book, Dunant sent the author copies of all the recent press discussing the founder of the Red Cross. The baroness replied warmly and immediately. 'You are one of us,' she wrote in October 1895, a discovery that filled her with an even deeper joy, she added, because the various Red Cross Societies had, until then, been 'adversaries of the peace movement, which can be understood because the institution is rife with military men, whose *raison d'être* is war.' Delighted to learn Dunant was alive, and shocked by 'the ingratitude of nations', she declared herself 'overwhelmed by the passionate desire to spare [her] contemporaries the shame of such an oversight'. She decided to pay him 'a blazing tribute' and leave him 'an endowment worthy' of his person and his work.[2]

---

[1] Dunant to Bertha von Suttner, 25 May 1896, UN Library, League of Nations Archives, IPM/FSP/Bvc, Fried/Suttner Papers, f. 182–203 (BGE copies). All letters from Henry Dunant to Bertha von Suttner come from these archives.
[2] Suttner to Dunant, 7 October 1895, BGE, Ms. fr. 2112, f. 112.

Here was someone who knew how to speak Dunant's language! Responding by return mail, he considered it an honour to 'be understood and appreciated by elite souls'. And with no textual transition, he stepped up to the plate – her plate: 'It was most definitely the horrors of war that inspired me to the work for which I was blessed to be the founder.' Wanting to show himself a worthy disciple of the pacifist cause, he listed out the numerous methods he'd already envisioned to facilitate world peace: arbitration between nations; the universal work of the Red Cross and the Samaritans; and an 'International Women's Alliance for Good', which would be patronized by queens and princesses.[3]

This was a bit more than the baroness had been asking for. Claiming she was already 'crushed' with work, she indicated she was not planning to join Dunant in his many projects, no matter how generous they might be.[4] But she offered him column space in her pacifist newspaper. She dubbed him a 'dear great man' and 'my great friend', and she rushed to the Austrian Red Cross with her project of a 'blazing tribute' and an 'endowment worthy'[5] of the man who so undeniably deserved it.

To her astonishment, the Austrian Red Cross received her rather coolly. They were also happy to inform her of the financial disasters suffered by her 'dear great man', the very disasters which had resulted in him losing not only his own assets but, in the words of Vienna's wagging tongues, 'the esteem of his fellow citizens'. They added that they had 'already given' 1,000 francs towards a new edition of his writings, and this was all they could do.[6]

Cut from the same cloth as Dunant, also an activist, also a victim of the very same jealousies, Bertha von Suttner wasn't a bit unnerved by what she herself deemed 'pitiful gossip'.[7] But it is likely she changed tactics at that moment. Since there was nothing to be had from the Red Cross, she would need another way of keeping her word.

Obviously, through pacifism. Dunant had again assured her, in his most recent letter, that this was now his most fervent cause: 'I

---

[3] Dunant to Suttner, 10 October 1895.
[4] Suttner to Dunant, 28 October 1895, BGE, Ms. fr. 2112, f. 115.
[5] Cf. letter of 7 October 1895.
[6] Suttner to Dunant, 7 March 1896, BGE, Ms. fr. 2112, f. 116.
[7] Ibid., f.118.

will say it loud and clear, I am even more a friend of peace and the peace societies than I am of the Red Cross, even if I founded that work with my entire soul!'[8] he wrote to her in February 1896. So why not take him at his word and, instead of honouring the founder of the Red Cross, find a way to compensate the pacifist and . . . perhaps gain something in the process?

On 7th March 1896, Bertha von Suttner relayed the Austrian Red Cross's disastrous reply to Dunant. Assuring him that, from her perspective, there was not 'the shadow of a doubt' regarding his honourability, she nevertheless asked him for 'a few details about the old business', and then ended her letter with a curious offer:

> If by chance, some significant sum would come about as the result of our action (us friends of peace) I make the following plea: I know that any money that would pass through your hands would end up serving some great charity [. . .] And well, since your heir will not be the Red Cross, as she has proven to be an ungrateful daughter and will not – we fervently hope – be called to utilize its riches again – let your heir be the work of peace – a work which you have prepared and which would be the crowning of your noble thinking.[9]

The friend of a friend

Twenty years earlier, the baroness had worked briefly as a secretary and then remained close to Alfred Nobel, the wealthy Swedish engineer and entrepreneur whose attempt to make explosives less dangerous to handle had inadvertently ended up perfecting the art of war. Inventor of dynamite, he was also a patron of the sciences and humanities. Bertha von Suttner had never stopped trying to convert her friend to pacifism. A generous man, he always met her requests for subsidies, even without any great conviction of his own. In a note accompanying the £80.00 he sent her on 31st October 1891, he gave the following argument:

---

[8] Dunant to Suttner, 24 February 1896.
[9] Suttner to Dunant, 7 March 1896, BGE, Ms. fr. 2112, f. 118.

I do not really see what large sums the League or the Congress of Peace might engender [. . .] It isn't the money, I think, but the programme that is lacking. Desire alone does not guarantee peace [. . .] Demanding disarmament is nearly making oneself ridiculous without any benefit to anyone. Asking for the immediate constitution of a court of arbitration is to be confronted with a thousand prejudices.[10]

Despite his doubts, he was nevertheless slowly won over to the cause. In September 1892, staying in Zurich while Bertha and her husband were participating in the International Peace Congress in Berne, he invited them to dinner. He wanted to know everything: 'Inform me, convince me,' he told them while folding his napkin across his lap, 'and then I will do something big for the movement.'[11]

Throughout supper and then over the following days, Bertha worked very hard. She informed him. And she convinced him. She had no way of knowing this would be the last time she'd ever see him: their paths would never again cross, despite numerous attempts to get together. But on 7th January 1893, a New Year card sent from Paris told Bertha von Suttner that her plea had been heard.

Dear friend,

Wishing you a happy New Year and to your generous campaign – which you are leading with so much strength to combat ignorance and foolishness.

I should like my testament to dispose of a part of my fortune by prizes to be distributed every five years (let us say six times in all, for if in thirty years, it has not been possible to reform the present system, there will be a total return to barbarism) to him or her who will have brought about the greatest steps in advancing the pacification of Europe.[12]

---

[10] Alfred Nobel to Bertha von Suttner, 31 October 1891, cited in Bertha von Suttner, *Memoiren* (Stuttgart and Leipzig: Deutsche Verlags-Anstalt, 1909), 239. The original letters from and to Nobel are in French. Parts of them are partially translated into English and available on the Nobel Prize website.

[11] Suttner, *Memoiren*, 270.

[12] Nobel to Suttner, 7 January 1892, Suttner, *Memoiren*, 272.

Alfred Nobel's promise did not quiet his friend's advocacy, she charged ahead, in letter after letter, to 'inform and convince him'. Knowing now that Dunant was still alive, she had the model she needed to overcome her overly realistic friend's hesitations: hadn't he beat the odds? A Swiss man without title or rank, with nothing but the strength of his conviction and his good manners – hadn't he succeeded, against all expectations and prejudices, to get ministers to sign up for a 'utopia'? In January 1896, she took up her pen to force the issue:

> If I had the means to act, I would achieve unhoped-for results. Look at Dunant – he founded the Geneva Convention. He did this by travelling from court to court, he saw every minister and every prince, he rallied them through his articulated belief – and he sacrificed his entire fortune to do this. But one must have a fortune to sacrifice one [. . .] You said to me in Berne (at supper, you remember), that you would be capable of dedicating two hundred thousand francs to the work if you believed it to be truly useful. And the day you [will have?] the faith, I know you would do – and even more – what you said. And so that this faith might overtake you, I continue to keep you up to date.[13]

Which is exactly what she did. The next month, February 1896, she came at him again. But Nobel wouldn't change his mind: he believed that only scientific progress could lead to peace. He was persuaded, for example, that the best way to pacify the world would be to discover the North Pole (the Andrée, Strindberg, Fränkel balloon expedition was imminent), because mothers enlightened by the advance of science would bring forth a greater number of civilized children to the world – decreasing the lust for war. With her charming honesty, Bertha von Suttner replied: 'It seems to me the lines of your progressive journey are rather curvy and complicated. Drawn straight, they would arrive more quickly at the goal.' The baroness then explained to Nobel that rather than waiting a thousand more years for the brains of our species to be finally developed – Bertha was a Darwinist – it would be more economical for him to give her

---

[13] Suttner to Nobel, 12 January 1896, Edelgard Biedermann (ed.), *Chère Baronne et Amie – Cher Monsieur et Ami: Der Briefwechsel zwischen Alfred Nobel und Bertha von Suttner* (Hildesheim: Olms, 2001), 164.

and her friends immediately what they needed for active propaganda work in favour of an international court of arbitration. And what better proof to support her thesis? Again Dunant. 'By virtue of his very straight line, Dunant had the world powers accepting the Geneva Convention in only four to five years.'[14]

In all truth, Nobel was already convinced. The man was single and had a weak heart. The year before, in Paris, he had established the third version of his testament. That document laid out the institution of several very generously endowed prizes. One of them was destined for the promotion of peace, as he had promised his friends in a letter in January 1893.

And yet at the very moment Bertha von Suttner was teasing him in that February of 1896, her friend Nobel had only a few months to live. His will would soon reveal its secrets.

Changing sides

Completely unaware of this friendship, Dunant diligently responded on 9th March 1896 to the two questions in Bertha von Suttner's last letter. The first: how would he make use of a large award? Before responding, he mentioned that he considered it a point of honour never to ask for anything for himself, but in the event that 'something' might be collected in his favour by the pacifists (what he'd deduced from Bertha's question, unaware of Alfred Nobel), he would happily leave them the capital and keep the interest for himself. 'With the interest, I would at least be able to buy my necessary linens and clothing, and more than anything I would be able to publish the work I care so much about.'[15]

And to her second question – regarding his financial misadventures – his response stretched across three consecutive letters. He provided a few details about his bankruptcy, which he explained as 'carelessness', as 'very big debts' and as 'slander'; but more clearly than ever here he connected his misfortunes to the undertakings of the 'fanatical Calvinists' who had been hounding him for thirty

---

[14] Suttner to Nobel, 27 February 1896, Biedermann, *Chère Baronne et Amie*, 171.
[15] Dunant to Suttner, 9 March 1896.

years. He must have believed that his Austro-Hungarian pen pal would have looked more favourably upon Catholics than Protestants.

Which was why he thought it wise to give his perceived persecutions a radically religious character. Those who remember how hard it was for the Red Cross to overcome the wariness of the Catholic countries might be surprised to hear its founder suspect the following motivations for his enemies: 'They never forgave me for the special protection of the bishops and cardinals, granted with such benevolence.'[16]

Hmmm – so the Geneva-born Red Cross had been founded under the paternalistic gaze of the prelates of His Holiness? Continuing in the same vein, Dunant told the baroness that an 1864 dinner at the home of a Catholic minister from Geneva, in the company of four bishops, had earned him the indignation of the entire 'Calvinist aristocracy', who then later insinuated that he'd converted to Catholicism in order to please Empress Eugénie.

The rest we know: in his letter to Suttner in May, he recounted the arrival of the Pope's autographed photo like it was the crowning achievement of his life; he even made a point to send her the few 'also precious' lines from the archbishop of Reims who had always shown 'the most precious interest' for his work.

This sudden devotion to Rome can, in part, be explained by Dunant wanting the Baroness von Suttner's attention and, through her, the rest of Austria's. After listing out his genuflections, he insisted she make them known to the larger public and to the Austrian clergy.

But did Dunant really earn Mrs Suttner's good graces with this sudden change of sides? Was he unaware that the Suttners were tenaciously fighting against anti-Semitism in Austria, which was raging beneath the averted eyes of the Catholic clergy? In March the baroness had sent him a response which should have tempered his pious outreach:

> The enmity which rages against you seems understandable to me because I know it comes from a religious fanaticism. This is the source of all iniquities – I see it daily in the actions of our good anti-Semites.[17]

---

[16] Dunant to Suttner, 9, 19 and 25 March 1896.
[17] Suttner to Dunant, 23 March 1896, BGE, Ms. fr. 2112, f. 120.

This phrase alone should have warned Dunant not to push the clerical note with the baroness, if his only goal was to please her. But in reality, another cause explains Dunant's anti-Calvinist fanaticism during the spring of 1896: a wound which the victim himself doesn't seem to have initially recognized. He continued his litany of misfortunes to Bertha von Suttner, incidentally mentioning:

> It took a quarter of a century to discover where this stubborn hostility was coming from. I knew of the hatred by the International Committee's president, but I didn't know on whom he relied; – the guilty party came himself to Zurich this autumn, where he betrayed and denounced himself through the very violence of his hostility.[18]

Dunant had not yet gotten over and would never get over the shock of Bourcart's revelations concerning Maximilien Perrot. To find himself so hated, after so many years, by a man he hadn't even thought about except as his long-ago valiant companion in the YMCA! The news had simply overwhelmed him. And once he'd got over his shock, the tide of his anger only continued to rise, carrying him away in a flood of rage against all the Christian 'unionists', the evangelicals, the Darbyists, the Pietists, and soon the entire Protestant world. In short, Perrot's visit to Swiss Germany had unleased all of Dunant's demons from their box. From that moment on, any Protestant sect would be suspected of being in cahoots with the enemy, and this would later determine all his campaign strategies – his channels, his supports, his relays. Dunant's surprising rush to bow to the Catholics is a direct result of his 'Perrot' trauma, at least as much as it was a desire to please Bertha von Suttner. After turning his back on the Red Cross Societies in order to circumvent Gustave Moynier's zone of influence, Dunant would now turn his back on the Protestant regions to avoid the landmines of Maximilien Perrot's evangelical network. For a man on a quest for a universal blessing, having to slalom between his enemies would be a tiring affair. But even with his rheumatism, his eczema, his chronic colds and chest congestion, with his incredible stubbornness and his fixed beliefs,

---

[18] Dunant to Suttner, 19 March 1896.

Dunant was a true force of nature. As long as he lived, he loathed his enemies, and his hatred kept him going.

The ladies of peace

The excerpts of *The Bloody Future* Dunant sent to Bertha von Suttner convinced her of the sincerity of his pacifism, and that it preceded their acquaintance by several years. It is in this summer of 1896 that we can see him move from theory into practice. Thinking he would find an immediate supporter in the baroness, he suggested a new incarnation of his International League for the Defence of the Family. This time the idea was to mobilize women beneath the auspices of an International League for Peace. His reasoning was simple: pacifist men had always stopped 'at a certain point of zeal and conviction',[19] he explained to the baroness, out of fear they would be considered unpatriotic or communist. But if a movement began with women, who could then force their beloved men to join the league, something 'impossible to refuse', it would then 'be a first step for each of them, a first step on the path we want all of humanity to take'. And so the League of Women would function as a kind of smokescreen or bait for the International League for Peace, because the people who might be 'stupidly prejudiced' against the second would certainly not be against a harmless women's alliance.

In line with his traditions, the league would be led 'aristocratically': the entire organization should be 'aristocratic, on all accounts'.[20] By emphasizing this point so much with the Baroness von Suttner (née Countess Kinsky von Wchinitz und Tettau), he must have believed he was addressing a sympathetic ear. Yet again, he was profoundly mistaken.

'You are deluded,' she curtly responded in July, perhaps exasperated with the old man's naivety:

> Unfortunately, regarding the peace movement, the aristocrats are still our enemies: it is among the ranks of my cousins that I find the most resistance to any propaganda – generals, courtiers,

---

[19] Dunant to Suttner, 6 July 1896.
[20] Ibid.

chamberlains, officers' wives see only nihilism and anarchy when we begin speaking of changing ancient customs.

Enroll the queens? But if they thought like us, the disenchanted baroness exclaimed, 'there would be no more war!' Furthermore, despite what Dunant seemed to think, his idea was anything but novel; several Ladies' Leagues already existed, and none had produced the marvellous 'snowball' effect of mass mobilization. We know your system, our female firebrand explained to the old man, we've tried it, and we've abandoned it, because it doesn't work. 'What happens is this: A sends the ball to B. B sends it to C, who sends it back to their mutual friend A. And instead of rolling, it turns back on itself.'[21]

She seemed to know what she was talking about. Unlike Dunant, who'd been forced out of the arena nearly twenty years earlier, the woman signing her letters with a simple 'Berthe Suttner' wasn't afraid to get her hands dirty, and she knew when it was time to roll up her sleeves. She was no entitled ambassador; she was an activist in both her grandeur and her humility.

Their various diverging opinions would not stop either of them from a tacit agreement to use one another. Henry needed Bertha for her energy, her confidence, and because she was his entry into the pacifist world – he would thank her affectionately at the year's end for the 'many useful and precious things' that came to him over several months because of her 'benevolent and persevering goodness', and without which he would 'probably be no longer in this world'.[22] Bertha von Suttner needed Henry to provide her pacifist cause with a whiff of 'the establishment', something the Red Cross ideally represented; a goal our passionate anti-war queen openly admits. What she wanted from Dunant, by giving him a byline in *Die Waffen nieder!* newspaper was precisely this: 'something that proves you are one of us and that in the white flag you see the outline of the red cross'.[23]

He would do exactly this. A first text was published in May 1896 with the candid headline, 'Small arsenal against militarism', taken

---

[21] Suttner to Dunant, 18 July 1896, BGE, Ms. fr. 2112, f. 122–3.
[22] Dunant to Suttner, 22 December 1896.
[23] Suttner to Dunant, 18 July 1896, BGE, Ms. fr. 2112, f. 124.

from his *Bloody Future* which was still without a publisher and which he was stubbornly keeping up to date in hopes of a publication opportunity. An open letter 'to the press' signed by Henry Dunant would appear in September, followed by a new excerpt from *The Bloody Future* in the summer of 1897, making the founder of the Red Cross a regular contributor to Bertha von Suttner's pacifist newspaper.

Meanwhile, Dunant was corresponding with a pacifist princess in Paris, Gabrielle Wiszniewska, who presided over the International League of Women for General Disarmament and who had convinced him to become honorary president for Switzerland. Dunant was clearly open to anyone and everyone at this point while dreaming of how he might now construct a vast movement uniting all these disparate groups around him. For the next five years, his preferred field would be pacifism. Hidden behind the closed shutters of his room on the second floor of the Heiden hospital, Henry Dunant, once again, was moving in the right direction.

Baby steps towards pacifism

For a man preoccupied with the fate of the world and an avid newspaper reader, Dunant only rarely, if ever, ventured into geopolitical matters in his correspondence. But his increasingly stimulating relationship with Bertha von Suttner was stirring his desire for more influence on current events. In July 1896, he sent her a small text on the 'Question of the East'. Now, what was this about? Since February of that year, a violent conflict had been raging in Crete between Muslim Turks and Christians. Faced with the threat of a crisis between Europe and the Orient, Dunant wrote an 'address to the nations of the Far East' offering a conspicuous tribute to Middle Eastern traditions and asking forgiveness for the wrongs committed against them by Europeans.

Intending his pacifism to be as pragmatic as possible, Dunant explained to Suttner that he was proposing 'a very simple idea', by which 'no one could claim that the Peace societies offer only utopian schemes': when two nations do not agree, they would defer their quarrel to an international tribunal, thus avoiding war. Their success would depend on a second very simple idea – 'that all Nations and Races help each other'. And finally, even simpler still: 'In this war against war, we will ask the women of all the world to give us their aide and their support.'

The author of this appeal, who was usually obsessively meticulous with his own texts, gave Bertha von Suttner as much freedom as needed to transform his prose as she saw fit: 'Do what will please you.'[24]

'What force and what fire!'[25] Bertha replied quickly. She was so blown away by Dunant's text she arranged for it to be published in *Die Zeit*, before signing it herself, alongside the author, for the congress in Hamburg in August 1897. In terms of public relations and media blitz, Dunant seemed to have finally found a worthy partner. Together, they could do anything.

On the financial side of things, however, collecting money from pacifists wasn't proving particularly lucrative: in July 1896, Henry Dunant could boast of receiving 25 francs from the Austrian Alliance for Peace, 10 francs from the Frankfort Alliance, and 10 francs from the one in Baden, near Vienna. To the baroness (certainly somehow behind these funds), he exclaimed his delight and confessed they'd procured him some superb oranges, and, in the spring, a basket of lovely wild strawberries, blessed antidotes to his 'insurmountable disgust for any food'.[26]

From time to time, he still received 50-odd francs from different Red Cross branches; he would eventually decide not to accept the 1,000 francs the Austrian Red Cross had told Bertha von Suttner they had already given, and why they refused any additional aid to Dunant.[27] Offended by what the baroness had reported to him, Dunant led a little inquiry and discovered that the person who represented Switzerland in Vienna was the same Alfred de Claparède who, twenty years earlier, had blabbed to anyone within earshot that Dunant had purchased *A Memory of Solferino* from a French officer. Now it was sure: Vienna was in the hands of Moynier and his cabal, and the 1,000-franc gift could only be one of their new traps. Dunant rushed to send it back where it came from.

---

[24] Dunant to Suttner, 27 July 1896.
[25] Suttner to Dunant, 31 July 1896, BGE, Ms. fr. 2111, f. 164.
[26] Dunant to Suttner, 27 July 1896.
[27] Cf. above, 'A new pen pal'.

From this point on, his mind was made up. Dunant now laid out new rules for gifts, rules which he distributed to one and all. Regretting the 'great error' of having expected support from the Red Cross Societies whose 'mission was <u>not</u>,' he underlined, 'to come to the rescue of their founder and promoter,'[28] he decreed that all donations should come from the people, who surely owed him as much.

'Mr Graeter, Mr Bourcart and yourself are almost the only ones who have understood that it is the greater public and not the Red Cross of various countries that should be addressed,'[29] he wrote to Müller on 17th July. Indeed, the Dunant Foundation, established that spring by Adolf Graeter and Rudolf Müller, was ostensibly placed under the thumb of the Stuttgart mayor, and not under some local or regional Red Cross. With this new offensive, Dunant was very directly getting involved; he was forming the battle plan himself, step by step.

First, launch a popular call for an 'honorary' donation in favour of the founder of the Red Cross, described as 'abandoned by everyone':[30] 'it is the people, and in particular the German people,' the call read, 'to honour one of its greatest benefactors.'

A good communicator, Dunant did not underestimate the power of the image. A small book written by one of the pillars of the German Red Cross, a certain Major Strantz, had recently come out in Berlin, and it fully restored Dunant to his role as founder. What was Dunant's next plan? A bookstore campaign:

> The provisory committee established in St[uttgart] should have a volume sent from Berlin to every Stuttgart bookshop and ask each one to place Major Strantz's book in the front window open to the first large title page because my portrait is beside it, and this portrait with the large title will attract the eye of every passer-by. The tissue paper over my portrait should be removed.[31]

What attention to detail and also what sense of media hype did this man still have even after being cloistered away for four years! But

---

[28] Dunant to Müller, 8 July 1896, BGE, Ms. fr. 5202, f. 78–9.

[29] Dunant to Müller, 17 July 1896, BGE, Ms. fr. 5202, f. 80–1.

[30] In German: *weltverlassen*. Stuttgart Committee's '*Aufruf. Deutsche Männer und Frauen*' facsimile in Amann, *Henry Dunant und Stuttgart*, 17.

[31] Dunant to Müller, 21 April 1896, BGE, Ms. fr. 5202, f. 35.

more than that, what an insatiable hunger for glory, further fuelled
by a feeling of injustice that cried for vengeance. With a poignant
blindness, given that a hundred journalists had been praising the
founder of the Red Cross for a year, he continued to claim he'd been
robbed of his work: 'Imagine that you, and Mr Graeter, Mr Bourcart,
Dr Altherr,' he wrote to Müller in July, 'you all know, but the public
does not, they don't know that I am who I am.'[32] Which is why
after the first broad public appeal, he wanted a second, and then a
third, each time bolstered with new and increasingly prestigious
names.

Thanks to the campaign orchestrated in large part by Dunant,
the Stuttgart appeal was an unexpected success. Large donations
came in from everywhere. Earmarking this money for something he
coveted more than fine linens and delicious strawberries, Dunant
had one intention and one intention alone: a beautiful edition of
The History of the Origins of the Red Cross, the German translation
of which Rudolf was just finishing.

Now so close to his goal, Dunant was very anxious that he might
die before seeing the publication of a work he considered akin to his
last will and testament. Everything that year made him so very tired.
He was suffering from pain that moved from the left side of his
shoulder over to his chest, and whether this was nerves or
rheumatism, it depressed him to the point of writer's block. He
complained to Müller, 'this is the worst because it's my only
distraction'.[33]

As diminished as he was, Dunant nonetheless continued to bury
his translator beneath pages and pages of new details, indispensable
corrections, additions that were essential to understanding the facts,
dates, names and citations meant to finally finish this interminable
publication. And all of it enhanced, in letter after letter, with a
neurotic summary of all the viciousness, tortures and villainies
suffered and already recounted a hundred times before, followed by
new plans of counter-offensives and grand delusions of vengeance
as Dunant's fear of dying prematurely reached its peak. Publishing
Müller's work was now more urgent than ever.

---

[32] Dunant to Müller, 17 July 1896, BGE, Ms. fr. 5202, f. 81.
[33] Ibid.

The origins of the Red Cross

The Stuttgart appeal brought in nearly 25,000 Goldmark.[34] A reason, if they needed one, to get the book out as quickly as possible. Dunant wanted to see it published before he died, and the money was now there to make this a reality.

Fully aware of how ungrateful this was, Dunant ended up dismissing the Winterthur Red Cross because its secretary, Johann Pfister, wanted to have Rudolf Müller's manuscript reread by Dr Altherr. The reason for this was clear to Dunant: Pfister must have received orders from someone higher up (the chiefs of the Red Cross) to verify that the book contained nothing too derogatory regarding Gustave Moynier. And to elude Dunant's suspicions, Pfister must have asked one of his good friends, Hermann Altherr, to do the work. It goes without saying that the devoted secretary of Winterthur, as thoughtful as he'd been towards Dunant, was sealing his own fate with this simple request. Suddenly, Dunant decided to have *The History of the Origins of the Red Cross* printed in Stuttgart under the sole authority of his friends Müller and Graeter, and no longer, as it had been settled for a long time, in Berlin under supervision of the Winterthur Red Cross. This was the end of a lovely friendship via correspondence: after two years of limitless devotion for 'the softening of a so honourable and noble old age'[35] – the very terms used by Johann Pfister – then two more years of indulgent patience for a difficult author, the dedicated secretary of the Winterthur Red Cross found himself politely let go. Does anyone find this surprising? Johann Pfister took it badly. He stopped writing, except to reluctantly acknowledge receipt one year later, in the name of his branch president, of the volume for which he had worked so hard and that Dunant had finally taken away from him.

Once the decision was made to do everything in Stuttgart, it was now up to Müller and Graeter, naturally, to take care of it all. Dunant's perception of being persecuted by the entire world meant that his remaining friends were saddled with an expectation of

---

[34] Amann, *Henry Dunant und Stuttgart*, 16. Amann estimates this sum corresponds to 2 million Deutsche Mark (approximately £650,000 in 2000).
[35] Pfister to Dunant, 16 September 1895, *Die Zweite wende im Leben Henry Dunants*, 126.

loyalty that bordered on subjugation. They gave it. Müller had already been bending over backwards for the last five years to meet his whims: first writing a short preface to Sonderegger's translation of *A Memory*, then translating the entire publication himself, and then completing not one, not two, but eight full chapters. Then the conference in Stuttgart, devised to give the founder his due attention; then the creation, with Graeter, of the Dunant Foundation; and now, the hunt for a new publisher, even though everything had been arranged in Berlin by the Winterthur Red Cross. Did Müller rebel? Not at all. And to top it all off, his third child had just been born; in homage to Dunant, he named the boy Heinrich.

But Henry was much too sick, too bitter, too deep inside his own obsessions to appreciate the extraordinary devotion this professor gave him. The only truly altruistic preoccupation Henry displayed towards Rudolf was about his health: half his letters included advice on how to make good plasters or, more radically, that he should abandon his classes, wife and children to take in the good mountain air. Other than this, Dunant was hardly interested in Rudolf's life. His congratulations on being appointed to the Royal College of Stuttgart took up all of two sentences in the summer of 1896; his gratitude that autumn for their having named a child in his honour took up half a sentence. All the rest of his letters are dedicated in part to the Machiavellian machinations of his enemies and in part to the additions that must be made to the work meant to ensure the gentle repose of his soul.

If the master wanted a new publisher in Stuttgart, then Müller would look for one. A first refusal came from a large German publisher, a setback Dunant immediately attributed to Genevan subversion. But Müller left him no time to indulge his nerves because he found a replacement solution: the editors Greiner & Pfeiffer, in Stuttgart, accepted the project for the first part of 1897. The only thing to do at that point was finalize the manuscript.

Easier said than done. Dunant had just decided to add an appendix to close the volume, comprised of all the tributes, compliments and 'the most marked authentic testimonies' he'd received over the last thirty years and which confirmed that he was definitely the sole and unique founder of the Red Cross and promoter of the Geneva Convention. Dunant made a point to tell Müller that this additional chapter was 'the one I feel most strongly about'; to such a point that he planned to have a few hundred examples printed separately: '[N]othing would make me happier, precisely because they're working so hard to prevent my resurrection.'[36]

A last-minute whim that would require a colossal effort from Dunant: he had to wade through hundreds of letters and copy them so he could send them to Müller. In addition to this, his constant preoccupation with being up to date meant that he kept wanting to add recently received letters, as long as they were from a slightly well-known name and contained any word liable to 'seal up the mouths of [his] contradictors'.[37] And though he had been panicking for the last few months that he might die before seeing the work finished, now he couldn't care less about slowing the entire operation down for another six months just to ensure his list of compliments was complete. What new thing might be secretly bothering him?

A blue-eyed something, that's what. The previous December had seen the passing of the Swedish Alfred Nobel, and there were already rumours circulating on the millions ready to spring forth from his will. Dunant, who read the *Journal de Genève*, learned on 3rd January 1897 that, as suspected, Mr Nobel's fortune would be used to create an international fund to encourage scientific research. Did this mean Bertha von Suttner had been deluded about the peace prize? On 9th January, the same newspaper upped the tension. The 1895 will from Paris, the only valid will, had been opened and published: alongside four scientific prizes and a literary prize, a sixth prize would be awarded 'to the person who has done the most or best to advance fellowship among nations, the abolition or reduction of standing armies, and the establishment and promotion of peace congresses'.[38]

Dunant became extremely excited. He wrote instantly to Müller to beg him to 'lean in the direction of the Peace Societies'. And, already predicting his friend Rudolf's objections, he added: 'If necessary, let the editor and printer grumble.'[39]

The first half of 1897 would be entirely dedicated to giving *The History of the Origins of the Red Cross* the most pacifist orientation possible. The book hadn't yet been printed: this was no time to let

---

[36] Dunant to Müller, 28 January 1897, BGE, Ms. fr. 5202, f. 102.
[37] Dunant to Müller, [no date, 1897], BGE, Ms. fr. 5202, f. 233.
[38] *Journal de Genève*, 9 January 1897.
[39] Dunant to Müller, [no date, 1897], BGE, Ms. fr. 5202, f. 233.

such an occasion pass! They must absolutely mention his continued efforts in favour of international arbitration, world peace, harmony between nations – even if none of this was directly linked to the history of the Red Cross! On 9th April, although the manuscript should have been long finished, Dunant was sending his apologies to Müller: 'My dear friend, you must see why – because of the Nobel business – I lengthened the appendix and filled it with numerous citations related to arbitration.' Reminding him that Baroness von Suttner had placed him 'in the ranks' and that the 'Peace Societies supported him in Europe and in America', he concluded: 'Therefore, in light of such an important goal, overspending and printer irritation are of no import.' [40] From this point on, his priority was set.

Poor Müller wasn't done with his troubles: following the battle for the text was the battle for the design. Dunant had always been obsessive about how his publications were presented, so much so that, in the hundreds of letters he'd received regarding *A Memory of Solferino*, compliments of the object often preceded praise of the content or the style. This time things were more complicated. He had decided to decorate the cover with an illustration. But what a fuss for a single drawing! Rudolf was insisting on a soldier, but neutral Henry didn't even want to consider the idea: what uniform and from what country? German? French? 'I do not want nationality nor confession *for me*; this means that for a book that is so profoundly full of my own mind – even if written by you – I obviously would not want to signal a preference already on the first page.'[41]

As always, the uncredited author knew exactly what he wanted. For the cover, he would not consider a plain Red Cross for even a second, he wanted it on an 'entirely white, and snow white, without shadows'[42] oriflamme and with its ends floating in the wind. He very much liked the aristocratic grace of the palm trees that decorated Mrs Suttner's book *Die Waffen nieder!* The same ones would suit him just fine. He also requested gilded copies for the crowned heads – there were at least forty among his top-tier

---

[40] Dunant to Müller, 9 April 1897, Ms. fr. 5202, f. 200.
[41] Dunant to Müller, 22 March 1897, Ms. fr. 5202, f. 164–5.
[42] Dunant to Müller, 17 March 1897, Ms. fr. 5202, f. 151.

dedications – pale green covers with a red spine for the other bound copies, and softbound for the larger public – in short, he left nothing to chance, so much so that at the very last moment, when he received the title page proof, he pretended to be on his deathbed to obtain a change because he did not like it. What did the cost matter!, Dunant repeated each week with the nonchalance of the nouveau riche: the Dunant Foundation would pay, it had been created for that.

No greener grass

Carefully and diligently managed by Graeter, the Dunant Foundation had enough money to satisfy its beneficiary's slightest desires. These were modest, but specific. A small lamp, 'with a powerful light',[43] as the one he'd received from the ladies of the Berne Red Cross wasn't any good. He also wanted a large-knit scarf in fine wool, grey if possible, to keep his ears and temples warm while he did his writing; a second one would be welcome to wrap around his lower back. And fruits, and good tea, and this was all. While he stayed in Heiden and saw no one, his needs remained simple.

There were many attempts to get him to leave the hospital, and none of them worked. Nevertheless, he still couldn't stand the region; his ten years of residence didn't stop him from continuing to vilify a population he believed was against him. Yet something kept him from leaving. When the banker Scholder-Develay and the secretary of the Swiss Red Cross Schenker found the perfect house in Zurich for him, he became convinced of an ambush from Perrot, Moynier and company. The year before, he had considered moving to Ludwigsburg to be near Ernst Neuffer, his architect friend who had helped him draw his diagrams. This project, too, was abandoned because the region didn't have enough mountains.

As 1896 ticked over into 1897, Graeter and Müller watched the Dunant Foundation's coffers swell, bringing them to suggest he set himself up comfortably in Stuttgart, where they could more easily take care of him. But they could do nothing but witness his hedging, his fear, his resistance: 'How can you imagine I could handle the

---

[43] Dunant to Müller, 8 December 1896, BGE, Ms. fr. 5202, f. 95.

fatigue of the travel when I can't even receive a visitor, and even the slightest thing excites me and gives me so much pain!' Dunant wrote to Müller in February 1897. And two days later again: 'If only I had stork or swallow wings, I would already be in Stuttgart; but I have a bad feeling about the trip, and one should never go against one's inner feelings.'[44]

The portrait he then drew up of what he would need in Stuttgart was enough to squelch the kind intentions of his friends for good. First, he would need to be taken there via car. 'I say: in a car, because I should not sweat, and I sweat for the slightest thing.' He would also require a 'daily meal of several courses'. He could go for walks, but he had to return to a warm room to change his clothes. 'Warm because I need sunlight at noon, and a warm heater in the room, but which is lit outside the room, I can no longer bear metal stoves.' He needed permanent access to hot water, and in his room, but without the annoying back and forth of servants. Finally, he would need two adjoining rooms so he could air them easily, since the 'slightest dust' irritated his throat, etc.[45]

Enough was enough: Müller wouldn't bring it up again. But charming Mr Graeter, who wasn't Dunant's daily confidant, came back fifteen days later with his jovial manner and the advice to soothe his throat pains by taking a trip to Haifa, in Palestine, where there was a very well-run European-style hotel. 'However, this is nothing but an idea one has when trying to help a dear friend,' he continued, as if already repenting of having said something foolish. He then went on to say how sorry he was that he would not have the pleasure of seeing Dunant move to Stuttgart or some other location 'closer to the Committee'.[46]

Any question of moving was soon put to the side. Even visits were becoming unmanageable. Dunant's psychological seclusion was worsening each day.

By now his door had been closed for a while to people he considered undesirable. But the hermit slowly became shy of even the people closest to him. Although still writing to Rudolf every day, Dunant began to push off his friend's calls. 'I feel too miserable for your visit

---

[44] Dunant to Müller, 22 and 24 March 1897, BGE, Ms. fr. 5202, f. 125 and 130.
[45] Dunant to Müller, 24 [February?] 1897, BGE, Ms. fr. 5202, f. 175–6.
[46] Graeter to Dunant, 15 March 1897, BGE, Ms. fr. 2111, f. 189.

to bring me any pleasure at this moment,'[47] he wrote in March 1897, while they were still correcting their book and exactly when a meeting would have been very useful. But no, he could not, it would be too much for him, his ailing heart would not handle it. Several days later, another visit was announced, and this time it had an even more dramatic effect. 'I was very ill and inconceivably and painfully weary,' he wrote to Müller on 12th March, 'which kept me from writing. And all this was brought on by the announcement that Baroness de Suttner and her husband were coming to visit me in Heiden.'[48]

She had gone to the International Peace Office in Berne and was delighted that her journey home could bring her face to face with the man with whom she had been so diligently corresponding for a year and a half. But Dunant, however long-winded in his writing, couldn't take any in-person encounters at this point. He panicked and wrote her three letters in quick succession, begging her not to come. But instead of sending a telegraph saying she would reschedule her visit, the baroness very calmly used the normal mail service, a stressful delay that ended up making him ill for an entire month.

Bertha von Suttner could never have imagined her friend's state of distress. Dunant spent each and every day fighting against his 'merciless enemies and creditors', who were spying upon his slightest movements. If he stepped across the threshold of his room, if he went out of his hospital, if he dared walk out into the streets of Heiden, or worse, if he dared go anywhere in Switzerland or in Europe or in the world, he would be at 'their' mercy. 'What they want is vengeance – I know this; and I want to avoid it. A hospital room is forbidden to them. That is why I stay here.'[49]

Dunant believed he was protected at the Heiden district hospital by a kind of medical immunity or a health cordon against his creditors. Neither Müller nor anyone else would attempt again to make him move. Also because Dunant's new resources now provided a luxury that had been out of his reach until then: in February 1897 a second room was made available to patient number one on Dr Altherr's register. From this point on and for the twelve years that remained of his life, there was no more need for Dunant to make

---

[47] Dunant to Müller, 1 March 1897, BGE, Ms. fr. 5202, f. 139.
[48] Dunant to Müller, 12 March 1897, BGE, Ms. fr. 5202, f. 141.
[49] Dunant to Müller, 24 February 1897, BGE, Ms. fr. 5202, f. 130–3.

any excuses about staying put in an environment he hated, among a population he disdained and in a region he detested.

A subjective alliance

Considering the exorbitant losses of Dunant's bankruptcy, his creditors had actually (and astonishingly) left him alone since 1867. He himself admits he hadn't received a single letter from them for more than thirty years. But no matter whether his persecutory delusions were founded or unfounded, he included both his creditors and those who were jealous of him among his 'enemies', even if these two groups had radically opposed motives, the first wanting to see him replenish his fortune while the others were holding out for no comeback at all.[50] However illogically, Dunant was persuaded (more firmly so since the business with Perrot) that his creditors from the *Crédit Genevois* and the Mons-Djemila Mills were being 'seconded' by Moynier's 'cabal' and Perrot's Pietist 'gang'. This connection was so tightly bound in his mind that he always paired them, speaking of 'enemies and creditors' or 'creditors and enemies'.

Perhaps a survival extinct explains this deliberate confusion. Most of the victims of his 1867 bankruptcy were people Dunant knew very well. How could he have lived with the shame of having deserted his nearest and dearest? Unable to do something about his debts, he did something about his creditors: with each passing year his own mind shifted them from the 'victim' box into the 'torturer' box, probably to alleviate his unbearable remorse. Which is how his poor creditors, duped twice over, found themselves among Dunant's 'merciless enemies', alongside his former rivals from the YMCA and

---

[50] One of the only indisputable links between the Red Cross and Dunant's creditors comes via Paul Maunoir, the son of Dr Théodore Maunoir, member of the initial Soldiers' Aid Society. This Paul Maunoir married the daughter of Thomas Mac-Culloch, one of Dunant's biggest creditors because it was with him that Dunant had guaranteed the loan of 300,000 francs from the *Crédit Lyonnais*, a loan that fell 100% back on Mac-Culloch; as we know, he died shortly after. Mac-Culloch's daughter and Maunoir form a pair that explicitly connect his former Red Cross colleagues and his creditors. Dunant was convinced – certainly correctly – that Maunoir's two sons especially hated him. But otherwise, any collusion between the two camps is mostly a fantasy. See (among other letters) Dunant to Müller, 24 February 1897, 12 and 19 March 1897, BGE, Ms. fr. 5202, f. 157–8, 142 and 132–3.

the Red Cross. Were the two sides really in cahoots for thirty years as he persisted to believe? There's no evidence to confirm this, even less so because the only six creditors who would show up in 1901 had no apparent connection with the Pietists or the Red Cross. Nonetheless, this diabolical alliance had solidified in Dunant's mind and nothing would ever unseat it.

Up to now, however, Dunant's fears had nothing behind them because his creditors had never had a reason to come calling. All his projects for financial gains had been hypothetical and never publicized – so there'd been very little risk of a sudden increase in the Genevans' appetites. But the situation had rapidly changed. Over the last six months, the international press had been focusing each week on a new donation in his favour. The latest had come from Russia's dowager empress, Maria Feodorovna, who'd just sent a 4,000-franc appetizer to a forthcoming annuity of the same amount. Although this Russian generosity might permanently remove his financial precarity, its immediate effect was to gravely disturb Dunant, who believed he could see an army of creditors rising up in the distance, ready to confiscate all his new gifts.

While fighting against these imaginary ghosts, Dunant cycled again through all the different phases of hope, distress and depression. He spent a few weeks convinced he might be able to reimburse his debtors in a single go, just as he'd hoped in the days of his first marvellous projects – the Universal Library, haemostatic bandages, lands in Palestine, etc. Baroness von Suttner then had a simple but genius idea: if every German Samaritan gave one Deutsche Mark, or even half a mark, to a fund in favour of the Red Cross founder, they would rapidly garner a sum of more than a million francs. They would sponsor a much-lauded action in favour of sickly or disabled Samaritans, and then the rest of the sum would enable Dunant to reimburse what he owed: 'It could only be considered honourable that I would like to pay off my debts; even debts that are over thirty years old,'[51] Dunant began to dream. And Dr Altherr, who first thought the idea was unrealistic, started to take it seriously and say it was viable. But who would actually get the project going? And how long would it take? Dunant eventually faced the facts: it was a marvellous idea, but completely impracticable.

---

[51] Dunant to Müller, 10 February 1897, BGE, Ms. fr. 5202, f. 113.

Sometime later, another scenario came into play. Burying himself in his bitterness, he decided his creditors had no more right to anything, and that anyway 'they are the ones who prevented [him]'[52] from repaying his debts. And so he returned to his customary psychological parade, transforming his victims into evildoers unworthy of his remorse. Two days later he was assailed by doubts: differences in cantonal legislation might mean his creditors did have some rights. This new panic was finally resolved a few days later with a radical decision: 'I have learned that the statute of limitations is thirty years ... I do not want to move from my hospital room before this limitation has been fulfilled, and I have no intention of advertising it.'[53]

His terror still lingered the next day. 'I must watch over myself like a hawk to avoid giving my creditors the slightest entry.' Rewriting history, he began to think that, in fact, his most voracious creditors had been 'more than reimbursed' by the 100,000 francs that came to them through the miniscule sale price of the Felfela quarry.[54] From this moment forward, he had a single obsession: make sure any donation sent his way could not be seized. And so, right when the very real possibility of reimbursing his debts actually did appear, Dunant decided to strike his creditors from his list of priorities – even if they still lingered in his nightmares, regrets and vindictive thoughts.

A new campaign

Written entirely by Dunant but translated and signed by Rudolf Müller, *Entstehungsgeschichte des Roten Kreuzes und der Genfer Konvention* (The History of the Origins of the Red Cross and the Geneva Convention) was published in May 1897. Dunant received the first copy in Heiden on 7th May, the day before his birthday. This was the deadline Müller and the printers had settled upon in honour of the publication's biological father; they managed to just barely meet it.

---

[52] Dunant to Müller, 3 February 1897, BGE, Ms. fr. 5202, f. 107.
[53] Dunant to Müller, 23 February 1897, BGE, Ms. fr. 5202, f. 127.
[54] Dunant to Müller, 24 February 1897, BGE, Ms. fr. 5202, f. 130–3.

The anonymous author was delighted. Thanks to the largesse of the Dunant Foundation, he got everything he wanted: a contemporary and luxurious edition with a solid hardcover and good paper, a lovely font, as well as the numerous additions and corrections that had significantly inflated the printer's invoice. The greenish grey cover worked a charm, and the palm trees were 'extremely well drawn and very prettily accompany the flagpole beneath the white flag'. He found the last chapter (that endless litany of laudatory quotations) 'admirable'. He had hoped to live long enough to hold this book in his hands; our elderly gentleman could now die in peace.[55]

This tranquility would last twenty-four hours. Catastrophe struck on his birthday. Dunant may not have been able to read German, but a mistake literally jumped off the page at him. The very first one at that! 'Franz Joseph II' instead of 'Franz Joseph I' had been printed in the first lines of the first chapter. An error of reign for a crowned head! How could courtier Dunant handle the shame of it, even when it was certainly his mistake. He wrote that very evening to his only saviour, his friend Rudolf Müller.

Following a charming preamble thanking him for his birthday wishes, then encouraging Rudolf to make a list of his costs – 'I ask you to note everything, I mean everything, otherwise I would be embarrassed and things would not be as I desire them' – , Dunant asked him 'as a start' to pay for a skilled copy-editor, 'or even an unskilled one, but who knows how to use a scraper' so that each of the superfluous *I*s might be erased – from each volume, without exception. He had tried it himself, Dunant added, and 'you can't see it'.[56]

This time Rudolf Müller must have put his foot down. No, he would not spend his evenings scraping pages by candlelight, nor would he pay for a skilled or unskilled copy-editor to erase the superfluous *I* from each Franz Joseph of each line seven of each first page of every single one of the 2,000 copies. At the very most he would ask the printer to glue a small *erratum* in each copy correcting the tragic error.

Dunant grumbled. He felt this would make the mistake 'even more noticeable'.[57] He tried to convince Müller. Then he gave up.

---

[55] Dunant to Müller, 7 May 1897, Ms. fr. 5202, f. 239.

[56] Dunant to Müller, 8 May 1897, Ms. fr. 5202, f. 240–1.

[57] Dunant to Müller, 25 May 1897, Ms. fr. 5202, f. 250.

The book would have a small *erratum*, it was already a miracle the printer hadn't sent Müller packing.

Once the books were corrected of their faulty *I* – without which, knowing the author as we do, all 2,000 copies would probably have been pulped – Dunant could launch his campaign. Two years had now passed since the wave of publicity unleashed by Baumberger's article in *Über Land und Meer*, and public attention had begun to wane; it was time to give it a little boost.

Since tried and trusted recipes are always the best, Dunant would proceed as was his custom. More comfortable than ever because he wouldn't publicly be known as the author, he sent the book to every single titled or untitled individual who might possibly be interested. At the top of the list were kings and queens, religious dignitaries (Catholic, of course), journalists (conservative, of course), celebrities of all kinds, and finally the committees of the Red Cross Societies of the entire world – except those that Dunant described as 'under Mr Moynier's slipper'.[58] As the thank-you cards and letters of congratulations came rolling in with recognizable names, he had them printed and sent them out again in all directions. As the press clippings appeared, he asked for twenty, fifty, even a hundred copies, making separate printings or copies in view of adding them to the famous 'appendix' of any future editions, an appendix that would double in volume for each new printing. From a small ripple to a tiny wave, from a tiny wave into a great swell, all this noise did indeed create a storm surge that would alter public opinion.

Initially, Dunant had only been thinking of reissuing *A Memory of Solferino*. As time passed and his desire for vengeance sharpened, he now wanted to checkmate his enemies by establishing himself once and for all as the sole and unique founder of the Red Cross and promoter of the Geneva Convention; this was the true purpose of *The History of the Origins of the Red Cross*. However, the last six months saw a new goal – the dream of a peace prize – hitching a ride onto his publication project. Promoting the book was no longer simply necessary, it was vital.

---

[58] Dunant to Müller, 8 December 1896, BGE, Ms. fr. 5202, f. 94.

A shock team

In the prime of his life, the author of *A Memory of Solferino* had been incredibly efficient at taking care of his own PR. But the Henry Dunant of Heiden was twice as old and could no longer frolic about from one town to another to ensure his work was being promoted. Not even close. When he was feeling particularly sociable, he ventured as far as spying through the half-closed shutters of his room to mutter insults about the farmers calling noisily to one another in the street. When he was seized with a truly sociable urge, he held the deaconess and head nurse Elise Bollinger at his side for an extra five minutes, or the cook Emma Rubeli for a few comments on the quality of the rice – the basis of all of his meals for the last five years.[59]

So how on earth did this devilish man manage his coup without leaving his two rooms on the second floor of the Heiden district hospital? How did he orchestrate a worldwide press campaign like the one that accompanied the publication of Rudolf Müller's *History of the Origins of the Red Cross and the Geneva Convention* during the second half of 1897?

An integral part of Dunant's genius is the absolute devotion he inspired both to himself and to his cause. A man who'd been refusing to see anyone for years – whether the president of Switzerland or Europe's poster girl for peace – still succeeded in assembling enough men and women who, out of respect, friendship, admiration or dedication, would pull out all the stops to add a few bricks to the construction of his monument.

The head nurse, Sister Elise Bollinger, was the first of his indispensable helpers. Since Dr Altherr no longer came to see him, she was his principal connection to the outside world. She chased off the drunks or children who might be shouting Swiss German nonsense under his window; she watched over his health, his comfort, his changing moods; most importantly she'd agreed to translate the letters he handed her every day with a contrite look after having struggled in vain to decipher them.

---

[59] For details about Dunant's daily life in Heiden, see Hermann Altherr, '*Henry Dunant's Letzte Jahre*' and Felix Christ, '*1908–1910, Dunants Letzte Jahre Lebenserinnerungen*', *Dunant und die Ostschweiz*, 39–53.

Speaking of devotion, Elise's niece Emma Rubeli should not be overlooked. Because Dunant was convinced, and had been for the last twenty-five years, that people wanted to assassinate him, he requested she either taste all his meals or prepare them in his presence. The special patient on the second floor took up so much of the poor woman's time that an assistant cook had to be hired.

But the most extraordinary loyalties came from a number of people he'd never even met, who spent their energy for him without asking anything in return.

Beginning in 1895, a certain Dr Idelson played a leading role in the new push to rehabilitate Henry Dunant. Dr Idelson – real name Valerian Smirnov – was a Russian refugee who'd been living in Berne since 1871. He was involved in the pacifist circles of Switzerland's capital city, home to the headquarters of the International Peace Bureau. Like many others, and following his colleague Bertha von Suttner, he was so sympathetic to this forgotten Henry Dunant that he mobilized 'a group of friends' in December 1896 to send a collective tribute to Dunant through letters, gifts and telegrams for Christmas and the New Year.[60] He was also the person who'd pleaded successfully for the miraculous annuity from Russia, considerably elevating Dunant's economic level starting from 1897. Eventually, along with Baroness von Suttner, Idelson decided to help Henry obtain 'this 300,000-franc Nobel Prize',[61] an outrageous project Dunant nevertheless took on board, as we know. As soon as *The Origins of the Red Cross* was published in May 1897, Idelson began scrambling to promote the book all the way from the Bernese Alps to the Ural Mountains. He enlisted the help of two Russian ladies in Berne for all varieties of copying and mailing tasks that the old man in Heiden was unable to do himself.

Henry recognized in this near stranger's astonishing commitment 'the benevolent perseverance of Madame the Baroness de Suttner'.[62] When the lady in question spoke of Idelson to Dunant, she simply called him 'our mutual friend'.[63] No matter the origins of this friendship, the fact is that until his premature death in 1900,

---

[60] Idelson to Graeter, 8 December 1896, handwritten letter in German (unknown source).
[61] Dunant to Müller, 1 March 1897, BGE, Ms. fr. 5202, f. 140.
[62] Dunant to Suttner, 22 February 1897.
[63] Suttner to Dunant, 8 March 1897.

Smirnov, alias Idelson, would support Dunant through all kinds of writing tasks, services, contacts and subsidies, not to mention that he most certainly inspired fifty Russian Red Cross branches to make Dunant an honorary member.

Through this peerless publicist Eastern Europe was now under control. Northward, where people were now turning their attention, there were two different fronts to consider: although the Nobel Prize headquarters were in Stockholm, the laureate of the Peace Prize, unlike the others, would be selected by the Norwegian parliament, the Storting. And so it happened that a certain Mrs Theorell was translating Swedish texts for Dunant and Müller while a young Miss Key, connected to several Norwegian parliamentarians, was discreetly preparing the field in Christiania.[64] In the Netherlands, a young and passionate journalist from Amsterdam, Christian Friedrich Haje, had already dedicated a long article in 1896 to the founder of the Red Cross in a popular weekly. Dunant, delighted by this tribute, asked Müller to send him proofs of *The History of the Origins*, which Haje immediately said he wanted to translate into Dutch. Success! Haje would serve as the Dutch relay on the sinuous roads towards Stockholm and Oslo.

The nerve centre of Dunant's campaign remained in Stuttgart, however, where the two pillars of the Dunant Foundation lived: Adolf Graeter and Rudolf Müller. Here again, the devotion of these two men – both were fathers and full-time professionals – proves the extraordinary charisma, even at a distance, of a man who was embittered, ill, shy of company, authoritarian to the point of tyranny and quick to feel offended. Both men continued their painstaking work to help Dunant walk up the steps onto the stage of the 'World's Great Men'. Graeter not only used the thriving foundation he'd created to pay for the numerous copies of Müller's book that Dunant siphoned away from bookshops to offer for free to the entire world, he continually negotiated Dunant's fear of his creditors and calmed his worries with incredible tact – both proofs of a rare and delicate affection. He was also constantly contacting newspapers so they might include press releases related to some new honour his friend Henry had earned. And all this for only the stingiest recognition from the very man reaping the rewards.

---

[64] Present-day Oslo. Norway was united with Sweden until 1905.

As for Müller, each day he received a list of names who must be sent the book, accompanied by another list of people who must be written to, journals to contact, letters to translate, articles to request and then forward to Heiden, etc. The secretary service he provided to Dunant must have taken up, at the very least, half of his time.

Had being isolated for so long made our elderly gentleman lose any sense of reciprocity? Not only was his gratitude scandalously below what his friends deserved, but he often teased them for nothing, got angry for mere trifles, accused them of mistakes that he himself had committed, harassed them for problems his own anxieties had created. Over the course of the five-year collective quest for the Nobel Prize, Idelson would be cursed for a mistake that was actually Dunant's, Haje would be judged as invasive, a money-grubber and awkward, Müller would be scolded for sending a letter he didn't actually write and Graeter would be treated (behind his back) as a mere peddler with no understanding of lofty causes, and this list doesn't even include Dunant's earlier whipping boys: the Sondereggers and Pfisters who were summarily fired after good and loyal services rendered. And no one thought for a moment to hold him accountable. They were all there, faithful, devoted, attentive, deferential, busy bees in the service of a tyrannical queen, as if getting that Nobel Prize into the hand of their friend had become as vital to them as it was to Dunant himself. The only one among his faithful followers who was less blindly docile than the others was Bertha von Suttner, and this earned her Dunant's eternal esteem.

The campaign bore fruit. On 30th December 1897, Henry Dunant received the Binet-Fendt Prize, an inaugural Swiss prize for 'the instigator of a civic action or a printed work judged the most liable to bring peace, harmony and mutual support to all citizens'.[65] Responsible for selecting the laureate, the Swiss government chose Dunant 'as the most qualified person to receive this distinction'.[66] This was indisputable recognition of his role as the founder of the Red Cross. It was also the occasion for another round of publicity: in the early days of January 1898, our laureate mobilized his entire team to send the news in every which way, to have it relayed by as

---

[65] Chancellery of the Swiss Confederation to Mr Henry Dunant, 30 December 1897, BGE, Ms. fr. 2111, f. 251.
[66] *Journal de Genève*, 31 December 1897.

many newspapers as possible, and then redistribute any of the relevant articles. Müller was requested to translate the prize announcement into German and bring the good news to Stuttgart's main newspapers for publication, against payment if necessary. 'I really want this to happen,' Dunant specified, eyes still looking north. 'This will be reprinted in other newspapers, until it reaches Norway. This is no time to rest.'[67] The day after the next, Stuttgart was no longer enough, all of Germany's newspapers needed targeting; Mrs Theorell and her access to Swedish newspapers should be engaged to the task. 'Without this, the prize means absolutely nothing,'[68] Dunant wrote categorically to Müller. But more than anything, he specified after four pages of detailed advice, no one must ever suspect he was the one waving the director's baton in this perfectly orchestrated uproar.

With Dunant behind them, there was very little risk that his troops would rest. Because Dunant's orders were now clear – 'no scrimping'[69] – no journal would refuse the paid insertion of news of the Binet Prize. Once the news had appeared, the Berne contingent – Idelson and his Russian assistants – got to work by having the best articles reprinted on flyers, improving the text if necessary; other team members translated it into the 'useful' languages – Swedish and Norwegian, for example – and off it went, another round of broad distribution to up the tension just another notch, then again redistributed by all of Dunant's agents across all of Europe. The great man 'abandoned by everyone'[70] had mastered the art of the media storm more than most of his contemporaries. The conquest of the Nobel was well on its way.

---

[67] Dunant to Müller, 3 January 1798, BGE, Ms. fr. 5203, f. 1.
[68] Dunant to Müller, 5 January 1798, BGE, Ms. fr. 5203, f. 4.
[69] Ibid., f. 5.
[70] Cf. note 30 above.

15

A Laurel-Crowned Finish
(1897–1910)

The age of his nerves

Bolstered after winning the first Binet Prize, Dunant found enough energy to keep riding the wave. There were still plenty of people throughout the world who didn't yet know 'that he was who he was'! Müller appears to have gracefully rolled up his sleeves for this publicity frenzy. During the first months of 1898, every week his mailbox received yet another list of people who should be sent a copy of *The History*. For Henry, the slightest pretext was grounds for a new parcel: Queen Regent of the Netherlands planning to abdicate? Princess Pauline engaged to the prince of Wied? An excellent reason to send them a book, even two! And of course, every one of these lofty targets sent their thanks via lovely letters that made their way into Dunant's precious 'Appendix' of compliments.

The following month our enterprising old gentleman focused on a new battle: a Swiss League for Human Rights for which he'd already written up the draft statutes and declared himself the president. The Dreyfus Affair was in full swing and it was the moment to publicly intervene.

Although he was still bubbling over with projects and new ideas, Dunant no longer had the stamina to complete the tasks they imposed. He was constantly tired, feeling low, flat. Depending on the day, his pains fluctuated: Monday, eczema; Tuesday, rheumatism; Wednesday, his head; Thursday, his heart; Friday, his nerves . . . and all week long a rage against the dreadful noise from the streets and the hospital,

coming from the drunks or the children Dunant continued to believe
were being paid by his enemies. Added to these pains was the near
daily recurrence of his multiple fears as well as his most intimate
sorrows, those he shared only with Rudolf, his sole confidant:
'Everything gives me a potentially fatal emotion; and the simple
arrival of January, that time of year when Mrs Kastner-Boursault died
in 1888, fills me with a feeling that is harmful to my health.'[1]

Léonie Kastner: an incurable wound. In personal papers probably
written around the same period, Dunant admitted what he had
never said before:

> This Lady never knew that, since 1876, I loved her. I would have
> thrown myself into the fire for her, and I am still mourning her
> loss. She died in January 1888. She loved me, too, I am now sure
> of this (and since 1872 or 1873). But how could I put myself
> forward, take even a single step, from my ruined and indebted
> position, when she was so rich, to the order of two million francs!
> It was impossible.[2]

Ten years had now passed since her death, and Mrs Kastner was not
forgotten. In September 1898, Dunant received a nice framed and
dedicated photograph from Archduchess Maria-Theresa of Austria-
Este, princess of Bavaria by marriage. 'This portrait made me very
happy,' he confessed to Rudolf, 'mostly because the archduchess
very much resembles Mrs Kastner-Boursault.'[3] As we will see later,
Dunant preferred portraits to the possibility of a flesh-and-blood
visit. Dunant was fearful of emotions, and nothing moved him more
than the physical presence of those he cared about. Since Mrs
Kastner had passed away, Rudolf Müller topped his secret list of
terrifying visitors. As any holiday became imminent, Dunant would
begin to double down on his health complaints, vehement excuses,
and distraught attempts to dissuade him. 'Just think,' Dunant wrote
to him the day before Easter 1898, 'that to avoid the slightest

---

[1] Dunant to Müller, 7 April 1898, BGE, Ms. fr. 5203, f. 26.
[2] 'Financial File', BGE, Ms. fr. 2116 G, f. 48. To the best of my knowledge this short
note has never before been published. It clarifies the relationship between Léonie
Kastner and Henry Dunant.
[3] Dunant to Müller, 6 September 1898, BGE, Ms. fr. 5203, f. 39.

emotion, I tidy my room myself, entirely, and only the *Oberschwester* brings me my meals and letters.'[4] As if Rudolf didn't know his friend had been living in a hospital for five years! But Dunant worried he had not been quite clear enough.

> The head has nothing to do with it, but the heart is far too sick to support anything; I have certainly become extremely nervous, but it's the fear of congestion – which is a too real fact. I would understand you might come in the summer because of the heat, to breathe the alpine air, but what would you do here in the winter? And then, you see, the people here are provoked by the Genevans, incited by their agents, and always ready to hurt me or damage me.[5]

Etc. One absurd argument followed by another, and the same list repeated three times each year, before summer, Christmas and Easter. Using all varieties of convoluted logic, Dunant stubbornly pushed away any possibility of a visit from his dearest friend, the man he wrote to nearly every day to discuss his nerves, his heart and his head but whom he obviously feared to see in person in case this might push him beyond what his emotional threshold could handle.

For his birthday on 8th May, Dunant would receive two pieces of good news from Müller. The first was that in honour of his seventy years, Rudolf had successfully placed several articles in some large German newspapers, but the best news was this: 'It was not possible for me to come see you during the holidays.'[6] Phew! Müller would not show up; he was already back in Stuttgart. Dunant could relax for the time being.

That same summer brought the threat of a new visit from the Müller family travelling in the Swiss Alps. But this time Rudolf ended up, rightfully, selecting the North Sea as their destination. Dunant dedicated plenty of ink to congratulating him on his choice and wished him happy travels with a joy large enough to be

---

[4] Dunant to Müller, 7 April 1898, BGE, Ms. fr. 5203, f. 26. The *Oberschwester* (Sister Superior) was the head nurse of the hospital.
[5] Ibid.
[6] Müller to Dunant, 6 May 1898, BGE, Ms. fr. 2112, f. 72.

suspicious, especially for someone he so depended on. But by the following day, he was lost. He had a thousand 'necessary or obligatory' mailings to do, a thousand small services to request. To whom else but Rudolf could he turn? While too emotional to be in his actual company, he couldn't last two days without him.

The Green Cross

Despite its protracted title, *The History of the Origins of the Red Cross and the Geneva Convention* deals with many other subjects. Anxious to profile himself as a candidate for the Nobel Prize, Dunant made sure the text included his favourite pacifist strategy: promoting the role of women in fighting the world's wars, miseries and misfortunes. Müller's book spends its last twenty pages – just before its concluding collection of tributes – describing in detail Dunant's two feminist projects.

The first project was the one he'd described rather unsuccessfully to Bertha von Suttner when their correspondence was first beginning. Dunant wouldn't let go of his idea that women were the only possible agents of harmony between individuals and nations. They alone, united into an 'aristocratic Confederation for the Good' and presided, of course, by a fleet of female sovereigns, could counter war, socialism, anarchy and 'brute force'.[7]

Dunant, still writing via Müller, was recycling the other feminist project he'd so laboriously developed five years earlier with Sara Bourcart and Pauline Gendre. Since then, both young women had completely given up: Miss Bourcart, now married, to care for her own family, while Miss Gendre was taking care of other people's children, travelling between the Netherlands and Russia as a governess for the offspring of high-society families. But Dunant's idea hadn't changed, and he presented it verbatim in chapter 9 of *The History*. The idea was to create, under a banner bearing a green cross, a movement in favour of women, mothers, widows and young girls to help them live with dignity, find work, defend their legal rights and ensure their independence. This assistance would be

---

[7] Dunant to Suttner, 10 October 1895.

offered by volunteer ladies, accessible through a dense network of charity offices recognizable from afar by their green cross – a sort of social and civilian sister of the Red Cross.

A direct beneficiary of the campaign surrounding Müller's book, the idea of the Green Cross managed to take hold. Grabbing the baton from the Misses Bourcart and Gendre, the daughter of a Belgian friend of Dunant's, Julia Belval, took the trouble to relaunch the idea exactly according to the plan written out in *The History of the Origins*. Between 1897 and 1898, she and her father were the instigators of several articles on Dunant and his Green Cross in both Belgian and French newspapers. Dunant also learned that the young woman had started a committee in Brussels; delighted, he corresponded with Miss Belval, giving her advice, basically dictating word for word the statutes she should give her committee, since this was a tune he knew by heart. He seemed to care a lot about the association's development, a little like it was his last child.[8]

To his greatest satisfaction, the idea kept gaining ground. Dr Idelson, a decidedly active proponent of Dunant's ideas, immediately solicited his own contacts to create a few satellite societies here and there, in Warsaw, in Moscow, in Berne and in Madrid. A St Petersburg baroness also wanted to form a committee. Dunant rejoiced. For the first time since 1863, one of his ideas was being translated into real activism. Everything was running smoothly, exactly as Dunant intended. For the moment.

But it didn't take long for something to go wrong. At the beginning of 1898, several people had already signalled to Dunant the existence of two Green Crosses formed before his, one in Austria for distinguishing alpine guides, and the other in France, used as an aid society for colonial soldiers.[9] Dunant didn't make a fuss and moved on to other things. But things grew more complicated in October. Miss Belval received a heated protest from the Berlin section of the International Federation for Aid to Young Women,[10] a slightly international and *very* Protestant association active in

---

[8] Dunant to Dr Jordy, 11 August 1898, Swiss National Library, Ms lq 1³, n° 6, BGE copy; to Müller, 16–17 October 1898, BGE, Ms. fr. 5203, f. 51. On Dunant's late feminism, also see Durand, '*Henry Dunant féministe*', 20–9.

[9] Dunant to Müller, 11 January 1898, BGE, Ms. fr. 5203, f. 9.

[10] *L'Union Internationale des Amies de la Jeune Fille*, founded in 1877 in Neuchâtel, Switzerland.

Switzerland, England, Scotland and the Netherlands, whose mission
was to protect young girls who went alone and without contacts
into unknown towns as servants, governesses, private tutors, etc.
The ultimate goal of this Pietist association was to spare young
women from the risks of debauchery, prostitution or exploitation,
keeping them in less lucrative but more Christian forms of
employment. These women were claiming primacy and exclusivity
of the green cross as an emblem, and also claiming that the goals of
the movement dreamed up by Dunant would only needlessly
duplicate their own; 'the Aid to Young Women', they concluded,
'would be forced to energetically protest'.[11]

This minuscule quarrel would be of no interest at all if it hadn't
so devastated Dunant. Throughout that entire month of October
1898, even while the fallout from the Binet Prize had again made
him the focus of all European newspapers, even though Müller's
book had established him as the founder of the Red Cross, and
despite the increasing rumours that he would be the future and first
laureate of the Nobel Peace Prize, Dunant took to his bed because
of an insignificant letter of protest from a few worried ladies in
Berlin. A microscopic spat indeed, but taking gigantic proportions
in Dunant's mind from the moment he looked at it through his own
personal lens, a prism which magnified all events with a religious
flavour and connected even tiny vexations to a worldwide plot
orchestrated by his enemies.

This protest from the Aid to Young Women had come from
Berlin. And for the last two or three years, Dunant had been nursing
a systematic mistrust of the Prussian capital city, the same for
Vienna. The very man who in 1866 had strutted alongside the royal
family of Prussia to see the troops return from Sadowa, the same
man whom Queen Augusta had sought to help in Paris in 1867, the
one the French had believed a spy for Prussia, had changed sides:
Prussia was no longer a friend. First, this was where one of his sworn
enemies, the recent ambassador to Vienna, Alfred de Claparède, had
spread the rumour while attached to the Swiss delegation in Berlin
that Dunant was not the author of *A Memory of Solferino*, nor the
true architect of the Geneva Convention. Already reason enough to

---

[11] Cited by Dunant in his letter to Müller, 28–9 October 1898, BGE, Ms. fr. 5203,
f. 61–4; half of this 4-page letter is about the quarrel with the Berlin 'Green Cross'.

strike an entire city off his map. Then Moynier's 'cabal' had turned Queen Augusta against him by telling her all kinds of horrors. And of course Berlin was a Protestant city, with very close and numerous connections to Geneva. And so, when Miss Belval had informed him that a letter had come from Berlin, he was already wary: before even knowing its contents, he suspected 'some machinations of the Calvinist ladies of Geneva and Neuchâtel'. Finally, when the indispensable Müller translated the letter for him, Dunant fell into a black anger, as if he could see an old skeleton jump out of the closet: 'The association of the Aid to Young Women in Geneva, Neuchâtel, Paris, London, Heiden, has hurt me beyond everything,' he wrote to Müller on 28th October, as soon as he had received the translation. 'These are enemies I will never forgive. Remember what I say now.'[12]

Ah, Rudolf must have thought, here we go again: here was yet another battalion appearing on a horizon already crowded with enemy troops. But what on earth could these ladies have done to Henry? Dunant only used insinuations and generalities, but he seemed to know the association in question extremely well, its goals, its methods and its shortcomings: 'many among these virtuous "friends" are after some kind of vengeance, by dispersing suspicions,' he said in a tone so concerned that one would swear he was one of their victims; 'when one of them has a retaliation to enact, there is no restraint in slandering in the most odious fashion, and their lies remain unpunished.'

What slander might he have experienced? In a later letter, without naming anyone, Henry told Rudolf an old story of neighbours back at the Paradies guest house in Heiden, who had been convinced that since there was no head of family around, Dunant had been courting the wife, the five girls and a niece! Were these tales propagated by the zealots of the Aid to Young Women? And the rumours of mistresses in all his ports of call – London, Paris, Stuttgart – might they have been relayed by some lieutenants in skirts of Max Perrot and the Evangelical Alliance? And what about the story of the Kastner daughter-in-law jumping out the window? Dunant claimed it was spread by the 'sanctimonious ladies' of London: might these be the same? He would say no more on the subject.

---

[12] Dunant to Müller, 28–9 October 1898, BGE, Ms. fr. 5203, f. 61–4, for the following citations as well.

Biographical clues

As benign as it may seem, the quarrel with the Aid to Young Women provides one or two useful biographical clues. Dunant's fury, which lasted until the end of that autumn of 1898, proves that he believed he was once or several times the target of this very charity. The rumours he relates, and which continued to make him shake with rage ten years later, are all about young women he's supposed to have seduced, or his mistresses, not to mention the numerous speculations relating to Mrs Kastner. Although there have been questions about celibate Dunant's sexual preferences, there is not a single sentence amid the thousands of pages of correspondence available to us which even hints at the idea, nor in the hundreds of insults that Dunant catalogues and recatalogues both meticulously and obsessively. He seems to have been the object of all forms of slander except the accusation of homosexuality (still penalized at that time), which is of note when discussing a man so soundly defamed for over fifty years. And if slights as insignificant as rumours about young women put him in such a state of disarray, there is every reason to assume he had nothing else potentially damaging lurking in the shadows, not in Heiden nor in London, Paris or Stuttgart.

But the episode with the Aid to Young Women highlights a second aspect of Dunant's life. At the height of the quarrel, he specifies that he'd only learned two years earlier about the 'fanatical actions' of this group of ladies. Yet, it was exactly two years earlier that Jean-Jacques Bourcart had filled him in on the shady dealings of the 'satanic' Perrot over the course of the last twenty-five years. The Aid to Young Women were certainly among this batch of revelations; Bourcart had much better access to such information, given that both his wife and daughter were close to the movement.

When cross-checking the secrets, dates and facts, it is clear that it was Dunant's dear friend Bourcart who regularly informed him about the behaviour of his enemies. How else could Dunant, cloistered away for ten years in Appenzell, sniff out each new clue to corroborate his fantasies of cabals and plots?

A former member of a Darbyist community that had kicked him out, Bourcart, like Dunant, harboured a serious distrust of his erstwhile religious fellows; but unlike Dunant, he still travelled quite a bit and had a large family and many friends who kept him abreast of the stories being passed among the Pietist and philanthropic circles. Furthermore, he began working with the Colmar Red Cross committee in 1899, which 'gave him the right to attend the Congress, where, until now,' he wrote to Dunant, 'you were being forgotten.'[13] Entirely devoted to his cause, he scrupulously forwarded any rumours to his friend; and Dunant, at his end, frequently requested information about such and such a person, or asked for a piece of evidence that might serve as proof against his enemies. As soon as the quarrel with the Aid to Young Women began making waves, for example, Dunant immediately wrote to Bourcart asking him to query Berlin's feminist circles about them, a task to which Bourcart eagerly agreed.

With complete loyalty, Bourcart fully identified with Dunant's desire for justice. A run-in with Perrot at the Basel train station? He immediately told his friend about it, and with a touching solidarity: '[He] pretended not to know me, carefully avoided my gaze and did not greet me. Too bad for him! Because I would have given him the good advice not to wait for his next life to make up for all the wrongs he's done in this one.' Same thing with Moynier: 'I haven't yet found the way to catch him'; and about his enemies in general: 'You must do something about it or authorize me via procuration to take legal action against your slanderers. I would happily do this at my own cost.'[14]

Contrary to reasonable Rudolf Müller, who quietly received Dunant's incessant complaints about his enemies, his suspicions and his hatreds, Bourcart seemed very willing to engage in Dunant's semi-fantastic world of demons. And for good reason. The transmission of thought, the influence of spirits, 'magicalism' and the cabal were pure sustenance for this man; he would never refuse to listen to Dunant's persecutory delusions, quite the contrary. 'I make incantations every day for you,' he would sign off, like this was an ordinary way to end a letter; 'I am quite absorbed in my mental combat in favour of all sorts of events and I am taking care of you every day,' he assured him another time.[15] They exchanged book recommendations on spiritualism, life after death and the

---

[13] Bourcart to Dunant, 23 February 1899, BGE, Ms. fr. 2115 N 1, f. 50.
[14] Bourcart to Dunant, 2 January 1898, 28 September 1896, and 1 December 1896, BGE Ms. fr. 2115 N 1, f. 39, 32 and f. 34.
[15] Bourcart to Dunant, 12 October 1899 and 8 December 1898, BGE, Ms. fr. 2115 N 1, f. 56 and 47.

Great All; Henry even prefaced one of Bourcart's publications. One day, the latter told Henry how he had stopped an 'unbearably painful enchantment' by using a steel point against some 'astral fluid'; another day he went off looking for 'the primary material of the philosopher's stone',[16] mentioned in a way someone else might mention heading off to pick mushrooms. The friendship between the founder of the Red Cross and the respectable army officer and Legion of Honour knight went far beyond normal earthly concerns.

An older letter, from 1895, brings an additional element to their rather esoteric relationship. With his usual honesty, Bourcart apparently justified himself for having spoken of Dunant publicly as a 'sick man', considering that he had good reasons to consider him as such:

> Now I must tell you that no one has convinced me that you are ill, except yourself. We spent months discussing possible names for your illness and we ended up deciding it was an 'enchantment' cast upon you by a horde of magnetizers in London.
>
> I have told several people that you became sick in the aftermath of twenty-five years of black misery and I will repeat this until you convince me of the opposite. Do not tell anyone that you are not ill, it would not be politic.[17]

So they had had time to discuss Dunant's obscure illness together 'for several months'. Where? When? Only Bourcart knew. He knew a hidden side of Dunant that neither the businessman nor man of the world, nor promotor of the YMCA or the Red Cross wanted to reveal: not just the esoteric part of him, revealed through his diagrams, not just the dark side of his misanthropy and his paranoia, but the hidden part of this mysterious 'illness' Dunant must have been treated for over 'several months', all traces of which he deliberately erased. Successfully as well. Except for his very close friends, except for Sister Elise of the district hospital who knew his mood swings, except for Mrs Altherr who'd found him 'a little deranged', and except for the prestigious visitors who were sent

---

[16] Bourcart to Dunant, 12 October 1899 and 8 December 1898, BGE, Ms. fr. 2115 N 1, f. 56 and 47.
[17] Bourcart to Dunant, 3 November 1895, BGE, Ms. fr. 2115 N 1, f. 26.

packing even after a long journey to see him, no one else suspected that the man who led a campaign for the Nobel Prize with such brio and rationality either was or had been so extremely fragile.

Captain's greeting

In September 1898, Henry Dunant received three small leaflets written in Norwegian. He could not guess at their specific content, but he didn't take long to recognize their importance. They had been sent to him from Christiania by Dr Hans Daae, army medical officer. The only recognizable words, 'Henry Dunant' and 'Solferino', indicated that they were somehow discussing him.

While on a field mission during the Greek–Turkish hostilities of 1897, Captain Daae had become desperate regarding the lack of Turkish military aid services; remembering Dunant's feelings during Solferino, he wrote to him shortly after his return to send a few of his press articles. What extraordinary luck that this Norwegian just showed up out of nowhere! Without a language in common with Daae, Dunant pressed Rudolf Müller to send him all sorts of documents and various suggestions in favour of his candidacy in Norway. At the same time, discretion was important. 'He should not think I was thinking of the Nobel situation,' Dunant candidly advised Müller; 'these northern people are a little slow.'[18]

However 'slow', it's likely all the same that Captain Daae would begin to suspect something: an invitation arrived three weeks later from Rudolf Müller to visit Stuttgart, all expenses paid! Dunant was counting on his eponymous foundation for the financing, and upon Müller for all the rest – host the captain, drive him around, show him the city, give him any documentation he might want to pass along, to members of the Nobel jury, for example ... 'We do not influence anything, nor anyone; we *are informing* the situation,'[19] Dunant insisted in his final recommendations to Müller.

There was no question, however, of receiving Dr Daae in Heiden. Dunant did not feel up to handling a visit of such importance. 'Do not let him think that I am senile,' Dunant specified to Müller, 'but

---

[18] Dunant to Müller, 22–4 October 1898, BGE, Ms. fr. 5203, f. 56–7.
[19] Dunant to Müller, 29 October 1898, BGE, Ms. fr. 5203, f. 66.

only unwell for the moment.'[20] By having refused any and all visits for so long, Dunant didn't dare show what he'd become, in his dressing gown in the midst of a mess of papers and books in his hospital room. 'If I had a grand apartment and all of life's comforts, it would not be so,' he defended himself. 'I could even receive visits every day; but as things are, that cannot be.'[21]

Coming all the way from Norway especially for Henry Dunant, Captain Daae insisted. Having seen enough of Stuttgart and its surroundings, he eventually decided to go and shake the hand of the Heiden hermit himself. But to his very great surprise, Dunant would not give in: upon this first visit, he stubbornly refused to allow him to climb the two floors of the hospital! The Norwegian army doctor would be summarily dismissed, just like the president of Switzerland, the president of the Red Cross and Baroness von Suttner. It was only upon his second attempt, a week later, that Dunant agreed to let him in.

A dense, cold fog had been hovering over town since early November. Because of his rheumatism and sore throats, Dunant hadn't opened his windows in fifteen days; overheated, his tiny little rooms must have been horribly stuffy and smelly. But he had no choice: it was in his room he must receive guests.

At his entrance, Henry was surprised: the captain was much younger than he'd guessed. Thirty-four, thirty-five, maybe? The same age he'd been when A Memory of Solferino had appeared. Since Mr Daae spoke no French, Dunant had asked Dr Altherr to mediate, a detail all the more irritating to him as the doctor hadn't bothered to see him for over two years, as if he wasn't worth the effort.

An hour later, Dr Altherr walked the captain back to the entrance; Dunant watched Mr Daae leaving through his half-open shutters at the window. He never skipped this ritual, revealing his reasons for doing so a few days later to Müller. While walking through Heiden towards the hospital, Mr Daae had met – luckily – a few people 'very well disposed' towards him:

But, this fact will explain why I tell all those who come from abroad: do not come see me. If Dr Daae had addressed himself

---

[20] Dunant to Müller, 22–4 October 1898, BGE, Ms. fr. 5203, f. 57.
[21] Dunant to Müller, 26 November 1898, BGE, Ms. fr. 5203, f. 75.

to someone else instead, these horrible people from here would do anything to denigrate and slander me.[22]

Hidden behind his shutters on the second floor, Dunant was making sure his visitors were spared any malicious assaults from his enemies or their agents. Above anyone else, it was vital that Captain Daae heard no spiteful gossip. That afternoon in November, while Dunant watched the captain's tall shadow melt into the fog, the Nobel Prize took its first decisive step towards a little town in the Swiss canton of Appenzell.

In formation

By the end of 1898, the events were lining up as if all the seeds sown over the last few years had begun to sprout at the same time. Over the summer, the young tsar of Russia Nicholas II had launched a proposal for an international diplomatic conference in favour of arms control, soliciting much enthusiasm from the pacifists but not the military powers. Utterly delighted, Bertha von Suttner wrote to Dunant to celebrate 'this sublime news',[23] news which Dunant immediately jumped upon as an occasion to centre himself, as publicly as possible and at the highest level, within pacifist ranks. Uniting his experience from the Red Cross of 1863, the Geneva Convention of 1864, the theses on arbitration and mediation he'd developed between 1871 and 1873, lessons learned from the Brussels conference failure in 1874 and even some of his apocalyptic interpretations, Dunant wrote a robust commentary on Russia's disarmament proposal, which he soberly entitled, '*La proposition de Sa Majesté l'Empereur Nicolas II*' (The Proposal of His Majesty Emperor Nicolas II). His text pleaded for a permanent institution for regulating conflicts, through arbitration, mediation and disarmament. The *Deutsche Revue* published his article in German in January 1899; by early March, Dunant and Müller had run out of the thousand copies they'd published separately for their own personal correspondence. A French edition followed, which Dunant

---

[22] Dunant to Müller, 26 November 1898, BGE, Ms. fr. 5203, f. 75.
[23] Suttner to Dunant, 7 September 1898, BGE, Ms. fr. 2112, f. 140.

arranged to be distributed to all the delegates to the international congress in The Hague, which opened in May 1899 to address the tsar's innovative proposals.

Much to the disappointment of the pacifists, and Bertha von Suttner most of all, a part of the conference in The Hague was also dealing with the Geneva Convention. The idea was to adapt its clauses to maritime wars, a subject which Empress Eugénie had already been looking at in 1867 when she invited Henry Dunant to the Tuileries, and which still had not been dealt with. Fearing that the legislation of war would only relegate peace to a lower level, Bertha von Suttner turned towards Heiden a few days before the conference was set to open: she asked Dunant to come out of the woods, to make a clear choice between the Red Cross and pacifism.

> All soldiers, statesmen and governments who aren't interested in discussing how to end war all line up behind the Red Cross and the Geneva Convention to clutter up the conference in The Hague [. . .] These gentlemen must be told that the people expect much more and that the founder of the Red Cross himself, who is in step with the times, also expects more.

And how did our imperious baroness insist Dunant prove his loyalty? Via open letter signed by the promoter of the Geneva Convention clearly asserting the priority of peace policies over legislating war. [24]

Dunant did as she requested: he could not do otherwise. But he wrote his open letter in such a way that he did not disqualify the actions of the Red Cross nor diminish the importance of the Geneva Convention. Instead of discussing either, he calmly repeated what he had said in his article: he pleaded in favour of a permanent office of mediation and arbitration.

Bertha von Suttner published Dunant's letter. But she had certainly wished for something stronger. Dunant's sidestepping may have been a factor in her decision later to support the founder of the International and Permanent League for Peace, Frédéric Passy, for the first Nobel Peace Prize. No matter her respect for Dunant, she would go on thinking that the French candidate, with his uncompromising pacifism, was the better recipient of a prize for peace.

---

[24] Suttner to Dunant, 9 May 1899, BGE, Ms. fr. 2112, f. 145.

For Dunant, however, the publication of his letter in the conference's daily newsletter further added to his visibility in The Hague, whose delegates would adopt two of his steadily defended principles: the extension of the Geneva Convention to maritime conflicts and the institution of a permanent – but not mandatory – tribunal for arbitration and mediation. When The Boer War erupted in South Africa shortly after the conference closed, Dunant would publicly get right back into the saddle regarding arbitration and mediation, not only through the press but in a highly documented report addressed to the captain of the Norwegian army, Hans Daae. Although confined to his hospital room, he remained in the international scene.

Leaving nothing to chance, Dunant also undertook a systematic verification of dictionaries and terminologies, continually offended to find his name wasn't always listed under the letter *D*. Loathe to claim for himself the honours he felt were his, he allowed his friend Rudolf to write to Larousse, Vapereau, Sax, Kurchner and other dictionaries of the time to require they insert his name and achievements.

The news coming from Norway was increasingly cheerful. In January 1899, Captain Daae published a long article in a Norwegian newspaper about his visit to Heiden, in which he concluded that the Nobel Peace Prize should definitely go to Dunant. In March, Dunant was named an honorary member of the Norwegian Society of Military Medicine, a title which Captain Daae assured him had never been given to anyone else. In April, Daae wrote to Müller with the news that a Norwegian newspaper had estimated that the Nobel Prize would be 'too weak a reward'[25] for Dunant. And in June, finally, Hans Daae published a little pamphlet on Henry Dunant, hoping this would get him a title of honorary member of the Norwegian Red Cross. Public opinion, in Norway at least, was nearly in the bag – even if it had no ultimate say when it came to the Nobel.

Surprises of translation

Everything would have been going better if Dunant's psychological fragility didn't spoil the upswing of his success. Among his most faithful supporters, the young and enthusiastic Christian Haje from

---

[25] Müller to Dunant, 26 April 1899, BGE, Ms. fr. 2112, f. 80.

Amsterdam had just spent two years completing the Dutch translation of Müller's (that is, Dunant's) book, a project which was obviously a delight for the author ever greedy for new publications about him. As the idea of the Nobel Prize had become more real over this period of time, Dunant felt it would be a good idea for Haje's book to include some more up-to-date information, like his recent commentary on the tsar's disarmament proposals. Encouraged by these additions, Haje then modified another two or three little things which Dunant, at first, considered a good idea. 'There's no harm in Mr Haje making an original work,' he wrote to Müller, who was probably shocked at the liberties the younger translator had taken with his book. 'It is good that in three or four languages there are some special publications, done with the right intentions, meaning truthful.'[26]

At the beginning of 1899, Dunant exhausted himself finishing up his article on Nicolas II. This was in January, when Mrs Kastner's death always returned to haunt him, he was morose and unhappy, both his heart and chest bothering him. Mr Haje's book arrived at this moment. It was very pretty: Dunant had insisted to Mr Graeter – a decidedly benevolent foundation cashier – not to scrimp on the costs of the binding, nor the forecasted print run of 1,000 copies. Extremely content, Dunant flipped through the book which he could read without too much trouble since, as we know, he was the author of the original text. With horror, he discovered that the young Dutchman had included two disastrous personal touches: a derogatory comment about one of the members of the International Committee of the Red Cross, and another about Parisians.

And off it went. Three months of suffering, of complaining, of threats that the situation would kill him. Three months arguing with Haje who didn't want anything to slow down the book's distribution, certainly not for two unfortunate sentences which he stubbornly claimed were fine. The discussion grew complicated because Dunant agreed entirely with Haje's sentences, but felt they were misguided, compromising and suicidal 'in this Norwegian moment'[27] – referring, of course, to the Nobel project. Unable to handle conflict anymore, all of Henry's strikes came muffled in kid gloves with Müller as an

---

[26] Dunant to Müller, 8 November 1898, BGE, Ms. fr. 5203, f. 70.
[27] Dunant to Müller, 12 January 1899, BGE, Ms. fr. 5203, f. 97.

intermediary. Haje held fast for several weeks, throughout which Dunant convinced himself the Dutchman had been put up to it by his enemies: 'These people truly thought the hot-headed young man would make some blunder in his text, which they intend to use to attack me.'[28] His demons were jumping so far out of their box they were clouding Dunant's foresight. But eventually the conflict was resolved: Haje would remove the two sentences, the two incriminating pages would be replaced, and the book could be redistributed, although the price of printing had now markedly increased.

After having cursed him left and right, Dunant now softened his tone towards Christian Haje. And moving from one extreme to the other, it even seems that for several months, the young man unseated Rudolf Müller from the topmost chair in Dunant's emotional pantheon. The letters for Stuttgart slowed as the letters for Amsterdam increased, grew longer and more confiding and intimate, paternal, opening with 'my dear and excellent friend', a greeting that no one else, not even Müller, had ever received. Like he had with Müller twenty years earlier, Dunant began inundating his young friend with advice on life, human relationships, social behaviours to follow or avoid, interspersed with the usual reports of his enemies' evil doings. The reconciliation was so spectacular that by the year's end they were busily establishing a new collaborative project: Haje would create a small volume in French from his book, in cooperation with one of his friends who lived in Orleans. Nothing could be better timed: up to this point France had been left out of Dunant's European resurrection, because he was lacking support from Paris's Red Cross circles. But it was now time to call upon France's good memories, which an unexpected event suddenly made possible: the Norwegian parliament decided to delay the Noble Peace Prize for one year, giving Dunant and his faithful a few extra months to spread his renown across all of Europe.

Return to the world

'The Storting resolution has not bothered me too much,' Dunant wrote to Müller in December 1899 after a silence of more than

---

[28] Dunant to Müller, 14–15 January 1899, BGE, Ms. fr. 5203, f. 106, 'Notes (Haje)'.

three months. 'At the same time, the Dreyfus affair has held me in daily suspense.'[29] His hope for a Nobel Prize had not only reawakened his need for recognition and his extraordinary communicative talents. It also awakened the best of him – his concern for human suffering, philanthropic intelligence, diplomatic sense and compassion. Long-time obstacle to his openness to the world, his personal misfortunes were now feeding his empathy. Beginning in 1897, Dunant had been passionately following the Dreyfus affair – not only because the injustice scandalized him, but because he recognized in the French military administration the tribe of malefactors who had persecuted him from 1870 to 1880. In April 1899, he was just as disgusted: 'You must surely be enlightened on the falseness of these people among the high command, on their vileness and baseness, their odious trickery,' he wrote to Rudolf. 'These were the very same people that turned everyone in London and on the continent against me and against the widow Kastner-Boursault.'[30] Six months later, the Boer War would upset him again, this time reinforcing his horror of all forms of fanaticism, and against Pietists in particular: 'It is an odious war, and these pietists are setting a frightening example on both sides.'[31]

The egocentrism of his last years would also crack in his personal relationships, enabling some real expressions of recognition – a welcome change following the amount of devotion he'd received. Several months earlier he had obtained – on his own initiative – an honorific distinction called *The Olga Orden* for Rudolf Müller and Adolf Graeter from the king of Württemberg. More recently, he showed sincere interest in a professional disappointment of Rudolf's, taking it to heart in a way he hadn't done so before. This was very out of step with the polite indifference he usually showed for his friend's private worries, other than his health. And for Graeter, he moved heaven and earth to help him get a title of Commerce Advisor to the King. Finally, in the spring of 1900, a small sentence appeared at the bottom of a letter to Rudolf Müller, surprising at first for its brevity: 'Death of Idelson: it's a loss.'[32] That's it? Nothing more for

---

[29] Dunant to Müller, 21 December 1899, BGE, Ms. fr. 5203, f. 163.

[30] Dunant to Müller, 8–11 April 1899, BGE, Ms. fr. 5203, f. 136.

[31] Dunant to Müller, 26 December 1899, BGE, Ms. fr. 5203, f. 165–6.

[32] Dunant to Müller, 5 May 1900, BGE, Ms. fr. 5203, f. 179–80.

a man he owed not only the return of his material comfort – the stipend from the tsar's mother had partly come through him – but who had been tirelessly devoted to the entire sweep of Dunant's causes, from peace in the Middle East to the Green Cross? But no: over the next few weeks, Dunant would show how extremely affected he was by this loss, to the point that he found it difficult to work. And although he'd never met the man, he wrote a lovely tribute to him a few weeks later in *L'Étranger*. Seeing his dear ones up-close still frightened him, but he was finally recognizing – from a distance – the exceptional scope of their devotion to him.

The last hour

As the new century opened, the pressure imperceptibly increased. The key to the whole situation was held by Hans Daae, but, as we already know, northerners shouldn't be jostled along. How to encourage him to take action without rubbing his integrity the wrong way? How to make him understand, without offending him, that all his expenses in favour of the cause would be reimbursed? For Dunant certainly wanted to make him his representative in Norway, but he could not decently ask him outright: 'I must be very tactful with him,' he wrote to Müller, 'because he is a man with much heart and he's not a businessman.'[33] For lack of a common language, Rudolf was an indispensable courier between Dunant and Daae, and so Dunant's correspondence was increasing again in the direction of Stuttgart. The professor hadn't overlooked his friend's extended silence while Dunant was so focused on Haje, and he couldn't stop himself from commenting on it. But this was no time for quarrelling: without Müller's obliging mediation, there was no Daae, and without Daae, there would be no Nobel. Henry stammered through his apologies and the incident was closed.

As if overtaken by a last-minute panic, Dunant began to worry that the mountain of documentation the Norwegian jurors were already buried beneath wouldn't be enough to make their choice. What if some of them didn't know German, but only French? Dunant was impatient for Christian Haje's French version to be

---

[33] Dunant to Müller, 18–19 May 1900, BGE, Ms. fr. 5203, f. 185–6.

finished, to which he'd already decided to add the ever-important 'Appendix' of compliments along with a new French edition of *A Memory of Solferino*. What good was the foundation's money, he explained to Müller, if he could not see 'a detailed *French* booklet'[34] published *in his lifetime*? He held fast to this idea like it was his final supper, in case he missed out on the Nobel: to be able to read about himself again in his own language, to be able to rediscover his own words in the only form fitting and for which they'd been written: published in black and white.

Rudolf agreed to everything. To save time, Haje's book would be published in French in Stuttgart, which meant Rudolf could check the final proofs and Graeter would pay the bills. Dunant was reassured, delighted, grateful. Soon he would have something new to drop over Norway, that Daae would hopefully translate in part for the journalists and, why not, for the parliamentarians as well.

But was there still time to influence opinion? Mightn't it be better to directly attack the true arbiters of the prize – the members of the Nobel Committee? In late 1898, after meeting Dr Hans Daae and in agreement with him, Rudolf Müller had already addressed himself to one of the best-known members of the committee, the poet Bjørnstjerne Bjørnson, whose response had been as friendly as it was discouraging. According to the regulations stipulated by Alfred Nobel, he explained, the prize Dunant was aiming for could only be given to a person who 'had brought the greatest contribution to peace during the previous year' and who, additionally, had worked *directly* for this cause.[35] Müller was careful not to transmit this response to his friend Henry who at the time was very busy writing his comments on Tsar Nicolas II's disarmament proposals: the news would have needlessly upset him. Furthermore, because the awarding of the prize had been delayed for a year, Müller could let some time pass in order to solicit Bjørnson a second time later on. Which is what he decided to do in the summer of 1900, this time with Dunant's knowledge.

---

[34] Dunant to Müller, 8 June 1900, BGE, Ms. fr. 5203, f. 192–3.
[35] Bjørnstjerne Bjørnson to Müller, 27 November 1898, cited and facsimile in Hans Amann, *De l'anonymat à la gloire, Henry Dunant et sa longue marche vers le Prix Nobel* (Heiden: Henry-Dunant-Museum, no date), 21–3.

In July, Müller sent Bjørnson a first long letter summarizing Dunant's work in general terms and announced a second letter would be coming the next month. Dunant gave Müller his primary materials but allowed him all the space he needed to put it together in the best way. Bjornson's response this time was already more encouraging:

Sir,
    I have just read your excellent letter and I'm looking forward to the second half. I will send both along to my colleagues. If Mr Dunant cannot have the first prize, there is one every year. I hope to see him rewarded.

And addressing himself to Müller, he added with great intuition: 'I admire your fine diligence.'[36]

It was admirable indeed. Having had to shorten his Tyrolean holidays because of a hurt foot, Müller took advantage of his early return, in August, to pick up his battle where he'd left it. A second mailing, this time much thicker than the first, left three days later for Christiania. While Rudolf had been resting in the Tyrol, Dunant had had time to sharpen his arguments against his hardline pacifist competitors, especially Frédéric Passy. His argument was simple: everything he'd accomplished in his life had been meant for no other goal but peace, yet via personal pathways, novel routes and progressive stages. Contrary to his competitors, he did not decry war, but had preferred to allow his book, A Memory of Solferino, to effectively demonstrate its horrors. The Universal Alliance, with all its chapters, subchapters, congresses, successful and failed conferences, had nonetheless paved the way for international arbitration and international mediation, to social peace between men, to the end of slavery.

For two months, Dunant worked tirelessly, sending new arguments to Müller every day to have him send them on to Bjørnson and his colleagues. By an unexpected stroke of luck, the Norwegian poet fell ill at the end of the summer, which prevented him from going to the Peace Congress in Paris he'd wanted to

---

[36] Bjørnstjerne Bjørnson to Müller, 9 August 1900, transmitted by Müller to Dunant, 17 August 1900, BGE, Ms. fr. 2112, f. 87.

attend. Since Bjørnson was known to be leaning towards France's Passy, this would have given the French an opportunity to gleefully destroy all of Müller's carefully constructed scaffolding in favour of Dunant. Instead, he remained at his farm in Aulestad to rest and received nineteen large-format new pages from Rudolf Müller, accompanied by twenty-one supporting documents. Forty years of Dunant's life distilled through a single lens: the goal of peace, endlessly pursued by our battlefield Samaritan.

Two visits

When the head nurse knocked at Dunant's door one afternoon in September 1900, the old hermit immediately guessed that something was up. There wasn't even enough time to invite her in; she was already standing in the middle of the room.

'It's the Archduchess!' she said. 'With her daughters! She's come all the way from Bavaria to see you!'

By now Sister Elise was very skilled at sending Mr Dunant's visitors away without consulting him, as he had stated he wanted none, no matter who they were. But this time, the ladies were so charming, so numerous, so elegant . . .

Dunant could not seem to decide to say no. Or yes. He seemed utterly perplexed.

'Bring her here, thank you. *Only* Madame. Yes, that's it, only the Archduchess.'

In real life, the Archduchess looked much less like Léonie Kastner than the photo she'd sent Dunant two years earlier. And yet, no other visitor could have overwhelmed Henry more since he'd moved to Heiden than Maria-Theresa de Modena, daughter of the East Austrian archduke and wife of the future Louis III of Bavaria. To have her witness the poverty of his room, the rustic furniture, the sad little teapot where he made his own tea and coffee, the almost unusable floor because of his piles of books and papers, to see this unresolvable disorder through her eyes, just to hear the rustling of her silk skirts over the floor, and her deliciously serious but playful French, to have her beside him, arranging his pillows for him, taking his hand and expressing her admiration for him . . . he was seized with such painful heart contractions that he felt almost compelled to send her away; but she was already almost at the door, graciously sparing him from all awkwardness. Before her final goodbye, she asked only to take his photo, not worrying over his hat nor the blanket covering his knees. Then she was gone in the same manner as she'd arrived, a whirlwind spinning in and out from another world, leaving the old man behind her in a million pieces.[37]

The timing could not have been worse. In the middle of writing his argument for the Nobel jury, right at the very moment his room was completely dishevelled by his papers! To make things worse, the proofs of Haje and Simon's book had arrived at the same time as if everything was conspiring to keep him from his work – both his pacifist biography for Bjørnson, and the little French volume he was so focused on. The Archduchess's visit on top of all this: how on earth would his fragile health and delicate heart handle it all? The autumn of 1900 made Henry Dunant feel as though he'd aged ten years. The slightest effort gave him pains from his head down into his arms, forcing him to stop working and keep still. He could only work during daylight hours, which were growing shorter each day. How could he keep this pace up for another year if, as Bjørnson was implying, the first Nobel might pass him by?

Well, his foot soldiers were certainly not planning on giving up. On 1st December 1900, Dr Daae visited Mr and Mrs Bjørnson. Following customary small talk and tea, the poet confirmed to the captain what he was afraid of: Bjørnson was holding out for his friend Frédéric Passy and was considering Dunant more for the second Peace Prize laureate, in 1902.

Upon hearing this, Mrs Bjørnson spoke, turning towards Dr Daae, but with a strange smile that made it seem she was truly addressing her husband:

> What luck, dear sir, that you have taken the trouble to come see us. Because you and I, we are fighting the same cause. I have told my husband several times: this Passy is quite good, but it's Mr Dunant who deserves the prize! And if you don't want to give it to Mr Dunant on his own, then well, you should give it to both of them![38]

---

[37] Dunant tells all about this visit first to Müller, 15 September 1900, BGE Ms. fr. 5203, f. 255 and to his brother Pierre three months later, 10 December 1900, BGE, Ms. fr. 2115 C, f. 126.

[38] Müller quotes Daae's letter about his visit to Bjørnson and what Mrs Bjørnson had told him. Müller to Dunant, 6 December 1900 BGE, Ms. fr. 2112, f. 91.

Leaving the Bjørnsons that evening, the good captain blessed the man for having chosen such a good wife. If he hadn't yet succumbed to her arguments, no doubt he would soon. That very evening, the captain wrote to Müller to recount that day's small triumph: at least half the Nobel Prize seemed to be within reach.

A few days later in Heiden, Müller's detailed summary of Dr Daae's mission threw Dunant into disarray. With his academic rigour, Rudolf could not have made their options any clearer:

1 continue to work towards the first prize for Dunant alone, something which Passy's favourable candidature made 'almost impossible';

2 accept that the prize be split in two, with the inconvenience of a reduced sum;

3 renounce work on the 1901 prize in favour of the entire prize in 1902.[39]

Dunant hadn't touched his meal since Sister Elise had left it for him with his mail. He needed to speak with someone! Why didn't Dr Altherr ever come to see him?

Struggling, he made his way from the sofa to his table. Being so unused to exercise, his legs were no longer trustworthy: they could get him from his bed to his window, or from his couch to his desk – that was it.

The letter he composed that day, 10th December 1900, with his life hanging in the balance, was to his brother Pierre. A heartbreaking letter in which his creditor worries returned in full force, pulling him by his hair back to the battlefield of his regrets.

'How can I reply? – If I did not have this mass of debt, I would be more than happy to share with Mr Passy.' Then, after a long detour revisiting previous misfortunes, he ended with this sombre note: 'Will I still be alive in December of 1902? That would be two full years [from now] [. . .] What shall I do? *That is the question.*' [40]

This final, vital reason – time – is what would win over his remaining reservations. Before the year was out, Henry Dunant

---

[39] Müller to Dunant, 6 December 1900 BGE, Ms. fr. 2112, f. 91.
[40] Dunant to his brother Pierre, 10 December 1900, BGE, Ms. fr. 2115 C, f. 126. The last sentence is in English.

readied himself to share the Nobel Peace Prize rather than run the risk of dying before it came around again. Since the Archduchess's visit, his chest pains sometimes lasted for several days. And so he resigned himself: 'The sooner, the better.'[41]

On 1st February 1901, thirteen candidates were in the running for the very first Nobel Peace Prize, meant to be awarded the following December. Frédéric Passy was still Bjørnson's favourite, and had the support from the peace societies, too. Two other Swiss pacifists were also being considered: Elie Ducommun and Albert Gobat, long-time activists and members of the International Office for Peace.

The dossiers had been submitted; all that remained was for the candidates to encourage as many recommendations as possible from various groups and organizations, who had until 31st March to make their preference known. Dunant's entourage got to work for a last push: Müller solicited the Württemberg deputies, Haje alerted the Dutch universities, Princess Wiszniewska pushed the female circles – so much so that letters of support for Dunant's candidacy rained down over Christiana. At this point, Dunant knew he could no longer change the course of events. Without missing a beat, he jumped onto another project in case the Nobel didn't come: another funding drive in his favour, either Norwegian, American, international, it didn't matter. An obsession for moral recognition *as* founder of the Red Cross was now replaced with an obsession for financial recognition *to* the founder of the Red Cross.

Rumours ran wild during that year of 1901. On 30th March, Dunant was astonished to read in the *Journal de Genève* that the *Swedish* parliament had supposedly awarded half of the Nobel Prize to the Central Peace Office in Berne and the other half to Frédéric Passy and the British William Randal Cremer. But he was so focused on his funding idea – at that moment in the US, Carnegie was handing out his millions and Dunant was optimistic about catching a few crumbs – that he barely commented on this unfavourable outcome: 'I am neither surprised nor even upset,' he wrote that very evening to Müller. In October the *Journal de Genève* announced that Mr Dunant had been 'proposed by 37 votes' and that Passy was just behind. In fact, these votes corresponded to the

---

[41] Dunant to Müller, 14 December 1900, BGE, Ms. fr. 5203, f. 331.

societies, groups and other authorities who had recommended a particular candidate to the Nobel Committee; Dunant had received the most support. While the Nobel Committee maintained a wall of silence, Dunant was already receiving congratulations from every direction, which gave him a taste of the ambiguous joy that was awaiting him: 'I am certainly very happy,' he admitted to Müller on 29th October; 'but my enemies, my creditors are on alert. And there are still about forty days.'[42]

But the rumours continued: on 4th December, another press release named Dunant the winner. Finally, on 10th December, 1901, five years to the day of Alfred Nobel's death, a telegram arrived in Heiden from Christiania. The text was brief; it was written in French.

It is the honour of the Nobel Committee of the Norwegian Parliament to inform you that it has awarded the 1901 Nobel Peace Prize to Mr Henry Dunant and Mr Frédéric Passy, one half to each, an approximate amount of 100,000 francs.[43]

Unusually, Sister Elise remained in the room while Dunant silently read the telegram. Then he read it again aloud, for her. The nurse wrung her hands while Dunant kept silent. 'We must tell Dr Altherr,' the head nurse said, just to say something.

The true price of the Nobel Prize

75,391 crowns, representing about 104,000 Swiss francs.

Considering the life Dunant had been leading for the last thirty-four years, at 1,200 francs a year, this was obviously a colossal sum. But it didn't even cover a fifth, or not even a tenth, of the debts he'd left behind him.

From the moment they'd launched their campaign, Rudolf Müller and Hans Daae had been preoccupied with the unresolvable problem of what to do with their candidate's debts should a lot of money come to him. On his side, Dunant was imagining all sorts

---

[42] Dunant to Müller, 29 October 1901, BGE, Ms. fr. 5204, f. 105.
[43] 10 December 1901, BGE, Ms. fr. 5204, f. 127 (copy by Henry Dunant).

of possible scenarios, but with so much hesitation that on 10th December 1901, no satisfactory solution had been adopted, to the greatest despair of the interested party. 'I so wanted all this to be decided ahead of time!' he lamented to Rudolf three days after the telegram.[44]

First, they needed to put the initial fire out: write to the Nobel Committee asking them to do nothing yet. But they seemed in a rush to give him the prize! Dunant began feeling oppressed and overwhelmed by the events. His first thought was to have the money transferred to Stuttgart: he sent Rudolf off to find a 'solid' bank. Once Rudolf found what he'd asked, he changed his mind: 'Now that I've thought about it, a State bank in Christiania would be better, because I've always wanted to go there to finish out my days.'[45]

Here was a bit of news! Dunant wanted to die in Norway now? Indeed, from the very day he'd been awarded the prize, he'd had one thing and only one thing in mind: become an honorary bourgeois of the city of Christiania. Between 16th and 18th December, he wrote twice to Daae with this idea, and promised he would come to thank him in person, accompanied by Dr Altherr. A man who hadn't even ventured to the first floor of his hospital in eight years? Had he suddenly lost his mind?

The end of December saw him begging Rudolf to 'come up with a small plan' to accomplish this new whim, which he was now pretending to care as much about as he had the Nobel Prize. Luckily for Rudolf, he wouldn't have enough time to start working. While Dunant was planning every detail of this new programme, a letter from Dr Daae was already en route for Heiden. Pragmatic, the captain politely swept away Dunant's request in a single paragraph: this title of 'honorary bourgeois' didn't exist in Christiania because it 'does not grant' local rights, and such a campaign would only lower Dunant in the eyes of the Norwegian people. In conclusion, Daae closed the discussion by asking Dunant 'not to think of it anymore'.[46] Exit Christiania.

What was Dunant hoping for with this idea of bourgeoisie? Was he seriously thinking of packing his bags and heading north? Might

[44] Dunant to Müller, 13 December 1901, BGE, Ms. fr. 5204, f. 128.
[45] Dunant to Müller, 17 December 1901, BGE, Ms. fr. 5204, f. 131.
[46] Dr Daae to Dunant, 30 December 1901, BGE, Ms. fr. 2112, f. 229.

we consider this in light of the fact that in Norway donations were unseizable, a law our bankrupt former entrepreneur had only just discovered?

It is very likely Dunant was convinced he could only fully enjoy his award in Norway. As one would expect, the fear of his creditors spoiled any excitement he might have had about winning the Nobel Prize. After much umming and ahhing, it was decided that the sum would be left in Christiania, under the watchful eye of Dr Daae; Dr Altherr, partly at the request of the laureate, had sent the Norwegian captain the necessary documents to transfer over responsibility. 'In terms of money,' Dr Altherr wrote on Christmas Day to his colleague, 'Mr Dunant has remained a child, and I am not far from thinking he would let it all slip through his fingers, God knows where. It is, thus, essential that you retain control.'[47]

Shortly after the Nobel was announced, a wire from Copenhagen asserted that Dunant's creditors had despatched a lawyer to Sweden to seize the prize. The sum, already on its way to Switzerland, would be returned to Stockholm immediately. But while this cable was being reprinted in the European press, a new article appeared in the *Dagblader*, a Norwegian newspaper, reporting it a hoax; with this 180-degree about-turn the press was now united in defending the laureate and his loot.

Curiously, much of this uproar did not reach Dunant. Having hoped, just a few months earlier, to win the prize in order to refund his creditors, he now felt that the Nobel Prize award should not go to them at all. The argument with which he persuaded himself, and all his nearest and dearest, was focused on the horde of creditors: whom should he serve first? Those who had remained silent, or those who had hurt him so much? Or should he distribute a little bit in all directions? Also, he no longer knew exactly how much he owed nor what rights his creditors had: how could he even begin to reimburse them?

To make things worse, in early 1902, Dunant was so traumatized by another issue that the fallout from the Nobel Prize went on the back-burner. During his Christmas visit to congratulate him for the

---

[47] Dr Altherr to Dr Daae, 25 December 1901, cited in Amann, *De l'anonymat à la gloire*, 30.

Nobel, Dr Altherr had inadvertently upset him. The story goes like this: sometime in 1895, the president of the Swiss Red Cross, Dr Staehelin, had promised Dunant a monthly stipend from that society. So as not to feel too indebted to the Red Cross, Dunant had asked Dr Altherr at the time to deposit the money in a Heiden bank and never mention it again. When Dunant casually asked the doctor, now seven years later in 1902, for an account of the small treasure he believed had been steadily growing over all this time, Dr Altherr informed him that the treasure hadn't increased by a single penny. Once the dowager empress of Russia had decided in February 1897 to give him an annuity, the Swiss Red Cross had judged this was enough, and had not raised a finger to find him any other resources, not in Switzerland nor in any other European Red Cross, contrary to what Dunant had believed all along.

Nothing from over the last fifteen years had shocked him as much as this little piece of news. 'This was so unexpected,' he wrote to Müller in early 1902, 'that for the last three weeks, I haven't been eating at all.'

Hadn't Bertha von Suttner called the Red Crosses 'ungrateful daughters'? Clearly she was right! Dunant could not forgive them. 'The duty – truly, yes, the duty of the Red Crosses, of all countries, shouldn't it have been to head up a general funding drive in each country?' he lamented again to Müller. 'Everything else seems very small compared to this iniquity. Iniquity is exactly the word.'[48]

But what did Dunant want exactly? He didn't even know himself. Since receiving the annuity from Russia, he'd been telling everyone he no longer needed anything. He'd also been claiming for several years that the money from the Red Cross shouldn't serve to honour its founder but to help wounded soldiers. At the same time, he resented his 'ungrateful daughters' for not throwing their millions at his feet, while he spent his time figuring out how to get them anyway – one buck per Samaritan, a universal funding drive, a gift from the world's pacifists, a monumental donation from Carnegie or Krupp, an appeal to 5 million women united in favour of disarmament, national collections in all countries, anything big, anything grand, but something! He obsessed day and night over the

---

[48] Dunant to Müller, 14 January 1902, BGE, Ms. fr. 5204, f. 142–4.

1.25 million francs[49] offered to Florence Nightingale (who was already rich!); only something of this scale could appease him and enable him, he continued to claim, to reimburse his debts.

Between 1901 and 1908, Dunant would continue to both secure his 100,000-Swiss-franc Nobel Prize money against the claims of his creditors and seek out the millions needed to reimburse them. But he was still stuck on the same psychological block he'd been stuck on since 1867: only an astronomical sum would enable him to pay back what he owed – a sum so large he could never obtain it, which meant he was actually free from his obligation. He would continue, even after the Nobel Prize and up until his death, hunting out the lottery ticket for the magic million he needed. 'You understand I will never give in,' he wrote to Müller about his creditors a month after obtaining the Nobel. 'And you know that my greatest desire is to pay my debt,' he continued, unaware of the paradox, 'that I have lived for that, overcoming everything in a vague hope, that has kept me going.'[50] This was a perfect summary of the problem at hand: he would never yield to his creditors, but maintained a 'vague hope' of reimbursing them.

Growing old and seeing death

Dying of old age involves witnessing a lot of death. Henry Dunant was no exception, despite his constant worries over the state of his own health. This macabre parade included both friends and enemies.

His old friend Ernest de Traz led the way, departing quietly in early 1900. After thirty years of silence, following the press uproar of 1895, Dunant's former comrade had obtained his address and written him in 1896, delighted at such a reunion. Henry's only reply was to send him his booklets and newspapers. Without a personal note. As if Geneva's curse had even tainted his childhood friendships, as if all these years of suffering forbade any softening gaze over his earlier years. Henry didn't weep for his friend's passing, believing he would soon follow.

---

[49] Dunant, *Mémoires*, 338. In fact, Queen Victoria gave her an award of £250,000 in recognition of her work.
[50] Dunant to Müller, 16 January 1902, BGE, Ms. fr. 5204, f. 151.

The indispensable Idelson departed that same year, while Dunant experienced his first chest pains. His associate Max Grazia from the Universal Library returned from oblivion only to then die in 1901, while Henry was fighting his congestion. His former ally turned enemy, Hermann Scholder-Develay, died of apoplexy in 1901, after losing his mind, while Dunant was suffering from a throat inflammation that made swallowing very difficult. Baron von Suttner passed away quietly at a congress in Monaco with his spouse in 1902, the year Max Perrot stopped haunting Dunant's nightmares, while the latter was experiencing strong pains on his left side. In the summer of that same year, his nephew Émile, 'literary hope of the family', died in the mountains at the age of 30, upsetting his uncle so much he could eat nothing but soup and boiled chestnuts. Princess Wiszniewska said her goodbyes to the pacifist circles in 1904, just as the *Daily Mail* and a series of French newspapers were claiming that Henry Dunant 'was dying'. That same year, Wilhelm Sonderegger left the hell to which Dunant had no doubt sent him and headed off to paradise; Daniel Dunant, his brother and unfortunate partner, passed away shortly after, in November, just when Henry started complaining of 'prostration' and 'general inflammation, endless fatigue and impossibility of handling the slightest contradiction'. The eczema on his right hand that had sent him on the rounds of the spa towns for years and years had completely disappeared with chamomile baths but had moved upward to his limbs with extra violence in 1906. The same year saw the death of Johann Pfister, twenty years younger than Dunant.

Was this his fountain of youth? Despite his sorrows, despite his illnesses, despite the general weakening that often prevented him from writing several days in a row, Dunant gathered all his remaining faculties for a last obsession: a large international fund in recognition of humanity's benefactor – himself. The publication of a small history of the Red Cross in English and several letters exchanged with Clara Barton, the founder of the American Red Cross, convinced him that this recognition would come from the other side of the Atlantic, an objective he seized upon during the spring of 1905. But the millions of dollars would never come – contrary to what he believed, America felt no obligation of a 'debt of honour' in his favour.

March 1906 saw the birth of a new hope. The head surgeon of the Swiss army, Colonel Mürset, who was also the Swiss government's delegate to the next conference to revise the Geneva Convention, honoured Dunant with a small visit. Writing to Rudolf that very evening of the 'great joy' he'd experienced, Dunant added: 'He thinks it's the right time to launch the worldwide funding drive which the late Dr Idelson had been focused on. He is passionate about it and has promised he will organize everything for Switzerland. He is indignant against my enemies. And told me, spontaneously, that I can count entirely on him.'[51]

When the abovementioned conference ended, in the early summer of 1906, Dunant seemed much less interested in the revision of the Convention he considered 'his Work' and more so in his new project for an international funding drive. 'The new Convention was signed on 6th July and it has thirty-two articles! It's much too much!' was all he said to Müller in mid-July. However, the same letter went on and on about the numerous kind messages sent from the Geneva delegates, and about their support for a worldwide collection. Captain Daae, present in Geneva, had even 'completely won over' the American delegate – 'the billionaires will follow the Royalties',[52] asserted the future beneficiary in a knowing tone.

But in the autumn of 1906, his euphoria vanished. On the Swiss side, the restorative desires of Colonel Mürset seemed to have decidedly cooled – gossiping tongues must have managed to dissuade him. As well as this, Hans Daae's lobbying with the American representative hadn't produced its desired effect. In Norway, on the other hand, the captain was very successful: he had encouraged his fellow citizens to gather money for the Dunant Foundation, which they were doing with a touching diligence. And so, after a year of various attempts to raise funds, Captain Daae was happy to inform Dunant that the ladies had gathered 35,000 francs. To which good Norwegian charity, Daae asked innocently, did Dunant want to send these funds?

Poor Dunant! The reality of his aura as benefactor finally struck him full force, like a firework hidden inside a sweet: Daae had not guessed that *he* was the intended recipient of all these noble foundations, fundraising and charitable collections. 'And so I must

---

[51] Dunant to Müller, 12 March 1906, BGE, Ms. fr. 5205, f. 35.
[52] Dunant to Müller, 14 July 1906, BGE, Ms. fr. 5205, f. 65–6.

turn to another group,' he wrote, pitiful, to Müller in early 1908; 'and so I thought of the Samaritans.'[53]

Up until the very end, Henry Dunant would envy the large reward given to Florence Nightingale after the Crimean War. And up until the end, he would be disappointed by any other honour he'd received. In 1902, the international conference of Red Cross Societies in St Petersburg had sent word of their congratulations to him; in 1903, the University of Heidelberg had awarded him an honorary doctorate; during the Geneva conference of 1906, he received testimonials of sympathy from all directions; finally, in May 1908, his 80th birthday saw an avalanche of accolades from around the entire world, which he still had enough strength to read and carefully tuck away for safekeeping. The first to write to him was the Queen Consort of Bavaria, the same Maria-Theresa of Modena, Archduchess of East Austria, who, by her resemblance to Léonie Kastner, had found a special place in his heart.

The others would follow: the entire Russian imperial family, King Haakon of Norway, the princess of Schleswig-Holstein, Prince Carl of Sweden and the entire Swiss Federal Council. Bertha von Sutter also wrote, to which Dunant sent this unbelievable response: 'People's eyes are starting to open about me.'[54]

The ultimate rival

Dunant would never get the international tribute he so coveted. In 1909, like a kind of ironic epilogue to his stubborn attempts, a letter arrived from his friend Baron Dutilh de la Tuque, the man whose life he'd saved in 1871. Two years earlier, Dutilh had asked him to support his candidacy for the Nobel Peace Prize. Discovering that he did not qualify (his pacifist work was not international enough), he came back in 1909 with a new idea: his friends were going to do all they could to get him a monetary reward through a 5-million-franc donation from Mr Carnegie. 'Will they succeed? If you might support my cause, it would be in the bag!'[55] Dutilh added hopefully.

---

[53] Dunant to Müller, 10 January 1908, BGE, Ms, fr. 5205, f. 101–2.
[54] Dunant to Suttner, 16 May 1908.
[55] Baron Dutilh de la Tuque to Dunant, 21 June 1909, BGE, Ms. fr. 2113, f. 314.

A loud burst of laughter must have resounded that day from the second floor of the Heiden district hospital. What a hilarious reversal, that *he* should be asked to help with a windfall he so very much wanted for himself! Amazingly blind to Dunant's real state of mind, the baron wrote to him a second time in June 1910, boasting of the 500,000 francs annual interest these millions would be able to ensure him, if only Dunant would consent to write all the requisite letters, or, if necessary, have Dr Altherr write for him!

Far from imagining he was plunging the knife in deeper into one of his friend Dunant's most painful wounds, Baron Dutihl would have the honour of being among Henry's last correspondents.

Dunant most certainly didn't have time to reply. Now was the moment to put his affairs in order. Heiden's summer was arriving with its high temperatures that doubled his congestion and his difficulty breathing. In the middle of July, he called for Dr Altherr and asked that he arrange for his nephew Maurice, Pierre's son, to come as quickly as possible.

The next day, Maurice found his uncle both very weak and very agitated. He wanted to make his will. Maurice called his father and another of his brothers. Twenty-four hours later, they were all gathered together at the foot of Henry's bed. His brother was struck by how thin Henry was; since his jaundice two years earlier, he hadn't regained any weight; his clothing hung on him, his cheeks were hollow, his eyes were sunken as though already focused on a dimmer world.

The dying man was only worried about his will: he was afraid he would pass before writing it, it must be done right away.

Easier said than done. His nephews encouraged him like busy midwives around a woman in labour: he needed to be helped and also had to do the job himself. His brother Pierre wanted to be part of the discussion, but because he was as deaf as a post, everything had to be repeated three times.

A few things quickly became necessary: the notary would be the one used by the family, Mr Cherbuliez whose father Dunant had known. Then he designated Maurice as his executor, because he understood his affairs and he spoke German, which would make things easier in Heiden, in Zurich, and even with Mr Daae.

The first bequests were easy: 13,000 francs to create a *Freibett* – a bed for paupers at the Heiden hospital; 10,000 francs would go to Dr Altherr and his wife; 4,000 francs to Sister Elise who had run so many postal errands for him, so much carrying of trays and translating of letters, so much listening to complaints! 2,000 francs to Emma Rubeli, who'd graciously submitted to the whims of his appetite and demands of his stomach. Rudolf Müller, Hans Daae and Adolf Graeter's widow would each receive 1,000 francs. Then a gift to a home for the blind, and another to the La Source nursing school founded by Valérie de Gasparin and her husband. Both institutions were incidentally located in Lausanne; not a single Genevan in the room would dare comment on this.

The division of fortune did not, however, exceed the sum of the interest accumulated by the Nobel Prize; the capital still remained like a sacred hill upon which no one wanted to venture even a first step.

Upon this question, Dunant kept silent a long time.

His brother Pierre would eventually find the most suitable solution: the decision was to decide nothing. The capital of the Nobel Peace Prize would not be bequeathed to any individual or for any particular use; in this way it was tacitly reserved for Dunant's creditors, in the event they showed up.

Once these provisions were written, Dunant could lie back and wait for death to come. He was hardly reading anymore. He could barely skim the headlines and the obituaries from the *Journal de Genève*. The 23rd August edition informed him of the death of Gustave Moynier; the following day a long article appeared dedicated to the man who was 'the true founder of the Red Cross', a eulogy Dunant suspected was written by the deceased himself. This would be his last indignation.

As the coolness of autumn arrived, he could wrap himself as tightly as he wanted in the white flannel dressing gown given to him by the ladies of Stockholm, he was constantly cold. And he could no longer eat: not rice gruel, not boiled chestnuts, nothing. 'Oh, but it is hard to die so slowly,'[56] he confided to Dr Altherr, who could do nothing for him.

Several days before his death, Dunant complained to his doctor that everything had gone black. Then, on 30th October, his state rapidly deteriorated. Dr Altherr could not be reached. Henry

---

[56] Dr Altherr, '*Henri Dunants Letzte Jahre*', *Henry Dunant et la Suisse orientale*, 53.

Dunant passed away in the presence of Heiden's Chief Nurse, Sister Elise Bollinger, and the cook, Emma Rubeli. He was 82 years old.

In an undated letter to Wilhelm Sonderegger, probably written sometime around 1890, Dunant claimed he wanted to be 'buried in the ground like a dog'. Two years before his death, he specified a desire for cremation in Zurich 'without any kind of ceremony'. On 2nd November, his coffin was brought by handcart from the Heiden hospital to the train station, where a wagon decorated in pine boughs by Heiden's Red Cross ladies was waiting. Escorted by his three nephews, Henry Dunant's body was then transported by train to Zurich, where his ashes would be laid to rest.

The ceremony was sparsely attended: his closest family members, several friends, representatives of Switzerland's largest Red Cross societies. Hans Daae had requested they wait for his arrival but Dr Altherr had refused.

Faithful to the specifications of the recently departed, there was no religious service. And no speeches. It was All Saints' Day. There was a thick and icy fog. Henry Dunant had finally reached the last Station on his own Way of the Cross.

Conclusion

After a life spent shunted between glory and despair, between a universal gaze and self-centred withdrawal, Henry Dunant leaves a single unanswered question: why him? Behind the pioneer of humanitarian law, behind the champion of wounded soldiers and prisoners of war, behind the peace activist, it would have been nice to discover a perfect man driven solely by a concern for his fellow human beings, operating out of humble kindness and modest charity, hovering well above all worldly goods and honours to the benefit of the less fortunate.

But that would not be Henry Dunant. There is no use denying the facts of his life. After his years of youthful piety, his social ambition slowly took the reins. And when his empathy was so forcefully challenged in the wake of the horrors of Solferino, it was not only a fervent young Christian who moved into action, but a man in the throes of building his career, weaving together his networks and chasing after land concessions.

And luckily so. If Henry Dunant had gone to Italy only by virtue of his zealous evangelism to give aid to his wounded brothers on the battlefield, he would have certainly done as much good on-site for that week in June of 1859; maybe he even would have written *A Memory of Solferino* upon his return. Then he would have distributed about fifty copies to his family, his friends in the YMCA, to General Dufour. End of story. The kings and queens, their chancellors and ministers, the journalists of Paris, Berlin and London would never have heard a thing, and Dunant's proposals would have suffered the same fate as those of his predecessors: stillborn on paper.

The Protestant influence within Dunant's initiative has often been highlighted. In the pragmatic reformism this implies, it would be 'typically' Protestant to focus on reducing the suffering of war rather than more radically attack the origins of the problem. Dunant's life indeed appears to corroborate this religious hypothesis in his turning towards the Pope and his bishops at the moment he swaps his Samaritan's flask for a pacifist's white flag. Yet, in stark contradiction to the Calvinist values of humility and discretion, the driving power of Dunant's ambition, of his unending quest for honour upon honour and, most of all, the absolutely uninhibited chutzpah which he used to achieve his goals have all been chastely minimized, to such an extent as to make his trajectory incomprehensible. So why him?

Definitely because his education and faith encouraged him to pay attention to the suffering of others, just as is taught by almost all religions and moral philosophies. But also because, unlike the reputedly austere Calvinism of his city, his own ambition did not forbid him from seeking success, honours and money.

The Red Cross and the Geneva Convention were not born simply by virtue of a good idea, even less so because Dunant was not the first to articulate it. The Red Cross and the Geneva Convention were born of an idea *carried* along by an unflinching tenacity rendered more effective because its humanitarian ideals were coupled with a goal of personal success. Dunant's avid social climbing – the entrepreneur in Algeria, the friend of kings and queens – may have often irritated his fellow Genevans. But *without* his outsized and fully assumed ambition, the Red Cross would never have been born, or would only have been born later, in another form and most surely not in Geneva.

When the disasters that followed his bankruptcy had destroyed all of Henry Dunant's social and professional hopes, what remained for him was the embittered selfishness of an old misanthrope more interested in maligning his enemies then respecting the peace and quiet of his friends. Here again, would it have been more acceptable for this biography to overlook the change in character of a man renowned as humanity's benefactor?

'It is clear you would have been better off dying in 1867; but God had probably destined you for some other cross,' wrote Jean-Jacques Bourcart to his friend in Heiden in November 1895. This comment aptly summarizes the incredible singularity of Henry Dunant's destiny. After following the Christian cross of his youth with such enthusiasm, after bearing aloft the Red Cross with all the strength of his convictions, Henry Dunant would shoulder the burden of bankruptcy, slander and exile – a third cross that would eventually bring about his resurrection. Bourcart was right: if Dunant had died in 1867, he would not have suffered such martyrdom. He would have only briefly known the glory of the Red Cross and the illusory success of his business exploits; he would not have had time to endure the tortures of public scorn, poverty, remorse, shame and hatred. He would not have been suspected of profiting off Mrs Kastner's fortune, he would not have been misled into outlandish philanthropic projects, he would not have finished his life depressed and paranoid in a hospital room. In the memory of his peers, he would have lived on forever as the exceptional being, the distinguished, charming, devoted, charitable and engaged man who had founded the Red Cross and launched the Geneva Convention. That's true.

But if Dunant had died in 1867, Gustave Moynier would have maintained the same steady course: he would have grabbed the reins of the Red Cross, erasing the name of his unworthy colleague, a man who had almost put their mutual cause at risk. And because nothing nor anyone would have shown up to remind the world of the vanished man, the amputation would have been complete. Henry Dunant would be no more known than Louis Appia or Théodore Maunoir; no street, no school, no hospital would bear his name.

'But God had probably destined you for some other cross.' This third cross, his forty years of misery, far from torturing him in vain, gave Henry Dunant the time and energy necessary to recover the paternity of the Work that had been taken from him. The severity of his disgrace in 1867, followed by the uninterrupted series of failures suffered between the age of 40 and 60 should have reasonably prevented him from any kind of comeback – his hole was much too deep. But remorse, anger and a desire for vengeance did the trick. All that he needed were friends devoted enough to bow to their master's tyranny, and the second miracle of Dunant's life could occur: to stand again among the great men of his time, all without ever leaving the top floor of the Heiden district hospital.

What Dunant achieved between 1862 and 1864 bears a first hint of genius: it's an irreproducible feat. Never again would an international treaty gather enough support and so quickly, being signed only two and a half years after its idea was first conceived.

If humanitarian genius exists, it can be found in the very content of Dunant's proposals. The idea of preparing aid services when they are not needed and then using them for other projects during times of peace may seem overly simple today. It is not. Despite an almost continuous state of war in Europe, the dominant philosophy regarding humanitarian aid prior to 1863 centred a state of emergency as the sole driver of activism; the permanence of the aid societies was at that point one of the most regularly criticized ideas within Dunant's project. The mutually beneficial relationship today between the ICRC, active in warzones, and the regional and national Red Cross societies, equally active in peacetime, proves the lasting pertinence of Dunant's vision.

Finally, the idea most seriously and courageously defended by Henry Dunant, although not completely novel, was no less revolutionary. The neutral status of aid teams, field hospitals and non-combatant soldiers does not correspond, no matter what the pacifists may have said, to a small cosmetic rearrangement of an otherwise tragic and inadmissible reality. This idea cuts directly across the political logic of war and hatred between warring parties in favour of the opposing logic of human brotherhood. The idea involves something both immense and very tiny: it is not a vision of the world, it is not a philosophical theory – it is a rule, a principle, a sacred pact which only has value when it is unanimously respected. Dunant's cleverness reveals itself not only in the historical audacity of his idea, but in having understood that it could be proposed *and* *accepted* at that very moment of history.

Today, the emblem of the Red Cross has become part of our daily life – from the household first aid box to the school infirmary – so much so that we often forget its meaning. Until certain events remind us. Brutally.

On 19th May 1992, Frédéric Maurice, delegate from the ICRC to Bosnia, was killed by a rocket launched into his vehicle near Sarajevo. The truck could not have been more visibly marked with the 'conventional and sacred' emblem to remind both sides of a warring conflict of the strict neutrality of humanitarian action and the respect it required. The convoy had received all formal guaranties of safety, from all sides involved in the conflict. To no avail.

Frédéric Maurice was 39 at the time; he was a dear friend of mine. The day of his funeral, in Geneva, in a cathedral bursting at the seams, a large Red Cross flag covered his coffin. It seemed to be proclaiming to all those in attendance that its idea and meaning still held – still held out, despite all the vicissitudes it had been made to suffer.

I thought often of that flag while writing this book. When detailing Dunant's obstinacy, his obsessions, his stubbornness, his determination and resilience, I was reminded that the Red Cross *is* his worthy heir, with its immutable principles, its tenacity and perseverance, despite all the misfortune and injustice in the world. It resists; it does not give up; it holds out as long as it can; and when it falters, it gets back up. This is its cross.

Faithful, in this as well, to the cross of its founder.

REFERENCES

The references included in this list are restricted to all sources cited in the text or other direct sources.

Complete bibliographies about Henry Dunant and the Red Cross can easily be found elsewhere, in all languages.

I. Unpublished sources

A. At the Manuscript Department of the Geneva Library (BGE):

- Handwritten memoirs, texts and notes by Henry Dunant, Ms. fr. 2071 to 2107; Ms. fr. 4501 to 4613; Ms. fr. 2116 G.
- Correspondence from or to Henry Dunant, or between others, Ms. fr. 2108 to 2115 A–N, P, R; Ms. fr. 4613; Ms. fr. 4615/1–2; Ms. fr. 5201 to 5212 (from and to Rudolf Müller).
- Documents about Dunant's will and the division of the Nobel Prize, Ms. fr. 2116 H/1 and 2.
- Family Dunant-Colladon correspondence, Ms. fr. 3257.
- Daniel Colladon Papers, Ms. fr. 3742.
- Family Boissier Papers, Ms. fr. 7504/13.
- Archives of the Dufour Foundation, Ms Dufour 166.
- Archives of the *Société évangélique de Genève*, Ms Soc. Ev. 49.
- Archives of the *Société de géographie de Genève*, Ms. fr. 7998/6.
- Copies of external archives from the following collections:
- Archives from the Institut Henry Dunant;

Bibliothèque nationale de Paris, corresp. Mgr Dupanloup, vol. 12 (about the *Alliance universelle*).

Bibliothèque historique de la Ville de Paris, Eugène Manuel file (about the *Société de Prévoyance*).

Oxford Rhodes House Library (about the Anti-Slavery Society);

UN Archives, Fried/Suttner Papers, IPM/FSP/Bvc (correspondence with Suttner).

B. At the archives of the ICRC (ACICR) in Geneva:

- the minutes of the Committee, AICRC A PV.
- the correspondence of the Committee, ACICR, A AF 20.
- CICR activities, 1st series, A AF 21, 1–5, 10.
- Old archives and Miscellaneous A AF 33 and A AF 34, 1–2.
- Letters from Henry Dunant, to various correspondents, A AF 44, 2–4.

C. At the World YMCA Archives in Geneva:

- World Alliance & General-T.1, Biographies: Dunant, Henri. 150th Anniversary. 1828–1978, Box Number 17.
- World Alliance & General-T.1, Biographies: Dunant, Henry, E – Box Number 18.

D. At the State Archives of Geneva:

Archives of the Geneva Society for Public Welfare, AP 241. 1 and 2.
Archives of the *Compagnie Genevoise des colonies suisses de Sétif*, AP 68.1.1–2, AP 68 2.1., AP 68.8.1.

E. At the Swiss Federal Archives, in Berne:

Archives of the Foreign Affairs Department, E2#1000/44, E2001A#1000/45.

II. Published sources

A. Official Records

Bulletin de l'Alliance universelle de l'ordre et de la civilisation, Recueil des documents publiés (1873), Paris: Aux Bureaux de l'Alliance.
Compte rendu de la Conférence internationale réunie à Genève les 26, 27, 28 et 29 octobre 1863 pour étudier les moyens de pourvoir à l'insuffisance du service sanitaire dans les armées en campagne (1863), Bulletin No. 24 de la Société genevoise d'Utilité publique, Geneva: Jules-Guillaume Fick.
Compte rendu de la Conférence internationale pour la Neutralisation du Service de Santé militaire en Campagne, réunie à Genève du 8 au 22 août 1864 (1864), handwritten copy at the ACICR, reproduced in *Revue internationale de la Croix-Rouge (RICR)*, No. 425, May 1954, 416–23; No. 426, June 1954, 483–98; No. 427, July 1954, 573–86.
Conférence internationale des Sociétés de Secours réunie à Genève les 10 et 11 août 1864 (en marge du 'Congrès de Genève') (1864), minutes at the ACICR, excerpts published in *RICR* (1954), No. 427, July 1954, 543–56.

Conférences internationales des Sociétés de Secours aux Blessés militaires des Armées de Terre et de Mer, tenues à Paris en 1867 (1867), Paris: Commission générale des Délégués and Imprimerie Baillière & Fils.

Congrès de l'Alliance universelle de l'ordre et de la civilisation (1872), Paris: Pougin.

Engel, E. (1865), *Rechenschafts-Bericht über die fünfte Sitzungsperiode des internationalen statistischen Congressen in Berlin*, 2 vols, Berlin: R. von Decker.

La Croix Rouge, Bulletin belge de l'Alliance universelle, Revue de la Charité internationale sur les champs de bataille et en temps de paix (1874), vol. 3, no. 3.

Le Comité international de la Croix-Rouge de 1863 à 1884 (1884), Geneva: Soullier.

Le Congrès de Genève: Rapport adressé au Conseil fédéral par MM. Dufour, Moynier et Lehmann, Plénipotentiaires de la Suisse (1864), Geneva: Imprimerie Fick.

Procès-verbaux des séances du Comité international de la Croix-Rouge, 17 février 1863–28 août 1914 (1999), in J.-F. Pitteloud, C. Barnes and F. Dubosson (eds), Geneva: ICRC and SHD.

'Statuts de la Compagnie algérienne' (1867), *Recueil authentique des lois et actes du gouvernement de Genève*, vol. 52, Geneva: Vaney.

'Supplément à la convocation d'une Conférence internationale à Genève' ([1863]1871), *Actes du Comité international de Secours aux militaires blessés*, Geneva: Soulier & Wirth, II.

Suprême tentative de conciliation & de paix entre Versailles & Paris, faite par M. le baron Dutilh de La Tuque en mai 1871 (1906), Paris: J. Dangon.

B. First-hand Accounts and Memoirs

Altherr, H. ([1828]1992), 'Henri Dunant's Letzte Jahre', *Das Rote Kreuz, May 1828*, reprinted in R. Durand (ed.), *Henry Dunant und die Ostchweiz*, 45–53, Geneva: SHD.

Arrault, Henri (1861), *Notice sur le perfectionnement du matériel des ambulances volantes*, Paris: [no publisher].

Baumberger, G. ([1895] 1993), 'Einiges über Henry Dunant und seine Werke', *Die Ostschweiz*: 10–20 September, reprinted *in extenso* in R. Durand, A. Bärtsch and G. Müller (eds), *Georg Baumberger, Die Ostschweiz, Henry Dunant*, 10–125, St Gallen and Geneva: SHD, Geneva and St-Gallen Red Cross.

Baumberger, G. ([1895] 1993), 'Eine Ehrenpflicht der Völker und Regierungen', *Die Ostschweiz*, 26 July 1895, reprinted in R. Durand, A. Bärtsch and G. Müller (eds), *Georg Baumberger, Die Ostschweiz,*

Henry Dunant, 31–4, St Gallen and Geneva: SHD, Geneva and St-Gallen Red Cross.

Bazancourt, Baron de (1860), *La campagne d'Italie de 1859, Chroniques de la guerre*, Paris: Amyot Éditeur.

Cambacérès, Duc de (1873), *Funérailles de Napoléon III. Procès-Verbal rédigé par le –*, Paris: Librairie générale.

Carette, Mme née Bouvet (1890), *Recollections of the court of the Tuileries*, translated from the French by Elizabeth Phipps Train, New York: D. Appleton and Company.

Cazenove, L. de (1869), *La guerre et l'humanité au XIXe siècle*, Paris: A. de Vresse.

Chaponnière, F. (1902), *Notices biographiques* (Max Perrot, Théodore Necker), Geneva: Union chrétienne de jeunes gens.

Chenu, Dr J.-C. (1869), *Statistique médico-chirurgicale de la Campagne d'Italie en 1859 et 1860*, 2 vols, Paris: Librairie militaire de J. Dumaine.

Déguignet, J.-M. (1904–5), '*Mémoires d'un paysan bas-breton*', A. Le Bras (ed.), *Revue de Paris*. Dickens, C. (1863), 'A Souvenir of Solferino', *All the Year Round*, 16 May 1863, 283–7.

Du Camp, M. (1889), *La Croix-Rouge de France*, Paris: Hachette.

Du Casse, Baron (1898), '*Le 5e corps de l'Armée d'Italie en 1859*', *Revue Historique*, vol. LXVI and LXVII, Paris: Félix Alcan.

Dunant, H. (1858) *Notice sur la Régence de Tunis*, Geneva: J. G. Fick (available on www.gallica.bnf.fr/BnF), facsimile by Société Henry Dunant, Geneva, 1996.Dunant, H. (1859), *Mémorandum au sujet de la société financière et industrielle des Moulins de Mons-Djemila en Algérie*, Geneva: J. G. Fick, or Paris: Renou et Maulde (available on www.gallica.bnf.fr/BnF)

Dunant, H. (1862), *Un souvenir de Solférino*, Geneva: J. G. Fick (facsimile by Slatkine Reprints, Geneva, 1980.)

Dunant, H. (1864), *La charité sur les champs de bataille, Suites du Souvenir de Solférino*, Geneva.

Dunant, H. (1865), *La charité internationale sur les champs de bataille*, Paris: Hachette.

Dunant, H. (1867), '*Le meilleur mode de faire parvenir aux prisonniers des secours en argent et en nature*', report submitted to the First International Conference of Societies for the Relief of Wounded Soldiers, in *Conférences internationales des Sociétés de Secours aux Blessés militaires des Armées de Terre et de Mer, tenues à Paris en 1867*, 2nd edn, 338–48, Paris: Baillière & Fils, Paris, first part (report reproduced in *RICR*, 412, April 1953, 279–88).

Dunant, H. (1872), *A proposal for introducing Uniformity into the Condition of Prisoners of War*, 2nd edn, London: Head, Hole &Co.

Dunant, H. ([1895] 1971), *Mémoires*, Bernard Gagnebin (ed.), Geneva: Henry Dunant Institute and Lausanne: L'Age d'Homme.

Falk, Th. (ed.) (1887), *Précis de la campagne de 1859 en Italie*, Brussels: Librairie militaire C. Muquardt.

Fonvielle, W. de (1882), *Georges Eugène Frédéric Kastner*, Paris [no publisher].

Giraudeau, F. (1873), *La mort et les funérailles de Napoléon III*, Paris: Amyot.

Haje, Ch.-F., and Simon, J.-M. (1900), *Les origines de la Croix-Rouge*, Stuttgart/Amsterdam: Lindheimer/Delsman & Nolthenius.

Ludwig, H. (1886), *Johann Georg Kastner, Sein Werden und Wirken*, Leipzig: Breitkopf & Härtel.

Lueder, C. (1876), *La Convention de Genève au point de vue historique, critique et dogmatique*, translated from German by the International Committee of the Red Cross, Elangen: Édouard Besold.

Moynier, G., and Appia, Dr L. (1867), *La guerre et la Charité, Traité théorique et pratique de philanthropie appliquée aux armées en campagne*, Geneva-Paris: Cherbuliez.

Moynier, G. (1888), *Les causes du succès de la Croix-Rouge*, Paris: Picard.

Moynier, G. (1903), *La fondation de la Croix-Rouge*, Geneva: Soulier.

Müller, R. (1897), *Entstehungsgeschichte des Roten Kreuzes und der Genfer Konvention, Mit Unterstützung ihres Begründers, J. H. Dunant*, Stuttgart: Druck und Verlag von Greiner & Pfeiffer.

Palasciano, F. (1864), *De la neutralisation des blessés en temps de guerre et de ses conséquences thérapeutiques*, paper presented on 1st October 1864 at the Medical Congress in Lyons, Lyons: Aimé Vingtrinier.

Perrot, M. (1857), *Appel aux jeunes chrétiens de tous les pays*, Union chrétienne de jeunes gens, Geneva: J G Fick.

Perrot, M. (1859), '*Calvin, ses élèves et les jeunes chrétiens d'aujourd'hui*' (opening speech), *Souvenir de la Seconde Conférence universelle des UCJG*, Geneva: Cherbuliez & Beroud.

Perrot, M. (1859), *Souvenir de la Seconde Conférence universelle des Unions Chrétiennes de Jeunes Gens (Genève, août 1858)*, Geneva/Paris: Jules Cherbuliez and Beroud/Grassart and Meyrueis.

Perrot, M. (1878), *Notice historique sur l'Union chrétienne de Jeunes Gens de Genève de 1852 à 1878*, Geneva [no publisher].

Saint-Félix, R. de (1865), *Le voyage de S.M. l'Empereur Napoléon III en Algérie et la régence de S.M. l'Impératrice, mai-juin 1865*, Paris: Eug. Pick (available on www.gallica.bnf.fr/BnF).

Staehling, C. (1884), *Histoire contemporaine de Strasbourg et de l'Alsace*, Nice: Gauthier.

Suttner, B. von (1889), *Die Waffen nieder!*, Dresden: Pierson.

Suttner, B. von (1909), *Memoiren*, Stuttgart-Leipzig: Deutsche Verlags-Anstalt.
Teissier, O. (1865), *Napoléon III en Algérie*, Paris-Alger-Toulon: Eugène Aurel.

C. Newspapers

Illustration (L'), Journal universel, 12 December 1863.
Journal de Genève (Le), many editions.
*Journal de la Guer*re, no. 11, 29 June 1859.
Journal des Tribunaux Vaudois (1868), no. 35, 5 September 1868.
Journal officiel de la République française, 13 September 1870. *Journal officiel de la République française*, 21 September 1870. *Journal d'Alsace*, 12 April 1881.
La Nature, Revue des Sciences, no. 36, 7 February 1874.
L'Ordre de Paris, nos 465 and 466, 17 and 18 January 1873.
Moniteur Universel (Le), Journal officiel de L'Empire français, 2 and 4 July 1859.
The Scattered Nation, 1 August 1866, C. Schwarz (ed.), Vol. 1, London: Morgan and Chase.
The New York Times, 'The Brussels Conference', 29 July 1874.

D. Reference Works*

Amann, H. (1992), *Henry Dunants zweite Heimat – das Appenzellerland*, Herisau: Verlag Appenzeller Hefte.
Amann, H. (1999), *Wilhelm Sonderegger – die rechte Hand Henry Dunants*, Heiden: Henry-Dunant-Museum.
Amann, H. (2000), *Frauengestalten um Henry Dunant*, Heiden: Henry-Dunant-Museum.
Amann, H. (2000), *Henry Dunant und Stuttgart*, Stuttgart: Deutsches Rotes Kreuz, Kreisverband Stuttgart.
Amann, H. (2003), '*Diagramme symbolique chronologique*', Bulletin de la Société Henry Dunant, 21, Geneva: SHD.
'*Avant le "Congrès de Genève", Lettres de Henry Dunant à Gustave Moynier*' (1954), RICR, 427, July: 587–600.
Biedermann, E. (ed.) (2001), *Chère Baronne et Amie – Cher monsieur et ami: Der Briefwechsel zwischen Alfred Nobel und Bertha von Suttner*, Hildesheim: Olms.
Boissier, P. (1963), 'The Early Years of the Red Cross', *IRRC*, 24, March: 122–39.
Boissier, P. (1973), 'Florence Nightingale and Henry Dunant', *International Review of the Red Cross*, 146.
Boissier, P. (1974), 'Henry Dunant', *IRRC*, 161, August: 395–419.

Boissier, P. (1978), *History of the International Committee of the Red Cross, from Solferino to Tsushima*, Geneva: Henry Dunant Institute and ICRC.

Bouvier, B. (1918), *Gustave Moynier*, Geneva: Journal de Genève.

Bugnion, F. (1977), *The Emblem of the Red Cross: A Brief History*, Geneva: ICRC.

Bugnion, F. (1988), '*La fondation de la Croix-Rouge et la première Convention de Genève*', in R. Durand (ed.), *De l'utopie à la réalité: Actes du Colloque Henry Dunant*, 191–223, Geneva: SHD.

Bugnion, F. (1989), 'The Red Cross and Red Crescent Emblems', *IRRC*, 272, October: 408–19.

Bugnion, F. (1994), *Le Comité international de la Croix-Rouge et la protection des victimes de la guerre*, Geneva: ICRC.

Bugnion, F. (2005), '*Genève et la Croix-Rouge*' in R. Durand (ed.), *Genève et la paix, Acteurs en enjeux, Trois siècles d'histoire*, 69–99, Geneva: Association Genève Un lieu pour la paix. English translation (excerpts) published in *International Geneva Yearbook* (2005–2006), Vol. XIX, 5–15.

Candaux, J.-D. (1978), '*Pour une nouvelle lecture des* Mémoires *d'Henry Dunant*', *Revue suisse d'histoire*, vol. 28, 1/2: 72–96.

Christ, F. (1983), '*Le pyrophone*', *Bulletin de la Société Henry Dunant*, 8, Geneva: SHD.

Christ, F. (1992), '*1908–1910, Dunants Letzte Jahre Lebenserinnerungen*', in R. Durand (ed.), *Dunant et la Suisse orientale*, 39–44, Geneva: SHD and Geneva Red Cross.

Cilleuls, J. de (1948), '*Un des précurseurs de la Convention de Genève de 1864: le pharmacien Henri Arrault*', *Revue d'Histoire de la Pharmacie*, 357–66.

Déjà cent ans! Aperçu historique de 100 années de l'Alliance universelle des U.C.J.G., 1855–1955 (1955), Geneva: [no publisher].

Dejung, E. (ed.) (1963), *Die zweite Wende im Leben Henry Dunants: 1892–1897, sein Briefwechsel mit der Sektion Winterthur vom Roten Kreuz*, 294. Neujahrsblatt der Stadtbibliothek, Winterthur: Ziegler & Co.

Dunant, H. ([1862, 1892] 1969), *Un souvenir de Solférino*, followed by *L'Avenir sanglant*, Lausanne: Institut Henry Dunant et L'Âge d'Homme.

Dunant, M. (ed.) (1918), *Les débuts de la Croix-Rouge en France avec divers détails inédits. Extraits des Mémoires de Jean-Henri Dunant*, Zurich/Paris: Orell Füssli/Fischbacher.

Durand, A. (1981), '*Un livre d'Henry Dunant écrit en collaboration avec le docteur Chéron*', *Bulletin de la Société Henry Dunant*, 6, Geneva: SHD.

Durand, A. (1989), 'La journée du 22 août 1864 à Genève', Bulletin de la Société Henri Dunant, 13, Geneva: SHD.

Durand, A. (2008), 'Gustave Moynier: retour à Genève et recherche d'une vocation', Cahiers du Centenaire, 4, Geneva: Association Dunant-Moynier 1910–2010.

Durand, R. (1975), 'Henry Dunant et sa famille', Bulletin de la Société Henry Dunant, 1, Geneva: SHD.

Durand, R. (1977), 'Henry Dunant féministe', Bulletin de la Société Henry Dunant, 2, Geneva: SHD.

Durand, R. (1982), 'Diagrammes symboliques chronologiques de quelques prophéties des saintes Écritures', Bulletin de la Société Henry Dunant, 7, Geneva: SHD.

Durand, R. (1983), 'Flash sur une année obscure', Bulletin de la Société Henry Dunant, 8, Geneva: SHD.

Durand, R. (1988), 'Le "non-événement" du 9 février 1863', Bulletin de la Société Henry Dunant, 10, Geneva: SHD.

Durand, R. (1988), 'Les prisonniers de guerre aux temps héroïques de la Croix-Rouge', in R. Durand (ed.), De l'utopie à la réalité, 225–97, Geneva: SHD.

Durand, R. (1989), 'Symbolique, éphémère et éternelle, la Croix-Rouge genevoise a 125 ans', Bulletin de la Société Henry Dunant, 12, Geneva: SHD.

Durand, R. (1991), 'La rencontre Dufour-Dunant', in R. Durand (ed.), Guillaume-Henri Dufour dans son temps 1787–1875, 384–96, Geneva: Société d'histoire et d'archéologie de Genève.

Durand, R., Bärtsch, A., and Müller, G. (eds) (1993), Georg Baumberger, Henry Dunant, Die Ostschweiz, Saint-Gall/Geneva: Sektion St. Gallen des Schweizerischen roten Kreuz/SHD and Croix-Rouge genevoise.

Durand, R. (ed.) (1997), 'La bataille de Solférino', in Le creuset de la Croix-Rouge, 21–31, Geneva: SHD and RCRCM.

Durand, R., Dunant, C. et al. (eds) (2003), Henry Dunant Citoyen de Culoz Français de cœur, Geneva and Culoz: SHD.

Durand, R. (2005), 'Les grandes manœuvres d'Henry Dunant pour conquérir le premier Prix Nobel de la Paix', in R. Durand et al. (eds), Genève et la paix Acteurs et Enjeux, Trois siècles d'histoire, 161–78, Geneva: Association Genève Un lieu pour la paix.

Durand, R. (ed.) (2007), La Tunisie d'Henry Dunant, Geneva: SHD.

'En marge du Congrès de Statistique, (Berlin, septembre 1863): Lettres de J. Henry Dunant à Gustave Moynier' (1954), RICR, 425, May: 424–8.

François, A. (1918), Le Berceau de la Croix-Rouge, Geneva and Paris: Jullien and Édouard Champion.

François, A. (1948), Aspects d'Henri Dunant, Geneva: Georg.

Gagnebin, B., and Gazay, M. (eds) (1963), *Encounter with Henry Dunant*, Geneva: Georg.

Geisendorf, Th. (1913), *Soixante ans de souvenirs, Notice relative à l'Union chrétienne de Jeunes Gens de Genève*, Geneva: UCJG.

Harouel, V. (2003), *Genève-Paris, 1863–1918: Le droit humanitaire en construction*, Geneva: SHD, ICRC and French Red Cross.

Heudtlass, W. (1962), *J. Henry Dunant, Gründer des Roten Kreuzes, Urheber der Genfer Konvention: Eine Biographie in Dokumenten und Bildern*, Stuttgart: Kohlhammer Verlag.

Humbert, G. (2018), *Faillite en Algérie*, Paris: Ampelos.

Lebègue, E. (1935), *Boursault-Malherbe Comédien, Conventionnel, spéculateur*, Paris: Félix Alcan.

Le Comte, G. (2003), '*Henry Dunant et/ou Maximilien Perrot*', in *Cent cinquante ans déjà . . . 1852–2002 Unions chrétiennes de Genève*, Geneva: Unions chrétiennes de Genève & SHD.

Lützelschwab, C. (2006), *La compagnie genevoise des Colonies suisses de Sétif*, Berne: Peter Lang.

Monnier, H. (1904), *Edouard Monnier. Souvenirs de sa vie et de son œuvre*, Paris: Fischbacher.

Mützenberg, G. (1984), *Henry Dunant le prédestiné*, Geneva: SHD.

Mützenberg, G. (1988), '*C'est là qu'Henry Dunant devint citoyen français*', *Bulletin de la Société Henry Dunant*, 11, Geneva: SHD.

Mützenberg, G. (1994), *Valérie de Gasparin, Une femme de style*, Le Mont-sur-Lausanne: Ouverture.

Perrot, A. (2003), '*Regards de Maximilien Perrot sur le début de l'UCJG de Genève*', in *Cent cinquante ans déjà . . . 1852–2002 Unions chrétiennes de Genève*, Geneva: Unions chrétiennes de Genève & SHD.

Pictet, J.-S. (1949), *The Sign of the Red Cross*, Geneva: ICRC.

Pictet, J.-S. (1963), 'The foundation of the Red Cross: Some important documents', *IRRC*, 23, March: 60–75.

Pourtalès, Y. de, and Durand, R. (1975), 'Henry Dunant, promoter of the 1874 Brussels Conference, pioneer of diplomatic protection for prisoners of war", *IRRC*, 167, March: 61–85.

Pous, J. (2020), *Henry Dunant colon affairiste en Algérie, pionnier du sionisme*, Paris: L'Harmattan.

Reynolds, P. (2017), 'Tunis the glorious: Report on the Regency of Tunis', in H. Boujmil, *In the Warm Shade of Tunisia* (Tunis: Nirvana).

Rombach, J.-H. (1988), 'Henry Dunant and the Anti-Slavery Society', in R. Durand (ed.), *De l'utopie à la réalité*, 344–52, Geneva: SHD.

Schedd, C. P. et al. (1955), *History of the World's Alliance of Young Men's Christian Associations*, London: SPCK.

Senarclens, J. de (2008), *The founding of the Red Cross, Gustave Moynier its Master Builder*, Geneva: Slatkine.

Sonderegger, R. (1935), *Jean Henry Dunant Revolutionär*, Zurich: Reso Verlag.

Suttner, B. von (correspondence), see Biedermann.

Tripet, M. (1991), '*La création de la Croix-Rouge*', in R. Durand (ed.), *Guillaume-Henri Dufour dans son temps*, Geneva: Société d'histoire et d'archéologie de Genève.

Wellis, M. (2013), *Unification and Consolidation of Germany and Italy 1815–90*, Cambridge: Cambridge University Press.

*Abbreviations

ACICR   Archives of the International Committee of the Red Cross (same abbreviation for all languages)

ICRC   International Committee of the Red Cross (CICR in French) *IRRC: International Review of the Red Cross*

RCRCM   Red Cross and Red Crescent Museum, Geneva

RICR   *Revue internationale de la Croix-Rouge et du Croissant-Rouge*

SHD   Société Henry Dunant (this Society has published since 1975 the *Bulletins de la Société Henry Dunant*, providing up-to-date scholarship and information on Henry Dunant)

UCJG   *Unions chrétiennes de Jeunes Gens*

YMCA   Young Men's Christian Association

INDEX